Peter Pan on Stage and Screen, 1904–2010

SECOND EDITION

PETER PAN ON STAGE AND SCREEN, 1904–2010

SECOND EDITION

Bruce K. Hanson

Foreword by Stewart Stern

McFarland & Company, Inc., Publishers

Jefferson, North Carolina, and London

Unless otherwise noted, photographs are from the author's collection.

LIBRARY OF CONGRESS CATALOGUING-IN-PUBLICATION DATA

Hanson, Bruce K.
Peter Pan on stage and screen, 1904–2010 /
Bruce K. Hanson ; foreword by Stewart Stern. — 2nd ed.
p.   cm.
Includes bibliographical references and index.

ISBN 978-0-7864-4778-7
softcover : 50# alkaline paper ∞

1. Barrie, J. M. (James Matthew), 1860–1937. Peter Pan.
2. Barrie, J. M. (James Matthew), 1860–1937 — Adaptations.
3. Acresses — Great Britain — Interviews.
4. Actresses — United States — Interviews.
I. Hanson, Bruce K. Peter Pan chronicles. II. Title.
PR4074.P33H36   2011   822'.912 — dc22   2011016253

BRITISH LIBRARY CATALOGUING DATA ARE AVAILABLE

On the cover: Hayley Mills as Peter Pan
(photograph by Tom Hustler, Ormand Street Hospital)

Manufactured in the United States of America

McFarland & Company, Inc., Publishers
Box 611, Jefferson, North Carolina 28640
www.mcfarlandpub.com

For Dale

Table of Contents

Acknowledgments

A book that chronicles the stage and film history of J.M. Barrie's most famous play could not have been written without the aid of many people. However, almost without exception, the enthusiasm and generosity that greeted me as I interviewed writers, performers and directors of productions of *Peter Pan* from 1924 through the present date was overwhelming, with each participant eager to share memories and anecdotes. It is my pleasure to thank the following people, some of whom have since departed this world, who shared their memories for this book: Mary Brian Tomasini, Elizabeth Charlap, Betty Comden, Sandy Duncan, Charles Eaton, Edward Ancona, Adolph Green, Mary Hunter, Josephine Hutchinson, Sondra Lee, Julia Lockwood, Mary Martin, Carl Meyer, Kathleen Nolan, Esther Ralston, Cathy Rigby, Jerome Robbins, Norman Shelly, Dinah Sheridan, Keith Stava, Sandy Stewart, Jule Styne.

Although Mary Martin was the first person I made contact with, my first *real* interview was with Betty Comden and Adolph Green, who good-naturedly allowed me to "Drop That Name" in order to obtain other interviews. In particular, Kathleen Nolan and Sondra Lee helped tremendously in understanding the daily turmoil the cast and crew experienced as they attempted to create a musical version of the play and then transfer it from California to Broadway to television. It was during one of our interviews that Kathy nonchalantly mentioned her ritual Saturday "morning brunches with Josie," or the "Wendy brunches." Inquiring, with fingers crossed, did she mean Josephine Hutchinson, she replied, of course, that they were great friends and in fact, Josie lived upstairs in the penthouse of the same building. Kathy arranged an introduction which led to another unforgettable interview.

The following people were also very helpful: David Drummond of Pleasures of Past Times on Cecil Court in London. His shop, one of the last of its kind, is a cornucopia of theatre ephemera and stories. Howard and Ron Mandelbaum of Photofest have been no less supportive this second go-round than they were the first. Their generosity and aid are always above and beyond what one should expect. Photographer Bob Willoughby was helping me with photographs until his death. His son, Chris Willoughby, graciously picked up where his father left off, allowing me to use several photos from the Mary Martin production. Also much gratitude to Simon Moss of www.stagememories.com, who not only enabled me to buy many of the illustrations for this book, but also offered advice for this edition. And many thanks to David Smith for offering vintage *Peter Pan* programs at vintage prices. They helped immeasurably with the London cast list appendix.

June Silver again agreed to the publication of several of her sister's lyrics which helped tremendously in understanding the musical journey that transpired. For the use of songs from their musical version of *Peter Pan*, I am extremely appreciative of George Stiles and Anthony Drewe.

My gratitude also goes to: Richard Bagehot, Esq., of Field Fischer Waterhouse Limited for aiding me in securing permission to use unpublished and rare Barrie material; Karin Nickeson and the helpful (and patient) staff of the Billy Rose Collection and the Rodgers and Hammerstein Archives of Recorded Sound of the Performing Arts Research Center at the New York Public Library at Lincoln Center; Melanie T. Christoudia and Barry Norman for their help with the earlier edition; Mitch Douglas of I.C.M. for bringing Eva Le Gallienne's "Playing Peter Pan" to my attention and for his solid advice; Eloise Armen for again allowing me to quote from Le Gallienne's beautiful "Peter Pan" essay; and Anne Kaufman Schnieder for her support, humor, and Le G's Peter Pan cap, sword and pipes which are still on display as I promised.

Thanks to Vincent Girourd, curator of the Barrie Collection, and Patricia Willis, curator of American literature, both at Yale Beinecke Library, who were helpful in locating rare Barrie scripts and other material. David Karpele of the Karpeles Manuscript Library Museum demonstrated extreme generosity in allowing me to use the stunning costume sketches from the early productions. Thanks to Christina De Poortere of the Great Ormond St. Hospital for arranging for the use of several beautiful photographs as well as helping me with cast lists of various British productions. Dick Patterson directed me towards several primary sources and Miles Kreuger of the Institute of the American Musical always had sound advice. Andrew Birkin allowed me to use photographs from his book, *J.M. Barrie and the Lost Boys*, my favorite book on the author. It was a pleasure to thank him in person at the 2004 celebration of Peter Pan's 100th birthday.

Stephen Reynolds of Ambassador Tickets arranged for me to meet with Alison Shaw, the box office manager of the Duke of York's Theatre. Alison not only took me on a personal tour of the whole theatre, she also upgraded my seat to enjoy *Arcadia*, which was playing in the theatre at that time. The beautiful theatre, still perfect for the intimacy that Barrie strove for in his play, does not require any microphones as the acoustics are perfect. I am grateful for their kind gestures.

Thanks also to Sylvia Morris, assistant librarian, the Shakespeare Birthplace Trust, the Shakespeare Centre, Stratford-Upon-Avon; Dr. Jeanne Newlin, curator of the Harvard Theatre Collection of Pusey Library at Harvard; and Hillary Ray of the Museum of the City of New York. As far as I'm concerned, Karl Michael Emyrs is the man who probably knows more about *Peter Pan* than anyone else. I am grateful that he shared his insight and expertise without any boundaries. Dr. Judith Gaines not only aided me with her editorial assistance during the early stages of the first edition of this book, she allowed me to adopt her computer when I most needed it.

I will always be grateful to Harriet Goldberg, my English teacher from New Dorp High School, who demanded the best her students could give. Marianne Simmonetti, a good friend and colleague, gave her time and talents as my personal secretary during the interview stages of research for the original book. I miss you, Marianne. Harvey Schmidt was supportive and enthusiastic right from the beginning. Had it not been for Harvey, I never would have met Mary Martin nor had so many wonderful illustrations. Thank you, Harvey, for your help and your beautiful music.

I would also like to express my gratitude to the following for their invaluable help: Michael Adams, Sheela Amembal, Simon Annand, Tim Bagley, Larry Baker, Sophie Baker, Ben Bagley, Andreas Brown, Rex Bunnett, Revinder Chahal of the V & A Museum, Elizabeth Charlap, Paul Charlap, Emily R. Colman, Dennis Colton, Betsy Davis, Richard Davis, Dorothy Decker, Paula Eisen, Diane Deigman, Doris Eaton Travis, George Fearon, Jack Gottlieb of Amberson Music, Susan Grushken, Catherine Haill, curator for the V & A Theatre Museum, Donna Hanson, Jane Klain, Jan Kreher-Policastro of NBC, Ken Mandelbaum, Alvin H. Marill, Deborah Marshall, Karin Nickerson, Daniel Peters of Hal Leonard, Inc., Robert Reisenberg, Abram Samuels, Ira Shapiro, Carol Siegel, Stephanie Sinclair, Delissa Slimp, Coordinator of Doss Heritage and Culture Center, Steven Suskin, Lynda Trapnell, Henry Wallengren, Lisa Ward, Jacob Watson, Suzi Williams, and Allen J. Wilson.

I still remember my students from the Florence M. Gaudineer School who influenced me more than they know to take on this project: Leslie (Wendy), Aaron (John), Nick (Michael), Jessica (Nana), Seth (Mr. Darling), Kelly (Mrs. Darling), Vincent (Peter Pan), Julie (Tiger Lily), Billy (Captain Hook), Kelly A. (Liza), Anita, Greg, and all those wonderful lost boys and pirates.

Thanks to my son, Drew, for his continued love and support, and thank you to Jessi Barnett, for that last minute typing.

Much of this would not have been made possible without the aid of two good friends: the late Robert Gable, for his photographs, ideas, advice, and contacts — thank you, Mr. Gable, I still miss you; and Richard Tay of Sepia Records, who not only exercised great patience with me as his house guest while I was doing research in London, but also treated me to plays, arranged interviews with theatrical personalities related to Pan and the Duke of York's Theatre, and contributed illustrations and theater programs, not to mention producing the *100 Years of Peter Pan* CD at my request. He also introduced me to Roy Busby, who, during tea at his lovely apartment in London, casually exited to another room only to emerge with a fantastic collection of photographs chronicling productions of *Peter Pan* from 1904 through 1986 and then stated, "Use what you want." His photographs are an important contribution to this book. Thank you, Roy, thank you Dennis Colton, too. And to Suzi Williams, who opened her home and her heart to my cause.

The idea for a new edition of this book originated with the late John McGlinn, during one of our endless midnight calls. At the time he was "cleaning up" the score and script to the 1954 musical version of *Peter Pan* for Samuel French and after which he hoped to restore the 1904 working script with its John Crook score.

In 1993, not too long after my first book was published, Stewart Stern sent a beautiful card to me, complimenting the book, and suggesting that we might be friends. Our letters, phone calls, emails, trading of gifts and far too few meetings will always hold a special place in my heart. I am honored to be his friend. Thimbles to you, Stewart.

Finally, words can not express the gratitude for the support, suggestions, consideration, enthusiasm, and sacrifices that Dale Neighbors has given for me and for this book. He continues to amaze me as my partner and as my best friend. I am the lucky one.

Foreword

by Stewart Stern

The ghost of the El comes banging down the tracks above Columbus Avenue, swaying at every curve, scattering soot on the street below and griming the windowsills it passes. It's a jungle gym of criss-cross girders with little Victorian stations of green iron at every stop. It keeps the street and the shops below in permanent low-rent darkness. I am with Mom. It will be my favorite day with her — out of my whole life. The rickety-buckety-buck of our El train careens past tenement windows, past the John Wanamaker department store, past the huge black Hippodrome where spectacles are shown before they build Radio City. I'm going to be eight in March. Next stop, 14th Street, and my mother is peering out the window as the wheels scream again. "This is the street where Uncle Adolph started!" my mother yells. "Down there was his Penny Arcade that grew up to be Paramount Pictures!"

(I can't believe she was only 32.) She has me clinging to her hand, skipping me down the steel stairs "to make the curtain." I wonder what curtain she's making without needle and thread and a thimble. My shoes beside her skippy ones go jump-jump-jump, all the way to the bottom and into the maw of the Civic Repertory Theatre, which she pronounces for me, then hurry-hurry-hurry to our seats way upstairs, and the dizzying height of the theatre dome and the dizzying fall to the people below make me hold all the railings very tight. There are many people on our bench so we are very close together and my leg is against her leg. I hold tight to the rail in front of me and make my mother spell what it says on the program. It says PETER PAN.

The people below have real chairs and the theatre is shrill with the voices of children and the shushing of moms as the lights are dimmed. Five old men come in and start to play five instruments, very happy music but a little sad too, and as the asbestos hisses up, my mother whispers, "That's the curtain we had to make." She makes me stop picking my nails.

There's a big dog on stage and I think there's a man inside. Things happen then: Mrs. Darling says goodnight, the night lights go out in the nursery and the big window blows open. Then into the gloom of the nursery, into silence deeper than the darkest night, into this blue hush, like a dark apparition, Eva Le Gallienne springs through the air with the buoyancy of a leaf on the wind and ends the parabola of her flight as softly as a conductor's baton coming to rest at the end of a note. Her smile is quick and seldom offered, but when it comes onto that brown as earth dirty-boy face, it has the sudden luminosity of numbers

1

on a radium clock. Her voice as she flies rings with the cold, careless bravado of a boy with a scraped knee who's pretending it doesn't hurt, and I suddenly know she's my brother.

At the curtain call, Le Gallienne, alone on the stage, sweeps off her hat in salute, spreads her arms wide, gives the first big smile of the afternoon, which is hers this time, not Peter's, then flies all the way up where we are on our cheap gallery benches at the very top of the theatre! All of our hands reach out to her: "Don't go!" we plead, "Don't go! Take us too!" And we hear her heartless laugh as she sweeps down and away, just missing the edge of the stage as the curtain falls. The lights come on and the kids are all chattering. But I have been changed forever. I know what to do with my life. I have a brother now to lead the way. Peter Pan is my brother. The actor inside will be me! I have loved Peter Pan all my life. He's even in *Rebel Without a Cause*.

My mother never laughed at me about it. She made me a Peter Pan suit as perfect as Le Gallienne's and I wore it everywhere except school. I'd lie on top of my bookcase in it, doing my homework with Peter's rubber dagger in my teeth in case Hook came into my room.

All children who saw Peter Pan wanted to fly! Until I was ten I dreamed of flying out my windows so many times that one morning I found my bare footprints in the snow on my window sill, FACING OUT! Over New York City! Eight floors up! Next day my dad had metal guards attached to every window in our apartment so I could never do it again!

One day on Uncle Adolph's golf-course, I was up in my usual tree, dressed as Peter and tootling on my pipes, when my father came along with a man I didn't know who had an English accent and wore knickerbockers. When he heard my tootling as he was about to hit the ball, he said, "Good Lord! That's the Pirate Song from Peter Pan! What's it doing in that tree?" My dad said, "It's just Peter, otherwise known as my son." The man peered through the leaves until he found me and we stared at each other for one long, meaningful moment, and I won! He said, "By George it IS Peter Pan! The REAL one! Bi-carbon-

Stewart Stern as Peter Pan (courtesy Stewart Stern).

ate of Soda, it IS!" That man with the accent turned out to be Sir William Wiseman, a friend of Barrie's, and a few weeks later a package came in the mail from London, a first edition of *Peter and Wendy*, autographed "To Stewart Stern. Kind regards from J.M. Barrie." I wished he had sent me a thimble in it, that silver thing you wear on your finger when you sew a button on, that Peter called a kiss. My letters from Eva Le Gallienne all had thimbles in them. She'd write, "Bless you, my dear. I send you a very nice thimble," and my letter from Betty Bronson had thimbles in it too. But not Elsa Lanchester's, who came down her flying wire like a black widow spider after its prey and acted the whole thing pretending to be Hitler at the age of six. Children looked to Charles Laughton for comfort all that season because he was only Captain Hook and not half so scary as Peter.

So I send thimbles to all of you, from the dozens of Peter Pans who've appeared in the play and the movies over the 106 years since it was written, and I send a special one to Mr. Bruce Hanson, the author of this magical book, which gathers into a pretend bouquet all of the stories and pictures of Peter that can be crammed between two covers, many of them his secrets until now. He has pinned them all up in the Wendy House at the top of his favorite Never-tree and guards them fiercely so he knows he's real and can never forget himself the way he forgets most things.

— Stewart Stern, 2010, Seattle, Washington

Stewart Stern is a screenplay writer best known for Rebel Without a Cause, The Ugly American, Rachel, Rachel, *and the teleplay* Sybil. Peter Pan *has been a major influence in his spirit and art: in* Rebel Without a Cause *James Dean is Peter, Natalie Wood is Wendy, and Sal Mineo, a Lost Boy. Mr. Stern teaches screenwriting in Seattle, Washington, where he lives with his wife, Marilee.*

Introduction

This book, with its cast of thousands and over a hundred years in the making, is intended as a celebration of the individual productions of the most popular children's play of all time and of the performers and other artists who have been associated with the various productions since 1904. It is not the story of J.M. Barrie. There are volumes of excellent biographies that analyze the playwright through his work and his life. Barrie was something of a mystery in his own time, and time has not been able to remove that shroud despite published attempts to understand the man behind the image. Let's face it: most geniuses have troubled pasts that we mere mortals find difficult to relate to, yet, oddly, many comment acidly with a matter-of-factness on the lives of these artists as if their private moments, their joys, and their anguishes were created for our entertainment pleasure alone to be pursued in a neatly formatted volume or two for biographical reading. Therefore, from the start the reader should be warned that while I might briefly narrate the life of J.M. Barrie, ultimately the play's the thing. When I say play, I do not mean just the script as written (or in this case, scripts) but rather a working text included in the framework of the other elements of theatre: actors, spectacle (costumes, sets, lights) and sound (music). Most importantly, this book examines the performers and the reactions of the audiences and critics of their day.

Let's end one misconception right now: the play was not derived from the book. Indeed, Barrie never wrote a book titled *Peter Pan*! He did, however, write a novel, published in 1902, called *The Little White Bird*, which introduced Peter as a baby who ran away from home seven days after he was born. This character was so unique that the author was compelled to develop him further in a play, *Peter Pan, or The Boy Who Wouldn't Grow Up*, which had its world premiere in 1904. In 1906 the chapters featuring Peter in *The Little White Bird* were published in a separate illustrated text called *Peter Pan in Kensington Gardens*, and in 1911 Barrie novelized his play into *Peter and Wendy*. Each venture met with great popularity, but before long, with three different versions of the story available, the public was confused about Peter's origin. The author only added to the enigma with his whimsical yet elusive explanations of the birth of Peter Pan.

"The difference between Peter Pan and his rivals," observed Roger Lancelyn Green, "is that, however hard it is to believe that they are mere characters of fiction, Peter alone has crossed the border-land of folklore. Even Alice is only three-dimensional: Peter Pan has broken into the fourth dimension of the imagination."[1] There are many children who have not read the book or seen the play or film, but everyone is familiar with this remarkable boy. Film makers have banked on this with such motion pictures as *Peter Pan*, *Hook*, and even *Finding Neverland*, each departing greatly from Barrie's concept and his life. No other piece of literature could be so drastically changed. For example, in *Hook*, Steven Spielberg, like everyone else, approached *Peter Pan* as an established myth that could be as relevant in the 1990s as it was in 1904.

Would Barrie have been pleased with the many alterations that have taken place with his favorite play, or for that matter, with his life? He certainly wouldn't have found reason to complain about versatile actor Johnny Depp playing his part in the 2004 film *Finding Neverland*, and why not? The actor gave a beautifully nuanced performance that compliments the playwright even as the film itself muddles the facts and timeline, something akin to Barrie's own practices. Certainly no one worked harder to nurture the concept of Peter Pan as a myth than the writer himself. As he wrote in The *Little White Bird*, "If you ask your mother whether she knew about Peter Pan when she was a little girl, she will say, 'Why, of course, I did, child.' And if you ask her whether he rode a goat in those days, she will say, 'What a foolish question to ask. Certainly he did.' Then if you ask your grandmother whether she knew about Peter Pan when she was a girl, she also says, 'Why, of course, I did, child,' but if you ask her whether he rode on a goat in those days, she says she never heard of his having a goat. Perhaps she has forgotten, just as she sometimes forgets your name and calls you Mildred, which is your mother's name."[2]

There are at least three reasons why people of all ages enjoy *Peter Pan*—the play, the flying, and Peter Pan himself. Actually, Barrie provided a fourth reason from a youngster sitting in his private box. "What I think I liked best," the boy said, "was tearing up the programme and dropping the bits on people's heads."[3] What always stands out is the personality and talent that each actor brings to the part of Captain Hook, Wendy, or even Smee. Above all, though, we remember Peter.

After seeing the play for the first time, we are especially aware of the actor playing Peter, and that performance usually remains the quintessential interpretation. But what of the past achievements of actors who played Peter and those who came after our first exposure to the play? With the exception of *Hamlet*, no other role has been as coveted by so many actors. Therefore, we will take a trip to the beginning of the 20th century, to a time when innocence was not confined to just the young, and we will continue to the present date with the ever-growing affection for Peter at a time when innocence and magic are deliberately shattered for the sake of "truth"—the truth of whoever happens to be profiting at the moment.

My own fascination with *Peter Pan* began in 1960 when at the age of seven I was allowed to stay up late with my brothers, Wayne and Mark, to watch the Mary Martin musical version on television. That evening, we had our baths before supper as our mother set up TV trays with our rocking chairs. Amazingly, on this special occasion, we were allowed to eat our meal in the living room (unheard of) while watching television (even more unheard of)! Our supper was also to be a treat: frozen chicken TV dinners! These small meals in compact aluminum trays were seen at that time as exotic departures from the homemade meatloaves and fried chicken dinners to which we were ordinarily accustomed. All of the rules were broken that night as I anxiously waited for something special to emit from our small eight-inch rounded television screen. The tension mounted when the Darling children were put to bed while their mother begged the night lights to protect them. And then it happened! Peter Pan once again flew into the Darling nursery, only this time to be witnessed by more people than any other event in history.

Of course I knew that Peter was really a woman playing at being a boy — Mary-What's-Her-Name! After all, we "baby boomers" were known for our sophistication. We had the common sense to allow ourselves to believe that *Howdy Doody, Kukla, Fran and Ollie, Sky King,* and *Roy Rogers and Dale Evans* were as real as the images locked in our televisions. We wanted the magic — we wanted to make believe. Thirty years later, when I received a telephone call from Mary Martin regarding an interview, I still believed. I remember being awed: "Peter Pan is calling me!" It was only after Mary asked me why my phone was unlisted and how much trouble she encountered in trying to contact me from Martha's Vineyard after leaving my phone number at her home in California that I came back down to earth. And yet, a few years later, when Heller Halliday casually mentioned that her mother took an instant liking to me from our few and all too brief conversations, I again was elated. "Peter Pan liked me!" You see, to my generation, Mary Martin was Peter Pan — she never grew old. And perhaps, neither did the other actresses who played Peter to nearly five generations before her. As for the generations that followed and for those to come, "children know such a lot now, they soon don't believe in fairies, and every time a child says, 'I don't believe in fairies,' there is a fairy somewhere that falls down dead."[4]

One of the problems I encountered in the first edition of this book was trying to curb my elation in my writing after interviewing artists such as Mary Martin, Comden and Green, Jerome Robbins, Josephine Hutchinson, Sandy Duncan and so many more. Hopefully, in this new and improved edition, I maintain certain soberness while examining the changes that have taken place in each major production of *Peter Pan* since 1904. I have also taken the liberty of replacing some illustrations and photographs from the first edition with others that are more insightful while also adding several new ones for their own sake. Finally, the reader of the first edition will notice other changes, including a few more interviews. Change is inevitable; in this case I hope that I have taken advantage of that inevitability to get things right, if not better than the first time. During J.M. Barrie's lifetime, changes in the script constantly occurred, often at the whim of the actress performing for that particular season. Even the 1928 published script was different than the acting versions used in England and at the Civic Repertory Theatre in New York City. Many productions were adapted in one way or another to suit the talents of the stars. Consequently, when I hear the statement that the musical of *Peter Pan* is not as good as the original, I ask, "Which original?" "What production?" and "Were you there?" Unlike a *Show Boat* or *Oklahoma!*, there is no definitive *Peter Pan*. James M. Barrie could never leave the play alone, and it seems, neither can anyone else.

Before long, we friends of Peter and lovers of his play will be disputing over the text as scholars do when a page of Shakespeare or a speech in Sophocles is in question.

—*Boston Tribune*, 1928

A whole chapter, indeed a considerable volume, could be written about the actors and actresses whose names have been associated with the play; some day possibly, a theatre critic may attempt a complete chronicle of the play and its players, and a fascinating book should be the result. Certainly no single play of modern times has a theatrical history remotely to be compared with it.

—J.A. Hammerton, 1929

1

James Barrie: The Man
Who Wouldn't Grow Up

*I sometimes feel about Peter that there is a little inner circle who would know
(as if it were a record of fact in which they had participated) the moment I
went astray with him.*

—J.M. Barrie, 1908[1]

In order to appreciate the history of the theatrical performances of *Peter Pan* it is necessary to briefly discuss the writer who invented it all, for despite the popularity of the folk hero, Peter comes from the mind of one man.

> All children, except one, grow up. They soon know that they will grow up, and the way Wendy knew was this. One day when she was two years old she was playing in a garden, and she plucked another flower and ran with it to her mother. I suppose she must have looked rather delightful, for Mrs. Darling put her hand to her heart and cried, "Oh, why can't you remain like this forever!" This was all that passed between them on the subject, but henceforth Wendy knew that she must grow up. You always know after you are two. This is the beginning of the end.[2]

The above passage is from James M. Barrie's 1911 novel *Peter and Wendy*. It is a combination of the author's natural talents for writing sentiment with tongue-in-cheek humor, but there is also a melancholy aspect that escapes many readers. Barrie's Peter Pan controls his own destiny; he chooses not to grow up. The author and his favorites among the boys for whose welfare he took responsibility did not have this luxury. The two boys had no voice in the matter as they both died violent deaths before they could truly grow up. As for Barrie himself, "It is as if, long after writing *Peter Pan*, its true meaning came to me," he inscribed in his notebook many years after he penned his most famous play. "Desperate attempts to grow up but can't."[3] Cynthia Asquith, his secretary, friend, and confidante, made it a point to state that the reader should not be allowed to take this random confession too seriously, yet authors Janet Dunbar and Andrew Birkin have both illustrated in their comprehensive biographies that his statement is lucid and quite tragic.

"All Barrie's life led up to the creation of Peter Pan," wrote *Pan* historian Roger Lancelyn Green, "and everything he had written so far contained hints or foreshadowings of what was to come."[4] Perhaps no one was more aware of this than Barrie himself. Born in Kirriemuir, Scotland, on May 9, 1860, he was one of the ten children of David Barrie, a linen weaver, and his wife, Margaret Ogilvy. Typical of even the poor inhabitants of that country, the education of the children was a major concern for both parents, although the primary focus for the mother was her second son, David. He was an extremely intelligent boy for whom she had great expectations. The eldest son, Alexander, grown, educated, and teaching at Glasgow, sent for his 13-year-old brother in order to help him win a scholarship. Although Margaret had great reservations about letting David leave her she finally relented and subsequently was stunned for life when the boy was fatally injured in a skating accident.

Six-year-old Jamie, as Lisa Chaney points out in her book, *Hide and Seek with Angels*, was already aware that he was not his mother's favorite and he must have been deeply hurt by the rejection he experienced after his brother's death. He later wrote that once while his mother was sleeping, she heard him stir and called out, "'Is that you?' I think the tone hurt me, for I made no answer, and then the voice said more anxiously 'Is that you?' again. I thought it was the dead boy she was speaking to, and I said in a little lonely voice, 'No, it's no' him, it's just me.'"[5] At his sisters' urging, Jamie tried to replace his brother by acting as much like David as he could. While this charade aided his mother, not to mention gaining the attention he craved, a deep wound was created that would have a significant impact on his writing and personal life. Margaret Ogilvy would spend the rest of her life mourning David; Jamie Barrie would grow older but David would always remain the boy who didn't grow up.

Jamie thrived on storytelling and drama and he would listen intently for hours as his mother told him stories of her childhood. His schoolmate, Charles Laing, would later remember how he would tell a story "with sparkling eye, full of the minutest detail and entrancing to the listener.... And I have no doubt that he heard it from the lips of some old body in Kirriemuir."[6]

James Mathew Barrie (photograph: Elliott and Fry, date unknown).

Family finances improved when his father accepted a managerial position for a commercial linen company and he could now afford to send James to Dumfries Academy. The boy already knew that he wanted to be a writer. While studying at the academy, he lived with Alexander, who was the inspector of the schools in the district of Dumfries. Here the boy discovered his love for cricket and, above all, the theatre. With a group of friends, he formed a pirate band that would meet by the river Nith. Their games of pretending led to the establishment of a small theatre group, the Dumfries Amateur Dramatic Club. The acting bug had bitten him. In an adaptation of a story by Fenimore Cooper, the boy played six parts. The group was highly criticized by a local clergyman as "grossly immoral," but the written support of prestigious patrons was sought out by the boys, which helped in the continuation of their productions. Barrie wrote his first play in Dumfries, *Bandelero the Bandit*, in 1877.

James's social life was not as stimulating as his life on stage. The young man was painfully shy. Standing about five feet tall, he was described by another student, Robert Galloway, as a "sallow-faced, round-shouldered, slight, somewhat delicate-looking figure, who quietly went in and out amongst us, attracting but little observation."[7] He was extremely uncomfortable with women, venerating them to a level that he could not possibly obtain. He particularly liked stage actresses.

Before long, the theatre group became the center of his life at school, and his work in other subjects suffered. It was obvious that James was not going to receive a scholarship to go to a university, so Alexander managed to make arrangements for him to attend Edinburgh University where renowned David Masson was professor of rhetoric and literature.

While at school Barrie became the drama and book reviewer for the *Edinburgh Courant*. After his graduation in 1882, he returned home where his sister, Jane Annie, implored him to apply for a "leader-writer" position with the *Nottingham Journal*. He worked in that capacity for a year while he also wrote a play and contributed stories to other journals. November 17, 1884, was to prove a turning point in his artistic career when the *St. James' Gazette* printed his short story, "An Auld Licht Community." Publisher Fredrick Greenwood requested more sketches of the Auld Lichts.

Against Greenwood's advice, Barrie moved to London in March of the same year. The next few years were a struggle financially but the young writer managed to write a book, *Better Dead*. Yet it was the Auld Licht sketches that brought him to the attention

Above: Jamie Barrie, age six, in 1866. *Right:* Age nine, in 1869 (courtesy Andrew Birkin, jm barrie.co.uk).

of the critics and the public. In 1888 he revised and compiled these works to form a new book, *Auld Lichts Idylls* (Old Light Ideals), which met with critical and financial success. However, that book was quickly overshadowed by *A Window in Thrums* (1889) and *The Little Minister* (1891), each work influenced not so much by Barrie's childhood observations but his mother's stories.

> The reason my books deal with the past instead of with the life I myself have known is simply this, that I soon grow tired of writing tales unless I can see a little girl of whom my mother has told me, wandering confidently through the pages. Such a grip has her memory of her girlhood had upon me since I was a boy of six.[8]

Margaret Ogilvy, published in 1886, tells the story of his mother as a young girl whose own mother dies when she is only eight, who raises her brothers, and takes care of the house. The biography moved the critics and book buyers, adding more to Barrie's purse. Yet the young writer's true obsession was with theatre. Barrie's first play to be produced in London, albeit a short one, *Ibsen's Ghost*, written in 1891, was hardly a success but its producer wanted a full-length play from Barrie. He delivered with *Walker, London*, which ran for 511 performances and served as an introduction to actress Mary Ansell, who would become the second most important woman in his life. His mother would always hold first place.

As with other beautiful actresses, the insecure little man placed Mary Ansell on a pedestal and subsequently a slow courtship followed. Had it not been for a serious illness that placed Barrie near his deathbed, it is probable that the marriage would have never taken place. Yet despite his badgering Mary to wed him, Barrie had his doubts about such a union. "Our love has brought me nothing but misery,"[9] he wrote in his notebook a few days before the wedding. He was particularly insecure with the idea of physical intimacy, and Mary Ansell later confided to actress Pauline Chase

J.M. Barrie's mother and the subject of his book, *Margaret Ogilvy* (courtesy Andrew Birkin, jmbarrie.co.uk, date unknown).

that their honeymoon was a nightmare. Did Barrie suffer from an incomplete puberty? Was there some physical deformation or a psychological problem? All we know is that the couple remained childless, which remained a sensitive subject for Barrie, who adored children, and for Mary, who wanted to be a mother. As if a foresight of a childless marriage, Barrie bought his wife a gift for consolation: a Saint Bernard puppy, which they named Porthos after a dog in George de Maurier's popular novel, *Peter Ibbetson.* The Barrie marriage appeared secure and proper to outsiders but both husband and wife were very unhappy. Ironically, it was during his marriage that Barrie wrote several of his most successful plays, *The Little Minister* (1897), *Quality Street* (1902), *The Admirable Crichton* (1902), *Peter Pan* (1904), and *What Every Woman Knows* (1908).

An inside look at their lives was provided by Barrie himself, in *Sentimental Tommy,* published in 1896, and its sequel, *Tommy and Grizel,* written four years later. Tommy Sandys is a boy who adores being a

David Barrie, the father of J.M. Barrie (date unknown).

child and can never really grow up. His marriage to Grizel fails because he is incapable of mature emotions. "He was a boy only," wrote Barrie in the second volume. "She knew that, despite all he had gone through, he was still a boy. And boys cannot love. Oh, is it not cruel to ask a boy to love?"[10] The tragedy of Tommy's inability to love his wife as a man was a reflection of the author's own life, yet from such pathos was raised a work of art. In fact, Barrie gave his literary figure, Tommy, the foresight of creating Peter Pan. "It was but a reverie about a little boy who was lost. His parents find him in a wood singing joyfully to himself because he thinks he can now be a boy for ever; and he fears that if they catch him they will compel him to grow into a man, so he runs farther from them into the wood and is running still, singing to himself because he is always to be a boy."[11]

The third most important woman in the author's life was Sylvia Llewelyn Davies, the daughter of George du Maurier. He met her at a dinner party where he watched as she secretly hid some desserts in her reticule. When confronted, Sylvia confessed that they were for her youngest child, Peter. Further conversation revealed that she was the mother of George and Jack, two small boys whom the Barries often encountered with their nanny during their daily walks through Kensington Park. He would entertain the boys by wiggling his ears, lifting one eyebrow, wrestling with Porthos, and making up stories with the boys

PLAYS

SENTIMENTAL TOMMY

WINDOW IN THRUMS

LITTLE MINISTER

Caricature artists had a field day with Barrie's small stature and large head.

Former actress Mary Ansell, the wife of J.M. Barrie, circa 1894 (courtesy Beinecke Library at Yale University).

as the heroes. He was immediately enchanted by the beauty and charm of Sylvia.

"There was never a simpler, happier family until the coming of Peter Pan,"[12] Barrie wrote of the Darling family in *Peter and Wendy*. In *J.M. Barrie and the Lost Boys*, Andrew Birkin borrowed Barrie's words to make an interesting analogy between Peter Pan and his creator. The Davies family was the prototype for the Darling family and, like their literary counterparts, their lives changed greatly with the visits of J.M. Barrie. In a short time, he began to show up frequently at the Davies home, much to the chagrin of Sylvia's husband, Arthur Llewelyn Davies, a young barrister. Barrie began writing to Sylvia, even addressing her by her middle name, Jocelyn, in order to create some sort of implied intimacy. Naturally, this irritated Arthur, as did Barrie's excessive generosity toward the boys. Arthur felt helpless as the successful writer burrowed his way into his family, acting as a surrogate father to the boys and confidant to Sylvia. Barrie's assurance that Sylvia was very much in love with her husband afforded him a level of comfort free of the challenge of sexual intimacy. However, sex or no sex, Barrie's time with Sylvia and the boys did little to improve his relationship with Mary.

Barrie was spending more and more time with the Davies boys, telling them many stories and taking them to the English pantomimes. The Edwardian pantomimes, so different from present-day productions, were presented as a Christmas treat for children, and included songs, comedy, a harlequin clown, flying and magical transformation effects all loosely tied together. The principal boy was played by a woman rather than a male child as she would be able to handle the many lines in the play and appear convincingly as a young male. Also, there were restrictions for the times allotted for juveniles on the professional stage, with nine o'clock as a curfew. In 1900 after seeing *The*

J.M. Barrie working on *The Little Minister* at Strath View, Kirrie, circa 1897 (courtesy Barrie's Birthplace — The National Trust for Scotland).

Babes in the Wood, Barrie wrote one of his own called "The Greedy Dwarf." It was acted out for the boys by Barrie and his wife; Gerald du Maurier, a popular actor and brother of Sylvia; Porthos; and Sylvia as the principal boy. Barrie carefully observed the children's reactions and recorded them.

The daily stories were continued, expanded, and embellished to include talking birds, fairies, and the boys themselves. At some point that no one could remember, Peter Pan became part of these adventures. Many of these stories were incorporated into a new novel, *The Little White Bird*, which was published in 1902. This book served as a written introduction to *Peter Pan*, a story within the story as narrated by a captain to a small boy, David, who was modeled after George Llewelyn Davies, the oldest of Sylvia and Arthur. Peter appears as a seven-day-old baby who runs away from home to live among the fairies on the island in the Serpentine River, which is part of Kensington Gardens. In this new fairy tale the narrator explains that all children start out as birds, eventually forgetting how to fly. Peter is content to live among the birds, believing that he is one of them, until he is informed by an old bird, Solomon Caw, that he is neither bird nor boy — he is "betwixt-and-between."[13] He eventually flies home only to discover that he has waited too long and that the window to his nursery is barred. Through his tears he spies on his mother holding a new baby.

Left: The beautiful Sylvia Llewelyn Davies in 1891, mother of the five boys who influenced Barrie to write the play *Peter Pan,* was also the sister of Gerald du Maurier, the stage's first Captain Hook (courtesy Great Ormond Street Hospital Children's Charity, London). *Right:* Arthur Llewelyn Davies, the handsome husband of Sylvia, who did not like J.M. Barrie's flirtations with his wife even though the writer was quite harmless. This photograph was taken in 1890 (courtesy Great Ormond Street Hospital Children's Charity, London).

The book also introduced a predecessor to Wendy in a little girl named Maimie who exchanged a thimble for a kiss with Peter. Foreshadowing the Wendy House in Peter and Wendy, a special house is built for Maimie by the fairies.

As interesting as the narrator's story is about Peter Pan, his telling of his relationship with the boy David, warm and whimsical, reflected Barrie's own desire to be a father as much as the captain's. There is no doubt that Barrie loved George just as much as the narrator loves David. In one of the passages David is allowed to stay overnight at the captain's home, who has set up a smaller bed in his bedroom. After giving the boy a bath and treating him to milk and a chocolate-covered biscuit, he retires him to the makeshift nursery in his own bedroom. Later, when the captain goes to bed David wakes up and asks:

"Is it going on now?"
"What?"
"The adventure?"
"Yes, David."
Perhaps this disturbed him, for by and by, I had to inquire, "You are not frightened are you?"
"I am not," he answered politely, and I knew his hand was groping in the darkness, so I put out mine and he held on tightly to one finger.
"I am not frightened now," he whispered.
"And there is nothing else you want?"
"Is there not?" he again asked politely. "Are you sure there's not?" he added.
"What can it be David?"

"I don't take up very much room," the far-away voice said.

"Why David," I said, sitting up; "do you want to come into my bed?"

"Mother said I wasn't to want it unless you wanted it first," he squeaked.

"It is what I have been wanting all the time," said I, and then without more ado the little figure rose and flung itself at me. For the rest of the night he lay across me, and sometimes his feet were at the bottom of the bed and sometimes on the pillow, but he always retained possession of my finger, and occasionally he woke me to say that he was sleeping with me. I had not a good night. I lay thinking ...

Of David's dripping little form in the bath, and how when I essayed to catch him he had slipped from my arms like a trout. Of how I stood by the door listening to his sweet breathing, had stood so long that I forgot his name and called him Timothy.[14]

In her book, *Hide and Seek with the Angels*, Lisa Chaney uses this passage to analyze Barrie's relationships with the Llewelyn Davies boys by noting the discomfort contemporary readers experience in the relationship between the captain and the boy. Upon reading her book, this writer was reminded of the lawsuit against singer Michael Jackson regarding the alleged seduction of a young boy by the singer at his Never Land estate. The parents of a young cancer victim had given their permission to allow their son to sleep over at the singer's house. Indeed, Jackson admitted that the boy slept in his bed, adding that he often slept with children but nothing sexual ever happened — that it was sweet and innocent. Although Jackson was acquitted of the charges, his reputation was stained for the rest of his tragically short life. Chaney warns her readers not to interpret Barrie's work or in fact his relationship with the Davies boys with our 21st-century frame of mind:

A great shift in understanding, in human intentions and consciousness, in assumptions of all kinds, has taken place since 1902, and interpreting the past by imposing our own attitudes and beliefs upon it is a dubious practice.[15]

While Chaney suggests that this passage from *The Little White Bird* offers modern readers a suggestion that Barrie was a pedophile, there is no evidence of such acts and she counters these arguments with a statement made by Nicholas (Nico) Llewelyn Davies to Andrew Birkin near the end of his life.

Of all the men I have ever known, Barrie was the wittiest, and the best company. He was also the least interested in sex. He was a darling man. He was an innocent; which is why he could write *Peter Pan*.[16]

One might argue that Nico was naively or keenly trying to preserve Barrie's image, but the youngest of the Davies boys had nothing to gain. He was bequeathed only 3,000 of the 173,000 pounds from the writer's estate. Also, with Nico admitting that he went through a phase of bisexuality in his youth, certainly he would have recognized any impropriety by his "Uncle Jim." No, when the Davies boys' own parents passed away they received from J.M. Barrie only unadulterated love, financial security, and, in many ways, an overbearing, almost maternal figure, for Barrie loved the boys as his own.

Barrie's passion for the Davies boys is best exemplified in his 1901 limited edition book, *The Boy Castaways of Black Lake Island*, a photo essay of make-believe adventures that the boys shared with Barrie's dog Porthos near his summer cottage at Black Lake. Limited indeed, as the book had a pressing of only two copies — one for Barrie and one for Arthur Llewelyn Davies. However, Arthur immediately lost his copy on a railway carriage, making the remaining copy (now housed at the Beinecke Rare Book and Manuscript Library at Yale University) Barrie's rarest book. Poor Arthur! He could not escape Barrie even in the summer, for his family spent six weeks vacationing near the Barrie cottage. Written as if narrated by Peter Davies, the adventure is a takeoff of classic shipwreck stories like *The Swiss Family Robinson* and *The Coral Island*, consisting of 36 photographs taken by Barrie of the boys playing at being pirates. As if in anticipation of his characters in the play *Peter Pan*, Barrie introduces Captain Swarthy as the prototype to Captain Hook and his dog, Porthos, as Nana's predecessor, who watches over the boys as they sleep.

> Even Tinker Bell has reached our island before we left it. It was one evening when we climbed the wood carrying Michael to show him what the trail was like by twilight. As our lanterns twinkled among the leaves Michael saw a twinkle stand still for a moment and he waved his foot gaily to it, thus creating Tink.[17]

Michael, born on June 19, 1900, makes a brief appearance in *The Boy Castaways* as the newest member of the Llewelyn Davies family. As beautiful a baby boy as could be allowed, Michael was soon to become Barrie's favorite.

For Christmas of 1901, Barrie treated the Davies boys to a Christmas entertainment, *Bluebell in Fairyland*. Written by Seymour Hicks, who also starred opposite his wife, Ellaline

A page from *The Boy Castaways* with (from left) Jack, George, and Peter Llewelyn Davies in 1901. It was published and with a very limited printing — two copies! The boys served as the impetus for the creation of the character Peter Pan (courtesy Beinecke Rare Book and Manuscript Library, Yale University).

Terriss, *Bluebell* was different from other theatrical fare for children of the period as it was not derived from a literary source and it presented a solid plot in the form of a dream. Amazed as Barrie was by the youngsters' delight, he was also impressed with how profitable a children's play could be. Surely he could also write a children's play of some quality.

All of the pieces of Barrie's life and writing were now being fused for his future masterpiece. During the next two and a half years there were many changes that would take place during the development of the new children's play, but a few remained constant. Mrs. Darling, the essence of motherhood, was found in Sylvia Davies, while Arthur was unfairly modeled into a cruel caricature as Mr. Darling, a man who has no time or patience for his children. Their daughter was named Wendy Moira Angela Darling, in honor of Margaret Henley, the deceased daughter of Barrie's friend, W.E. Henley. The six-year-old, one of several of the author's favorite children, had a special nickname for Barrie: "my Friendy." Since her childish speech prevented her from pronouncing her *fr*'s properly, it came out as "my Fwendy" or "Wendy." In a few years this would become one of the most popular names for girls. Moira was the same name he used in his play *Little Mary*, and Angela was in honor of a cousin of the Davies boys, who also just so happened to be one of the daughters of Gerald du Maurier, the first Captain Hook.

The names of the Davies boys were also used, with George becoming Mr. Darling's first name, Jack becoming John Napoleon Darling, and Michael becoming Michael Alexander Darling. The middle name of Alexander was soon replaced with Nicholas for Nico, who was born to the Davies family on November 25, 1903. Peter Davies's name was given to the hero of the play, but he did not serve as a single model for Peter Pan. "I made Peter by rubbing the five of you violently together, as savages with two sticks produce a flame," wrote Barrie in 1928 as part of his dedication to the published version of *Peter Pan, or The Boy Who Wouldn't Grow Up*. "That is all he is, the spark I got from you."[18] He states that he does not remember writing the play that was influenced by so many of the adventures and stories he shared with the Davies boys. "What was it that made us eventually give to the public in the thin form of a play that which had been woven for ourselves alone?"[19] Poetic and sentimental as he sounds, Barrie always was able to separate feeling from the real-life events that he was writing about. When his sister Maggie's fiancé died after falling from a horse that he had given the couple as a wedding present, the writer within was always present and jotted down an idea for a novel:

> After death, a character [a la Maggie] talks beautiful resignation, &c. Yet what is the feeling at heart? A kicking at the awfulness? A bitterness? Work this out in novel, showing how almost no one in these cir[cumstances] gets at other's real feelings. Each conceals from the other.[20]

Barrie recorded many important events in his life. No one incident resulted in the birth of Peter Pan. He is a combination of many experiences, acquaintances, and the desire to tell a good tale. Barrie was shrewd enough to use life experiences to create art.

Captain Hook is one of the most evil villains ever created for a children's play. Interestingly, he was originally envisioned as a cruel schoolmaster, someone to whom many children could relate and love to hate. In fact, this idea was not discarded until the play was well into rehearsals. Below is a passage from an early script where Smee meets Hook outside the Darling house at the end of the play.

> HOOK: That's why I'm a schoolmaster — to revenge myself on boys. I hook them so, Starkey, [indicating how he lifts them by waist] and then lay on like this! When it was found what a useful hook I had every father in Merry England clamoured for my services.[21]

Hook plans to keep an eye on Wendy until she meets again with Peter so that he may catch the boy truant.

With the exception of Noodler, the pirates' names were derived from literary figures or actual pirates. Noodler was given his name after John Kelt; the actor portraying him had amazing rubber arms. Tinker Bell was called Tippy in the early drafts, and while most of the lost boys were given nicknames of the period, Slightly was the only boy given a last name, Slightly Soiled, from a note that his mother pinned on his clothing for the laundry cleaners. As for the Twins, they are a direct influence of the twins used in *Bluebell*, although they are given no names as Peter cannot tell them apart.

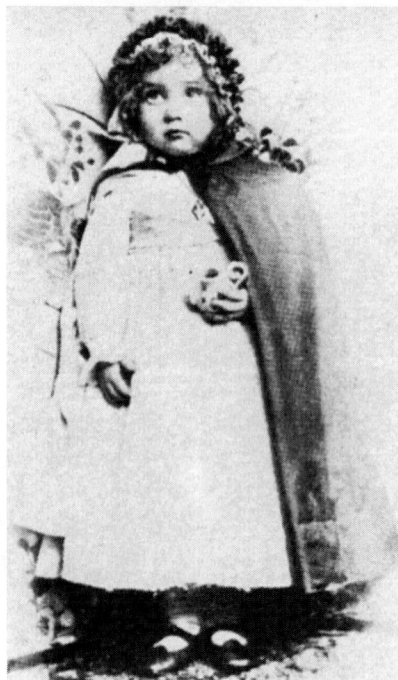

Top, left: Barrie later gave this photograph of eight-year-old Michael Llewelyn Davies, Barrie's favorite, dressed as Peter Pan in July 1908, to sculptor Sir George Frampton as a model for the statue in Kensington Gardens. Frampton chose a more tranquil look, which displeased Barrie (courtesy Great Ormond Street Hospital Children's Charity, London). *Right:* Nicholas "Nico" Llewelyn Davies, the youngest brother, around the age of four, in 1908 (courtesy Great Ormond Street Hospital Children's Charity, London). *Bottom:* Margaret Henley, the child who inspired the creation of the name Wendy. Margaret, who called Barrie her "fwendy," died at age six but has been immortalized since by every girl named Wendy. She is seen in this very rare photograph wearing the cloak that would be replicated for the stage actresses playing Wendy during seventy years of London productions of *Peter Pan* (courtesy Great Ormond Street Hospital Children's Charity, London).

When Barrie completed the first script it was merely titled "Anon-A play." He was sure that his American friend and producer, Charles Frohman, would not be interested in a theatrical venture that would be prohibitively expensive with its large cast, many set changes and special effects. He read the play to actor-producer Beerbohm Tree, who was renowned for his elaborate productions at His Majesty's Theatre but not only was Barrie's play rejected, Tree went so far as to tell Frohman that Barrie had gone mad with his latest writing. But Frohman was known for taking chances, a luxury he enjoyed and could afford. In addition to his lucrative theatre business in the States, Frohman also rented the intimate Duke of York's Theatre in London, which to him resembled a drawing room.

Wrote Daniel Frohman and Isaac Marcosson in their biography of impresario Frohman:

> No two men could have been more opposite. Frohman was quick, nervous, impulsive, bubbling with optimism; Barrie was the quiet, canny Scot, reserved, regressed, and elusive. Yet they had two great traits in common — shyness and humor. As Barrie says: "Because we were the two shyest men in the world, we got on so well and understood each other so perfectly."[22]

It was only a matter of time before Frohman was confronted by the Scotsman during his annual trip to England, when, according to his brother, the two met for dinner at the Garrick Club in London. Barrie seemed nervous and Frohman asked what was wrong.

> "Simply this," said Barrie. "You know I have an agreement to deliver you the manuscript of a play?"
> "Yes," said Frohman.
> "Well, I have it, all right," said Barrie, "but I am sure it will not be a commercial success. But it is a dream-child of mine, and I am so anxious to see it on the stage that I have written another play which I will be glad to give you and which will compensate you for any loss on the one I am so eager to see produced."
> "Don't bother about that," said Frohman. "I will produce both plays."[23]

The second play was *Alice-Sit-By-the-Fire*, which, despite the casting of Ellen Terry in the title role in London and Ethel Barrymore in the U.S., played very short seasons and was quickly forgotten. Frohman was not too concerned for he was sure that the "other" play would be a perfect vehicle for an American actress under his contract: Maude Adams.

Barrie could not have found a better producer than Charles Frohman. Known as the Little Napoleon for his toughness and shrewd business deals, the producer was a child at heart with the theatre world as his playground. He took chances with material that other producers would not touch and maintained a cheerful attitude when a play did not work. For instance, he brought a play, *Held by the Enemy*, to San Francisco at a very great expense, yet when the critics tore the show apart Frohman was undaunted.

> "Look what the critics have done to us," said (the playwright) Gillette, gloomily.
> "But we've got the best of it," replied Frohman, with animation.
> "How's that?" asked Gillette, somewhat puzzled.
> "*They've* got to stay here."[24]

Frohman was enthusiastic about Barrie's new play right from the beginning and he showed his excitement with his purse. According to his brother Daniel:

> When Frohman first read *Peter Pan* he was so entranced that he could not resist telling all his friends about it. He would stop them in the street and act out the scenes. Yet it required the

Left: J.M. Barrie and his second dog, Luath, a Newfoundland (courtesy Andrew Birkin, jmbarrie. co.uk). *Right:* The Duke of York's Theatre, home of *Peter Pan* for ten years.

most stupendous courage and confidence to put on a play that, from the manuscript, sounded like a combination of circus and extravaganza: a play in which children flew in and out of rooms, crocodiles swallowed alarm-clocks, a man exchanged places with his dog in its kennel, and various other seemingly absurd and ridiculous things happened.

But Charles believed in Barrie.[25]

Frohman decided to produce a London production of the new play not only for its own sake but also as a test for a vehicle for an American production with Maude Adams as her busy schedule would not permit her to take on such a project until the 1905 season. Earlier, Barrie had written to Adams about the progress of his new play. Informally it was referred to as "Peter and Wendy" but Barrie was toying with the title *The Great White Father*. According to Andrew Birkin, Frohman suggested the simple *Peter Pan* as the title for the play, but Daniel Frohman gave all of the credit to Barrie.

The original title that Barrie gave the play was "The Great White Father," which Frohman liked. Just as soon as Barrie suggested that it be named after its principal character, Frohman fairly overflowed with enthusiasm. In preparing for "Peter Pan" in England, Charles was like a child with a toy. Money was spent lavishly; whole scenes were made and never used. He regarded it as a great and rollicking adventure.[26]

While Frohman was excited about his new "toy," the new play was much more to Barrie than a game like "Hide and Seek," or, for that matter, just another play. No, this new work was an obsession — a conglomeration of "youth, joy and freedom," of all that he held dearest. And ready or not, *Peter Pan, or The Boy Who Wouldn't Grow Up* was finally on its way into production.

Poster by Ben Nicholson with Great Big Little Panther advertising the original production of *Peter Pan.* Ben's father, William Nicholson, designed the sets and costumes for the play. Ben was ten when the poster, painted a few years before, was printed. He was cross with J.M. Barrie because he never received any payment for the design. The missing heading or the lower piece had the information about the play (V & A Images/Victoria and Albert Museum, London; © 2010 Artists Rights Society (ARS), New York / DACS, London).

2

Nina Boucicault and
the First Peter Pan

But to me Peter Pan *has always been much more than a fairy play for children. The fairy trappings are only a setting for the development of a serious idea. From beginning to end the story is rather wistful commentary on human nature, taking as its theme the supreme selfishness of man and the supreme unselfishness of woman.*

— Nina Boucicault, 1923[1]

For years Nina Boucicault was remembered by London audiences as being the best of all Peter Pans. Barrie sustained this belief years later when he advised another actress how to approach the role: he told her that Peter should be either a lovable tomboy, as his favorite actress, Pauline Chase, portrayed him, or the whimsical, fairy creature that Nina Boucicault made him. But memories last only as long as a lifetime and today, almost 100 years later, we each have our own favorite Peter Pan. Only one thing remains constant — Nina Boucicault was the first actress to play Peter Pan.

We know the background that led to the writing of the play, but was Barrie thinking of Nina while he was writing? At one point he corresponded with Maude Adams stating that he wrote the play for her and with her in mind. Still, even then he was not sure which part he wanted her to play. Later he approached Ellaline Terriss to play Peter with Seymour Hicks as Captain Hook. The talent and popularity of the husband-wife acting team, not to mention their success with *Bluebell in Fairyland*, must have influenced him to some degree. Mrs. Hicks was pregnant, however, and her husband did not want to appear without her, although he later starred as Hook in 1938. Barrie was enamored with several other actresses and it would difficult to assess if he was thinking of one in particular to play Peter, least of all Nina Boucicault. No, if any character from *Peter Pan* was inspired in any way by the performer who would eventually play him, it was probably Captain Hook. In 1964, Christopher Calthrop wrote to Nicholas Davies inquiring if his father, Donald Calthrop, a nephew of Dion Boucicault and an actor who had worked with Barrie on several occasions, was the original source of inspiration for Captain Hook. Nicholas responded:

> I would say that J.M.B. only on the rarest occasions had an actor or actress definitely in mind while he was writing a book: Elisabeth Bergner certainly for *The Boy David*: Gaby Deslys certainly for *Rosy Rapture*: but always the part came later, came, probably, at the rehearsal stages when J.M.B. took an unusually active part in moulding and rewriting and so on.
>
> From what he told me — and it was frequently pretty difficult, if not impossible, to know what he really meant — it was highly desirable if not, indeed, essential that the man to play Captain

Hook should also be Mr. Darling. Ideally, he would say, Mrs. Darling should be played by someone impossibly young to have children as old as John and Wendy and Mr. Darling should really not be all that much older. So that, although I remember well his affection for your father and high appreciation of his acting: and am, of course, aware of the connection with Dion Boucicault [producer of *Peter Pan*] on whom J.M.B. depended a great deal: I would, I'm afraid, be certain enough that if anyone at all was in J.M. B.'s mind for Mr. Darling as he created the story, it would have been in the shape of Gerald du Maurier, the original of course as Captain Hook and Mr. Darling, who was, as you probably know, my mother's brother. As you will also know the story/stories evolved out of tales told to my brothers, and indeed, while the published version of the play is dedicated to my brothers and myself, the book of *Peter Pan in Kensington Gardens* is dedicated to my father and mother as well. My mother was the real spur, so it would seem, possibly, most natural that her devoted brother, Gerald, should always have been somewhere in the mind of the author.[2]

Nina Boucicault as Peter Pan, crying because he can't get his shadow to stick. Duke of York's Theatre, 1904 (photograph: Ellis and Walery).

Gerald du Maurier had already achieved stardom in several plays, including Barrie's *The Admirable Crichton* and *Little Mary*, and was yet to create his greatest triumph in *Dear Brutus* when he was asked to play Captain Hook. In addition to being an excellent actor, he also had the distinction of being uncle to the Davies boys and the youngest son of their grandfather, George du Maurier.

In the biography *Gerald*, his daughter, Daphne du Maurier, wrote:

When Hook first paced his quarter-deck in the year of 1904, children were carried screaming from the stalls, and even big boys of twelve were known to reach for their mother's hand in the friendly shelter of the boxes. How he was hated, with his flourish, his poses, his dreaded diabolical smile! That ashen face, those blood-red lips, the long, dank, greasy curls; the sardonic laugh, the maniacal scream, the appalling courtesy of his gestures; and that above most terrible of moments when he descended the stairs and with slow, most merciless cunning poured the poison into Peter's glass. There was no peace in those days until the monster was destroyed, and the fight upon the pirate ship was a fight to the death. Gerald was Hook: he was no dummy dressed from Simmons' in a Clarkson wig, ranting and roaring about the stage, a grotesque figure whom the modern child finds a little comic. He was a tragic and rather ghastly creation who knew no peace, and whose soul was in torment; a dark shadow; a sinister dream; a bogey of fear who lives perpetually in the grey recesses of every small boy's mind. All boys had their Hooks, as Barrie knew; he was the phantom who came by night and stole his way into their murky dreams. He was the

Seymour Hicks as Dickie and Ellaline Terriss as Bluebell in *Bluebell in Fairy Land*, a Christmas pantomime from 1901. Barrie wanted the husband-wife team for the leading roles in *Peter Pan* (photograph: Rotary Photograph, E.C.).

Left: A portrait of Gerald du Maurier, the first Captain Hook, circa 1904 (photograph: Lissie Caswall Smith). *Right:* A rare illustration of Gerald du Maurier as Captain Hook, by David Wilson from 1905 (courtesy Roy Busby).

spirit of a lonely spirit that was terror and inspiration in one. And, because he had imagination and a spark of genius, Gerald made him alive.[3]

Gerald du Maurier not only provided the new play with his talent but also with his attraction at the box office. The part of Peter was another story, demanding great sensitivity and athletic prowess. Ironically, Dion Boucicault did not have to look far. Continuing with the pantomime tradition, Peter, the principal boy, would be played by an actress — none other than the director's own sister, Nina Boucicault. Hardly a newcomer to the theatre, Nina, who was born on February 27, 1867, made her first stage appearance in 1883 in her father's American production of *The Colleen Band*. Nine years later, the Strand Theatre featured her London debut in *The New Wing*. In 1892 she played Kitty Verdun in *Charley's Aunt* and continued in the role for two years. Except for a seven-year hiatus in the 1920s, Nina was

Right: A contemporary portrait of Nina Boucicault, circa 1900 (photograph: Rapid Photograph Co.).

Nina Boucicault as Peter Pan (courtesy Great Ormond Street Hospital Children's Charity, London).

seen on the stage almost every season until she made her last appearance in 1936. She died on August 2, 1950, at age 83.

Nina previously created another Barrie character, Moira Loiney, in the minor success *Little Mary*, which opened on September 24, 1903. Almost four decades later Denis Mackail wrote of the performance as Moira:

Not Beautiful. Or you don't think so for a minute or two. But then her voice and movements do rather more than the trick. If Barrie writes something that raises a slight shudder in print, Miss Boucicault only has to say it and your heart turns over three times while tears trickle from your eyes. This gift and others she will be bringing, in only a little over a year now, to the creation of the first stage Peter Pan.[4]

Everything about *Peter Pan* was unconventional — including rehearsals. Hilda Trevelyan, the actress to play Wendy, did not know that she would be flying until she was asked to take out a life insurance policy. She later recalled that "Barrie never read the play to the cast. We worked on one scene at a time, none of us knowing what was going to happen next."[5] The press as well as the cast was kept in the dark. Barrie himself was of little help to Nina as she tried to figure out just who *was* Peter Pan. Nina wrote in 1923:

When I first began to study the part of Peter Pan, I remember going to Sir James Barrie and asking him, since I was to be the first Peter, if he would tell me something of his conception of the part and how it should be played. I thought that he would naturally have a great deal to say on the subject, that he might perhaps explain to me how he visualized Peter, and give me his ideas as to how the character should be developed. But I was doomed to disappointment. "Peter is a bird," he said to me in that quiet, level voice of his, "and he is one day old." And that is all I had to go on. At rehearsals, it is true; he would drop an occasional hint, but if one wanted to ask him a question one could never be quite sure of finding him. At one moment he would be sitting in the stalls, and the next he had slipped out in his elusive way and disappeared.[6]

The part of Wendy was of equal importance to Barrie and had to be played by an actress of equal stature. Hilda Trevelyan, born on February 4, 1880, was such an experienced actress. She made her theatrical debut at age nine and retired 50 years later after creating the original roles in *What Every Woman Knows* and *A Kiss for Cinderella*, as well as Babbie in *The Little Minister* and Tweeny in *The Admirable Crichton*. As far as Barrie was concerned, she was the best. "You are Wendy," he wrote years later, "and

Hilda Trevelyan as the first Wendy in a 1904–05 portrait (photograph: Ellis and Walery).

there never will be another to touch you."[7] For several years no one had the opportunity to challenge her, for she continued to play Wendy until the 1907-08 season, then came back to play her again in 1909, 1911, and 1914. Hilda died on November 10, 1959.

Dorothea Baird, the actress chosen for Mrs. Darling, was very popular in her day and had appeared in Barrie's *The Wedding Guest* in 1900. Five years later she originated the part of Trilby opposite Beerbohm Tree's Svengali. Mrs. Darling's oldest son, John, was portrayed by George Hersee, who appeared not only in *Quality Street* but also in *Bluebell in Fairyland*.

For the part of Smee, George Shelton was selected. In addition to his many years of experience as a character actor Shelton was also in Barrie's first London production in 1891, *Ibsen's Ghost*, as well as *Walker, London* and *Quality Street*.

The part of Smee would become his most famous role, one that he would continue to play until 1929, missing only two seasons. Shelton explained:

> There have been two great reasons for my long association with Peter Pan. The first of these is my love for the play and the part of Smee. The second one I must keep to myself. Having been connected with the stage for over fifty years, one cannot expect to be much in demand. Consequently, I welcome each revival of Peter Pan with great pleasure, looking upon it, as my old friend, Chance Newton, once said, as "my old age Peter Pansion."[8]

Of the Lost Boys, two actresses went on to fame: Christine Silver, who played Nibs, and Pauline Chase, an American actress who earned great popularity as the "Pink Pajama Girl." It is more than likely that her success in that show prompted Barrie to include a special dance in *Peter Pan* that allowed her to demonstrate her terpsichorean talents with pillows while wearing pajamas.

George Shelton credited Dion Boucicault's direction for much of the success of the play. He wrote:

> Those who have enjoyed *Peter Pan*— and they are legion — will remember the divisions of the stage, the flying feats of John Napoleon Darling and his family, and so on. I wonder if they can realize what each one of these scenes meant in the beginning, when ways and means had to be devised by which all should work smoothly, and the frequent change of picture be effected without waits interminable in length. Truly, this was a great piece of work for any man to undertake and carry through successfully. Nor did Dion Boucicault's task end here, for when the scenery was in train there

Winifred Geoghegan as Michael Darling, 1904 (photograph: W. Fulkner & Co.).

It's Smee! was the title of George Shelton's autobiography, which was published in 1928. The actor played the role, except for two seasons, from 1904 until 1929 (photograph: Ellis and Walery, 1905).

were still the rehearsals of the play itself to organize. During that time Boucicault must have spoken every word of the text, sung every note of the music, and danced every step of the dances many times over. I think that in the whole long experiences as a producer — and he has had many successes in that field — Boucicault can never have surpassed this effort.[9]

Nina remembered:

I shall never forget the strenuous times we had during rehearsals. Fifteen to eighteen hours a day was nothing uncommon, and before they were over both Sir Gerald du Maurier and I lost our voices. It was the first production of the play and there were so many points that needed constant rehearsing. Apart from the actual play, the flying, the lighting, the dancing had each to be rehearsed separately until it was perfect, and often there would be calls for three separate rehearsals at three different theatres in the course of the morning.[10]

The play was to premiere on December 22, 1904, but mechanical problems delayed the start. Even when it opened five days later, it was necessary to omit two and a half scenes.

The following is based on a description given to Roger Lancelyn Green of that first evening's performance:

The first few moments of the play prepared the audience for an extraordinary evening at the theatre. A small girl in a maid's costume stepped in front to of the curtain to cue the conductor to play the opening music.

The programme has Act I of the play beginning Scene I, Outside the House, although this is no more than a glimpse of a painting of a house, which quickly goes up revealing Scene II — Inside the House. In a nursery Mr. and Mrs. Darling are preparing to go out for the evening. Mrs. Darling is hesitant to leave her three children, Wendy, John, and Michael, this evening. She explains to her husband that a small boy has appeared at their window and that one evening he left his shadow. Her husband has no patience for his wife's story or for Nana, the dog that cares for the children. The dog is brought outside to her kennel. Before Mrs. Darling leaves she sings the "Lullaby" to her children, a 17th century song with music by John Crook, a staff composer and conductor for the Duke of York's Theatre who wrote most of the music for the play.

While all the children are asleep Peter Pan returns and with the aid

Dion Boucicault (left), the first director of *Peter Pan*, and his leading actor, Gerald du Maurier, circa 1904 (photograph: J. Beagles & Co.).

Henry J. Ford's costume design for Nina Boucicault, 1904 (courtesy Karpeles Manuscript Library Museum).

of his fairy, Tinker Bell, a flickering stage light, he finds his shadow. He cannot make it stick and soon his sobbing awakens Wendy. After she sews it on for him, he does a shadow dance. Peter then tells her about Never Never Never Land (in later versions of the play the fairy land would be shortened to Never Never Land and finally to Never Land). Wendy is so pleased with the things that Peter has to say about girls she offers him a kiss but resorts to giving him a thimble

LULLABY.

from "Peter Pan."

WORDS 17th CENTURY.   MUSIC BY JOHN CROOK.

"Lullaby," a seventeenth-century lyric, was set to music by John Crook for Mrs. Darling to sing to her children.

The Song of the Pirates.

"The Song of the Pirates." Words by J.M. Barrie and music by John Crook.

"The House We Built for Wendy." L. to R. Joan Burnett (Tootles), George Hersee (John), Phyllis Beadon (Second Twin), A.W. Bascomb (Slightly), Hilda Trevelyan (Wendy), Nina Boucicault (Peter), Winifred Geoghegan (Michael), and Pauline Chase (First Twin) on stage during the 1904–05 season of *Peter Pan* (photograph: Ellis and Walery).

when he reveals his ignorance about kisses. Peter then gives Wendy an acorn button, which she attaches to a chain around her neck. Peter convinces Wendy to go back with him but she asks that her brothers also be permitted to go. Peter teaches the children to fly around the nursery and then they fly out the window to Never Never Never Land.

Act II, The Never Never Never Land, introduces the Lost Boys and their enemies, the Pirates and Captain Hook, in the first scene called The House We Built for Wendy. The Pirates sing "The Song of the Pirates" and it is revealed that the pirate king obtained his hook when a crocodile ate his hand.

Tinker Bell, jealous of Wendy, flies ahead of the children to warn the Lost Boys of the coming of the Wendy-Bird. They shoot her down only to find out from Peter that he intended her to be their mother. Luckily, the arrow hit the "kiss" Wendy is wearing and she is not dead. The boys build a house around their sleeping mother.

The curtain comes down while Scenes 2 and 3 are being set. Because of the time needed to move the elaborate sets, Captain Hook comes out in front of the curtain to offer his imitations of famous actors pretending to be pirates. The curtain goes up and reveals the Redskins' camp in front of a drop cloth where we are introduced to Great Big Panther and his daughter, Tiger Lily, during an Indian dance.

Scene III, Our Home Underground, shows the boys living underground, guarded by the Indians. A lively pillow dance is followed by a story from Wendy as she puts the boys to sleep. Her story describes the joy that they will bring to their parents when they fly home. Peter groans and explains what happened to him.

> PETER: Wendy, you are wrong about mother. I thought like you about the windows, so I stayed away for moons and moons and moons, and then flew back, but the window was barred, for my mother had forgotten all about me and there was another little boy sleeping in my bed.[11]

Wendy realizes that it is time to go and Peter asks Tinker Bell to lead them home. As they leave they are kidnapped by the Pirates who had driven the Indians away. Hook sneaks down to

Miriam Nesbitt as Tiger Lily in 1904–05.

poison the medicine of a sleeping Peter. After the captain leaves, Tink tells Peter that his medicine is poisoned. However, he does not believe her and just as he is about to take the medicine, Tinker Bell drinks it. Realizing that she is dying, Peter begs the audience to save her by clapping their hands to show that they still believe in fairies. Tink lives and they're off to rescue Wendy.

Act III, We Return to Our Distracted Mothers, begins with Scene 1, The Pirate Ship, where Wendy and the boys are in captivity. Hook orders all of the boys to walk the plank after Michael and John decline his offer to join his crew and swear, "Down with King George." Peter arrives just in time to save them. When all fails, Hook jumps off the ship to the waiting crocodile. The curtain falls and rises again to show a tableau of Peter dressed as a triumphant Napoleon.

Scene II, A Last Glimpse of the Redskins, shows a pirate, Starkey, as a prisoner of the Indians, tied up and forced to play a concertina. "Oh, miserable Starkey," he cries until the Indian Panther threatens him to change to tune to "Oh, happy Starkey." Then Smee, Hook's first mate, arrives followed by the crocodile. Starkey softly plays his instrument as the reptile falls asleep. Smee calls inside its mouth to see if his captain is really in there.

SMEE
Avast, belay, inside! D'ye hear?
My captain Hook, yo-ho!
Oh are you still a pirate bold,
Or have you gone below?

(After Song, SMEE finds hook in Crocodile's mouth. Takes it out. It gives two snaps.)

Ah, it got him! The gentle Captain is inside! Thus crime is punished and all villains die! Oh! Tempora! O mores! O cui bono? Cui!

Scene III, Home, Sweet Home.—The children return to their mother.[12]

The omission of scenes, a delayed opening, and the continued exhaustive rehearsal schedule would be daunting for any cast and crew. In 1939 Nina Boucicault wrote to Eric Johns of *Theatre World*:

> I am afraid we were all so tired with the very long and heavy rehearsals of "PAN" that I was somewhat bewildered on the first night. Fog had held up most things and indeed the "Tree Tops" scene was not done for nearly a month after the first night.[13]

Nina was indeed tired, for what seemed like a month for the "Tree Tops" addition was in fact a matter of days. However, the cast was overwhelmed by the response of the audience on opening night. Nina wrote:

Top: The Pillow Dance. L. to R. Joan Burnett (Tootles), George Hersee (John), Pauline Chase (First Twin with her legs in the pillows), Hilda Trevelyan (Wendy), Winifred Geoghegan (as Michael in the hanging basket), Christine Silver (Nibs), and Nina Boucicault (sitting as Peter) in the underground home. 1904 (photograph: Ellis and Walery). *Bottom:* The Home Underground. Wendy tells a story during the 1904-05 season. L. to R. Pauline Chase (First Twin), Phyllis Beadon (Second Twin), Joan Burnett (Tootles), Alice Dubarry (Curly), George Hersee (John), Winifred Geoghegan (as Michael, sitting on the floor), Christine Silver (Nibs), and Hilda Trevelyan (Wendy) (photograph: Ellis and Walery).

But that first night brought us our reward. The gasp of surprise that greeted me as I flew in through the window and the enthusiasm at the end of the first act were well worth all the hard work. The audience were [*sic*] splendid; I don't think they missed a single point.[14]

In point of fact, Peter did not fly in the nursery. Below is an excerpt from the original script:

[MUSIC #3: PETER'S ENTRANCE]

(NIGHT-LIGHTS out 1, 2, 3 to Music Cue)

(The room is now dimly lit by night-lights and fire. Pause. Then night-lights go out one by one to music. Suspense. TINKERBELL [*sic*] light. Then TINKER BELL darts in. All that enters under this name is a flame of light not much larger than a human finger — it flashes about the room, zig-zagging hither and thither in air, then it lights on jug L. and disappears.)

(LIMES P.S. on PETER on)

(When TINKER BELL is in the jug PETER PAN appears as before, undoes window, lifts sash, comes in, closes window)

(LIME OFF)

(Runs down C., is frightened, crosses above MICHAEL's bed, runs behind curtain where wire is put on, he emerges, crosses to above Michael's bed. MICHAEL turns in his sleep; he flies to mantel. John turns. PETER flies back to above Michael's bed, then hides behind curtain again when the wire is removed — he then comes down C.)

(BELLS)

PETER: (In low voice, jumps on chair L.C.) Tinker Bell! Tink, where are you?[15]

Hilda recalled:

I shall never forget waiting to make my entrance on the first night, at the moment when it dawned on the audience that the dog "Nana," airing the pajamas before the nursery fire, was really the Nanny. The shout of joy that went up from the house simply beggars description. The audience was seeing something new, and how they relished it! They liked the flying, too, especially as *Peter Pan* was the first production in which flying was actually part of the play. The familiar flying ballets, so popular in pantomime, were not an intrinsic part of the story, as were our aeronautic efforts in Barrie's play.[16]

Nina continued:

I remember that I had been rather anxious about the scene where Peter appeals to the audience to clap if they believe in fairies. "Suppose they don't clap?" I had asked. "What do I do then?"[17]

Nina was not the only one concerned about the clapping. Dion instructed the musicians in the orchestra to initiate the clapping if the audience was slow upon their cue. Incredibly, the spectators, made up of mostly adults, including theatre critics, applauded wildly, bringing Nina to tears. She remembered:

John Kelt performed in the role of the pirate, Noodler, for 28 seasons between 1904 and 1934.

The Battle on the Pirate Ship during the 1904-05 season. L. to R. Winifred Geoghegan (Michael), Nina Boucicault (Peter), A.W. Bascomb (Slightly), Hilda Trevelyan (Wendy), Alice Dubarry (Curly), Gerald du Maurier (Captain Hook), Pauline Chase (First Twin) and Phyllis Beadon (Second Twin) (photograph: Ellis and Walery).

But clap! I think everyone in the house believed in fairies. And I am sure the play took them by surprise ... the play was so utterly different from any other play that the audience, I fancy, were swept off their feet.[18]

Most of the critics, along with the audience, were also swept off their feet in the intimate atmosphere of the Duke of York's Theatre. One paper's headline with the heading "Mr. Barrie's 'Peter Pan'—Tomime," said:

The piece which last night kept a crowded audience at the Duke of York's in ecstasies is less a play than a playground. A playground in which Mr. Barrie's impish sense of fun may disport itself to the fullest. The story is of little moment. Peter Pan is half human and wholly fairy by turns.[19]

The *Morning Post* declared:

Peter Pan is not so much a play as a spree and never has Mr. Barrie spreed to better purpose.... The first act was, for all its impish waywardness, truer to home and nursery than any other act we can recall.[20]

The Daily Telegraph said:

The *Peter Pan* amalgam, as is of the oddest and most contrary ingredients, is in its essential qualities, a play of such originality, of such tenderness, and of such daring, that not even a shadow of doubt regarding its complete success was to be discerned in the final fall of the curtain.... It is so true, so natural, so touching, that it brought the audience to the writer's feet and held them captives there.... We have unfortunately to endure a "front scene" as meaningless and as exasperating as it is paltry. The only excuse for its introduction, if excuse it can be considered, is that it

Top: The Pirate Ship. The Napoleonic Tableau mimicking the famous painting by Sir William Quiller Orchardson. L. to R. Alice Dubarry (Curly), Phyllis Beadon (Second Twin), Pauline Chase (First Twin), Winifred Geoghegan (Michael), A.W. Bascomb (Slightly), Joan Burnett (Tootles), Christine Silver (Nibs) and Nina Boucicault (as Peter dressed as Napoleon after the surrender of Captain Hook) (photograph: Ellis and Walery, 1904–1905). *Bottom:* A print of *The Surrender of Napoleon to Great Britain* by Sir William Quiller Orchardson (1832–1910).

27/12/04

Duke of York's Theatre.
ST. MARTIN'S LANE, W.C.
Proprietors ...   .   Mr. & Mrs. FRANK WYATT.
Sole Lessee and Manager   ...   .   CHARLES FROHMAN

EVERY AFTERNOON at 2, and EVERY EVENING at 8,
CHARLES FROHMAN
PRESENTS
PETER PAN
OR
THE BOY WHO WOULDN'T GROW UP.
A Play in Three Acts, by
J. M. BARRIE.

Peter Pan ...	Miss NINA BOUCICAULT
Mr. Darling	Mr. GERALD du MAURIER
Mrs. Darling	Miss DOROTHEA BAIRD
Wendy Moira Angela Darling	Miss HILDA TREVELYAN
John Napoleon Darling	Master GEORGE HERSEE
Michael Nicholas Darling	Miss WINIFRED GEOGHEGAN
Nana	Mr. ARTHUR LUPINO
Tinker Bell	Miss JANE WREN
Tootles	Miss JOAN BURNETT
Nibs	Miss CHRISTINE SILVER
Slightly	Mr. A. W. BASKCOMB
Curly (Members of Peter's Band)	Miss ALICE DUBARRY
1st Twin	Miss PAULINE CHASE
2nd Twin	Miss PHYLLIS BEADON
Jas Hook (The Pirate Captain)	Mr. GERALD du MAURIER
Smee	Mr. GEORGE SHELTON
Gentleman Starkey	Mr. SYDNEY HARCOURT
Cookson	Mr. CHARLES TREVOR
Cecco (Pirates)	Mr. FREDERICK ANNERLEY
Mullins	Mr. HUBERT WILLIS
Jukes	Mr. JAMES ENGLISH
Noodler	Mr. JOHN KELT
Great Big Little Panther	Mr. PHILIP DARWIN
Tiger Lily (Redskins)	Miss MIRIAM NESBITT
Liza	Miss ELA Q. MAY
(Author of the Play)	

Redskins, Pirates, Crocodile, Eagle, Ostrich, Cat, Pack of Wolves, by Misses Mary Mayfren, Victoria Addison, Moira
Creegan, Gladys Stewart, Kitty Malone, Marie Park, Elsa Sinclair, Christine Lawrence, Mary Maddison, Gladys
Carrington, Laura Barradell, Daisy Murch. Messrs. E. Kirby, S. Spencer, G. Malvern, J Grahame. Masters S. Grata,
A. Ganker, D. Ducrow, C. Lawton, W. Scott, G. Henson, R. Franks, E. Marini, P. Gicardo, A. Biserga.

ACT I.—OUR EARLY DAYS.	ACT II.—continued
Scene 1.—Outside the House. (Painted by Mr. W. Hann, designed by Mr. W. Nicholson).	Scene 2.—The Redskins' Camp. (Mr. W. Hann)
	Scene 3.—Our Home under the Ground.
Scene 2.—Inside the House. (Mr. W. Harford).	ACT III.—WE RETURN TO OUR DISTRACTED MOTHERS.
ACT II.—THE NEVER, NEVER, NEVER LAND.	Scene 1.—The Pirate Ship. (Mr. W. Harford).
Scene 1.—The House we built for Wendy. (Mr. W. Hann).	Scene 2.—A last glimpse of the Redskins.
The Curtain will here be lowered for a few moments.	Scene 3.—Home, Sweet Home.

The Play produced under the Direction of Mr. DION BOUCICAULT.

| General Manager ... ... (For CHARLES FROHMAN) ... ... | W. LESTOCQ |

The Esquimaux, Pirates and Indian Costumes designed by Mr. W. NICHOLSON, and executed by Messrs. B. J. SIMMONS, 7, King Street,
Covent Garden. Miss Boucicault's Dress designed by Mr. HENRY J. FORD. Miss Baird's Costumes by Madame HAYWARD 64, New Bond St.
Miss Trevelyan's Dresses designed and executed by SHERA, 17, Sloane Street.   The Dances invented and arranged by Mr. W. WARDE.
The Music composed and arranged by Mr. JOHN CROOK.   The Flying Machines supplied and worked by Mr. G. KIRBY.   Properties
supplied by Mr. LOUIS LABHART, 12, Queen's Square, W.C.   Stage Mechanist Mr. H. THOMPSON.   Electrician, Mr. C. HAMBLETON.
Property Master, Mr. W. BURDICK.

| Stage Manager ... ... DUNCAN McRAE | Musical Director ... ... JOHN CROOK |
| Business Manager ... ... | JAMES W. MATHEWS |

Extract from the Rules made by the Lord Chamberlain
(1.) The name of the actual and responsible Manager of the Theatre must be printed on every play bill. (2.) The Public can leave the Theatre
at the end of the performance by all exit and entrance doors, which must open outwards   (3.) The fire-proof screen to the proscenium
opening will be lowered at least once during every performance to ensure its being in proper working order. (4.) Smoking is not permitted in the
Auditorium. (5.) All gangways, passages and staircases must be kept free from chairs or any other obstructions, whether permanent or temporary

ICES TEA AND COFFEE can be had of the Attendants.

An extremely rare program from the opening night of *Peter Pan* on December 27, 1904. Note that
there are no advertisements in the side borders and that the last scene is "Home Sweet Home," the
Darling nursery.

affords Mr. Gerald du Maurier an opportunity of imitating the bearing and style of Sir Henry
Irving, Mr. Tree, and Mr. Martin Harvey: but that Mr. Barrie should have feathered an interlude
so unworthy of his brilliant talent is wholly and entirely incomprehensible. The sooner it is
replaced by something of a fresher and more exhilarating character the better it will be for play
and author.[21]

Said the *Illustrated Sporting and Dramatic News*:

Miss Nina Boucicault both acts and looks Peter Pan admirably, and Miss Hilda Trevelyan is
simply marvelous as the very young heroine.[22]

Du Maurier was also praised for his roles:

Mr. Gerald du Maurier makes a spirited Mr. Darling, but the part, though requiring very delicate
handling, is comparatively short. He has greater chances as Hook, of whom he gives a splendidly
high-coloured impersonation. It is not often that an actor catches his author's meaning so completely.[23]

The critic from *The Morning Post* went on:

In *Peter Pan* Mr. Barrie again relies not on any real dramatic interest but on his marvelous powers of keeping you amused in the theatre. Mr. Barrie is the only living writer, except perhaps, Mr. Bernard Shaw, who can build palaces of entertainment on an unsubstantial basis.[24]

The critic also found that

the play is admirably acted. Miss Nina Boucicault is excellent as Peter, and preserves the half-human, half-fairy character with exquisite skill.... Miss Hilda Trevelyan is most delightful and sympathetic as Wendy, and Master George Hersee and Miss Winifred Geoghegan are also excellent. All the other characters are well rendered, but we must specially mention the Smee of Mr. George Shelton and the First Twin of Miss Pauline Chase, who performed a most remarkable dance with each foot in a pillow. Great pains have been taken with the mounting and with the stage management, while the crocodile and some of the other animals are immense.[25]

One of the most famous reviews was quite negative, coming from Barrie's friend, Anthony Hope, who "sat unmoved throughout the performance, and at the end was heard to remark: 'Oh, for an hour of Herod!'"[26] Yet, overall, the response to the new play was overwhelmingly positive:

Top: The cover of the Duke of York's Theatre Program, 1904. *Bottom:* Mrs. Darling (Dorothy Baird) being comforted by Nana (Arthur Lupino) in the nursery (photograph: Ellis and Walery, 1905, courtesy Roy Busby).

Top: The Darling family reunited: (from left) A. Lupino (Nana), George Hersee (John), Gerald du Maurier (Mr. Darling), Winifred Geoghegan (Michael), Hilda Trevelyan (Wendy), and Dorothea Baird (Mrs. Darling) (photograph: Ellis and Walery, 1905). *Bottom:* The "How to Know Your Mother" scene was added four days after opening night. This photograph is unusual as the scene would later be deleted from the play (photograph: Ellis and Walery, 1905).

Duke of York's Theatre.

ST. MARTIN'S LANE, W.C.

Proprietors .... Mr. & Mrs. FRANK WYATT

Sole Lessee and Manager .... CHARLES FROHMAN

EVERY AFTERNOON at 2.30, and EVERY EVENING at 8 30,

CHARLES FROHMAN

PRESENTS

PETER PAN

OR

THE BOY WHO WOULDN'T GROW UP.

A Play in Three Acts, by
J. M. BARRIE.

Peter Pan	Miss NINA BOUCICAULT
Mr. Darling	Mr. GERALD du MAURIER
Mrs. Darling	Miss DOROTHEA BAIRD
Wendy Moira Angela Darling	Miss HILDA TREVELYAN
John Napoleon Darling	Master GEORGE HERSEE
Michael Nicholas Darling	Miss WINIFRED GEOGHEGAN
Nana	Mr. ARTHUR LUPINO
Tinker Bell	Miss JANE WREN
Tootles	Miss JOAN BURNETT
Nibs	Miss CHRISTINE SILVER
Slightly	Mr. A. W. BASKCOMB
Curly	Miss ALICE DUBARRY
1st Twin	Miss PAULINE CHASE
2nd Twin	Miss PHYLLIS BEADON
Jas. Hook	Mr. GERALD du MAURIER
Smee	Mr. GEORGE SHELTON
Gentleman Starkey	Mr. SYDNEY HARCOURT
Cookson	Mr. CHARLES TREVOR
Cecco	Mr. FREDERICK ANNERLEY
Mullins	Mr. HUBERT WILLIS
Jukes	Mr. JAMES ENGLISH
Noodler	Mr. JOHN KELT
Great Big Little Panther	Mr. PHILIP DARWIN
Tiger Lily	Miss MIRIAM NESBITT
Liza	Miss ELA Q. MAY

(Members of Peter's Band)

(The Pirate Captain)

(Pirates)

(Redskins)

(Author of the Play)

Beautiful Mothers, Redskins, Pirates, Crocodile, Eagle, Ostrich, Cat, Pack of Wolves, by Misses Mary Mayfren, Victoria Addison, Moira Creegan, Gladys Stewart, Kitty Malone, Marie Park, Elsa Sinclair, Christine Lawrence, Mary Maddison, Gladys Carrington, Laura Barradell, Daisy Murch. Messrs. E. Kirby, S. Spencer, G. Malvern, J. Grahame, Masters S. Grata, A. Ganker, D. Ducrow, C. Lawton, W. Scott, G. Henson, R. Franks, E. Marini, P. Gicardo, A. Biserga.

ACT I.—OUR EARLY DAYS.
   Inside the House. *(Mr. W. Harford).*
ACT II.—THE NEVER, NEVER, NEVER LAND.
   Scene 1.—The House we built for Wendy. *(Mr. W. Hann.)*
     The Curtain will here be lowered for a few moments.
   Scene 2.—The Redskins' Camp. *(Mr. W. Hann)*
   Scene 3.—Our Home under the Ground. ,,

ACT III.—WE RETURN TO OUR DISTRACTED MOTHERS.
   Scene 1.—The Pirate Ship. *(Mr. W. Harford).*
   Scene 2.—A last glimpse of the Redskins.
   Scene 3.—How to know your Mother.
   Scene 4.—Outside the House.
   Scene 5.—The Tree Tops. *(Mr. W. Hann.)*

The Play produced under the Direction of Mr. DION BOUCICAULT.

General Manager *(For CHARLES FROHMAN)* .... W. LESTOCQ

The Esquimaux, Pirates and Indian Costumes designed by Mr. W. NICHOLSON, and executed by Messrs. B. J. SIMMONS 7 King Street, Covent Garden. Miss Boucicault's Dress designed by Mr. HENRY J. FORD. Miss Baird's Costumes by Madame HAYWARD 6¾ New Bond St. Miss Trevelyan's Dresses designed and executed by SHEBA, 17, Sloane Street. The Dances invented and arranged by Mr. W. WARDE. The Music composed and arranged by Mr. JOHN CROOK. The Flying Machines supplied and worked by Mr. G. KIRBY. Properties supplied by Mr. LOUIS LABHART, 12, Queen's Square, W.C. Stage Mechanist Mr. H. THOMPSON. Electrician, Mr. C. HAMBLETON. Property Master, Mr. W. BURDICK.

Stage Manager .... DUNCAN McRAE | Musical Director .... JOHN CROOK
Business Manager .... JAMES W. MATHEWS

Extract from the Rules made by the Lord Chamberlain
(1.) The name of the actual and responsible Manager of the Theatre must be printed on every play bill (2.) The Public can leave the Theatre at the end of the performance by all exit and entrance doors, which must open outwards (3.) The fire-proof screen to the proscenium opening will be lowered at least once during every performance to ensure its being in proper working order. (4.) Smoking is not permitted in the Auditorium. (5.) All gangways, passages and staircases must be kept free from chairs or any other obstruction, whether permanent or temporary

ICES TEA AND COFFEE can be had of the Attendants.

A revised program dated January 9, 1905, which reflects the changes that occurred as of December 31, 1904. Note the addition of "The Tree Tops," the official last scene of the play. And now only one space is vacant for advertising.

> We now have to consider why it was that the audience, ourselves included, enjoyed "Peter Pan" more than any piece produced for many months. It is because of Mr. Barrie's marvelous fertility in humorous and pathetic touches. A dramatic outline, such as we have described, would, in other hands, have produced an intolerable mass of irritating padding. With Mr. Barrie, when he chooses to be sportive, the padding becomes the life and soul of the piece.[27]

On December 31, four nights after the opening, the omitted scenes were put in their place. Scene III of the last act was changed from "Home, Sweet Home" to "How to Know Your Mother." This was an embarrassingly sweet scene where several beautiful women gather in the Darling nursery to claim their lost boys. Slightly is unable to find his mother until Liza reveals that he is her son because she can feel it in her bones. The actor playing Slightly was a tall comedian named Archie Baskcomb who provided the last laugh of the evening as he reached out to hug his mother, Liza, played by the tiny Ela Q. May, and missed way above her head.

The mechanical problems being solved, a small house was now able to be lifted to provide the intended ending—Scene V, The Tree Tops. The gigantic wooden wheels are still in the sub-basement of the Duke of York's Theatre, laying dormant these many years. Scene IV, Outside the House, ends with Mrs. Darling agreeing to allow Wendy to visit Peter once a year to do his spring cleaning. She closes the window with Peter on the outside, kisses him through the window, and exits the room. Then Wendy says goodbye to Peter.

WENDY: (Opens door and is going) You won't forget me, Peter, will you. Before spring cleaning comes?

PETER: No.

WENDY: (Going again, then turns) Give me a thimble, Peter. (They kiss) Oh, Peter, how I wish you were littler so that I could take you up and squdge you. Good-bye.

(Kiss again)

PETER: Good-bye.

(Wendy runs into house)

(Peter exits R.)

(Music Cue No. 56)

(Eliza enters from L. with Harlequin Wand. Crosses to C. Shows wand to audience, taps door, and exits L. dancing to Music)

(Segue Music)

SCENE V

Ready Bells for Lights to commence coming up. RED WARNING LIGHT under stage for Doll's House, 2nd RED LIGHT under stage for Doll's House to come up when Doll's House MUSIC commences. READY to give electrician the Cue for LIGHTS UP in Doll's House.

Segue MUSIC

The Scene changes to the Tree Tops. The tops of a great wood of firs are seen, the idea being that we look down on the wood from on high. Beyond is a great blue sky. Not seen at present, are nests which are really fairy houses, to be lit up presently inside by connection with unseen electric wires. Nightingales unseen, sing. House appears up trap when lights full up. LIGHTS appear in house, doors open. LIZA comes out, wire is fixed. WENDY stands L. of door. PETER sits R. of door.)

LIZA: Well, goodnight, Miss Wendy.

WENDY: (At door) Tell mother the spring cleaning is getting on very nicely. You really do like the house?

LIZA: Of course, it's small, Miss Wendy.

WENDY: It is small. Peter, don't bite your nails. But, you see, it isn't as if we meant to entertain.

LIZA: Quite so, Miss.

(Getting on broom, ready to fly)

WENDY: And it's rather noisy in the evening. You see, those nests are the fairies' houses and they light up at bath time, and fairy children are so naughty in their baths that the row they make is positively deafening.

WARNING FOR CURTAIN. DITTO FOR CHIMNEY SMOKE TO DOLL'S HOUSE

LIZA: One can't have everything.

WENDY: That's just what I say. Most people of our size wouldn't have a house at all. Good-night.

LIZA: Good-night, Miss. Home!

(Amid hand waving, she flies away on broom and disappears L.)

(WENDY and PETER sit on the steps of the house, PETER playing pipe. Clocks of fairy houses begin to be lit up. Chattering of bells increases. There can be hundreds of lights as there are many small ones among the trees on back cloth. Bells chatter is great — some fairies flit about. WENDY and PETER wave handkerchiefs to audience as:)

THE CURTAIN FALLS

WENDY and PETER come in front of ground rows for Curtains.[28]

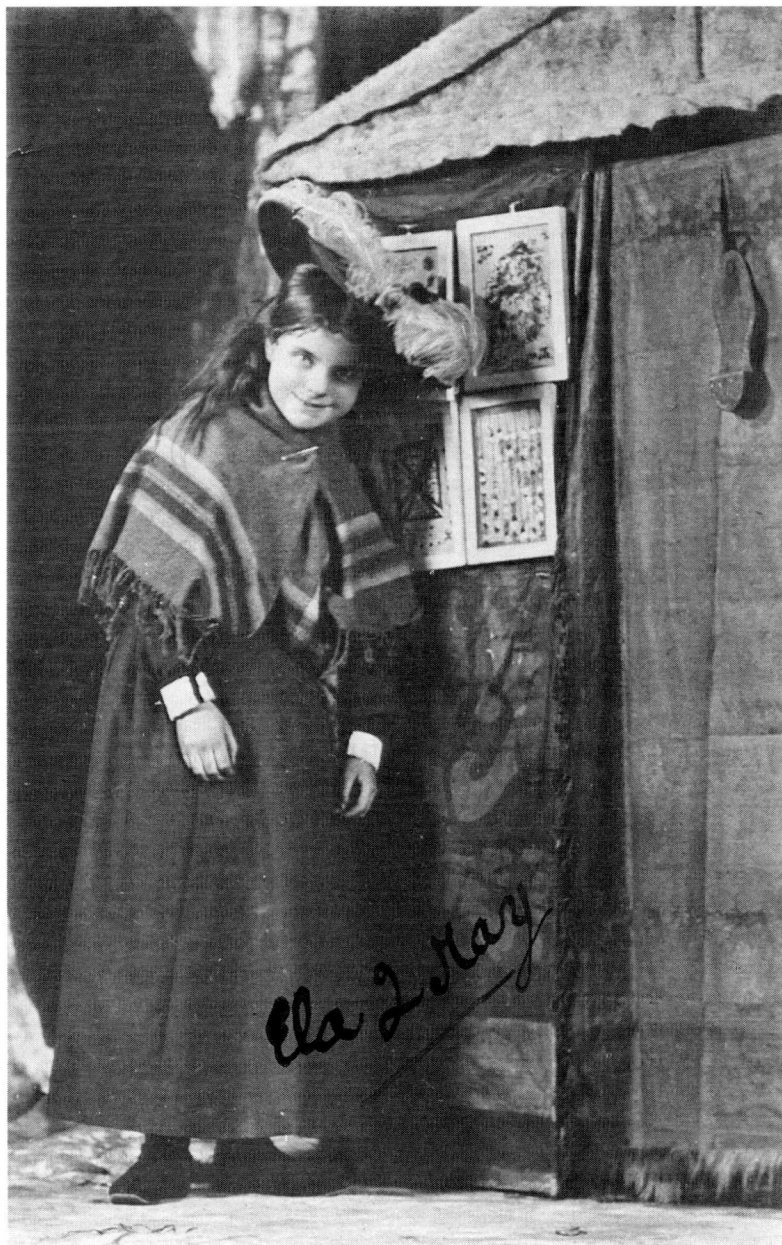

Ela Q. May as Liza. Ela's name would often be misspelled as "Ella" during her career. In 1906 and 1907 she would play Wendy on the *Peter Pan* tour of the provinces (photograph: Ellis and Walery, 1905).

The additions did not alter the critics' fond opinions of the play, as seen in this review:

Dear Mr. Barrie,

There is only one word for your new play, and that is — Larks! All through it is a delightful spree.

You have the secret of making us grownup people feel like the children for whom you wrote *Peter Pan or The Boy Who Wouldn't Grow Up*. It is true we enjoy your ingenious entertainment with a difference. To us it is a rollicking burlesque with dashes of tender sentiment.

To them it is much more real, and I expect, much more enthralling. They can believe, without any difficulty, in the activity of Peter Pan, the boy who ran away the day after he was born, because he heard his parents discussing what he should be when he grew up, and because he wanted to remain a little boy all his life.

... My advice to everyone who has children is to take them to the Duke of York's Theatre without delay. Those who have no children should immediately borrow some for the afternoon. They will find that they get a rare pleasure out of watching their little companions enjoy your quaint inventions, and there will be something wrong with them if they do not enjoy the piece on their own account as well.

... In spite of themselves they laugh at Mr. Gerald du Maurier, both when he is the fantastic parent of three little children, and when he is enjoying himself immensely as the Pirate King. He certainly is very funny indeed, and funny in the most natural and artistic way.

... I do not suppose that children will be greatly entertained by Mr. du Maurier's imitations of Sir Henry Irving, Mr. Tree, and the rest. But there is no doubt about their instant appeal to the elder portion of the audience. Children, again, may find the talk between Peter and Wendy about playing at being the father and mother of the little family that lives underground rather beyond their comprehension. Even I could bear a little priming in this direction.

But, for the rest, I would not sacrifice one line or one gesture of Miss Hilda Trevelyan or of Miss Boucicault. Even now I can hardly believe that eleven year old Wendy in her long nightgown and short frocks was played by a grown-up girl. Even now I think there must be some mistake when I read on the programme that Peter Pan is in private life a young lady whom I know to have been married for several years.

They and all the rest play their parts in exactly the right spirit of dainty and amusing make-believe. The whole piece is the best lark I have had for a very long time. So believe me, dear Mr. Barrie, yours gratefully.[29]

Sandwiched between all of the positive press was a most disturbing review written by Max Beerbohm:

Undoubtedly, *Peter Pan* is the best thing he has done—the most directly from within himself. Here, at last, we see his talent in its full maturity; for here he has stripped off from himself the last flimsy remnants of a pretense to maturity. Time was when a tiny pair of trousers peeped from under his "short-coats," and his sunny curls were parted and plastered down, and he jauntily affected the absence of a lisp, and spelt out the novels of Mr. Meredith and said he liked them very much and even used a pipe for another purpose than blowing soap-bubbles. But all this while, bless his little heart, he was suffering. It would be pleasant enough to play at being grown up among children of his own age. It was a fearful strain to play at being grown up among grown-up persons.... Now, at last, we see at the Duke of York's Theatre, Mr. Barrie in his quiddity undiluted—the child, as it were, in bath, splashing, and crowing as it splashes....

Mr. Barrie is not that rare creature, a man of genius. He is something even more rare—a child who, by some divine grace, can express through an artistic medium the childishness that is in him.

Our dreams are nearer to us than our childhood, and it is natural that *Peter Pan* should remind us more instantly of our dreams than of our childish fancies. One English dramatist, a man of genius, realized a dream for us: but the logic in him prevented him from indulging in that wildness and incoherence which are typical of all but the finest dreams. Credible and orderly are the doings

"PETER PAN," THE NEW PLAY BY MR. J. M. BARRIE,

AT THE DUKE OF YORK'S THEATRE.

SKETCHES BY RALPH CLEAVER.

The first cast of *Peter Pan* as seen through the pen of Ralph Cleaver for *The Sketch*, January 4, 1905.

of Puck in comparison with the doings of Peter Pan. Was ever, out of dreamland, such a riot of inconsequence and of exquisite futility?...

 Mr. Barrie has never grown up. He is still a child, absolutely. But some fairy once waved a wand over him, and changed him from a dear little boy into a dear little girl. Some critics have wondered why among the characters in *Peter Pan* appeared a dear little girl, named in the programme "Liza (Author of the play)." Now they know. Mr. Barrie was just "playing at symbolists."[30]

 Ouch! Perhaps Mr. Beerbohm was on the right track but it's quite conceivable too that considering Barrie first approached Beerbohm's brother about producing the play and was refused, Mr. Beerbohm was by now suffering from too many "sour grapes."

 The parts of Peter and Captain Hook were exceedingly taxing on their stars. On January 29, 1905, Nina missed her first performance and her understudy, May Martin, took her

Nina Boucicault as Peter Pan, playing his pipes with Hilda Trevelyan as Wendy listening intently during the "Tree Tops" scene. The scene was not performed until four nights after the play opened as the huge wooden wheels built to lift the tree house suffered from technical difficulties. Deep in the bowels of the Duke of York's Theatre, the wheels are still in place, perhaps awaiting Peter's return (photograph: Ellis and Walery, 1905).

place. By the end of the run Martin had replaced an exhausted Nina, although, according to Hilda Trevelyan, Nina performed on April 1, 1905 — closing night.

> Despite its sensational success, none of us realized that *Peter Pan* would be revived until Nina Boucicault gave her curtain speech on the last night, announcing, much to our surprise and delight, that it would be done again the following Christmas.... Once more I played "Wendy," a part which I was to play over a thousand times.[31]

Most of the principal players of the original cast were brought back to repeat their roles eight months later except for Dorothea Baird and "Nina," according to Denis Mackail:

> whose exhausting part had nearly killed her last year, but who had rested and recovered and was prepared to face it again, had learnt now that another little boy, or actress, had taken her place. There were reasons, of course, though none of them could ever reflect either on her or what she had done. Barrie was now an autocrat, whose word and whose whims were law, and professionally speaking he could do anything for any actress that he chose. There was something, at any rate, that he saw as a reason in this case, and accordingly Miss Boucicault vanished — but will never be forgotten.[32]

We can only speculate why Barrie wanted another actress for the part of Peter. Perhaps he was unhappy that Nina had missed so many performances. Or, maybe, Barrie sought to make the first Peter Pan as elusive and ethereal as lost childhood, with only memories that improve with age. Fifty years later, writers were still writing prose of rhapsody regarding Nina Boucicault's Peter Pan, still comparing any newcomers to her legendary performances. Years later, in 1939, Nina wrote:

> For my own part I was very afraid as I had never done anything like it before, and did so hope I should not let them all down. After my scene with "Tinker Bell" (underground) I felt they liked it — and perhaps me — but I never realized that anyone would remember that I played it thirty years after.[33]

3

Maude Adams: Peter Pan
Lands in America

My Dear Maudie,

I have written a play for children, which I don't suppose would be much use in America. She is rather a dear of a girl with ever so many children long before her hair is up and the boy is Peter Pan in a new world. I should like you to be the boy and the girl and most of the children and the pirate captain. I hope you are coming here before summer is ended and I also hope I may have something to read you and tell you about. I can't get along without an idea that really holds me, but if I can get it how glad I shall be at work for little Maudie again.

—J.M. Barrie, April 18, 1904[1]

When Maude Adams received J.M. Barrie's letter she believed that she would be playing the part of Wendy, a role, no doubt, inspired by Margaret Ogilvy. As Adams's knowledge of Peter Pan would only have been from *The Little White Bird* and his world in Kensington Gardens, the actress had no idea what the play was about. Maude described her first encounter with *Peter Pan, or The Boy Who Wouldn't Grow Up*:

One afternoon last year, while I was playing *The Little Minister* and *'Op o' me Thumb* at the Empire Theatre, Mr. Frohman called to have a talk about plans for my coming season. He told me that he had *As You Like It* in mind for me, also another Shakespearean play and one of the old comedies. He said he would on the following afternoon show me some of the scenes in the Shakespearean plays and we could then decide upon the one in which I would appear. Meanwhile, he gave me the manuscript of *Peter Pan* to read, because it was a play by Mr. Barrie.

I read the play after going home, and was so completely won by the character of dear Peter and so thoroughly interested and thrilled by his numerous adventures that I fell in love with him at once. In the evening, when I saw Mr. Frohman at the theatre, I said: "The Shakespearean plays and the old comedy that we spoke of are all right, but I would like to act Peter Pan." That is how I come to be acting in another Barrie play this season, but that is not all of the story. The season before last, when I was in London, Mr. Barrie said to me one day: "A character which is in my mind I propose to make a play of, and that character has come to my mind through you."

I thought no more of the remark until I was reading *Peter Pan* that afternoon, when it came back to me, and I seemed at once to feel and understand its meaning. For while I read *Peter Pan* it seemed that nothing I had ever read before, nothing I had ever imagined and no play in which I had ever appeared had appealed to me so strongly or inspired me with such full and direct happiness and with such anxiety to appear in it. Every line of it thrilled me, and as I passed from scene to scene an affection for Peter grew and took hold of me, until I was perfectly wrapped in a spell of desire to be Peter Pan himself. Mr. Frohman, I believe, said nothing to Mr. Barrie about my eagerness to play Peter until he met him last spring in London. After that meeting he sent me word that Mr. Barrie has said:

"Whether or not Miss Adams was to play Peter Pan I did not know, but I am going to send her word that it was she who inspired the writing of the play." And so what was in my mind with regard to the play, the part and myself was really true.[2]

Perhaps Maude actually believed her over-simplified account of the origin of *Peter Pan* but we know that Barrie began writing the play as an extension of his stories with the Llewelyn Davies boys. Perhaps Frohman never told her that it was he who insisted that Barrie write the role of Peter for his leading American actress. Or maybe, just like today, the origins of great art get muddy as each participant tries to take credit before the public eye. Whatever the case, we do know that Barrie was quite infatuated with Maude Adams; that he later gave her the master script with a special written dedication; and that, conscious or unconscious, Adams influenced his work on the play to some degree.

Maude Adams was already a respected actress in Frohman's roster since 1890 (their contract was bound by a handshake) when Barrie first met her in 1896. However, Frohman was looking for a vehicle that would make her a star while also establishing her as a profitable stage personality. Luckily, Frohman knew that Barrie had been try-

Top: Maude Adams as Peter Pan in 1905. Through the years she played the role in New York and on tour until 1917 (photograph: Sarony). *Bottom:* "Little Maudie Adams" as Adrienne in *A Celebrated Case*, 1879.

ing to convert his popular novel *The Little Minister* for the stage before the inevitable unauthorized stage adaptations appeared. Barrie was stuck; he didn't believe anyone could play the character of Babbie, the Minister's wife, as he envisioned her.

During a rare visit to the United States, Frohman arranged for Barrie to see his production of *Rosemary*, which was playing at the Empire Theatre on Broadway. "'There,' said he when the final curtain had fallen upon Maude Adams, to an accompaniment of 'bravos,' 'is the woman to play my Lady Babbie.'"[3] Frohman was not exactly surprised. He had envisioned the teaming of his star with the Barrie heroine when he gave him the tickets to see the play. Still, it took a considerable amount of convincing by Frohman and his secretary, Elizabeth Marbury, for the writer to go further: to lengthen the part of Lady Babbie, thereby converting the play into a stage vehicle for Maude Adams. Not only did Barrie adapt the play to suit Frohman's needs, he also was receptive to the producer's many suggestions during the rehearsal period.

The Little Minister opened as a moderately successful play but within the period of a few months it became a hit. The *New York Times* stated that Adams's "personal charm was never more potent and she was satisfying to the most exacting taste."[4] On the other hand, a critic from the *Herald Tribune* wrote,

> Miss Adams will be a better Babbie in a week hence. She was clearly nervous. Her sudden alterations of seriousness and gaiety will gain ease and effect. That Miss Adams knows what should be done in such places no one doubts.[5]

By the time the play opened in Boston, the reviews had changed from lukewarm to ecstatic.

> Nearly the whole triumph of the thing is due to Miss Adams. Her gay mischievousness, her sudden dashes and spurts of coquetry, her consciousness of her woman's power and the helplessness of the little minister, her gift at swift dryness of speech, and with and through all her quaint and taking personality which gives to every word and movement a pretty girlish piquancy and grace — these avail completely to turn the regard of her audiences.[6]

Maude did not achieve overnight success in her climb toward stardom. Born as Maude Adams Kiskadden on November 11, 1872, she began her career at the age of nine months. She described her auspicious beginning to writer Perriton Maxwell:

> My mother was playing in a dramatic stock company in Salt Lake City, and one of the pieces put on was a farce called *The Lost Child*. The infant in the play got into bawling tantrums one night, and the manager was on the point of ringing down the curtain and "calling off" the performance, when he spied my precious self cooing in the arms of my nurse as we waited for my mother in the passage to the street. The child in the farce had to be brought in a tray carried by a bewildered waiter, and without so much as "by your leave" to my astonished mother, the desperate stage-manager whisked me from the hold of my nurse, plumped me on the waiter's tray, and literally pushed the man, tray and child into view of the audience.
>
> And that audience! A month-old infant had just been taken off the scene, only to reappear in a few minutes miraculously grown into a lusty nine-month-old child. The transformation was so sudden, so unexpected that the house rocked with laughter, while I sat comfortably on my tray crowing with glee at the cheerful noise and evidently pleased with the spectacle of so many merry faces. In the jargon of the press agent, I had made my "initial appearance in contemporaneous drama."[7]

Maude's mother, Annie Adams, distant kin to John Adams, and her father, James Kiskadden, decided that their daughter would no longer be exposed to the stage. Yet daughter, like mother, was hooked on acting. She made her official stage debut as "La Petite Maude" in *La Belle Russe* and over the next decade she appeared in *Oliver Twist, A Celebrated Case, Pinafore* (as Little Midshipmite), and *Uncle Tom's Cabin* (as Little Eva), always billed as "Little Maude Adams." By 1888 she was listed in the credits as Miss Maude Adams in Charles Hoyt's *The Paymaster*.

"There's a charming little girl in Hoyt's new play," wrote a reviewer about *The Paymaster*. "I think her name is Adams, or something like it. She's different."[8] What was different about Maude Adams was the combination of her individual, winsome charm, her naturalness on stage, her distinct appealing voice, and a physical beauty that photographs still reveal as classic. Before Hoyt, who was also her manager, could fully appreciate the prize he had in this young actress, Annie Adams had convinced Charles Frohman that Maude would be perfect for his stock company. She was cast in the role of Dora in *Men and Women* by David Belasco and H.C. DeMille.

Realizing Maude's potential, Frohman was bent on making a star of his new acquisition. Known as the "star maker," Frohman often found humor in his title, as exemplified in a simple cartoon he sketched of himself shouting to the moon, "I will make a star of you yet!"[9] Two years later Maude was elevated to leading-lady status opposite John Drew, one of the most popular leading men of the period, and they continued with great success in a series of plays that showed off their best assets.

Maude was awarded her first starring role with *The Little Minister*. Denis Mackail wrote:

It was the riotous triumph of *The Little Minister* that made Barrie and Miss Adams such allies. Which if either of them really felt indebted to the other will probably never be known; for both had temperaments, and both had good grounds for taking more credit than they might openly

Left: The exquisite beauty of Maude Adams is exemplified in this portrait (date unknown). *Right:* Maude Adams as Lady Babbie in *The Little Minister* by J.M. Barrie in 1897. The actress made a niche for herself in the sentimental heroine roles written by J.M. Barrie.

admit. Yet here, with this staggering success to set it off, was the beginning of another close friendship — and most profitable association too. Miss Adams became a private heroine, and another object of sentimental devotion. It was eighteen years after that performance of *Rosemary* before Barrie next saw her on the stage, though in the interval she had starred for him in America over and over again. But whenever she took a holiday on this side of the Atlantic, there he was to squire her, to flatter her, to employ his old and ingenious wiles again. Very possessive and rather mysterious about it to all others — perhaps so as to heighten the romance. Always spoke of her as Miss Adams, even to those who knew her better than himself. But if you were to gather that she was royalty, you were also to gather that it was he who stood nearest the throne.[10]

Before she was to portray Peter Pan, Maude was seen in *Romeo and Juliet* (prompting Barrie to write to her, "Are you listening, or have you gone off with your nose in the air and your hand on the arm of Mr. Shakespeare?"[11]), *L'Aiglon*, Barrie's *Quality Street*, and *The Pretty Sister of Jose*. It was during a revival of *The Little Minister* in December 1904 that Frohman was anxiously waiting in his country home in White Plains, New York, for the news about Peter's opening night in London. At some time around midnight his secretary called and read a cablegram from Frohman's London agent, William Lestocq: "Peter Pan all right. Looks like a big success."[12]

Frohman was elated. That summer, even as Barrie was writing revisions for a second season in London, an American version based on the script of the first season was being planned. Meanwhile, Maude studied for the part from the script Frohman had given her.

The way she prepared for the part was characteristic of her attitude toward her work. She took the manuscript with her up to the Catskills. She isolated herself for a month; she walked, rode, communed with nature, but all the while she was studying and absorbing the character which was to mean so much to her career. In the great friendly open spaces in which little Peter himself delighted, and where he was king, she found her inspiration for interpretation of the wondrous boy.[13]

If Frohman was delighted with the London production, he was ecstatic with the American presentation. Not only had his gamble paid off with financial success, but he also had exclusive rights to a children's play of genuine artistic merit. *Peter Pan* opened on Monday evening, November 6, 1905, to extremely enthusiastic reviews.

The *New York Times* headlined the theatre page with "A Joyous Night with 'Peter Pan,'" "Maude Adams Triumphs as 'The Boy Who Wouldn't Grow Up,'" and "An Exquisite Dream Play — The Fanciful Barrie at His Best."[14] The review continued:

Maude Adams is Peter. Most ingratiatingly simple and sympathetic. True to the fairy idea, true to the child nature, lovely, sweet and wholesome. She combines all the delicate sprightliness and the gentle, wistful pathos necessary to the role, and she is supremely in touch with the spirit of it all.[15]

The *Times* critic concluded:

All New York may not believe in fairies, but there is no doubt last night, when Tinkerbell [*sic*] is dying that the audience in the Empire, irrespective of age or condition, had gotten back very near to second childhood.[16]

Raved the *New York Herald Tribune*:

Miles away from the beaten paths of Broadway drama was the exquisite bit of fairyland which Maude Adams unlocked in Mr. J.M. Barrie's phantasy [*sic*] play Peter Pan, before a brilliant audience in the Empire Theatre last night. To theatergoers surfeited with the stale dramatic conventionalities which pass for real life in the theatre, was like a drought of fresh air, a sight for sore eyes.[17]

The *Tribune* critic continued:

> What the play would be without Miss Adams it is difficult to say. She was the chief medium by which it was made alive last night. It seemed made for her and she for it. As Peter Pan ... she was a Puck, an Ariel and a blithe child all in one.[18]

Maude was honored with a note from Mark Twain:

> It is my belief that *Peter Pan* is a great and refining and uplifting benefaction to this sordid and money-mad age; and that the next play on the boards is a long way behind it as long as you play Peter.[19]

Peter Pan was recognized as perfect children's entertainment for any age but it was not Barrie's hand alone that made it the perfect vehicle for Maude Adams. In 1929 a critic for the *Boston Transcript* disclosed the following:

The cover of the Empire Theatre program, where *Peter Pan* opened on November 6, 1905.

> Truth to tell, it was hardly Barrie's play ... that Miss Adams acted. Rather she appeared in a version of her own in which speeches were shifted because she fancied them; characters, like Wendy, subordinated lest they should draw too close to the star-part; the whole piece conformed to her wishes or necessities. Within the frame of the script she wove a Peter quite as much out of her own fantasy as off Barrie's sheets — the player versus the playwright, with the victory where, in this land of "personality," it usually lies. The public applauded long and loud.[20]

Barrie certainly must have been aware of the "tinkering" with his play as Frohman was not averse to making changes in his scripts to suit the actors. Nonetheless, he added his voice to the cheers:

Peter (Maude Adams) and Nana (Charles Weston) in a publicity photograph from Act I in *Peter Pan*; they actually never shared a scene together (photograph: Hall, 1905).

22 March 1906

My Dear Maudie:
   ... How splendid all the accounts of your Peter are. Even Babbie surely is getting jealous, and she could not go to the Never, Never Land and make a row were it not (she says) that after all he is a boy, and she had always a weakness for boys herself. I feel sure you are the most entrancing little boy that ever was by sea or shore, and I hear of things you do in the part which are so absolutely what Peter did that it makes me gay. There never was such a girl as you for finding out what her author was up to. I must see you as Peter, and so, dear Maudie, good-night.[21]

Not all of the praise was awarded exclusively to Adams. Wrote the *New York Times* critic:

But though she is the centre of it all, there are several others in the cast who but deserve more space for praise than can be spared just now. Especially Mildred Morris (Wendy), whose task to hers was perhaps the most difficult; Ernest Lawford, who in his dual role of Papa and Pirate developed the proper ferocity to suit the case, and his chief bloodthirsty assistant, Thomas McGrath, who was also most excellently ferocious, contributed a share to the generally sympathetic acting, while the dog, the crocodile, and the rest of the live stock were — well, they were very much like life.[22]

Mildred Morris, the daughter of character actor Felix Morris, was born in 1887 and soon followed in her famous father's footsteps by becoming a competent juvenile performer. She appeared as a boy in *Two Little Sailor Boys* and the 16-year-old won enough praise for her portrayal as Becky, the scullery maid in *The Little Princess*, to be cast in Richard Mansfield's productions of *Prince Edward* and *Richard III*. Frohman caught her performance in the Shakespeare play and cast her as Wendy. She later co-starred with Mary Pickford in *The Foundling*. Mildred and her sister, Felice, collected 19th and early 20th-century autographs of theatre personalities, which were bequeathed to Princeton University in 1961. One of her last public appearances was on opening night of *Peter Pan* with Jean Arthur in 1950.

In addition to Captain Hook, Ernest Lawford had the distinction of being the original Charley in *Charley's Aunt*. The English actor had been educated at Oxford for a career in law but changed professions at the age of 24 when he made his 1890 stage debut in *As You Like It* with Lily Langtry. For several years he was cast in juvenile roles in Shakespeare's plays. He arrived in the United States in 1904 to play in *The Coronet of the Duchess*, which was quickly followed by *Peter Pan*.

A few critics managed to find fault with Barrie's play, with one criticizing the producer for not using all children in the boys' roles.

The four real children who act in the play are most satisfying and delightful, but they serve to accentuate the painful shortcomings of the imitation boys.... The haunting contralto notes of Miss Adam's rich voice sound damningly womanly when Peter talks to Wendy, John Napoleon and Michael Nicholas.[23]

Another reviewer for the New York *Daily Tribune* praised Maude's presence with a left-handed compliment:

sprightly ... indicative of sweetness and mirth, and graced by the allurement of pretty ways. As an actress, Miss Adams is incarnate mediocrity — for she possesses neither imagination, passion, power, depth of feeling, or formidable intellect, and her faculty of expressive impersonation is extremely limited; but as a person she is piquant, interesting and agreeable, and, in such a play

"Peter and Wendy" (Maude Adams and Mildred Morris) from the first Broadway season, 1905-1906 (photograph: Hall).

Maude Adams and her Wolves in Act II—The Never Never Never Land (photograph: Hall, 1905).

as *Peter Pan*, which is an amiable fabric of whim and fancy, devised for the amusement of children, she is shown to advantage.[24]

Of course, as always, there were severe detractors, such as the critic from *The Evening Sun*:

From the beginning of its second act, Peter Pan inevitably challenges comparisons with plays like *The Wizard of Oz* and *Babes in Toyland* and fails to show either the spirit of fun or childhood which made both these pieces a delight to children of all ages. It will be very interesting to watch the effect of this play on its first audience of children. The one thing a child demands before all else in either a story or a play is a narrative clearly told. And that is one of the things which they will not find in *Peter Pan*.[25]

He continued:

As a novelty Peter Pan may prove a "go." Certainly nothing quite like it has ever been seen here. But as a fairy story or as an embodiment of the lost delights of childhood it must rest for its artistic success entirely on its first act. For an artist of Miss Adams's standing this play seems like a waste of time.[26]

Ernest Lawford received mixed reviews, with *The World* stating that he "did amazingly well"[27] while *The Evening Sun* wrote:

A clever actor in certain roles, Mr. Lawford was utterly at sea last night on the pirate ship. His lisp was the first thing which should have been made to walk the plank, and in his ferocity he was not nearly half so fierce as some of the little boys.[28]

There were several distinct differences between the American production and its British counterpart: references to England's monarchy were substituted by the "Stars and Stripes" and the president of the United States and there was no impersonation scene for the actor playing Hook. Also, and of far greater significance, according to several accounts, including that of Maude Adams's biographer Phyllis Robbins and this one by Mildred Morris, the ending was altered for the star.

And now we come to the last performance at the old Empire Theater. It is the Tree-top scene, and the crowded house is hushed; the flute-notes sound like the twitter of birds, the canvas tree-tops are shadowy and real in the dim blue of the spot-lights. *Peter* and *Wendy* step sadly into the little house and are slowly lowered. Not a word breaks the stillness to-night, until the house commences to rise. *Wendy* tries to swallow the lump in her throat. "Good-by, Wendy, until spring-cleaning time!"

Now the green-clad boy is standing alone at the doorway, waving his last farewell, while the audience rise in a body, cheering; and then from each side of the stage troop out the company, singing "Auld Lang Syne;" "Indians" whooping, everyone waving, and *Peter* just looking at them all, unable to make the quivering lips form a smile. And so we leave "him."[29]

Whereas in London, Peter and Wendy came out together for their bows, Maude made her curtain call alone. Incidentally, Peter's attire, designed by none other than Maude Adams herself, influenced the fashion industry with the popular "Peter Pan Collar."

Maude enjoyed singing and this play presented a perfect excuse to showcase her musical talents, although at the expense of Wendy's character, who, in the London version, sang the following while preparing the boys for bed:

Left: A cabinet card of the period depicting Maude Adams as Peter Pan. She designed her hat and costume, which introduced the popular "Peter Pan Collar" in ladies' fashion (photograph: Sarony, 1905). *Right:* Ernest Lawford without makeup in 1931 (Photofest).

John Anderson my Jo John
When we were first acquaint
Your looks were like the raven
Your bonnie brow was brent
But now your brow is bald, John,
Your locks are like the snow,
But blessings on your frosty pow,
John Anderson, my Jo.[30]

The song, an 18th century ballad "John Anderson" by Robert Burns, makes perfect sense, for as soon as Wendy is finished singing Peter utters a cry:

WENDY: Peter, what is it?

PETER: (C.) I was just thinking — it's only make-believe, isn't it, that I'm their father?

WENDY: (Pained) Oh, yes.

PETER: You see it would make me seem so old to be their real father.

WENDY: (Rises,) (Crosses to him) But they are ours, Peter — yours and mine.

PETER: (Anxious) But not really.

WENDY: (Moves nearer to Peter) Not if you don't wish it, Peter —

PETER: I don't.

WENDY: Peter, what are your exact feelings for me?

PETER: Those of a devoted son, Wendy.

WENDY: I thought so! (Crosses sadly to above fire and sits looking into it)

PETER: You're so puzzling. Tiger Lily's just the same — (TIGER LILY is attracted, then goes down R. D. tree. All INDIANS listen). There's something she wants to be to me, but she says it's not my mother.

WENDY: No, indeed it isn't.

PETER: Then what is it?

WENDY: It isn't for a lady to tell.[31]

A rare photograph from 1906 depicting Maude Adams in Peter's winter hunting costume. On Never Never Never Land the four seasons coexist on the four corners of the island.

Here, "John Anderson" provides the impetus for Wendy to become homesick while at the same time fusing the pathos of the boy who would not grow up with subtle humor.

While Peter remains ignorant of love — romantic and physical — Wendy begins to realize that there is more to life than Never Never Land.

Maude chose to sing instead, "Sally in Our Alley" a popular and bawdy song written by Henry Carey around 1726.

> Of all the girls that are so smart
> There's none like pretty Sally;
> She is the darling of my heart,
> And she lives in our alley.
> There is no lady in the land
> Is half so sweet as Sally;
> She is the darling of my heart,
> And she lives in our alley.
>
> Her father he makes cabbage-nets,
> And through the streets does cry 'em;
> Her mother she sells laces long
> To such as please to buy 'em;
> But sure such folks could ne'er beget
> So sweet a girl as Sally!
> She is the darling of my heart,
> And she lives in our alley.
>
> When Christmas comes about again,
> O, then I shall have money;
> I'll hoard it up, and box it all,
> I'll give it to my honey:
> I would it were ten thousand pound,
> I'd give it all to Sally;
> She is the darling of my heart,
> And she lives in our alley.
>
> My master and the neighbors all
> Make gave of me and Sally,
> And, but for her, I'd better be
> A slave and row a galley;
> But when my seven long years are out,
> O, then I'll marry Sally;
> O, then we'll wed, and then we'll bed —
> But not in our alley![32]

The song was first introduced on the stage at the Drury Lane Theatre in London by Mrs. Willis, a leading lady and singer, on May 20, 1717. How it was interpolated in *Peter Pan* was explained in a review from the *Boston Transcript* the following year.

So they lived for a while in the Never, Never, Never Land. High up over the house underground, the Indians sat on guard, under the trees, and Tiger Lily sat with them and watched for Peter to come back from his hunting. And underneath was Wendy mothering the boys. She put Michael in a basket that hung from the wall, because if she was to be a mother, she must have one baby in the cradle, and he was the littlest. Seven though there were to care for, she gave them their supper, which was very noisy and let them meet their father, who had given Tiger Lily a thimble-kiss, and came down through the tree. When Peter, who was all in white now, found that the boys had been good, he let them rummage his pockets for sweets. And when they had eaten the sweet stuff, he sang them the old song of "Sally in Our Alley" because it was Saturday night, when even the fathers and mothers are carefree. Then they danced, danced with pillows on their legs, while he talked sagely to Wendy of the care of seven, and she as sagely of his flannels and his medicine.[33]

Peter Pan played for 31 consecutive weeks or 237 performances, making it the longest continuous engagement that Maude Adams had ever played in New York. The season closed on June 10, 1906.

The following autumn she toured with the play, and while in Boston there was a surprise addition:

> The popularity of Peter Pan will undoubtedly be redoubled by the announcement that a new act is to be added to the play during the last two weeks of its Boston engagement, which begins tomorrow night. The new act, "Marooner's, or the Mermaids' Lagoon," describes the exploits of Peter Pan, by his friends and his enemies, in the open ocean. It is a recent composition by J.M. Barrie, and is written in his best characteristic vein — a delicate interweaving of the serious, the comic and the grotesque — such as only Barrie can conceive. Tomorrow night will be the first time the new act has ever been performed upon the American stage. It is only lately that sufficient time has been gained in the staging of *Peter Pan* to make possible any addition to an already lengthy evening's entertainment. Mr. Barrie's new act is placed between the second and third acts of *Peter Pan*— between the act called "The Never-Never Land" and the third act, "Our Home Under the Ground."[34]

The play sailed into New York with the additional act in place and was welcomed back by audiences and critics alike. A Christmas Eve review found:

> At the Empire Theatre last night a multitude of Peter Pan's old friends took "the first turn on into morning" to the Neverland. It was a fitting journey for Christmas Eve, and those who went upon it had some new adventures, as delightful as any surprises that ever came out of a Christmas stocking.

Maude Adams possessed a small but lovely singing voice, which was used effectively when she sang "Sally in Our Alley" to the Lost Boys as depicted in this 1906 photograph from the play.

Earth, air and fire have already been placed at the service of "Peter Pan." It remained for Mr. Barrie to add the one missing element — water — to his great Myth of the Nursery. If he forgot in the first writing that greatest joy of the boyish heart — swimming — he has amply atoned for his negligence in this revised version.

Here the marvellous [*sic*] Peter fulfils his promise to show Wendy and her brother "real mermaids with tails," and brings them to the Marooner's Rock, swimming through the sea "the same as a dog."[35]

Adams's *Pan* became one of the most successful touring companies in the United States. "It was on the road tour of *Peter Pan* that occurred one of those rare anecdotes in which Miss Adams figures," wrote Isaac Marcosson.

Frohman had a curious prejudice against the playing of matinees by his stars, especially Maude Adams. A matinee was booked at Altoona, Pennsylvania. Frohman immediately had it marked off his contract. The advance-agent of the company, however, ordered the matinee played at the urgent request of the local manager, but he did not notify the office in New York. When Charles got the telegram announcing the receipts, he was most indignant. "I'll discharge the person responsible for this matinee," he said.

In answer to his telegraphed inquiry he received the following wire:

> *The matinee was played at my request. I preferred to*
> *work rather than spend the whole day in a bad hotel.*
>   Maude Adams[36]

The actress commissioned a theatre car, the only one of its kind to be built in 1907. "The car," reported the *Boston Herald*, "is to be a combination of living apartments and a completely equipped theatre for the rehearsal of scenes and one act pieces. It will be known as the 'Tinker Bell' and will cost from $25,000 to $30,000 when fully furnished."[37] The interior plan for the car was illustrated as well.

In 1907 a song by Jerome Kern and Paul West was added for Maude to sing in *Peter Pan*. It was customary for Frohman to insert American songs by up-and-coming songwriters in his plays of British origin. Kern first came to the attention of the critics three years earlier when he wrote some material for Julian Eltinge, a female impersonator, in *Mr. Wix of Wickham*. "Who is this Jerome Kern," asked critic Alan Dale, "whose music towers in an Eiffel way above the average, hurdy-gurdy accompaniment of the present-day musical comedy?"[38] Audiences did not find out immediately as Kern spent the next few years doctoring other composers' musicals. Finally, in 1911, he was given credit for the first time with "The Red Petticoat." His first hit show, *The Girl from Utah*, opened in 1914 and established Kern as a new force in the world of musical comedy. While the song "Won't You Have a Little Feather," Kern's contribution to *Pan*, was relatively small, his name would be associated with the play again in 1924.

Young Jerome Kern, a favorite composer of Charles Frohman, contributed the song "Won't You Have a Little Feather" to the 1907 production. Seventeen years later he would write several songs for a spectacular Broadway version of the play (Photofest).

Maude Adams in *What Every Woman Knows* by J.M. Barrie, 1909.

The original sheet music indicates that the vocal part was followed by a dance, so it is quite probable that this music accompanied the famous pillow dance that appears to have been performed by Maude.

> Two little birds southward going
> Flew to a tree for a storm was blowing
> One found a nest all feathered and warm
> But one was left in the storm
> So he shivered and shook till the other bird
> His weak little trembling twittering heard
> And she cried "Poor Chap"
> My nest is warm
> You'll catch your death in that dreadful storm
>
> Won't you have a little feather from my little nest
> If your little nest is bare?
> It's a nice little feather for the wint'ry weather
> And I have feathers to spare
> It's a selfish little bird I've always heard
> Her feathers who will not share
> So please have a feather from my little nest
> If your little nest is bare?

Peter Pan joined Maude's repertoire with Barrie's *Quality Street*, *The Little Minister*, and *What Every Woman Knows*, making her association with the playwright extremely profitable for both. When Frohman developed the Theatre Syndicate, he was able to use Maude's popularity as a weapon against independent theatre owners. He sent the *Peter Pan* company to San Francisco to woo audiences away from other theatre companies, including the great Mrs. Fiske's. That same year, a bigger "hit" attacked the area when the great earthquake of 1906 struck. Maude donated the entire receipts of her 200th New York performance as Pan to the Relief Fund.

Other theatrical successes continued for Adams, including an extravagant 1909 pageant of *Joan of Arc* at the Harvard University Stadium and *Chanticlee*r, her favorite play.

Peter Pan officially flew back to New York on December 23, 1912.

> There was a welcome homecoming at the Empire last night when *Peter Pan* was greeted by his adorers. The charm of this wonderful play never dies, and the popularity of Miss Maude Adams never can wane. Everyone loves the actress, and when she appeared coming through the window into the little children's sleeping room the applause stopped the play for minutes.... *Peter Pan* surely can take its place in the dramatic Hall of Fame as one of the most popular plays ever produced in this country.[39]

Three years later, Adams graced Broadway once more with what was to be her farewell run of *Peter Pan*. Opening on December 22, one member of this production was young Ruth Gordon, who many years later would win an Academy Award for *Rosemary's Baby* although for this writer the true prize is her portrayal of the eternally youthful and ever optimistic Maude (not in any way related to Adams) in the film *Harold and Maude*. Praised by the *New York Times* for her portrayal of Nibs, Gordon wrote to her parents:

> After my dance Miss Adams beckoned me to take three bows and our orchestra leader Henri Deering stood up and applauded. Gratifying after all I've been through. And Miss Adams has no jealously like Alice Claire Elliott says many stars have. My cup runneth over and I guess when you read this, yours will too.

Then came the final curtain with Miss Adams alone in the tree top house after waving goodbye to Wendy who flew home and everybody including the cast were crying when down came the curtain to thunderous applause and we all took our rehearsed bows, then rushed back and stood in the wings. That means just out of sight in the scenery. Miss Adams took one of her calls alone then came over and said "Nibs" and led me on and while the audience applauded she broke off a rose from the immense bouquet that had been passed over the foot lights and handed me a long-stemmed American Beauty rose that must have cost I don't know much and I will treasure and preserve forever.[40]

A decade later, Gordon met Adams quite by chance during a break in rehearsals. Remembered Gordon:

She recognized me instantly. Out of sheer nervousness, I think, I asked if she would like to see the rehearsal.... She would. Whereupon, with such graciousness as only Miss Adams could have muttered, she turned to the lady who was with her and said: "We were together in *Peter Pan*."[41]

In the years following the death of Charles Frohman, Maude Adams introduced other Barrie heroines in *The Legend of Leonora* and *A Kiss for Cinderella*. However, the great epidemic of influenza during the tour of the latter struck Adams with a ferocity that kept her from even thinking about performing on stage for over a year, although many of the theatres were closed themselves. Barrie wrote on February 13, 1919:

Miss Adams not well, hasn't been playing for months and won't before autumn. It makes a mighty difference in my income![42]

When Maude finally gained the strength to resume her career in 1920, she found that her contract with the Frohman Company terminated, so she began negotiations with its new parent company, Famous Players. Meanwhile, she anxiously anticipated the arrival of Barrie's new play, *Mary Rose*, a haunting ghost story almost the female counterpart to *Peter Pan*, which was to open in New York on Christmas night. At the same time Barrie was negotiating the film rights to several of his plays with the Famous Players Company. Barrie received a letter from his American representative, Lewis Delafield.

A Kiss for Cinderella, which ran from 1917 through 1918, was to be Maude Adams's final appearance in a play by J.M. Barrie and her last stage appearance until 1931.

September 2, 1920

As respects the contract filming of your plays between yourself and the Famous Players Company (dated August 19, 1919) I have never seen a copy of the instrument, nor did I have any reason to suppose ... you had given any sort of film rights to *Peter Pan* to that corporation.

Apart from Miss Adams's curious feeling of reverence for the play ... she would be bitterly hurt and disappointed if that play should be filmed by the Famous Players-Lasky Corporation while she is still upon the stage...

I am not by any means sure that Miss Adams's wish that you should reserve Peter for her is reasonable from an everyday standpoint.

But none of us, I suppose, is altogether reasonable about things that touch life most closely, and if in Miss Adams's nature to look at this sort of question as coolly and as impassively as I do, it is quite certain that she could never metamorphose herself into Peter or Lady Babbie, or Cinderella.[43]

Mr. Delafield cabled Barrie:

FROHMAN, INC, DECLINE TO MAKE CONTRACT WITH ADAMS FOR MARY ROSE UNLESS SHE WILL RELINQUISH THE RIGHT TO PRODUCE PETER, MINISTER, OR ANY OTHER PLAYS OF YOURS DURING THE TIME OF THE PROPOSED THREE YEARS CONTRACT ... ADAMS HAS MADE EVERY REASONABLE CONCESSION WITHOUT SUCCESS. SHE CANNOT THEREFORE PRODUCE MARY ROSE.[44]

The very same day Maude wrote a letter to Barrie:

Apart from all these negotiations which have been a great ... disappointment to me, I want to send some word to remind you of my affection for you and of my gratitude for all you have done for me; and to tell you that you must not feel badly on my account. Of the success of the play there can be no doubt and you will not be happier in its success than I shall be.

Love,
Maude[45]

Barrie wrote in October 1920:

It is now settled between the Frohman Co. and Miss Adams that she does not play Mary Rose. Sad to me, but I can see they couldn't hit it off together.[46]

Adams signed with Mitchell Erlanger but stayed off the stage while she pursued on her own the film rights to *Peter Pan*. Of course, almost all of the major studios were also interested in filming the play and it was just a matter of time before it would see its way to the large but silent screen. In a letter dated August 3, 1920, Maude wrote to Barrie:

I have not liked being a dog-in-the-manger about the moving-pictures for *Peter*; especially during my illness it has seemed dreadful to me that you should be deprived of the large sums that *Peter* would bring you. For several months I have interested myself in a process which would make it possible to do pictures in color, which, of course, would give beauty and take away the monotony of black and white. In the meantime another process has been completed which would make it possible now to do *The Little Minister*. I should like more space for *Peter*, it is not absolutely necessary, but I am told that further adjustments will give more space. I have had some moving-pictures taken of myself and they are not quite bad as you think, but before the end of this month I hope to have some pictures done in color — then I shall know exactly what I can do. Perhaps you will let me know if you would care to have me do *The Little Minister* and *Peter*, provided that they be done well and beautiful.[47]

Two months later she again wrote to Barrie:

As I wrote you I am very keen about pictures in color, but if nothing satisfactory should come in color I am quite willing to try one or two scenes in black and white to see what can be done with me. I should prefer to try at first in *Peter's* own scenery, but if that should not be right, we could do some of the snow scenes this winter and wait for the other scenes until spring or summer. If the color schemes come to anything then I am sure the play will be better in its own theatre clothes and so far as I personally am concerned the sooner it can be done the better for me. I don't look so much older, but I *am* older. It would be the making of the play if you would come and direct it ... I doubt very much that the Famous Players Company would care to do the play in colors because of the necessity of a different sort of projecting machine ... I don't know whether these (black and white) pictures express the limitations of the medium or the lack of experience of the people who put the pictures together; it is probably the former but I shall know more about it within the next six weeks.

> Love,
> Maude[48]

On October 18, Adolph Zukor, president of Famous Players-Lasky Corporation, offered Adams the role of Peter, writing:

> I want you to believe that I am making the suggestion for you to take the part in the very best of faith and that we would conscientiously endeavor to do everything possible to have you appear to as good advantage as you have upon the stage and will stop at nothing to make the production a credit to you.[49]

Adams met with Daniel Frohman, who, now associated with Famous Players, wrote a letter to Zukor listing her concerns for the proposed film regarding color, the possibility of Barrie directing the film, and several other points:

> 1st — As to her possible plan of playing "Peter Pan" in the regular theatres of which she is yet in doubt.
> 2nd — The project of her appearing in the picture of "Peter Pan."
> 3rd — The matter of adopting Barrie's suggestion which he made to her to the effect that a boy of considerable qualifications be engaged to play "Peter Pan" in the picture.[50]

Zukor wrote back to Adams asking her to consider producing, which meant effectively directing the film version. While Maude had broached this subject with Barrie, it is highly unlikely that the actress in her could tolerate someone else doing *her* role. Finally, after much correspondence, Maude Adams relinquished her rights to play Peter Pan.

Dear Mr. Zukor:

> After the most careful consideration of the suggestion contained in your letter of October 18th, that I should produce "Peter Pan" upon the screen for the Famous Players Lasky Corporation, I have reached the definite conclusion that it would be inexpedient for me to do so.
> Let me assure you of my appreciation of the courtesy implied in your offer.

> Yours sincerely,
> Maude Adams[51]

Barrie had been uncomfortable with the informal negotiations between Adams and himself, choosing instead to go through the Frohman Company. It is also apparent that, as author of *Peter Pan*, his interests in the success of a film version did not necessarily include it as a vehicle for Maude Adams. For this he was perfectly justified, as film would only emphasize what Maude already knew but could not admit to herself: that she was too old for the role. Certainly in retrospect, a filmed version with Adams would have been of historical significance in terms of recording one of the greatest stage actresses of early 20th century in her greatest role but as art it would have been a great miscalculation for *Peter Pan*. Film had still not found its voice and Maude's appeal, indeed her art, depended on all of the tools an actor can bring to a role. The turn of events left her heartbroken, keeping her off the stage for over a decade.

During her remaining years Maude made several attempts to set her life on paper. She also experimented with camera lights for color film in Schenectady, New York, which paid off— at least for G.E. The lights she developed were strong enough for color film but she did not patent her ideas thus gaining none of the profits. An out-of-court settlement of $500,000 could have been won; however, Maude declined and referred to it only once, on paper, which was found among her belongings when she passed away. She stated simply, "I was an idiot!"[52]

A radio re-creation of Peter Pan was scheduled in 1937 but Maude was replaced by Eva Le Gallienne when she became ill. The following year, on December 15, Maude played the role on a New York station, WEAF. Earlier that same year, she assumed a teaching position at Stephens College and accepted an invitation from David O. Selznick to test for a role in the film *The Young in Heart*. While the screen test was successful, Maude felt that the role was not suited to her talents and suggested Minnie Dupree instead.

Her last years were spent in retirement with her companion of 46 years, Louise Boynton, who, a few years older than Maude, passed away in 1951. Maude died two years later on July 17, still working on her autobiography. It is rather ironic that Barrie never saw Maude Adams as Peter Pan. Perhaps it is better that no filmed record exists for audiences to judge the talents of one of the most popular actresses ever to grace the stage, for film, with all its abilities to capture nuance, cannot do justice to the over-the-top-performances necessary for the stage. All that remains of Maude Adams is some film footage from her screen test, a couple of worn records at the Library of Congress of her radio performance as Lady Babbie, a multitude of photos and programs, and the legend. And maybe, just maybe, somewhere in an old radio station or storage basement there lays a stack of shellac radio transcriptions of Maude's radio performance as Peter Pan.

On December 19, 1931, after attending a performance of *The Merchant of Venice*, Alexander Woollcott wrote:

Maude Adams was one of the most popular American actresses of her day. This extremely rare portrait was taken around 1914 by Gertrude Kasebier, who, famous for her use of *chiaroscuro*, was one of the most influential American photographers of the early 20th century.

Sitting as one unresisting spectator in the largest audience I have seen in any theatre in many a season, I found myself yielding to the spell of a music familiar, dear, and ineffably touching. It was the music of a speaking voice I had not heard in years nor ever thought to hear once more. It was the voice — unchanged and changeless — of Maude Adams. And the sound of it filled me with an almost intolerable nostalgia for a day that is not now and can never be again.[53]

4

Cecilia Loftus and the Mermaids

I think it is in the combination in him of the mature knowledge of a man
and the wonderful imagination of a child that the secret of Peter Pan's charm
lies. But neither Peter nor his creator is really capable of explanation. Fairies
were never meant to be explained.

— Cecilia "Cissie" Loftus, 1923[1]

Peter Pan had proved itself in London, and while it was being tweaked for the services of Maude Adams in the States, Charles Frohman was preparing the play for a second Christmas season at the Duke of York's Theatre.

It appears that the casting decision for the role of Peter came rather late, as Cecilia Loftus was not offered the role until November 1905. She recalled:

My first introduction to Peter Pan was when I went to see Maude Adams, the American Peter, play the part in New York. I thought what a glorious part it must be to play, with no idea that I should ever play it; but by an extraordinary coincidence I received a cable from Mr. Charles Frohman the very next morning, asking if I could sail immediately and play Peter Pan in London. I rushed to the cable office, cabled that I was sailing at once, left America within a couple of days, crossed the Atlantic in a state of dreadful anxiety lest something go wrong at the last moment and, still hardly able to believe in my good fortune, found myself interviewing Sir James Barrie and Mr. Boucicault at the Duke of York's Theatre. I was rather frightened at meeting Sir James, but I soon discovered that he was as shy and as timid of me as I was of him.[2]

Cecilia (Cissie) Loftus, a young actress from Glasgow, Scotland, was a popular music hall entertainer with a remarkable talent for mimicry. The product of variety artists, Ben and Marie Loftus, Cissie was born on October 22, 1876. It was during a vacation from her convent school in 1891 that she served as a temporary replacement for her mother's backstage maid at the Oxford Music Hall. The 14-year-old would stand in the wings watching the different variety acts with great interest, particularly the imitations of some of the performers. Convinced that she could do better, she persuaded the theatre manager to give her a chance mimicking famous entertainers like Henry Irving, Ada Rehan, and Sarah Bernhardt.

Years later she remarked:

I had a trick voice. I couldn't do anything with it as myself, but I could make it accurately copy the speech or singing of anyone else. When Sir Arthur Sullivan asked me to sing for Marchesi I wasn't able to produce a note, so I imitated a celebrated singer, and Marchesi wanted to train me for opera.[3]

Enrico Caruso was amused at her takeoff of his singing, as were Eleanor Duse, Maude Adams, and Ethel Barrymore at her imitations of them in their famous stage roles. Despite her success, Loftus was anxious to act on the legitimate stage and decided to give up her enormous salary to appear in Justin Huntly McCarthy's *If I Were King.* Henry Irving caught her performance and asked her to appear opposite him in *Faust* as Marguerite at the Lyceum in 1903. That same year she played Ophelia to E.H. Southern's *Hamlet.*

Cissie eloped with McCarthy when she was 17, continuing to grow artistically and in stature on stage. Off stage she enjoyed writing verse and was often seen in the company of Aubrey Beardsley, Max Beerbohm, and E. W. Mason. Ironically, with all of her impressive credits, Cissie Loftus is best known as the "second" Peter Pan. Like all who followed her, Cissie had her *Peter Pan* stories.

> Of the play I particularly remember one incident which might have had a tragic end. When Peter flies he must always take off from exactly the right spot or he will fly in the wrong direction. There are marks on the stage to guide him, but on one occasion I missed the mark and was swung crash into the scenery, but so skillfully were the wires manipulated that I swung, without touching anything, straight through the window at the back of the stage through which I entered.[4]

During the second season, audiences that came back for a second dose of Pan were surprised with the addition of Act III. "There are mermaids, Wendy, with long tails,"[5] he promises in Act I. In place of the Indian scene, a new act was added in which Peter takes Wendy and the boys to Marooner's Rock (in 1928 Barrie moved the apostrophe: "Marooners' Rock"). It is a fantastic place with mermaids and a pelican protecting her eggs in her floating nest. Barrie edited some of Hook's lines from Act II and snugly fit them in the new act.

> "The game's up!" moans Hook. "Those boys have found a mother."
> "What is a mother?" asks Smee.[6]

His captain points to the floating nest to explain. "The nest must have fallen into the water, but would

Top: Cecilia "Cissie" Loftus, the second Peter Pan, in 1905 (photograph: The Philco Publishing Co.). *Bottom:* A formal portrait of Cissie Loftus, circa 1905.

the mother desert her eggs? No!"[7] The boys delight in teasing the mermaids and share a humorous song with a baby mermaid and her mother:[8]

Mermaid Sings:	When waters of the never-land are naked to the moon,
	Then wakes the fair mermaid-en from her sleep in the Lagoon,
	And I raise my coral mirror my drooping locks to tend,
	But the part of me I'm proudest of, is at the other end.
	The mermaid's tail,
	The mermaid's tail,
	It fans us when we're hot,
	We whisk it thus! If we are pleas'd,
	And so! If we are not,
Mermaid Chorus:	When swimming thro' the green lagoon,
	We hoist it as a sail,
	And when we take to flirting,
	It fascinates the male.
	No lady would dress in skirts
	If she could show a tail.
Baby Mermaid:	Who turns this way? If mortals I must go!
	Turn answer! Legs, or tails?
Peter:	A merman I, with my tail on high,
	In a way that most allures,
	I humbly wish, O famous fish
	To pay my respect to yours
Boys:	We accompany him and all of us swim,
	With our beautiful tails as lures,
Baby Mermaid:	You're awfully cool,
Peter:	I'm rather cool,
	With your tail I so want to play.
Baby Mermaid:	Then please to write, Mama tonight,
	And ask her if I may.
Boys:	Yes, that would be better,
	He's writing the letter,
	How we wonder what he'll say!
Peter:	Dear mermaid may your daughter play,
	At tails tonight with me?
	I wish she would and now conclude,
	With kindest wishes, P.
Boys:	That cannot fail to pull her tail,
	What will the answer be?
Mermaid:	Dear sir, who wrote? Received your note,
Baby Mermaid:	Oh say that he may tum
Mermaid:	My leave you've got,
	Don't make her hot,
	Yours faithfully, her mum.
Boys:	Oh lucky we, her tail to see,
	The mermaid bids us come.

The humor is interrupted by a fight with the pirates, who wound Peter and abandon him with Wendy, leaving them stranded on a rock with the threat of a rising tide. They are

Rosamund Buryn as the Mermaid and Geraldine Wilson as the Baby Mermaid in the new Marooners' Rock scene during the second London season of *Peter Pan* in 1905.

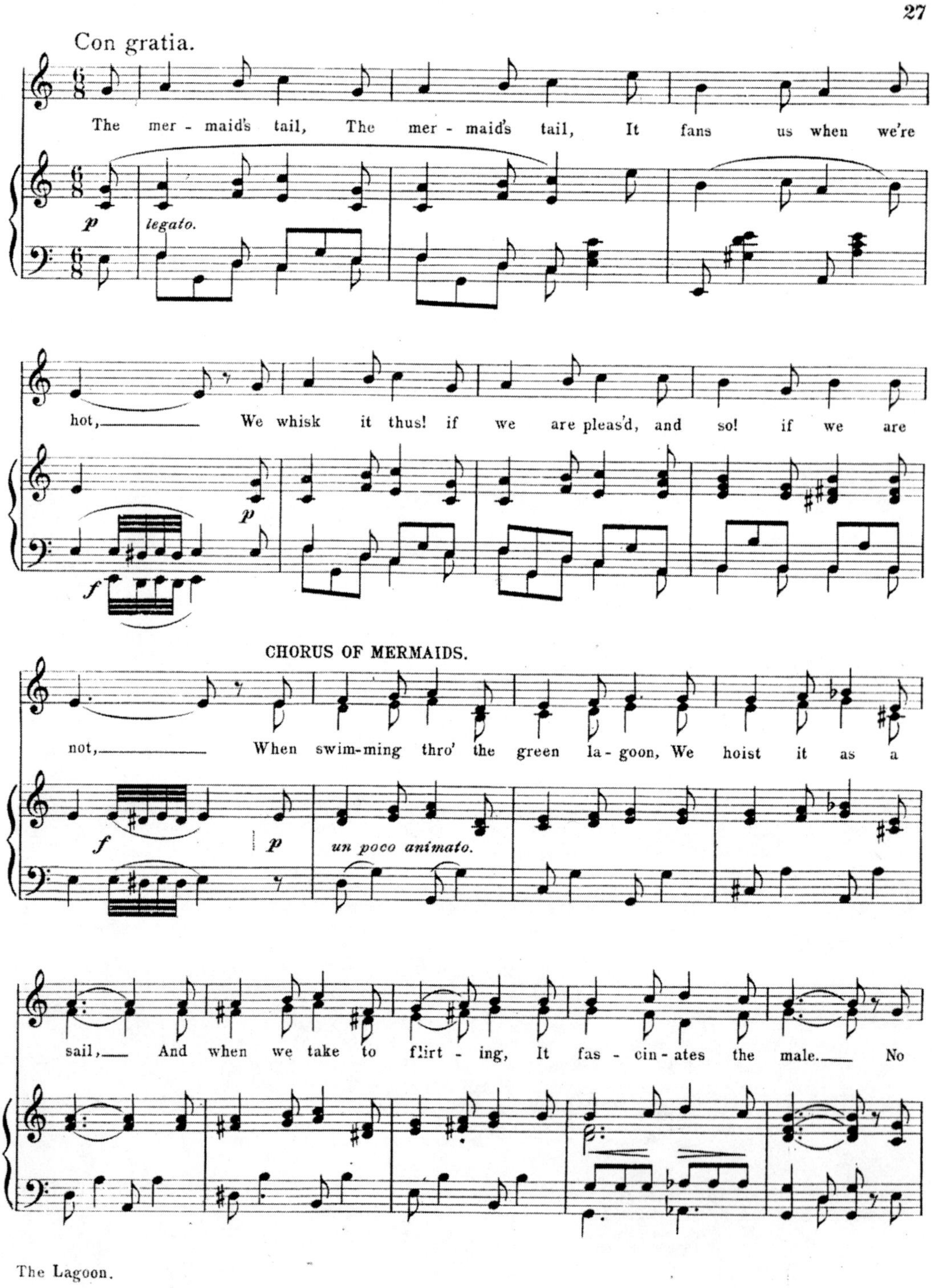

27
Con gratia.
The mer - maid's tail, The mer - maid's tail, It fans us when we're
legato.
hot, We whisk it thus! if we are pleas'd, and so! if we are
CHORUS OF MERMAIDS.
not, When swim-ming thro' the green la - goon, We hoist it as a
un poco animato.
sail, And when we take to flirt - ing, It fas - cin - ates the male. No
The Lagoon.

"Song of the Mermaids." Lyrics by J.M. Barrie and music by John Crook.

too tired to fly but Wendy is saved by Michael's kite, with Peter remaining behind with no hope of being rescued. "To die will be an awfully big adventure,"[9] he says.

Of course Peter cannot die. Barrie steals from himself by adding a solution he used in *The Little White Bird*. Peter takes the nest from the bird and uses his jacket as a sail, floating away from danger.

Several reviews were quite critical of the new addition. They were disappointed with Peter's lack of compassion for the mother and her eggs. Careful not to offend, Barrie revised the scene the following year, with a more sensitive Peter carefully placing the eggs into a pirate's hat before sailing off. The contented mother sits again protecting her eggs.

Another change takes place on the pirate ship. The few lines Hook recited at the opening of the scene have become part of a soliloquy, stuffed with those now memorable phrases: "How still the night is.... Nothing seems alive.... All mortals envy me, yet better perhaps for Hook to have had less ambition.... Oh, fame, fame! Thou glittering bauble..."[10]

Like Nina Boucicault,

The new act, with Peter Pan (Cissie Loftus) and Wendy (Hilda Trevelyan) trapped on Marooners' Rock (photograph: Ellis and Walery, 1905).

Cissie Loftus starred in *Peter Pan* for only one season but her career spanned more than 50 years. She appeared in the *Ziegfeld Follies* and made her motion picture debut in 1913, yet a year later she was unemployed and could not find work for the next decade. In 1923, she

"Peter and Wendy": Cissie Loftus and Hilda Trevelyan in *Peter Pan*, 1905–06 (photograph: Ellis and Walery).

was charged with possession of illegal drugs, which she explained were needed to relieve the pain caused by the premature birth of her child. She was given one year's probation. That same year she enjoyed the personal success of appearing at the Mecca of vaudeville houses, the Palace Theatre on Broadway. Her imitations of Mrs. Fiske, Harry Lauder, and Nora Bayes delighted her audiences and brought her standing ovations. The Loftus career once again bloomed and Cissie was featured in many plays, including *Becky Sharp*, *Uncle Tom's Cabin*, *Merrily We Roll Along*, *The Holmes of Baker Street*, and *The Wooden Slipper*. She also appeared in several motion pictures including *East Lynne*, *The Old Maid*, *The Blue Bird*, and *Hers to Hold*.

Cissie returned to the stage again in 1938 for a series of Sunday concerts at the Little Theatre. At first the public was shocked by the appearance of the actress, now looking much older with her shocking white hair, but her imitations of popular artists of the day, Gertrude Lawrence, Fanny Brice, Beatrice Lillie, and even Noël Coward, were wickedly funny.

Cissie Loftus died of a heart attack on July 12, 1943. Roger Lancelyn Green — who had the good fortune of seeing every actress to appear as Pan from 1904 until the mid–1950s, as well as acting in the 1943 *Peter Pan* touring company as Noodler — wrote that

Cissie Loftus as Peter Pan, which she played from 1905 to 1906 (photograph: Ellis and Walery (courtesy Roy Busby).

Cecilia Loftus, the second Peter, lacked her predecessor's uncanny, eerie qualities, but was more boyish and elfin — characteristics even more apparent in her understudy Pauline Chase, who played for a few performances at the end of the tour before tackling the part in earnest the following Christmas.[11]

5

Vivian Martin and the Unknown Peter Pans

It was while I was playing Peter Pan that I became fascinated with Barrie, and oh, I think he is delightful with his delicious humor and that pathos that grips me more than real tragedy.
— Vivian Martin, 1919[1]

When Marilyn Miller assumed the role of Peter Pan for his spectacular return to Broadway, it might have appeared that she was the second actress to appear in that part in the United States. Comparisons to Maude Adams were inevitable and for many the idea of anyone trying to challenge the memories of Adams's portrait of the boy who wouldn't grow up was ludicrous. Therefore, it came as something of a surprise for this writer when he discovered that not only did another actress play Peter before Miller, but that she also played the part at the same time as Adams, and that she was hired by Charles Frohman — in a juvenile company!

Vivian Martin was almost 15 years old when she came out of retirement to play Peter Pan. Born on July 22, 1893, near Grand Rapids, Michigan, she had previously attained great success as a child actress in Richard Mansfield's company. Her first stage role was in *Cyrano de Bergerac* and she made her Broadway debut in *Little Lord Fauntleroy* in 1903. Mansfield suggested she leave the stage to go to school and come back to work for him in a few years. In 1907 she was preparing to leave her school in Greenville, Michigan, to return to Mansfield's company when she received word of his death. Devastated by this news (and perhaps more so by the thought that her career was over), she was surprised when Charles Frohman contacted her and requested that she come to his office for an interview. He met with Vivian and her parents and a second meeting, sans her parents, was scheduled. A newspaper article of the day detailed the conversation of that meeting.

"What do you want do?" he asked.

"I used to think I wanted a dramatic part," replied the young girl, "but now I believe I would like to try musical comedy."

"Why musical comedy?" asked Frohman. "Your training has been dramatic."

"But I think the chances to rise fast are greater in musical comedy," replied the ambitious girl.

Mr. Frohman thought this over and then said: "Come around tomorrow and I will see what I can do for you."

When she arrived on the scene the next day at rehearsal hour he asked her: "How would you like to play in *Peter Pan?*"

Vivian Martin as Peter Pan, 1907 (Photograph: Marceau).

"I would like it," she answered, "but how long would it be before I could hope for a leading role?"

"The part I have picked for you is the part of Peter Pan himself, which Miss Adams is now playing," answered Mr. Frohman with a sly grin. The answer nearly took away the breath of little Miss Martin, but she promptly accepted the role and the astute Mr. Frohman has expressed himself as decidedly well satisfied with the result.[2]

Vivian Martin, as Peter, and Violet Hemming, as Wendy, toured just outside of New York City in 1907. Most theatre historians are prone to state that the role of Peter exclusively belonged to Maude Adams during the first decade of performances of the play in America.

Eva Lang toured the U.S.A. in *Peter Pan* in 1909 (courtesy Roy Busby).

"I had a wonderful season as Peter Pan," remembered Martin in 1919. "It was such a whimsical, fanciful thing and so popular that it was a joy to play it. I had met Maude Adams, for my father was in her company, but I did not see her as Peter until several seasons after I had played it, and what a treat it was! I shall never forget it."[3]

Papers of the day stated how pleased Frohman was with Martin's performance, yet she was never invited to return to the role, nor was she to play it in New York. She did come back to Broadway in 1910, where she continued to meet with success in several plays throughout the 1910s and 1920s. Vivian signed with the Famous Players-Lasky Company and was featured in a few silent films, including *Unclaimed Goods* in 1918 and *Louisiana* the following year. She later married William Jefferson and died on March 16, 1987, at age 94.

Playing opposite Martin was another youngster, Violet Hemming, who was making her American stage debut as Wendy. Violet was born in England to a theatrical family. Only 12 when she appeared in *Peter Pan*, she next had the lead in *Rebecca of Sunnybrook Farm*. Her first adult part was in *Disraeli* with George Arliss, which she repeated on the screen in 1932 with Arliss and Bette Davis. In the years following, Violet became known for her comedic talents. In 1945 she retired to marry Bennet Champ Clark, a federal judge, and did not return to the stage until nine years later, after which she continued to appear on Broadway and in stock. She died on July 5, 1981.

As surprising as it was to discover another actress playing Peter Pan during those early years, it appears that Frohman leased the rights to the play in other parts of the country as well. In 1910, "Eva Lang and Company" was found touring the West Coast in the play. Beverly West also toured with the show in 1912 with Isoldi Illian as Wendy and Jane Tyrrell playing Mrs. Darling as well as reading a prologue. Perhaps these performers were not as well known as Maude Adams but they are still a small part of the theatrical history of *Peter Pan*— the touring companies — which is appropriate to be recorded here.

6

Pauline Chase and an Afterthought

It is a very curious fact that when Mr. J.M. Barrie imbued Peter Pan with everlasting youth, by some strange gift of magic he also bestowed upon those fortunate enough to be destined to play the part of "the boy who wouldn't grow up" an everlasting enthusiasm for the role, and, personally speaking, although I have been Peter Pan on over a thousand occasions, I fell to-day even more in love with my part than when I attended the first rehearsal which was — it's wonderful how time flies, isn't it? — actually just over seven years ago.

— Pauline Chase, 1913[1]

"Every December a terrifying ceremony takes place before *Peter Pan* is produced," wrote Pauline Chase, "and this is the measuring of children who play in it. They are measured to see whether they have grown too tall, and they can all squeeze down into about two inches less than they really are, but this does not deceive the management, who have grown frightfully knowing, and sometimes they frown horribly at you and say, 'We shall pass you this year, but take care, madam, take care!' and sometimes you are told, 'It won't do my lad; you are grown out of knowledge. We are sorry for you, but — farewell!' Measuring day is one of the tragedies of Peter Pan."[2]

There was a certain irony that the younger cast members of *Peter Pan* were unaware of: they were adrift in a tragedy about a boy who will never grow up and yet sooner than they wished they had to come to terms with the reality that they were too old to appear in the play any longer. However, Pauline Chase did not have to worry about losing the role of Peter as she was adored by the critics, audiences, and Barrie himself. "There are only two possible ways of playing Peter," he stated to Edna Best in 1920 when she went to his flat for his advice on approaching the role. "Either he must be the whimsical, fairy creature that Nina Boucicault made him or he must be the lovable tomboy of Pauline Chase. There is no other way."[3] Pauline played the part for some 1,400 performances; not bad for an actress who in 1903 was known only as the "Pink Pajama Girl" from her role in *The Liberty Belles*.

Born in the U.S.A. in Washington on May 20, 1885, Pauline Chase made her stage debut in 1898 in *The Rounders* at the Casino Theatre in New York. Two years later she was playing juvenile roles in *The Belle of New York* and *The Lady Slavery*. Charles Frohman, impressed with audience reaction to the vivacious pajama-clad blond, hired the actress to appear in a London production of *The School Girl*. From then on, with occasional visit to the States, Pauline Chase enjoyed a successful career on the English stage.

It came to no one's surprise that Dion Boucicault added a pajama-costumed dance for Pauline's character of the First Twin in *Peter Pan*, which cemented the Pink Pajama image

Pauline Chase as Peter Pan, 1906–1914 (photograph: Bassano).

for the two years she "danced" the role. During the second season, while understudying for Cissie Loftus, she toured in Edinburgh when Loftus wired the management of a sudden illness. Pauline was to go on in her place. Reminiscing in 1913 she wrote:

> Just before I was going on the stage a certain member of the company stopped me in the wings and said:
> "Would you feel more nervous than ever if Mr. Barrie chanced to be sitting in front?"
> "Good heavens!" I said, growing pale through my make-up at the thought. "If Mr. Barrie were to be in front I think I should faint with sheer fright."

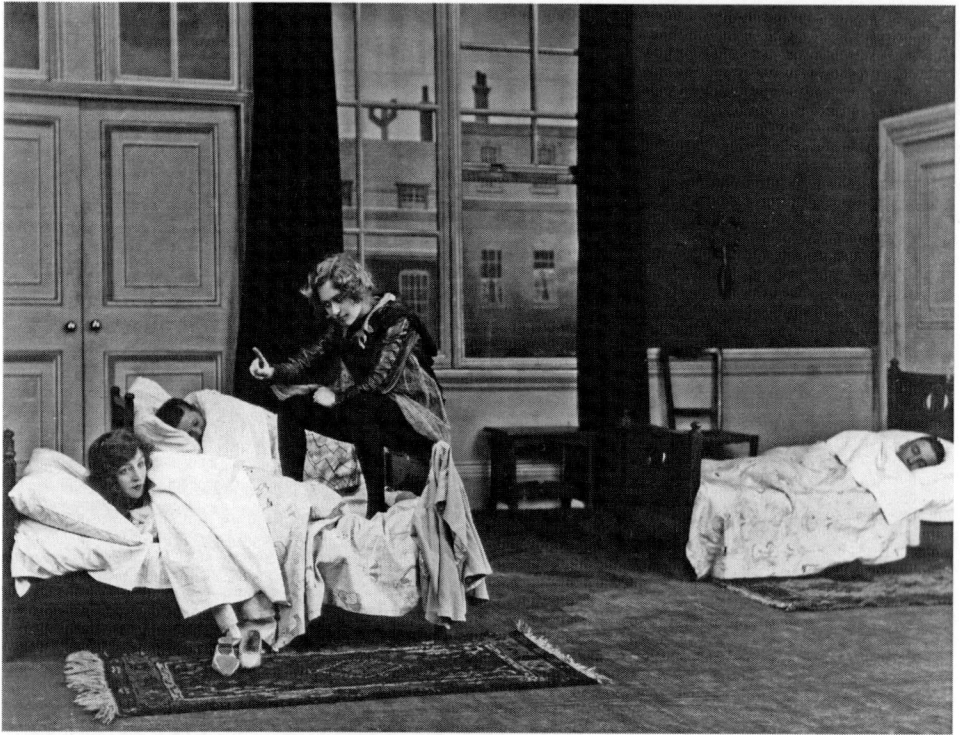

Top: Peter Pan (Pauline Chase) visits the Darling children in the nursery (photograph: Bassano, 1906). *Bottom:* Perhaps the rarest of all *Peter Pan* programs, Michael's Programme was created for an afternoon performance in the nursery of Michael Llewelyn Davies in 1906 when he became too ill to go to the theatre for the annual London production. In the film *Finding Neverland*, it was changed as a performance for a dying Sylvia, Michael's mother, who passed away in 1910. The cast was the "Growing Up Company" with J.M. Barrie listed as the Cabman.

Pauline displaying Peter's spider's web costume (photograph: Bassano, 1906).

"Well, you'll be saved that unpleasant experience," was the reply, "because he can't possibly have had time to travel from London to Edinburgh."

So for the moment I felt reassured; for, you must know, to take up the leading part in the play at a few minutes' notice is an ordeal which the most experimented actress would regard as terrifying in the extreme.[4]

Much like those early film musicals where the understudy goes on to become a star, Barrie was indeed in the audience and immediately offered her the role of Peter for the 1906 season. However, ten years later Pauline remembered how she was offered the role of Peter with an entirely different scenario:

The second year I understudied Peter and when Miss Cecilia Loftus was ill at Liverpool Sir James Barrie and Charles Frohman came to Liverpool to see me play the part. They told me that if they were both pleased with my performance they would send me a piece of paper at the end of the performance (as they had to catch a train back to London) with an X on it. I received the piece

Top: Pauline afloat in the Pelican's Nest (photograph: Bassano, 1906). *Bottom:* "Wendy's Sampler" was a special drop-curtain created for the play in 1908. It featured the alphabet at the top and tributes to Hans Christian Andersen, Charles Lamb, Robert Lewis Stevenson, and Lewis Carroll. In the middle is Pauline Chase as Peter afloat in the bird's nest.

of paper at the end of the first act; so I knew then that I was to play Peter the next Christmas in London — and I played it for 8 years, twice a day in London, and then went ... on tour. I played the part, 1,400 odd performances, which is more than twice as anyone else has ever played the part.[5]

"Her Peter Pan lacks something of the histrionic skill of Nina Boucicault, the original Peter Pan," declared the *Morning Telegraph* of Pauline's performance, "but such shortcomings were compensated for by her graceful delicacy and charming childishness, which captivated the audience."[6]

"Miss Chase is wonderfully light and graceful and brings to the part a delicious childishness," agreed the *Daily Mail*. "There is piquancy, too, in her slight American accent."[7]

And finally, from the *Daily Chronicle*, "Perhaps one might say that as a picture Miss Chase brings Peter Pan nearer to being a boy fairy than any of her predecessors."[8]

Denis Mackail's account of Pauline Chase's acting is similar to Green's:

A Peter who will never achieve Miss Boucicault's sexlessness, for he or she is far too pretty, but a Peter who never ceases to transmit the happiness and gaiety which she always feels in the part. "I'm youth, I'm joy, I'm a little bird that has broken out of its egg." That is Miss Pauline Chase's greatest line, for whenever she says it, it is almost the literal truth. She hardly plays anything else, but here — always excepting Miss Boucicault — she is incomparable and irreplaceable.[9]

During Chase's reign, a few changes occurred. Gerald du Maurier's schedule could no longer permit him the luxury of playing a short season in the perennial favorite. His part was divided between two actors

Pauline sharpening Peter's knife to fight Captain Hook (photograph: Bassano, 1906).

with A.E. Matthews cast Mr. Darling and Robb Harwood as Hook. Harwood received excellent notices (Mackail called him "the next best of all Hooks"[10]), but the fascinating parallels between Mr. Darling and Hook were lost (although Andrew Birkin makes a point that Barrie initially conceived Dorothy Baird to play Hook as well as Mrs. Darling, thus adding more impact to one of Barrie's thrown-out titles, *The Boy Who Hated Mothers*). Another change, much more fascinating, occurred as a result of inquiries from Barrie's friends, colleagues, and even the young actors in the play as to whatever became of Peter and Wendy as she grew older. Hilda Trevelyan explained how he responded:

> It was always the same. "A story please" that is how it ran. Mr. Barrie would sit down solemnly & told his captives [*sic*] a story that generally was made up on the spur of the moment. These ultimatums for stories I believe was the birth of a one act play that he wrote called An Afterthought which is the epilogue to the immortal Peter Pan. It was produced at the Duke of York's Theatre, and enjoyed a run of exactly one night. It was secretly rehearsed by J.M. Barrie as its production was to be a surprise for his great friend and manager, Charles Frohman, who was present at the performance. There was only one manuscript, the original one as written by the Author. This was the Prompt copy & Production copy all in one. The production of the Afterthought took place on the last night of the 3rd Christmas Season at the Duke of York's theatre.
>
> When the curtain fell on *Peter Pan* for the last time that season, the Tree Tops were quickly swept away and Mr. and Mrs. Darlings' nursery took their place. In the prompt-corner with manuscript in hand stood the author and producer, ready to help should anyone forget what they had to say. The curtain rose and "discovered" were a grown-up Wendy with her hair done on top of her head, and dressed in a fashionable ball gown. In a bed nearby snored rather feebly a dog, who was very tired and fast asleep. It was Nana who was

Hilda Trevelyan returned to the role of Wendy in 1909. Portrait drawn by Frank Haviland for *The Illustrated London News*.

so old and feeble that she had really got beyond being a nurse anymore. On another bed was a child called "Jane," daughter of Wendy. That was the glimpse the audience got when the curtain rose.

As the play proceeded the nursery window opened itself unaided and in flew Peter Pan, in his usual manner. He had called to fetch Wendy to do his spring cleaning. Time to Peter Pan means nothing; it is something he cannot understand. It seemed to bewilder him to find Wendy all grown up and with a little girl of her own. Wendy told him all that had hap-

Top: Peter (Pauline Chase) and Wendy (Hilda Trevelyn) in the House in the Tree Tops (photograph: Bassano, 1906). *Right:* In 1907 John Hassall created six posters depicting scenes from *Peter Pan* that were sold in the lobby of the Duke of York's Theatre. One of his works, "The Wendy House," was adapted for the cover of the programs for the next few years.

PETER AND JANE

"An Afterthought: Peter and Jane." Illustration by F.D. Bedford from Barrie's 1911 novelization of his play. Although performed only once during Barrie's lifetime in 1907, the author included the scene in *Peter and Wendy* and the script was published posthumously in 1957. By that time the scene was already known in the U.S. as it was part of the Mary Martin musical.

pened since they had last met and it was quite a shock to him when he heard that "Slightly Soiled" had married a Lady and become a Lord. When the curtain fell on that first and last night of the Afterthought Mr. Barrie walked on to the stage and thanked the cast for playing so well and as he thanked Wendy for her performance, he slipped the original manuscript into her hand and pressed it.[11]

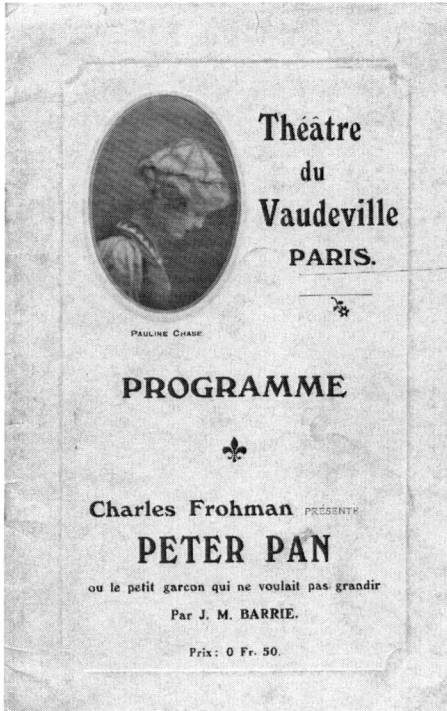

Théâtre
du
Vaudeville
PARIS.

PAULINE CHASE

PROGRAMME

Charles Frohman présente
PETER PAN
ou le petit garcon qui ne voulait pas grandir
Par J. M. BARRIE.

Prix: 0 Fr. 50.

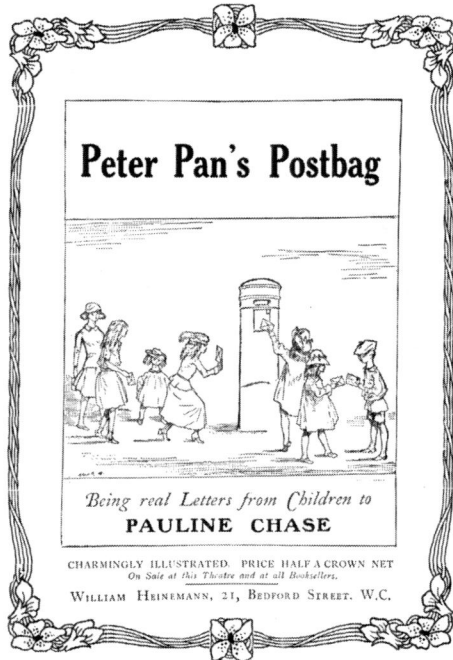

Peter Pan's Postbag

Being real Letters from Children to
PAULINE CHASE

CHARMINGLY ILLUSTRATED. PRICE HALF A CROWN NET
On Sale at this Theatre and at all Booksellers.
WILLIAM HEINEMANN, 21, BEDFORD STREET, W.C.

Every copy of the book sold in this Theatre autographed by
Miss PAULINE CHASE

Left: Peter flew across the Channel for an engagement in Paris in June of 1908. In addition to the program illustrated here, a 12-page pamphlet, "L'HISTOIRE DE PETER PAN," was distributed so that the French-speaking audience could follow the story. The cast made a return engagement in 1909. *Right:* An enterprising Pauline Chase received Barrie's permission to have her autographed book, *Peter Pan's Postbag*, sold at the Duke of York's Theatre starting in 1909, the year the book was published.

The addition was unveiled on February 22, 1907, and was introduced by Tessie Parke, earlier seen as the mermaid and now playing Jane. Hilda Trevelyan played the grown-up Wendy. The scene was met with a 15-minute period of applause!

In June 1908 *Peter Pan* arrived in Paris for two weeks of special performances at the Theatre du Vaudeville. The audience members were provided with small 12-page booklets, "L'Histoire de Peter Pan," as well as a theatre programme. The performances were so well received that the following year the company returned for an extended five-week run. On opening night Barrie and Frohman each had their own box. "Frohman was overjoyed at its success, and Barrie, naturally, could not repress his delight. What pleased them most was the spectacle of row after row of little French kiddies, who, while not understanding a word of the narrative, seemed to be having the time of their lives."[12] Like the actresses playing Peter before and after her, Pauline Chase received a large volume of letters from children as well as adults. In 1909 she compiled a few for a publication, *Peter Pan's Postbag*, which was sold at the Duke of York's Theatre with the actress's inscription. One of those letters was from Michael Llewelyn Davies:

> Dear Peter Pan thank you very much for the Post Card you Gave me I am Longing For some more of them and I have sent you A picture of the Little House For you And Nik-o thinks he can fly But he Only tumbles about ~~his~~ he sends his Love.
> From Michael[13]

Two Peter Pans were celebrated in *The Illustrated London News* on December 22, 1906: Zena Dare on tour and Pauline Chase in London.

Sharply contrasting with the success of *Peter Pan* was the disintegration of Barrie's marriage and also the Davies family. Arthur, diagnosed with cancer, was quite concerned about the financial security of his family but Barrie assured the dying man that they would be cared for. He died on April 18, 1908. Meanwhile, as Barrie immersed himself further into the Davies family, the neglected Mary Barrie was having an affair. Oddly, when Barrie was informed about the situation, he wanted to forget the whole thing and to continue going on as they had. This was too much for Mary, who wanted a normal marriage and children. Thus, against her husband's wishes, she filed for a divorce, which went to court in October 1908. Barrie was asked by his lawyer to refrain from seeing Sylvia until after the divorce was complete. Admirably, Mary did not bring up her husband's relationship with Sylvia during the proceedings. She knew only too well the limitations of her husband's love for the woman, for any woman. It had been rumored during Barrie's lifetime that he was impotent, with one jokester calling him "the boy who wouldn't go up,"[14] although Mary told Hilda Trevelyan that the couple enjoyed "normal marital relations"[15] early in their marriage. Andrew Birkin published a letter Mary Barrie had written to Peter Davies years later. "J.M. Barrie's tragedy was that he knew that as a man he was a failure and that love in its fullest sense could never be felt by him or experienced, and it was this knowledge that led to his sentimental philanderings." She continued, "One could almost hear him, like Peter Pan, crowing triumphantly, but his heart was sick all the time."[16] True to his generous character, Barrie helped his ex-wife years later when she was in financial trouble.

Just two days after the divorce was granted it was discovered that Sylvia, still mourning the loss of Arthur, also had cancer. Barrie was by her side constantly while the truth of her condition was kept from her. She succumbed to the disease on August 27, 1910, with the secure knowledge that Barrie would provide financially for the boys, keeping them together

"To Die Would Be an Awfully Big Adventure." Zena Dare as Peter Pan on Marooners' Rock. It's quite probable that Zena's photographs as Peter were only second in quantity to those of Pauline Chase. The actress would play Mrs. Darling in 1932 (photograph: Bassano, 1906).

"Silence all, for a mother's last words to her children." Act V. The Pirate Ship, as illustrated by Charles Buchel in 1912. Depicted are E. Holman Clark as Hook, George Shelton as Smee, and Mary Glynne as Wendy.

as a family rather than splitting them up between relatives. However, in her will she also requested that the boys be cared for in their home by their devoted nurse, Mary Hodgson, to be joined by her sister, Jenny. In a remarkable move, Barrie provided Sylvia's family with a copy of her will in which he had changed the name Jenny to Jimmy. Even more incredible is that the relatives did not bother to ask to see the original will even though they were distraught at the idea of Barrie acting as the boys' legal guardian. Perhaps, though, monetary considerations prevailed as no one but Barrie was financially secure enough to keep the boys together and enrolled in their expensive private schools. George was now 17 years old, Jack was 16, Peter was 13, Michael, 10, and Nico, 6. While George and Michael, in particular, loved Barrie, George, like Peter and Jack, was reluctant to call him Uncle Jim. The boys continued to go to boarding school, with the exception of Jack, who joined the navy. Their summers were spent with their guardian in the country.

In October 1911 Barrie published the book *Peter and Wendy*, which included the closure of *An Afterthought*. A

Winifred Geoghegan returned to *Peter Pan* as Curly for the 1907-08 season (courtesy Roy Busby).

Michael Llewelyn Davies dressed as Peter Pan, playing with J.M. Barrie in July of 1906. Barrie had a series of photographs taken of Michael for sculptor Sir George Frampton to use as a model for the statue in Kensington Gardens (courtesy Great Ormond Street Hospital Children's Charity, London).

magical read, the book allows the reader to experience the characters through their thoughts as well as much of the dialogue of the play. That same year Barrie commissioned sculptor Sir George Frampton to create a statue of Peter Pan for Kensington Gardens. Photographs of Michael Davies at the age of six were given to the artist for inspiration, but ultimately they were not used. Although Barrie was unhappy with the results, he secretly had the statue

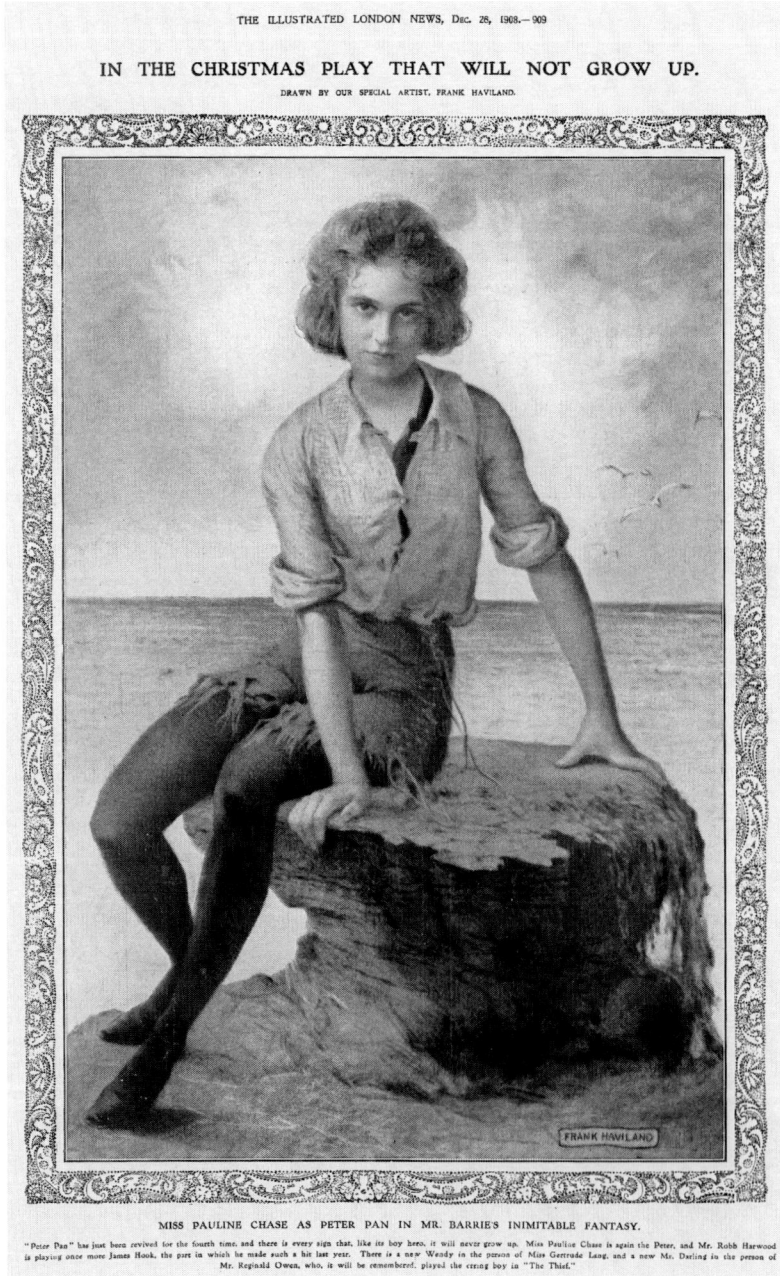

THE ILLUSTRATED LONDON NEWS, Dec. 28, 1908.—909

IN THE CHRISTMAS PLAY THAT WILL NOT GROW UP.

DRAWN BY OUR SPECIAL ARTIST, FRANK HAVILAND.

MISS PAULINE CHASE AS PETER PAN IN MR. BARRIE'S INIMITABLE FANTASY.

"Peter Pan" has just been revived for the fourth time, and there is every sign that, like its boy hero, it will never grow up. Miss Pauline Chase is again the Peter, and Mr. Robb Harwood is playing once more James Hook, the part in which he made such a hit last year. There is a new Wendy in the person of Miss Gertrude Lang, and a new Mr. Darling in the person of Mr. Reginald Owen, who, it will be remembered, played the erring boy in "The Thief."

Pauline Chase: "The Play That Will Not Grow Up." Portrait drawn by Frank Haviland for *The Illustrated London News*, December 26, 1908.

placed in the park, where it remains to this day. Many were surprised and pleased by the addition of the statue to the landscape but there were also those detractors who were upset at what could be conceived as the writer's self-glorification.

One of England's most treasured entertainers — actor, writer, singer, composer and lyricist — was Noël Coward. Long before he wrote and appeared in such sophisticated fare

Maie Ash took the role of First Twin in 1906 when Pauline became the star of the play (photograph: Dover Street Studios.

Top left: Maidie Andrews was the Second Twin in the Second Touring Company in the 1906-07 season (photograph: The Philco Publishing Co.). *Top right:* Phyllis Embury was the Second Twin in the London production in 1906 and 1907 as well as in the main touring company in 1907–08. *Bottom:* Philip Tonge as Michael in the Princess Theatre in Manchester in 1906. (He is perhaps most famous in later life for his portrayal as the twitching psychiatrist in the original film version of *Miracle on 34th Street*.)

such as *Private Lives, Bitter Sweet, Tonight at 8:30*, and *Sail Away*, Noël Coward was a Lost Boy. Cole Lesley wrote:

The Duke of York's Theatre was packed with children when Noël went for his audition, all of them accompanied as he was by their mothers and, like him, all burning with the same ambition — to get into *Peter Pan*. When Noël's turn came they both went up on to the stage but Mrs. Coward "kept well in the background as I always did, such good policy...." Dion Boucicault, who was taking the audition, called out, "Only one verse," but when Noël and the accompanist stopped he again called out, "Go on. Go on!" and Noël did go on, to the end of the song. Mr. Boucicault asked Mrs. Coward what part Noël wanted; she rather daringly asked for Slightly and even more boldly asked for four pounds a week. He told them to go away and come back in an hour, which time they spent feverishly walking about. Mrs. Coward wrote (after he had granted both her requests) that he was a nice kind man, with the most charming manners....

The *Observer* thought Noël excellent in the part and

Noël Coward played Slightly at the Duke of York's in 1913 and 1914 (courtesy Roy Busby).

another critic wrote, "The immortal Slightly, as acted by master Noël Coward, is quite a young boy [the older A. W. Bascomb had previously played him] and his grave pretence at wisdom is all the funnier."[17]

Years later, Noël and his companion, actor Graham Payn — who played Curly in 1931 — and Cole Lesley — his secretary and friend — often used dialogue from *Peter Pan* in their everyday conversation:

"A little less noise there," "And now to rescue Wendy!," "Straight on till morning," were in everyday use as were "that is the fear that haunts me," and "oh the cleverness of me!" Much of it could be shortened and used as a code: "That's Nana's bark when she smells danger," for instance. A *sotto voce* "Nana bark" from Noël to, say, a business meeting, would be enough to warn Graham and me to beware.[18]

During her tenure as Peter Pan, Pauline Chase appeared in other plays, such as *The Little Japanese Girl* by Loie Fuller, the American skirt dancer who adapted the play from the Japanese; *Our Miss Gibbs* during a triumphant return to New York in 1910; and *Man and Superman* in 1912. She remained close to Barrie and he became her godfather, giving her away when she wed Captain A. V. Drummond in 1914, which resulted in her retirement from the stage.

Pauline remained fixed in the public's eye as Peter Pan for many years after she gave up the stage. Even with three children of her own she would be asked to don Peter's costume for charity events. On June 16, 1928, she appeared again in that role for *The Pageant of Peter Pan*, a celebration at Sefton Park in Liverpool in honor of a duplicate Frampton statue for that park. The elaborate pageant included small children dancing around the statue as fairies, but the highlight of the day occurred when Pauline accidently fell into the lake. Her fondness for the role never waned. She christened her country cottage "Tree Tops" and had a small replica of Peter's stage

Walter Gross as John on tour at the Princess Theatre in Manchester in 1906.

In May 1928, Pauline Chase once more donned a Peter Pan costume for a celebration in honor of Barrie's famous character in Sefton Park, Liverpool. The statue she is seen with is a duplicate of the Kensington Gardens original. However, Chase's costume was not her original but rather one that was created to resemble the statue.

house built for the birds, placing it high in a treetop. For many years she would come to London with her children to see *Peter Pan*.

Pauline Chase died on March 3, 1962, at the age of 76. Almost 50 years since she had appeared on the stage as Peter had passed, yet she was remembered fondly by the press as Barrie's favorite *Peter Pan*.

7

Marilyn Miller:
The Ziegfeld Treatment

It may sound strange, but I never want to grow old. I never want to see the day when I cannot sing and dance as I can now. I cannot bear to think of myself being middle-aged, with all my success behind me. The picture of a dear, gray-haired old lady by the fireside doesn't appeal to me.
— Marilyn Miller, 1922[1]

She was the darling of the Jazz Age; she possessed youth, beauty, a sparkling personality, and an enormous talent for dancing. Although her singing voice was merely adequate, her great charm pushed her songs over the footlights and into the hearts of her audiences. For more than a decade she was the ultimate "Ziegfeld Star," the toast of Broadway. Her three film appearances at the dawn of sound offer little evidence of her talents, and her only recordings, a collection of nursery rhymes to be found on 78 rpm records, not much more. Yet there must have been something special about this performer to generate such excitement, for as jaded as we might be about the tastes of earlier generations you must remember that Miller's was the Broadway of the Gershwins, Cole Porter, Rodgers and Hart, and Jerome Kern.

My good friend, Robert Gable, who passed away a few years ago, was the only person I ever met who actually saw Marilyn Miller perform on stage. "She was an angel!" he said simply in trying to explain her now elusive charms. A few years ago, while teaching the history of musical comedy to my I. B. (International Baccalaureate) theatre students, I showed a couple of clips from Marilyn Miller's first motion picture, *Sally*, which was filmed in 1929. Miller's handling of the Jerome Kern classic "Look for the Silver Lining," with her thin, reedy soprano voice, was an immediate turn-off, but then, when she offered her eccentric interpretation of the tune with Joe E. Brown, my kids sat up and took notice. A short while later, as she performed a lively version of "All I Want to Do, Do, Do, Is Dance," a student, Erin, with some dancing experience herself, exclaimed, "That lady can dance!" Miller's dancing abilities were perhaps better expressed by film historian, Richard Barrios, who wrote, "Miller was not technically flawless by any means; her arms sometimes flail in ungainly fashion, sometimes her posture is oddly stooped, and her tap work is too determined to be effortless. These liabilities she overcomes with two hallmarks of the irreplaceable performer: she seems to love what she's doing, and she makes it impossible and unnecessary to look anywhere in the frame except at her."[2] In the musical number "I'm Just a Wild, Wild, Rose," the only portion of the film to have survived in color, Barrios elaborates on Miller's appeal:

106

The camera follows Miller as she dashes madly about the set, spinning, throwing off high kicks with abandon — there's probably more energy in this scene than in any other film made that year. It's the same type of full-figure dance photography that Astaire would later demand, and as a coupling of performer and medium it's precisely what musical films were and are supposed to be about. Miller finishes with a grand flourish, flinging roses at her admirers; across all these decades, the admiration is still warranted.[3]

Marilyn Miller as Peter Pan, 1924, at the Knickerbocker Theater (photograph: Art Edeson).

Marilynn Reynolds was born on September 1, 1898, the name "Marilynn" derived from her grandparents' names, "Mary" and "Lynn" Thompson. Her mother, Ada Reynolds, married a second time shortly after her first husband deserted her and their four children. Her new spouse, Caro Miller, was a well-rounded vaudeville entertainer who eventually added Ada, Marilynn, and her two older sisters to his act, the Columbians. Much of Marilynn's training, self-discipline, and drive for perfection came from her stepfather, whom she detested. He was extremely short-tempered and strict in his rehearsals, yet despite his frequent use of corporal punishments for unsatisfactory performances, Marilynn's happiest memories of childhood were those moments on the stage. As her dancing improved, the child developed a unique talent for impersonations that included Nora Bayes, Lillian Russell, Eva Tanguay, and even Bert Williams! When she was five years old her name was legally changed to Marilynn Miller; she eventually dropped the second "n."

To avoid the strict child labor laws in the top cities of the United States, Caro Miller booked the family act abroad. While Marilyn was performing in London, impresario Lee Shubert of the Shubert Brothers spotted the youngster and signed her for *The Passing Show of 1914*, just one in a series of revues that poked fun at fads and personalities of the day, a showcase that well suited Marilyn's talents. As the Columbians were breaking up as an act (Marilyn's sisters were getting married), Caro signed his 15-year-old stepdaughter to a Shubert contract for $75 a week, neglecting to mention that she was underage.

During this period, Marilyn trained extensively in ballet, acrobatic dancing, and tap. When *The Passing Show of 1914* opened on Broadway at the Winter Garden, a star was born. "The real hit of the entire performance was little Miss Marilyn Miller," raved *The Telegram*, "who is youthful and pretty, who dances as if she enjoyed it, and who as an imitator approaches very closely to Miss Elsie Janis."[4] Three months after the opening, the new star turned 16, the legal age for a minor to perform at night.

The following year Marilyn appeared in another *Passing Show* to even more ecstatic reviews, with the *New York Review*'s Colgate Baker citing her as "one of the daintiest, prettiest, and cleverest girls on the American stage. She is a vision of delight at all times."[5] The critic for the *New York Dramatic Mirror* concurred, writing that "Miss Miller made the hit of the evening with her adorable smile and blithesome dancing. Her reception at her every appearance was deservedly uproarious. The gain she has made the past year in poise and assurance has made her personality even more awesome."[6] The next showcase, *The Show of Wonders*, was a much more sumptuous production with even greater personal reviews for Marilyn. Unfortunately, it was during a rehearsal for this show that she suffered a nose injury, a splintered bone, that would cause great pain for the rest of her life.

Marilyn came to the attention of Florenz Ziegfeld, through, of all people, his wife, Billie Burke. In retrospect, Burke must have seen the irony in that introduction as Ziegfeld was notorious as a womanizer. However, recognizing her husband's strengths and weaknesses, Burke often looked the other way during his many brief affairs. This tolerance was not in the least due to her assurance that she always held the trump card in the form of their daughter, Patricia. Astute as she was, Burke immediately recognized the charm and youthful vitality of Marilyn Miller as a possible asset for her husband's famous *Follies*. Unknown to

his wife, Flo Ziegfeld had been monitoring Marilyn's progress for some time. He was in need of a beautiful headliner to replace Olive Thomas, who left the stage for the movies. During the run of her show, *Fancy Free*, in 1918, Marilyn was approached by the Ziegfeld organization. Luckily, her original contract with the Shuberts was invalid since she was not yet 16 when she originally signed. Despite generally poor reviews for her singing and acting abilities in *Fancy Free*, Ziegfeld was bent on making her his star.

In *The Ziegfeld Follies of 1918*, Marilyn performed a "Yankee Doodle" dance and shared the bill with Eddie Cantor, Will Rogers, and W.C. Fields, but it was a young and handsome featured performer, Frank Carter, who received most of her

The 5 Columbians. Ada Reynolds and her husband, Caro Miller, with her three daughters. Marilyn Miller, the youngest, is at the bottom. Circa 1908.

attention. They fell in love and received excellent notices for their *Follies* contribution. In particular, Marilyn's impersonation of Billie Burke in "Mine Was a Marriage of Convenience" was greeted with howls of laughter.

Ziegfeld was not too happy with the prospect of a marriage between his two young stars; he had professional (and perhaps personal) plans for Marilyn that did not include Carter. In addition, her parents did not approve of the young man, refusing him admittance into their home, where Marilyn was still living. One of the few ways that the couple could find solitude during their time off from the theatre was at rallies promoting the sale of war bonds. At one of these rallies, Marilyn sold $1.25 million worth of Liberty Bonds!

During a break in rehearsals for the 1919 entry of *The Ziegfeld Follies*, Marilyn and Frank Carter tied the knot. Ziegfeld, furious, promptly fired Carter, but he was quickly signed up by the Shuberts for a new musical, *See Saw*. Both husband and wife received excellent reviews for their respective shows and set up housekeeping. After the initial Broadway engagements, their shows went on tour, eventually meeting in Chicago. During their reunion, Carter secretly purchased an expensive Packard automobile that Marilyn had admired. Following the tour he planned to drive it home to her with his friends. He never made it; he was killed instantly when the car flipped over after attempting a very sharp turn.

Marilyn was devastated. After the funeral she continued with her *Follies*

Fifteen-year-old Marilyn as seen in *The Passing Show of 1914*. Three months after the revue opened at the Wintergarden, Marilyn turned the legal age of sixteen to perform nightly (photograph: White Studio).

commitment but was miserable when not on the stage. She went to Europe to rest when her show closed and, at Ziegfeld's request, studied voice and acting. Her next project was going to be something special.

Sally opened in 1920 to the best reviews that Marilyn had ever received. This was

A quintessential image of Marilyn: on her toes. Circa 1920.

extremely important since the entire show, a book musical, revolved around her character. No expense was spared in the Cinderella story of a young waif who is raised by waiters to eventually become a "Ziegfeld girl." The music was composed by the producer's favorite composer, Jerome Kern. Everyone expected fine dancing from Marilyn, but they were pleasantly surprised by her singing voice, especially singing "Look for the Silver Lining":[7]

A heart full of joy and gladness
Will always banish sadness and strife.
So always look for the silver lining.
And try to find the sunny side of life.

According to her biographer, Warren C. Harris:

There was a hush for a moment as the last note died, followed by a storm of applause. Again and again, Marilyn had to repeat the chorus, and each time she sang it there was that awed silence before the ovation. The plea for practical optimism was obviously the kind of sermon audiences wanted to hear in that time of postwar depression. Performance after performance, the response was always the same.[8]

Ziegfeld awarded Marilyn with the best contract ever given to a musical comedy ingénue: 10 percent of the gross receipts against a guarantee of $2,500 weekly. The Ziegfeld-Miller teaming spelled magic at the box office but not off stage. Marilyn was seeing a movie star, Jack Pickford, Mary's actor brother. Ziegfeld

Marilyn Miller dressed to sell war bonds in 1918.

was worried, and with good reason. Olive Thomas had married Jack Pickford a few years before and then died mysteriously in Paris. According to the French police, she accidentally had taken bichloride of mercury tablets that she mistook for sleeping pills. However, it was rumored that Pickford and Thomas were taking illegal drugs and she died from an overdose. Whatever the circumstances, Ziegfeld held her husband responsible for her death and now was worried about losing Marilyn. Ironically, his interference only strengthened the relationship and Marilyn and Jack married at the famous Hollywood estate, Pickfair, in 1922.

During the first few months of the marriage, Ziegfeld, Jack, and Marilyn provided the press with a field day as they publicly

Marilyn Miller going over her music with her conductor at a rehearsal for *Sally* in 1920.

hurled insults and accusations until finally her husband suggested that Marilyn not renew her contract with the showman. According to Marjorie Farnsworth's book, *The Ziegfeld Follies*, another reason to split was that Marilyn wanted to play Peter Pan and Ziegfeld felt she couldn't do it. Warren Harris cites the personal conflict as the end of her professional relationship with Ziegfeld.

Charles Dillingham wasted no time in offering Marilyn a contract with an attractive salary and the guarantee of an extravagant musical spectacular to be built around her talents. However, since planning would take at least a year, he suggested starring her in a revival of *Peter Pan*. She readily accepted and negotiations were begun with Barrie in 1923. Basil Dean, a close friend of the playwright who also directed several productions of the play, was asked his opinion of Marilyn's potential. Dean had seen her in *Sally* and reported back that her great talents and pixie quality were perfectly suited for the part.

During the negotiations it was learned that a film version was also in production, but Dillingham decided to proceed with his plans, reasoning that most people would rather see a live and colorful performance of the play rather than a silent black-and-white film. Furthermore, the publicity generated by the film could only improve business for all. It was a decision he would regret.

Everything about this Broadway production of *Peter Pan* suggested a Ziegfeld extravaganza — minus Ziegfeld. Over $300,000 was spent in re-creating the lavish sets and costumes originally used in the Maude Adams version. Unwittingly, Dillingham was setting his star up for comparisons

Left: Marilyn and Frank Carter, her first husband, in 1919. *Right:* Marilyn and Jack Pickford, her second husband, circa 1922.

with Adams by going this traditional route. Even some of the photographs of Marilyn in costume have her in traditional poses made famous by Adams. Basil Dean took the traditional approach to directing the play. Charles Eaton, who played John, remembered that almost 50 percent of the actors were English, brought in an attempt to legitimize the production. As Charles was interviewed over 65 years later, his memory might have exaggerated the amount, but Donald Searle, who played Slightly, was a member of the English *Peter Pan* company. In fact, Searle also played the same role on and off again in English tours (1915–1920) and in London (1921–1923), and was acknowledged by Basil Dean in the program for his assistance.

The John Crook score was played by a full-sized orchestra under the direction of Milan Roder, and Marilyn's numbers, "The Pillow Dance" and "The Indian Dance," were arranged by Alexis Kosloff of the Metropolitan Opera House. Jerome Kern supplied several songs, including "The Sweetest Thing in Life" with lyrics by B.G. DeSylvia and "Won't You Have a Little Feather," the song Kern had written with Paul West for the Maude Adams touring company.

Charles Dillingham, a former partner of Charles Frohman, produced *Peter Pan*. Dillingham was Ziegfeld's rival (date unknown).

"Just think of me following Maude Adams in that wonderful play," Marilyn told the press in an interview that reads like it was written for Ruby Keeler in a Busby Berkley film. "I honestly get the shivers when I think of opening night. But it's something I've dreamed of doing since childhood — and, if work and study count for anything, I know I'm going to make good."[9]

Rehearsals did not run smoothly, though, as Marilyn's conception of the play conflicted greatly with Dean's, with Dillingham backing Marilyn. Eventually what emerged was a production that was not a musical and certainly not the play as envisioned by its creator. Yet when *Peter Pan* opened out of town in Buffalo it garnered excellent reviews.

According to the *Buffalo News*, "She won completely an audience that filled every seat of the Majestic.... Miss Miller brings us a new Peter Pan and wins triumph in a new friend."[10] Echoed the *Buffalo Express*, "A performance of sheer delight."[11]

Peter Pan opened on Broadway at the Knickerbocker Theater on November 6, 1924,

Peter (Marilyn Miller) and his Wolves (photograph: White Studio, 1924).

but the New York City critics were not as impressed as their upstate counterparts. The *New York Post* noted:

> In writing about *Peter Pan* it is necessary, perhaps, to put on several pairs of gloves as a precaution against hurting either present feelings or older memories.
>
> It was not that she made you remember Maude Adams — at least, not after the first few minutes. It became, soon after it began, simply a test of Miss Miller's powers as an actress; it became a struggle between her and the part, not a three-cornered affair with Miss Adams included.[12]

The *Post* critic concluded:

> Here is again merely the old matter of interest. Miss Miller doesn't interest you in herself, so she can't very well interest you in *Peter Pan*. It appears of slight importance whether or not she is on the stage.
>
> And *Peter Pan* without Peter was exactly what it turned out, with the help of the critics, to be — Peter panned.[13]

There was this note from Heywood Broun:

> There are few in the world who dance like Marilyn Miller, and Peter Pan should not be one of them. He dances because he is happy and gay and not because he has been to ballet school.[14]

The critics were also displeased with the added songs, finding Marilyn's performance of them "brittle and sharp" and adding that they belonged instead in a musical revue.

In *Life* magazine, Robert Benchley summarized what many felt:

> The fact that a script like that of *Peter Pan* could fall into the hands of people who didn't know last January that Marilyn Miller could never be Peter Pan, beautiful and graceful as she is, any more than Mary Eaton or Julia Sanderson or seven hundred other beautiful and graceful ladies could ever be a Peter Pan, shows exactly what is wrong with the commercial theatre to-day and what will probably be wrong with it tomorrow. The fact that people should be allowed to present this play who would interpolate a Broadway song-hit into it, shows exactly what is wrong with the world.[15]

The song Benchley was referring to was "The Sweetest Thing in Life." He continued:

Marilyn in another Pan costume (photograph: Art Edeson).

That song hit was particularly revolting. It was bad enough when *Peter* sang it to *Wendy* as they sat by the fireplace, a tawdry affair on the order of "Look for the Silver Lining," about Home being the best little thing after all. But all through this, and all through the rest of the disheartening performance, we sat waiting for the final curtain, when *Peter* stands among fireflies in the tree-tops waving good-by, because we didn't see how they could spoil that. This scene might, we hoped, recapture something of the original charm.

And when it finally came, and the curtain started descending, on that memorable picture, what happened? The orchestra began plugging the song-hit just as they do at the final curtain of a musical comedy, and to the strains of this Tin-Pan Alley whistler, the most fireproof asbestos that we have ever seen came slowly down on our shattered temple.

"Shattered temple" because, most unforgivable of everything, Mr. Basil Dean and the rest of them made us see that "Peter Pan" isn't really so splendid after all. Even had some one more suitable than Miss Miller played the role, we doubt whether we could have kept our illusions about it. It is just plain dull in great, long stretches. It is even worse in others. Aside from the moment when Little Carol Chase, as *Liza*, drawing herself up to her full three feet, said "Pooh!" with such and force and artistic fire as to throw herself completely off her balance, we got scarcely a thrill from the words Barrie had written.[16]

Wendy (Dorothy Hope) sewing on the shadow of Peter Pan (Marilyn Miller) (photograph: White Studio, 1924).

He concluded:

> Perhaps the fault was not entirely Miss Miller's, or Barrie's, or Mr. Basil Dean's. The trouble probably lay in our having once been fifteen and, being fifteen, having seen Maude Adams.[17]

None of the new songs were listed in the program; only John Crook's name appeared. However, Dillingham was determined to have a hit song in the play. Much ado was made when Wanamaker's department store decided to have Marilyn sing "The Sweetest Thing in Life" on a live radio broadcast that would be transmitted to London on December 10, 1924, but a sudden cold caused her to back out at the last minute.

If Marilyn's Peter was not embraced by the critics, she was not alone. Most agreed that "Wendy scarcely emerged per Dorothy Hope." Heywood Broun wrote:

> I do not mean to be severe about the actress who does Wendy for she is probably an excellent player, but this is not her role. With the possible exception of Mrs. Fiske I can not think of one less appropriate. Here the fault is not that of the actress, but of Basil Dean. It is silly and unfair to ask anybody who is not distinctly childlike in quality to play the part.[18]

Broun felt that

Top: The original sheet music cover for "The Sweetest Thing in Life" by Jerome Kern and B.G. DeSylva. In the 1940s, Buddy G. DeSylva would head Paramount Pictures while Kern moved on to bigger (and better) things such as *Roberta* and his masterpiece, *Show Boat. Bottom:* Cartoon from *Daily Mirror*, November 8, 1924.

the present Hook is not the unctuous ruffian created by Ernest Lawford. Edward Rigby is fine as Smee and Violet Kimble Cooper has no trouble with Mrs. Darling, but on the whole, *Peter Pan* has been badly cast for the revival.[19]

Dorothy Hope disappeared from the entertainment scene, but the same cannot be said of British actor Leslie Banks, who played Captain Hook. Banks made his English stage debut in *The Merchant of Venice* in 1911 and his first New York appearance was in *Eliza Comes to Stay* at the Garrick Theatre in 1914. For 40 years the actor crossed back and forth across the Atlantic to appear in *Goodbye, Mr. Chips, Life with Father*, and his biggest hit, *Springtime for Henry*. He made his film debut in 1932 in *The Most Dangerous Game* and immediately became one of the busiest actors on the screen, appearing in almost 75 movies, including *Fire Over England, The Man Who Knew Too Much, 21 Days, Jamaica Inn*, and *Henry V*. He also served as the president of British Equity.

The last time Broadway witnessed a Leslie Banks performance was in the musical *Lost in the Stars*, which opened in 1949. He died on April 21, 1952, at age 61.

One other actor in *Peter Pan* who bears mentioning is Charles Eaton, who was the younger brother of another Ziegfeld star, Mary Eaton, the most famous member of the Eaton stage family. Although barely a teenager by the time he appeared with Marilyn Miller, Charles was already a veteran of the stage and screen. At the age of three he was cast by the Shuberts in *Blackbirds*, and at ten he was in *The Ziegfeld Follies of 1921*. That year he made his first film, *Peter Ibbetson*, with Wallace Reid and Elsie Ferguson. Then he returned to Broadway in a revue playing Romeo opposite one Miriam Battista in the balcony scene; he was only 12 but the critics were amazed at the depth of his understanding of Shakespeare's tragic figure.

Four years after *Peter Pan* Charles scored his biggest hit as Andy Hardy in the Broadway play *Skidding*, which later became a popular film series with Mickey Rooney. During the late 1920s he was one of the busiest juveniles on Broadway. When interviewed by this writer in 1991, Charles reminisced about the joy of working with Marilyn, stating that she was extremely talented, very professional, and very popular, with stage-door Johnnies waiting each evening for Marilyn's exit from the

A 1932 portrait of Leslie Banks, who played Captain Hook opposite Marilyn Miller (Photofest).

Marilyn as Peter bids goodbye to Wendy (Dorothy Hope) and the Lost Boys. Charles Eaton, a famous child actor of the period, is second from the left (photograph: White Studio, 1924).

theatre. "But then, we all had our stage-door Johnnies," he chuckled.[20] Charles also relished the Crook score, even singing the "Pirate Song" in full during our conversation. Although plagued with illness in his later years, Charles joined his sister Doris Eaton for the annual New York City Easter Bonnet AIDS Benefit, where, at the age of 88, he performed "Ballin' the Jack." Doris, who was 96 at the time, later wrote:

> Now there is only Charlie and me of the seven Eatons. We are having happy times together again as we did when we were children traveling on the road in *Mother Carey's Chickens* so many years ago. Charlie has never lost that sense of childhood wonder and discovery, nurtured by his early life in the fantasyland of the Broadway theater. After all, he played in *Peter Pan*! I surmise that he still thinks that all the world is a stage and that we — people he deals with every day — are the somewhat peculiar characters playing around on it. He is kind, thoughtful, not wanting to be a burden to anyone, and he contributes his keen sense of humor to his observations about the crazy antics of the world we seem to be living in. He is still able to engulf us in laughter. How very grateful I am that it has worked out for Charlie and me to be together in these precious years of our lives."[21]

Charles died on August 15, 2004, while Doris continued dancing (including her dancing appearance in the 2004 PBS documentary, *Broadway*) until her death on May 11, 2010.

Only one performer was able to captivate the critics: Carol Chase, who played Liza. Broun said she "played superbly,"[22] and Alan Dale, distinguished critic of the *New York*

Liza (Carol Chase), Peter (Marilyn) and Wendy (Dorothy Hope) on the steps of the "House in the Tree Tops" (photograph: White Studio, 1924).

American, felt she "made a hit as Liza with her tiny voice, and her cunning presence."[23] But a star vehicle cannot depend upon the excellent reviews gathered by as minor a character as Liza.

    Alan Dale actually enjoyed the new production, in fact even more so than the original. He wrote:

> Our good friend, the new Generation, had a new *Peter Pan* all to itself last night at the Knicker-bocker — a *Peter Pan* speeded up to meet the jazzizious moods of to-day, a *Peter Pan* gorgeously set in all the wizardries of opulence, and good taste. It was indeed a new *Peter Pan*. Those who had memories of Maude Adams missed from the latest Barrie heroine, the wistfulness, the sweet aloofness, and dainty unselfconsciousness and the irresistible charm that Miss Adams gave to the

role. Last night they saw a delightful young woman known as Marilyn Miller, who had her own ideas and her own fig-yure [*sic*].

Miss Miller was not wistful; nor was she diaphanous, spirituelle [*sic*] or eerie. She was a nice, jolly, material girl, with no nonsense about her—an ice-cream-dosed Peter Pan—well nourished.[24]

Dale also felt that

Miss Miller, moreover, had it one over Miss Adams with her dancing. She gyrated and she cavorted deliciously. She looked like an elongated Ariel, as she flitted about. Then she sang with a voice—a real voice, a voice that had quality, and creaminess, and tone. Oh, such a different Peter Pan. Perhaps she even wasn't *Peter Pan* at all, but Marilyn Miller, which is pleasant enough.[25]

He continued:

But towards the close of the third act, you began to like her for herself, and Barrie and Maudie go hang! She was so very healthy, so beautifully plump, so well molded, so gracefully agile, and so lissomely alert.[26]

Dale, usually a perceptive critic, must have been thinking with another part of his anatomy; his enthusiasm for Marilyn's "charms" only made the other critics seem more objective. Despite the generally poor reviews and a short run, the play broke all kinds of attendance records.

It is rather a shame that Marilyn or any popular singer of the day did not record the two Kern songs.[27] Ironically, a song, "Peter Pan (I Love You)," was allegedly written in her honor and was recorded by many musical groups of the 1920s. However, in other countries the same song was published in honor of Betty Bronson, star of the film version in most movie houses by that time.

To counter the negative reviews, Dillingham devised several gimmicks to attract audiences, including contests, puzzles in the newspapers, and charity benefits. Marilyn frequently gave silly interviews with some rather absurd intentions:

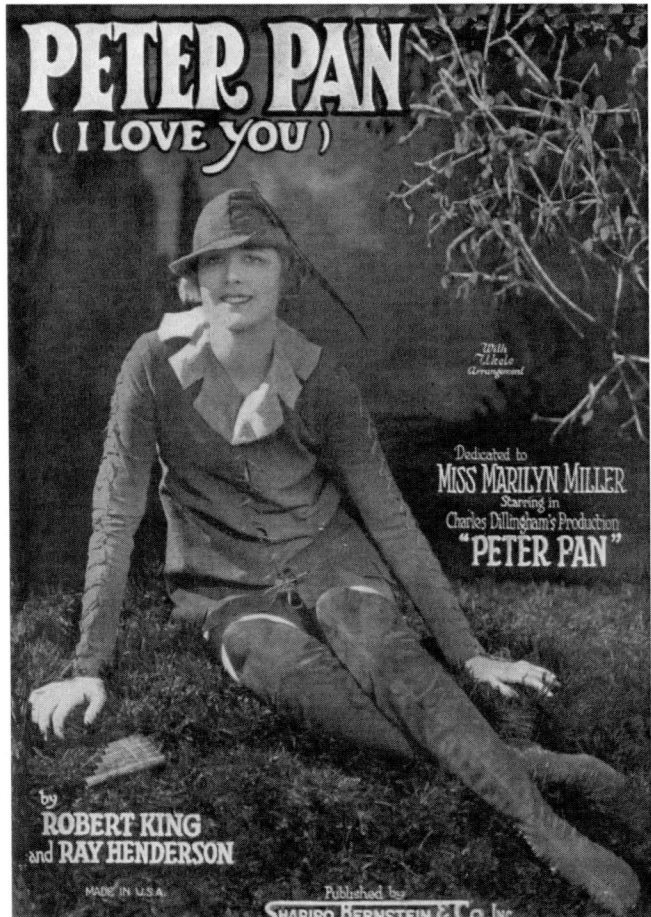

"Peter Pan (I Love You)," a 1924 song dedicated to Marilyn Miller by its writers, Robert King and Ray Henderson. They also dedicated the song to Betty Bronson, who was in the silent film.

I will show Peter grown up and making real love to Wendy. And of course they will marry in the last act. The second act shows Peter as a young man living in a big city — London or New York, as you please, though the name of the city is not given. The act shows how difficult he finds it to adapt himself to modern life, but he is made to realize that the only way he can win Wendy is to settle down like any other human being.[28]

The sculpture of Marilyn Miller as "Sunny" still adorns the I. Miller Building on Broadway in New York City (photograph: Author, 1992).

Peter Pan ran for 96 performances before going on the road. Dillingham hoped to at least break even with his investment, but the film version cut deeply into the play's receipts and the tour was cut short.

Had Marilyn's career ended with *Peter Pan* she would probably not be remembered today. However, the next vehicle, *Sunny*, was specifically tailored for her talents — a simple story, a great score by Kern (including "Who?"), fantastic sets, a circus background, and a short title reminiscent of *Sally*. Her marriage to Jack Pickford was basically over, although they were not divorced until 1927; Pickford was too laid back for a hard-working performer like Marilyn. He died in 1932 of multiple neuritis, but before he departed, he was to marry one more Ziegfeld girl, Mary Mulhern, who also divorced him. Meanwhile, Marilyn was back on top with a hit and her career continued to flourish. In 1928 she appeared in *Rosalie* and then she went to Hollywood, where she filmed *Sally* for $100,000, the highest salary ever given a Broadway star up to that time. Movie mogul Jack Warner was extremely enthused with Marilyn's film potential, although part of that enthusiasm might have been because they were romantically involved at the time. He signed her to a three-picture deal. *Sally* was not quite the money-maker that Warner had hoped, so Marilyn was only paid $50,000 for her next picture, *Sunny*. She made one more picture after that, *Her Majesty Love*.

Marilyn, extremely frugal with her money, was one of the few not hurt by the Depression, which turned out to be a double blessing as she was unable to work during the last few years of her life. The chronic sinus condition had worsened the point that her last show, *As Thousands Cheer*, despite being a hit, had very little Marilyn in it. She met her last husband, Chet O'Brien, who was 11 years younger than she, in this show; the press was not kind about their age difference.

In 1935 an operation to alleviate some of the pain from her ailment was botched up when the doctor cut too deeply into her skull, thus subjecting Marilyn to many infections. She grew progressively weaker and tired easily, causing her to reject the lead role of the ballerina in *On Your Toes*. Disagreement over billing also prevented her from appearing in the film spectacular *The Great Ziegfeld*, where she would have re-created one of her famous *Sally* numbers. Neither her husband nor her sisters had any idea of the seriousness of her illness, but according to Marjorie Farnsworth Marilyn knew the end was near. On a cold day in early March of 1936 Marilyn was shopping with a friend when she spotted a blue silk dress. Marilyn insisted they stop to buy it as she was going into the hospital the next day. When her friend wondered aloud if Marilyn wanted to wear it when she left the hospital, she replied that she wanted to be buried in it, as she was certain she would not leave the hospital alive.

Her sisters accompanied her to Doctors Hospital in New York on March 12. Marilyn was alert and in good spirits so they felt it safe to go on a small trip to visit their parents. Her doctor told the press that she only needed rest, but Marilyn slipped into a coma on March 20 and died on April 7. There was no autopsy, but the probable cause of

Marilyn in the title role of Charles Dillingham's musical extravaganza, *Sunny*, at the New Amsterdam Theatre in 1925. A few years ago the *New York Times* ran a story that stated the sculpture of Miller on Broadway depicted her in her Peter Pan costume and not Sunny's. However, this photograph clearly shows it is indeed *Sunny*.

death was a result of the sinusitis operation the year before.

Marilyn was buried in Woodlawn Cemetery, next to Frank Carter. While the image of Marilyn will remain as she wished — young and beautiful — her mausoleum is aged, with its roof caving in. Nine years before her death, a poll was taken for the most popular performers in the United States. The four winners were sculpted by A. Stirling Calder with the statues placed on the then-new I. Miller Building on Broadway and Forty-sixth Street. According to the inscription below the statue, Marilyn was depicted as her character in *Sunny*, her most famous play after *Sally*. In 1999, the *New York Times* reported that the costume was "Peter Pan, Not Sunny,"[29] with the writer stating that Calder found Marilyn's *Peter Pan* costume more appealing than her *Sunny* costume, therefore immortalizing Marilyn Miller as Peter Pan. This was an enticing thought for this author, to

The ever youthful Marilyn Miller as "The Boy Who Wouldn't Grow Up" (photograph: Art Edeson, 1924).

end this chapter illustrating Peter Pan as perhaps Marilyn's favorite role, but a photograph of Marilyn dressed as a harlequin clown from *Sunny* proves that is not the case. Today, amidst the noise of taxis, construction machines, and the steam shooting out from nearby manhole covers, remain the four sculptures: stage actress Ethel Barrymore, opera singer Rosa Ponselle, film star Mary Pickford, and the musical comedy star who never wanted to grow old, Marilyn Miller, as *Sunny* as ever.

8

Betty Bronson:
The Silent Treatment

I loved Peter. I am a lot of Peter myself. But I am at least a little different.
It isn't fair. They look for Peter, not for me. I am grateful to Peter. But he's
like a poor relation — he hangs around so!
— Betty Bronson, 1925[1]

When the Lasky Company took over controlling interest of the Frohman empire, one of their priorities was to transform *Peter Pan* to celluloid form. While several other companies had tried to convince Barrie to sell, he finally gave in to the Famous Players in 1921. The public's anticipation over the project was heightened when it was announced that Barrie himself would be staying in Hollywood during the filming. He also wrote a film scenario that Denis Mackail called

twenty thousand words of the most carefully rewritten scenario, with all the subtitles, and a mass of fresh visual detail which to anyone but a film producer and his attendant experts must surely have seemed like a gift from heaven. It's authentic, it comes from the one and only source of the saga, who took enormous trouble over it, and never forgot for one moment the special medium for which it was meant.[2]

The scenario begins:

The first picture we see is of Peter riding gaily on a goat through a wood, playing on his pipes (a reproduction of the painting in my possession). He suddenly flies on to a tree in the inconsequential way of birds. From this he flies over a romantic river, circling it with the careless loveliness of a sea-gull. He as suddenly re-lights on his goat and rides away playing his pipes, his legs sticking out cockily.... This incident should show at once that film can do things for Peter Pan which the ordinary stage cannot do. It should strike a note of wonder in the first picture, and whet the appetite for marvels.[3]

From the first frame of Barrie's treatment, Peter was to be portrayed as a long-established myth, as in the book, *Peter and Wendy*.

Barrie follows this with the Darling nursery scene, but he uses portions of his book to open up the scene for the film. Mr. and Mrs. Darling walk down a snow-filled street to a business supper. Later, they are convinced by Nana, who has broken loose from her rope, to hurry home as the children are in danger.

The parents and Nana burst into the nursery just in time to see them disappear. From the window they watch the children flying over the house-tops.[4]

Here Barrie outdoes himself with an exhilarating flight scene:

> The flight to the Never, Never Land has now begun. We see the truants flying over the Thames and the House of Parliament. Then an ordinary sitting of the House of Commons, faithfully reproduced. A policeman rushes in the august Chamber and interrupts proceedings with startling news of what is happening in the air. All rush out to see, the Speaker, who is easily identified by his wig, being the first. They get to the Terrace of the House and excitedly watch the flying group disappear.
>
> Then the children flying over the Atlantic. The moon comes out. Wendy tires, Peter supports her.
>
> Then they near New York. The Statue of Liberty becomes prominent. They are so tired that they all alight on it. It is slippery, and they can't find a resting place. At first we should think it is a real statue. Then we should get the effect of the statue mothering them by coming to life, to the extent of making them comfortable in her arms for the night.
>
> This should be one of the most striking pictures.
>
> Next we see them resume their journey. They cross America, with Niagara seen.
>
> Then they are over the Pacific, where the Never, Never Land is.
>
> We see the island all glorious and peaceful in a warm sun. We see the whole of it as in a map, not a modern map but the old-fashioned pictorial kind with quaintly exaggerated details.[5]

We can clearly see the love that Barrie poured into this adaptation. It is rich in visual details that could never be seen on stage and even more Barrie charm and wit had been added for this proposed film adaptation.

While Barrie's screen treatment was taking shape, Famous Players launched a well-publicized search for the actress to play Peter, announcing that the author would have the final choice. Many

Betty Bronson as Peter Pan finding his shadow. Although only 17 years old when she won the prize role from under the noses of established actresses such as Mary Pickford and Lillian Gish, Betty Bronson was chosen by James Barrie to play the role in the first film adaptation in 1924.

photographs and screen tests were sent to London for his consideration. Filming, however, was not to begin until 1924.

Despite the fact that she had appeared as only an extra in a few films, 17-year-old Betty Bronson knew from the start that she was the only person to play Peter Pan on the screen. Born Elizabeth Ada Bronson in Trenton, New Jersey, on November 17, 1907, she left East Orange High School and convinced her parents to let her move to California to aid her career in films. Her father decided that the whole family would move there too.

Before she moved to California, she appeared in a few films made in New York. In a 1930s manuscript for an aborted autobiography, Betty elaborated on her first attempt to get into the movies:

> I went over to the Paramount studio in Long Island for an interview with the casting director. When I appeared at the studio I pinned my hair up and tried to

Mary Pickford was just one of many Hollywood stars who wanted the role of Peter in the film version. Known for such youthful characters as *Rebecca of Sunnybrook Farm*, Mary had several photographs taken of herself in Peter Pan garb in hopes of landing the role (date unknown).

look as old as possible. And it was quite discouraging to me when the casting director said he had a part that would suit me perfectly, that of a twelve-year-old in a picture, *Java Head*. Although this was not exactly what I had visualized myself playing, I was delighted that I was actually to have a part in a picture. It meant that my career as an actress was really to have a beginning.[6]

After the move to California, Betty heard that *Peter Pan* was to be made into a movie and relentlessly campaigned for the part to any Lasky official who would listen. Director Herbert Brenon finally permitted the youngster to be tested.

I felt very sad and tearful as I returned to the wardrobe to change from my costume and felt that I had made a failure of it.[7]

Brenon went to London to show the best screen tests to Barrie and he was still there when Betty was offered a contract.

I felt when that took place that I had probably been chosen for Peter Pan or at least that I was to play Wendy. The contract was for a hundred and fifty dollars a week for a year and then two hundred and fifty for the second year or so, for five years.[8]

Jesse L. Lasky, the head of Paramount, was cabled by the playwright:

BETTY BRONSON CHOSEN TO PLAY THE ROLE OF PETER PAN — REGARDS — BARRIE.[9]

When the picture was completed, the studio realized that it had a hit on its hands and Betty was rewarded with a $5,000 bonus.

"We had decided on a pert kid named Mary Brian, when along came another unknown,

Above: Peter was a popular fellow in 1924. This rare magazine photograph shows Mary Hay in costume for the film *New Toys*, in which she co-starred with her husband, Richard Barthelmess, who many felt would have made the perfect Peter. *Right:* Actress Viola Dana as Peter, 1924. Dana designed a Maude Adams/ Peter Pan lamp that she sold through the mail. While photographs exist with the prototype, this author has yet to see an actual lamp.

even better suited to the part," Lasky confessed later. "Betty Bronson was given the lead and Mary Brian shifted to the role of Wendy."[10]

"No, no, I was never considered for Peter!" Mary Brian exclaimed when I told her Lasky's story in 1991. "Betty had already been chosen for Peter. They wanted me to be the little house mother. I was much more that type than Peter. Everyone else had been set for their parts and they made a screen test and signed me immediately and we went to work almost immediately."[11]

Top: Producer Jesse Lasky, Betty Bronson and *Peter Pan* director Herbert Brenon, 1924. *Bottom:* Peter (Betty Bronson) attempting to stick on his shadow with soap, 1924.

Esther Ralston, who played Mrs. Darling and had met her costar the day before their first rehearsal, confirmed this story:

I was judge for a beauty contest for Miss Los Angeles or something.... I kept looking at this little dark-haired girl with long curls. She was about fourteen years old and I kept saying to the other judges, "I like that little girl down at the end. She's got personality. She's beautiful." They said, "She's too young." I said, "She may not be Miss Los Angeles but she certainly can be Miss Personality." And that's the title we gave her.
    The next day I was called on the set to meet the cast of Peter Pan and who did I meet, Louise Dantzler, only she had a new name now. She was Mary Brian.[12]

Mary elaborated:

We had come out from Texas; my mother's sister was living out there. Through people that she met, they said that they were looking for little people for the fairies. You would never see their faces but they would just be flying about. So they asked me if I'd come over. That was Al Kaufman

Wendy (Mary Brian) sews on the shadow for Peter (Betty Bronson). 1924.

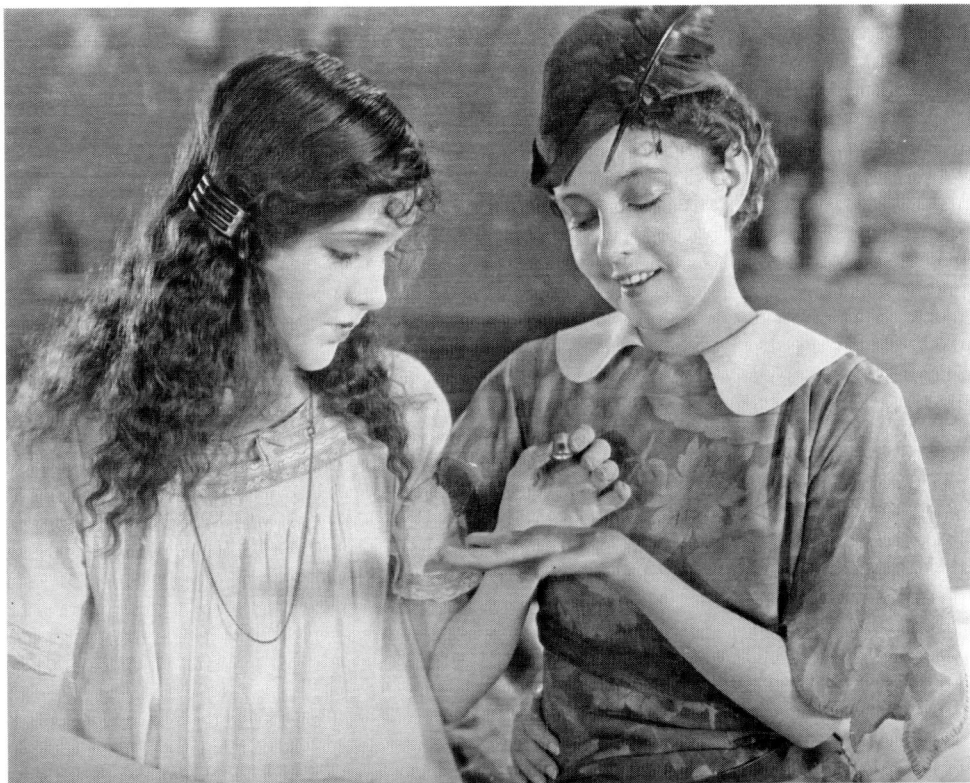

Wendy (Mary Brian) gives Peter (Betty Bronson) a "kiss" in the form of a thimble. 1924.

who was Mr. Lasky's brother-in-law and an executive at the studio, but that's what I went in for. When Herbert Brenon saw me and talked to me, he was recovering from an eye operation. I walked into this dark room because he could only have a light on the person he was interviewing. I didn't know that I was up for Wendy. After we talked, he said, "Is that you own hair?" I said, "Yes and you can pull it if you want to." They called me back and I made another test with Betty and then it was decided right after.

Of course, this was the first thing that I had ever done. I had nothing to compare. They had decided to go with unknowns. Betty Bronson had done a few things but as long as she was playing Peter, they thought that if Wendy and the little lost boys were all unknowns to the audience it would seem more like a fairy tale. That was the reason I got the break. Herbert Brenon, who picked me, was one of the better directors at that time. It was wonderful for me because I was his choice to play Wendy.[13]

The casting of Esther Ralston as Mrs. Darling surprised no one more than Esther herself. She was only 24, much too young to be the mother of Wendy. Sixty-seven years later she still remembered the day that she was cast.

I was working with Tom Mix wearing a Stetson hat with a gun on each hip when my agent called me about a part at Paramount as a mother. I said, "Who me, a mother?" He said, "No, no, the director, Herbert Brenon, feels every child thinks of his mother as a young girl. And they want a young girl to play the part." So I went over to Paramount on my noon hour and met Walter Wyman and Jesse Lasky.

I heard Jesse Lasky say, "Walter, you don't think of this cowgirl as Mrs. Darling?" He said, "Wait a minute," and called the wardrobe department. "I have a Miss Ralston down here and

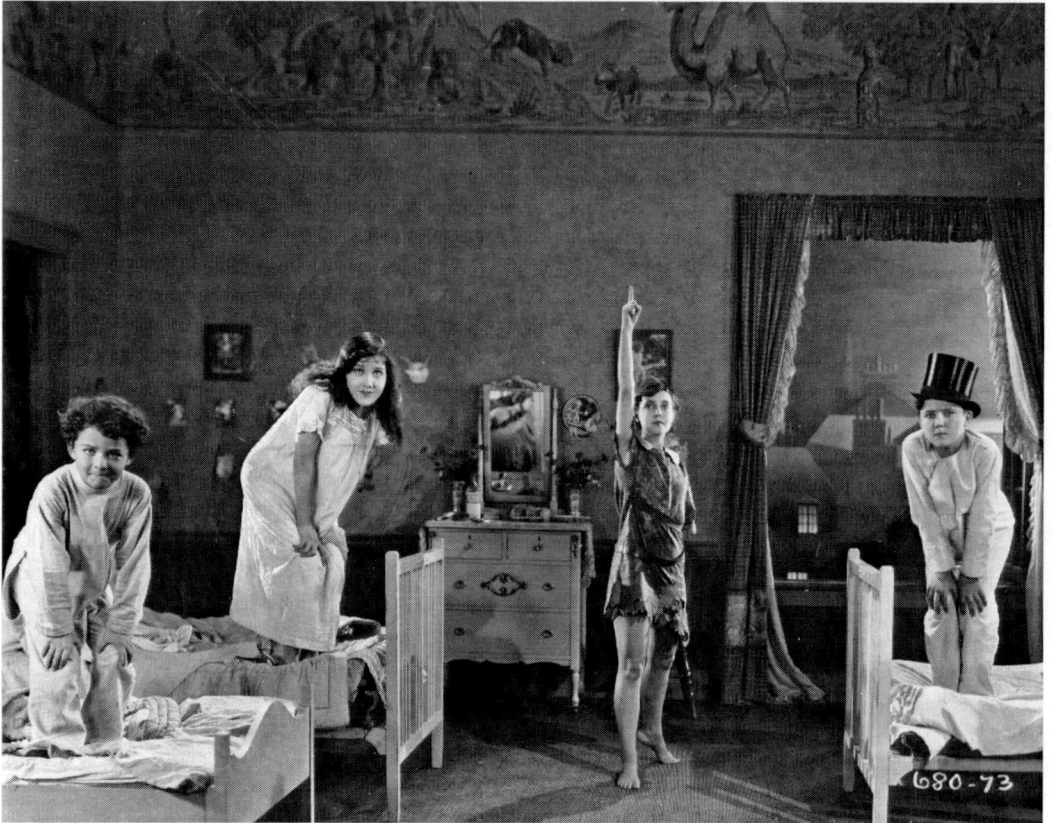

"Now try, try from the bed." Philippe de Lacy (Michael), Mary Brian (Wendy), Betty Bronson (Peter Pan), and Jack Murphy (John). 1924.

we want to test her for the part of Mrs. Darling. Do you think you can make a lady of her in fifteen minutes?" So, of course they made a lady out of me in fifteen minutes and I got the part.[14]

Ernest Torrence, a film villain of the period, took the role of Captain Hook. He had costarred in several prestigious films, including *The Hunchback of Notre Dame* and *Ruggles of Red Gap*, before this important assignment and he would go right into talkies with *The Cuban Love Song* and *Sherlock Holmes*.

The screen's foremost "Oriental" actress, Anna May Wong, played Tiger Lily. The Chinese American actress had a long career in films that began in a 1922 Technicolor film, *The Toll of the Sea*, and flourished in such films as Douglas Fairbanks's *The Thief of Bagdad* and Josef von Sternberg's *Shanghai Express*. Unfortunately, many of her films were "B" pictures that found the actress typecast in stereotypical roles for Asians in that period. Despite this, she was the first international Chinese movie star. Anna May worked on radio and television but sadly passed away in 1961, only 56 years old.

Animal actor George Ali was Nana and the crocodile. By the use of strings running from the head of the dog costume through the whole body, Ali was able to move the eyes,

Opposite, top: Ernest Torrence as Captain Hook outside the Wendy House. 1924. *Bottom:* Anna May Wong as Tiger Lily, 1924 (Photofest).

Philippe de Lacy as Michael riding on Nana. 1924.

Left: George Ali played Nana. 1924. *Right:* The audience was allowed to see Tinker Bell, as played by Virginia Brown Faire, for a few moments. One wonders how many other actresses were considered for the role as Virginia certainly had her "name" going for her (photograph: E.R. Richee, 1924).

mouth, ears, and tail. This was particularly effective as Nana demonstrates sadness at the loss of the children. Just as we are able to sense a dog's emotions in real life, Nana's half-closed eyes and drooping ears convey mourning.

For the first time, Tinker Bell would be played by a human, Virginia Brown Faire (yep, that was her name!). Her few scenes were shot with giant sets that brought the appropriate pixie touch to the film.

With an excellent cast and a handsome budget, *Peter Pan* began filming in September 1924 and was completed and edited in time for the Christmas holiday season, opening at the Rivoli Theatre in New York where it was accompanied by a prologue, *The Storm*, and an animated short, *Out of the Inkwell*. The reviews were some of the best that Peter ever received. The *New York Times* led the praise:

> That wonderful, ecstatic laughter, tinkling and beautiful, just the laughter that Barrie loves to hear, greeted Herbert Brenon's picturized version of *Peter Pan* yesterday afternoon in the Rivoli. Again and again the silence of the audience was snapped by the ringing laugh of a single boy which was quickly followed by outbursts from dozens of others, some of whom shook in their seats in sheer joy at what they saw upon the screen.... Obviously inspired by his discussions with Sir James Barrie, Mr. Brenon has fashioned a brilliant and entrancing production of this fantasy.... It is not a movie, but a pictorial masterpiece which we venture to say will meet the approval of the author.[15]

"I cannot strike. There's something stays my hand." Peter (Betty Bronson) surrounded by the Lost Boys with Wendy (Mary Brian) on the ground after being shot by an arrow. 1924.

The *New York Times* critic found Betty Bronson to be

> a graceful and alert Peter Pan. She is youth and joy, and one appreciates that she revels in the role. Her large eyes are wide with wonder when she first greets Wendy and she is lithe, erect and straight of limb when she fearlessly fights the horrible Captain Hook on his pirate craft.[16]

He also observed:

> Captain Hook is impersonated by Ernest Torrence, who is as effective as he can be as a gruff pirate whose voice is not heard.... Esther Ralston is comely as Mrs. Darling, whose mouth is "full of thimbles." Mary Brian makes a charming Wendy, and Phillippe de Lacey and Jack Murphy are effective in their respective roles of Michael and John.[17]

Peter Pan was part of the *New York Times'* Best Ten Films list of 1924 and Betty Bronson was cited by almost every critic as the chief asset of the film. Wrote James R. Quirk:

> The more we think of Betty Bronson, the more we marvel at her perfect performance. Not only the expression in her face but the way she stood and walked, and the grace that she showed every instant caused us to feel that she was truly an ethereal child who never could grow up. And anybody who can do that is, in reality, Peter Pan.[18]

What did Barrie really think? Denis Mackail wrote that it was "a great pity, and a considerable disappointment to the author; for the version which finally reached London at the

Michael (Philippe de Lacy) is forced to walk the plank by Captain Hook (Ernest Torrence). 1924.

end of 1925 was always, for him, the wrong kind of success. He reverted to detachment, and one recalls that he wouldn't even go round to the Tivoli — a mere step from his own front door — to see the talking picture of *The Little Minister* ten years after that."[19]

Seen today, the 1924 *Peter Pan* stands as a testimony to the silent-film era, yet it was not the film its author had envisioned. For some incomprehensible reason the producers discarded Barrie's scenario! To give them credit, they did take a few of his ideas and these are shining moments in an otherwise conventional screen translation of the play. As for rest, it is merely a retelling of the stage play with an unusually rigid camera. Except for the location footage of the pirate ship and the mermaids on the beach, the movie takes on the look of a filmed stage play. Brenon decided not to shoot the famous "To die would be an awfully big adventure" lagoon scene, therefore relegating the mermaids to little more than scenery. However, they do find the crocodile to help save the children from Captain Hook.

Screen Scrapbook to advertise the screening of *Peter Pan* locally. 1925.

Peter's first entrance, on film, into the nursery becomes uneventful as he steps into the window rather than making a bigger impact by flying. The nursery scene seems much too long and claustrophobic, but the actors had to suffer more as they waited considerable amounts of time between takes. Esther Ralston remembered a humorous incident on one of these occasions.

> We were standing; I had my daughter, Wendy, on one arm, my son, John, on another arm, and Michael, who came to about my waistline. We were standing close together with our arms around each other and we were waiting for the camera man to focus and get the correct lighting. Well it was a little long, at least five or ten minutes. All of a sudden Mr. Brenon said, "Lights, camera, action!"
>
> I let out a scream! And he said, "Cut, cut! For heaven's sake, Esther, what's the matter? What happened?"

Esther Ralston as Mrs. Darling (center) reunited with her children (from left) Wendy (Mary Brian), Michael (Philippe de Lacy) and John (Jack Murphy). 1924.

I said, "Michael, he bit me in the stomach!" And the director said to young Michael, "No matter how long you have to wait, or how bored you get, you are not to bite Miss Ralston again!"[20]

It is the charm and youth of the actors playing the children that save the nursery scene from becoming completely maudlin. By sticking to the stage directions, Brenon prolonged the scene with actions that were not necessary for the film. For example, on stage Nana's barking causes the children to hide behind the curtains, which was necessary for the attachment of their flying wires. However, this same routine in the film is just not needed. Rather than editing in the flying, Brenon seems to have shot a continuous scene, therefore using this same curtain device to no avail.

Mary Brian defended Brenon's choices:

It was done according to tradition. I think that so many people are familiar with the play that they would miss certain things if it had been done quite differently. It's like people with opera. They don't want anything left out.... It wasn't usual at that time, but Herbert Brenon ... really wanted us to speak the lines from the script and from the book. And that we tried to do.[21]

As for the assumption that the movie was filmed in sequence, Mary assured me that this was not the case as she also explained the mechanics behind their flight.

At that time the wiring wasn't perfected as it is now. They had planks across the cross beams up above the set. Men with piano wires would run across these tracks and we would fly from one place to another. But they were so complicated that they would have to change the tracks up there for each of us. So we were put to bed there on the set in the nursery until they changed the flying direction. I would almost finish with that and I'd get a certain amount of sleep there, my mother was with me. Then we would just go home and clean up to be ready to go to San Pedro.[22]

She went on:

The Pirate ship was down in San Pedro, and we had to go down very early in the morning so that we would be shooting by the time the sun came up. So we had hours that people would never think about doing anymore. Because this was my first I thought, "Well this is the way they make pictures!"[23]

Mary continued to make pictures until the early forties. She also did some work on Broadway, including *Three After Three* with Mitzi Green, Simone Simon, and Jack Whiting. During World War II she was busy entertaining the troops in Europe and the South Pacific. Later she married George Tomasini, noted film editor for the Hitchcock classics *Rear Window* and *Psycho.* When *Peter Pan* was being adapted for Mary Martin some 30 years later, Mary was approached by the producers.

They wanted me to open the second act, "Wendy Grow Up." The only thing was I was doing television at that time and I couldn't do it. I'm sorry now that I couldn't have made arrangements; that would have been great fun.[24]

Captain Hook (Ernest Torrence) orders Smee (Ed Tipling) to bind Wendy (Mary Brian) to the mast.

Peter Pan retained special memories for Mary Brian, who was in the midst of directing workers to clear trees from her yard when we conducted our interview almost 20 years ago.

I hadn't seen it for years. I knew that it was *Peter Pan* but I didn't know it was going to be a classic all through the ages. I had never seen the stage play. Everything was like a fairy tale to me when you have never been before a camera before. About five or six years ago, I guess it was, Eastman showed it in one of

Top: Peter (Betty Bronson) saying farewell to Wendy (Mary Brian), 1924. *Bottom:* Esther Ralston as the fairy godmother and Betty Bronson as Cinderella in *A Kiss for Cinderella*, 1925.

the Century City Theatres with a full orchestra. They asked me to come. It was really quite a thrill to see this beautiful hand tinted film. I was quite impressed.[25]

Mary Brian, born on February 17, 1906, passed away on December 30, 2002, during the traditional season for Peter's annual visits.

Esther Ralston continued to work for many years in film, radio, and television. She also appeared in another movie with Betty Bronson, Barrie's *A Kiss for Cinderella*. In 1985 the 83-year-old actress published a very candid autobiography. She died on January 14, 1994, at the age of 92, maintaining a close friendship with Mary Brian from the day they met until she died.

As for *Peter Pan*, Betty Bronson enjoyed an immediate but all too brief stardom in some of the most important films of that era. Both she and the film *A Kiss for Cinderella* were lauded by the critics. The *New York Times* reported:

> Hers is a truly wistful characterization, in which there comes a smile in daring to hope and trust, a tear creeping to the eye in pity for something, a dread of the hour of midnight, the gratification expressed at the sight of the Prince, whose face is not that of a stranger, after all. She is captivating in every scene, pathetic to the point of making one look at her through a mist of tears.[26]

Her scenes in *Ben-Hur* were also praised despite the part being not much more than a cameo appearance. Again quoting the *New York Times*:

> A most astounding performance happens in the initial chapter of this picture. It is of a girl who was practically unknown on the screen eighteen months ago. She here delivers a portrayal of the Madonna that is gloriously beautiful. At first you may wonder who this young actress is, for her appearance is completely changed in the brief performance she gives here. She is none other than Betty Bronson, the girl who was selected to play the title role of *Peter Pan* a little more than a year ago, and who won further laurels by her impersonation of the slavery in Barrie's *A Kiss for Cinderella*. In both these films she was a pert, lively, skittish little creature, fantastic, impudent, or impish.[27]

Other films, such as *Are Parents People?*, were good but soon the quality of the scripts offered diminished. In *Classics of the Silent Screen*, Joe Franklin gave a perceptive analysis of the actress's career:

> The real tragedy of Betty Bronson's career is that she ar-

Betty Bronson as the Virgin Mary in *Ben-Hur* in 1924.

rived on the screen just a few years too late. *Peter Pan* should have been the zenith of one phase of her career, not the beginning of it. Had she arrived on the scene just ten years earlier, in that age of innocence when honest sentiment, whimsy, fantasy, and Cinderella themes were not deemed old-fashioned and out of touch with the times, what a star she could have become.[28]

Betty appeared in a few talkies, notably *The Singing Fool* and *Sonny Boy* with Al Jolson, and endured until 1937 with her last feature, *The Yodelin' Kid from Pine Ridge*, which starred Gene Autry. She then retired to become a full-time wife and mother. During the 1960s, Betty returned to the screen to make cameo appearances in films like *The Naked Kiss* and *Evel Knievel*.

Upon reading several reviews of the films that she made after *Peter Pan*, one finds that the critics unintentionally helped end her career through their insensitive typecasting. PETER PAN IN CINDERELLA or PETER PAN AS THE VIRGIN MARY were among the headings of film reviews. It is no wonder that Betty complained to reporter Myrtle Gebhart of their unfairness, yet the latter ironically chose to title her story, "Peter Pan's Rebellion."

Betty Bronson died on October 21, 1971. Earlier that year she made an appearance on "The Merv Griffin Show," a popular "talk show" of the period, along with other stars from the silent-film era. DeWitt Bodeen remembered that last appearance: "Betty was so alive when I saw her that evening," he wrote, "laughing and clapping her hands in delight, just as she did when Lasky informed her that J.M. Barrie had selected her to play Peter Pan, and she danced around the room, repeating, "'I'm the luckiest girl in the world.'"[29]

Left: Betty Bronson as Peter Pan, 1924. *Right:* Betty Bronson, still lovely in her later years, circa 1971.

9

Jean Forbes-Robertson and
Other English Lasses

*She has only to appear in any character and before she has crossed the stage
you feel that you are in the presence of a spirit whose excess of fineness cannot
escape the world's pain, of a soul importunate for things not of this earth,
and in Herbert's phrase, something "divinely loose" about her.*
— James Agate, 1926[1]

Each actress playing Peter Pan has naturally had her own interpretation of the part complete with its idiosyncrasies. Sometimes, however, these interpretations were carried to an extreme, thus affecting the playwright's vision. Noël Coward, who played the role of Slightly again in 1914, gave a humorous account of Madge Titheradge's performance as Peter to his biographer, Cole Lesley. Titheradge was the first actress to play the role in London after Pauline Chase vacated the part. Wrote Lesley:

> Miss Titheradge was a dramatic actress of enormous power, and in the scene when Tinkerbell will die unless we all applaud and help to save her, she asked, "Do you believe in fairies?" and commanded, "Say quick that you believe!" so ferociously that little children whimpered and clung to their mothers instead of clapping their hands, and Miss Titheradge never played Peter Pan again.[2]

On June 13, 1913, Barrie was honored with the Baronet title, becoming Sir James. With the advent of World War I in the summer of 1914, Barrie's world as he knew it would be drastically changed. He had begun to write *Rosy Rapture*, a revue intended for French music-hall sensation Gaby Deslys, which involved extensive use of motion-picture film. Barrie and all of the Davies boys, particularly 21-year-old George, were infatuated with the French star. George and Peter, then 17, enlisted in the Special Reserve of 60th Rifles, while Jack, 20, was already in the Navy. On March 15, 1915, George, the soldier, was shot through the head in Flanders. Just four days earlier, in his last letter to George, Barrie tried to comfort the young man who first influenced him to write of Peter Pan's adventures in Kensington Gardens:

> It was terrible that man being killed next to you, but don't be afraid to tell me of such things. You see it at night I fear with painful vividness. I have lost all sense I ever had of war being glorious; it is just unspeakably monstrous to me now.[3]

Among George's possessions was a copy of *The Little White Bird*, which he had bought on leave just before going back to the front.

Top, left: Jean Forbes-Robertson as Peter Pan (photograph by Sasha). Jean played Peter for nine seasons between 1927 and 1936. *Top, right:* Madge Titheradge at the Duke of York's for the 1914 season (photograph: Wrather & Buys, courtesy Roy Busby). *Above:* Jack Llewelyn Davies in uniform in 1914. John Napoleon Darling was named after Jack (courtesy Great Ormond Street Hospital Children's Charity, London). *Right:* George Llewelyn Davies in 1913, two years before his death in World War I. George's name was used for Mr. George Darling (courtesy Great Ormond Street Hospital Children's Charity, London).

Three months later Charles Frohman went down with the *Lusitania* while on his way to London to help Barrie with *Rosy Rapture*. Daniel Frohman described the last moments on the *Lusitania* from an account given by a survivor, actress Rita Jolivet:

> The great liner began to lurch. Frohman now said to Miss Jolivet: "You had better hold on the rail and save your strength."
>
> The ship's list became greater; huge waves rolled up, carrying wreckage and bodies on their crest. Then, with all the terror of destruction about him, Frohman said to his associates, with the serene smile still on his face:
>
> "Why fear death? It is the most beautiful adventure of life."
>
> Instinctively the four people moved closer together, they joined hands by a common impulse, and stood awaiting the end.
>
> The ship gave a sudden lurch; once more a mighty green cliff of water came rushing up, bearing its tide of death and debris; again Frohman started to say the speech that was to be his valedictory. He had hardly repeated the first three words —"Why fear death?"— when the group was engulfed and all sank beneath the surface of the sea.[4]

Upon Frohman's death, the Daniel Mayer Company took over as perennial producer of *Peter Pan*, beginning with a lease at the New Theatre in London. In 1919, George M. Cohan's daughter, Georgette, played the role, with Edna Best taking over in 1920. During the rehearsals Barrie added some charming dialogue for Michael and Mrs. Darling:

MICHAEL (as he is put between the sheets): Mother, how did you get to know me?

MR. DARLING: A little less noise there.

Top: Peter Llewelyn Davies in 1916. Although Barrie wrote that he created Peter Pan by metaphorically rubbing the five Davies boys violently together, Peter Pan was named after Peter Davies, which the young man viewed with disdain (courtesy Great Ormond Street Hospital Children's Charity, London). *Right: Peter Pan* producer Charles Frohman on board the ill-fated *Lusitania* on May 1, 1915. In the film, *Finding Neverland,* Frohman, as played by Dustin Hoffman, was depicted as Barrie's antagonist in terms of making the play a reality but in real life he was Pan's champion right from the beginning. It was reported by a survivor that Frohman's last words were "Why fear death? It is the most beautiful adventure in life."

MICHAEL (growing solemn): At what time was I born, mother?

MRS. DARLING: At two o'clock in the night-time, dearest.

MICHAEL: Oh mother, I hope I didn't wake you.[5]

The most devastating day in the life of J.M. Barrie was May 19, 1921, when Michael Llewelyn Davies, his favorite, drowned in the river Thames at Sanford Pool at Oxford. The 21-year-old, who had never learned to swim, had been bathing

Top, left: Unity More as Peter at the New Theatre, 1915–16, 1916–17 (courtesy Roy Busby). *Bottom:* Eva Embury played Peter on three tours from 1916 through 1918. In 1983 Catherine Haill compiled Embury's letters and photos for a charming book, *Dear Peter Pan. Above:* Fay Compton, New Theatre, 1917 (courtesy Roy Busby).

Left: Faith Celli as Peter and Isobel Elsom as Wendy, New Theatre, 1918. *Right:* From 1919, Georgette Cohan, the daughter of George M. Cohan, as Peter Pan (courtesy Roy Busby).

in the pool with his close friend, Rupert Buxton, when he began to have trouble staying afloat. It was reported that Buxton tried to aid Michael, only to be taken down as well. However, those closer to the young men suggested that it might have been a joint suicide between lovers. Michael, the most sensitive son of Arthur and Sylvia, was in many ways like Barrie: talented, prone to writing verse, and often deeply contemplative. The differences were his age and his beauty. Just six months earlier Barrie had convinced him to go back to school at Oxford rather than quitting to study painting in Paris. It was a decision that would haunt Barrie for the rest of his life as he mourned "the lad that will never be old."

On 7th Nov 1922 I dreamt that he came back to me, not knowing that he was drowned and that I kept this knowledge from him, and we went on for another year in old way till the fatal 19th approached again & he became very sad not knowing why, and I feared what was to happen but never let on — and as day drew nearer he understood more & thought I didn't — and gradually each knew the other knew but still we didn't speak of it — and when the day came I had devised schemes to make it impossible for him to leave me yet doubted they could help — and he rose in the night and put on the old clothes and came back to look at me as he thought asleep. I tried to prevent him going but he had to go and I knew it and he said he thought it would be harder if I didn't let him go alone, but I went with him, holding his hand and he liked it and when we came to the place — that pool — he said goodbye to me and went into it and sank just as before. At this point I think I woke but feeling that he had walked cheerily into my room as if another year had again begun for us.[6]

Henry Ainley as Captain Hook with Edna Best as Peter at the St. James's Theatre in 1920 (courtesy Roy Busby).

In 1923 Gladys Cooper was cast as Peter and immediately confronted Barrie with alternatives. She wrote:

"I wonder where Peter got his high boots from. Did he go to Clarkson?" I asked at one lunch. Barrie pondered for some time, and then said: "Well, what do you propose?" Result: I got my own way and played Peter in a pair of old shoes of John's [her son]. The same with shorts. I asked

A snapshot of nineteen-year-old Michael and Nico Llewelyn Davies, sixteen, taken on April 19, 1920. Barrie used Michael's name for the first name of the youngest Darling sibling while Nico's full name became the youngster's middle name; thus Michael Nicolas Darling (courtesy Great Ormond Street Hospital Children's Charity, London).

Sir James where he got them — result, I was allowed to wear an old pair of flannel shorts belonging to Gerald du Maurier. By taking thought — and Barrie out to lunch — I even managed to get the fight between Peter and Hook changed. I said it was "silly" for them to fight with wooden swords, and so it came about that when Franklyn Dyal [Captain Hook] and I had our fights we used real sabers.[7]

Stewart Stern, a friend of Cooper's, wrote that "she invented the first flight in through the window, always wrote the word MOTHER on the palm of her hand to remind herself what she was escaping and looking for, and also told me she always had a roughly bandaged knee because boys usually do."[8]

Cooper was invited to play Peter again in 1924, only this time her Wendy had personal connections to Barrie and the play. Angela du Maurier, cousin to the Davies boys and daughter of Gerald, complained in her journal:

> Another thing that horrified me was the exceedingly dirty (or so I thought) old clothes I had to wear! No new wardrobe for a hardy annual like Peter Pan! My diary quotes that my senses revolted at "clothes dreadfully shabby, ghastly old shoes."[9]

During one performance, Angela crashed during the flying scene right into the footlights and off the stage. She wrote:

Top, left: Franklyn Dyall as Hook, Adelphi Theatre, 1923 (courtesy Roy Busby). *Bottom, left:* Allan Whittaker, who played Slightly four times between 1925 and 1928, signed this autograph with a self-portrait caricature. *Above:* Gladys Cooper as Pan at Adelphi Theatre in 1923 and 1924 (photograph: Sasha, courtesy Stewart Stern).

A more uncomfortable, nerve-shattering and painful experience I have never had. There was a hush throughout the house, quite obviously it was thought I was seriously injured, if not killed. The next few moments are hazy because I do not know just what did happen, but I recovered my "wind" which had been knocked out of me, and when I came to I realized from the orchestra pit that my understudy had been hurriedly pushed on. In great pain I crept under the stage and up, and came in collision with old X. Our heads met and the impact of that was even worse than the hurt I received in the fall into the orchestra. As bad luck would have it, poor Daddy [Gerald du Maurier] chose that moment to pop around to see the end of the performance and was met by an hysterical "Wendy's gorne!"...

When I felt certain I was going to be neither sick nor faint I gave the signal that I'd go on again. Poor Wendy II crept off the stage, and I crept back via the prompt corner, into my bed where luckily Wendy had to lie for a good five minutes in peace and silence. The ovation which greeted me was almost frightening. The audience stood up and clapped and yelled, and with tears running down my face by then (from emotion not pain), I blew them all a kiss, and then the play went on.[10]

With the 23rd edition of *Peter Pan* in 1927 came a breath of fresh air in the form of Jean Forbes-Robertson, the daughter of the famous actor, Sir Johnston Forbes-Robertson, and actress Gertrude Elliot. Jean, born in London on March 16, 1905, made her stage debut in her mother's production of *Paddy the Next Best Thing* in South Africa in 1921 but with the stage name of Anne McEwen. After touring New Zealand and Australia, she returned to England in 1925 to make her London debut in *Dancing Mothers*. The critics started to take note of her when she played Helen Pettigrew in *Berkeley Square* and Juliet in *Romeo and Juliet* in 1927. St. John Ervine wrote:

Dorothy Dickson played the Shaftesbury Theatre in 1925 and the Adelphi Theatre in 1926.

> For my part, I have never in a long course of playgoing, during which I have seen many Juliets, witnessed anything so beautiful as Miss Jean Forbes-Robertson's performance in the Balcony scene. She gave us here the young girl newly acquainted with affection, opening out to high and lovely passion, the very "bud of love" proving itself to be a "beauteous flower." Her expression is extraordinarily mobile; she has a singular ability to illuminate her slightly somber face with fleeting smiles, and with the least movements she betrays a medley of emotions. When Romeo first kisses this Juliet she shyly draws back as his lips touch hers, not because the importunate

youth is displeasing to her, but because some delicate apprehension fills her mind. But when she resolves her doubts and has allayed her fears, she pours her affection out, not unmaidenly, but with young and innocent ardor. This was Juliet on her balcony, for me at all events: my imagination was here fulfilled.[11]

In addition to sharing many of her famous father's attributes, Jean also shared his insecurities with an audience and people in general. It wasn't easy to have such theatrical luminaries as parents, yet despite her shyness and fragility, Jean became an actress of great skill with many adoring fans. In 1927 she stepped on the stage for the first time as Peter Pan, a role that she would continue to play until the 1934–35 season, vying with Pauline Chase for longevity in part. Wrote a critic for *The Era*:

Personally, I think she is the best Peter I have seen. She is a boy with youth and vigor and fun, and yet she is fey. Her wings are those of the imagination, and she is at home in the Never-Never-Land.[12]

A critic for *The Times* found:

This Peter is full of fiery beauty; he sparkles with vitality; he gives a magic to Wendy's house that we have not known it to possess. Here is a Peter who is at the farthest possible remove from a principal boy in a pantomime, whose vitality is something altogether different from rollicking high spirits, who hovers most brilliantly between the joy and melancholy of boyhood, and the different joy and melancholy of the immortals.[13]

Jean suggested to Barrie additional lines to further Peter's fairy qualities. When Wendy discovers that Peter has no mother she jumps up to hug him.

PETER: You mustn't touch me. No one must ever touch me.

WENDY: Why?

PETER: I don't know but I think if you were to touch me I shouldn't be here.[14]

Barrie liked the suggestion so much he also modified the published version of the play with the addition.

For eight seasons the critics continued to find new phrases to describe the experience of seeing this gifted actress play Peter. In 1928, critic Charles Morgan wrote:

Top: Jean Forbes-Robertson played Peter at the Palladium in London as well as tours through other cities across England (photograph: Bertram Park, courtesy Great Ormond Street Hospital Children's Charity, London). *Bottom:* Jean as a teenager, circa 1921.

It has been thought enough for Peter to be boyish and sprightly and full of "go"; it has been forgotten that, in spite of his human parentage, he has, by long association with fairies, become

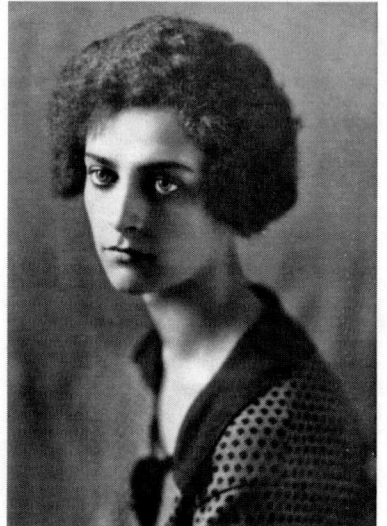

more than half fairy himself. It has been forgotten that he is an immortal with more of the powers of the immortals in him than an ability to fly in the air. Now Miss Forbes-Robertson's restored him to his own kingdom.[15]

A critic for *The Era* noted:

Mr. George Shelton, fortunately, is still here as Smee. What "Peter Pan" would ever do without him is unthinkable! Our Nonconformist pirate is adorable.[16]

A young unknown actor named Sydney Boulton played the part of Slightly when the play toured the regions in 1928 with Sheila Moloney as Peter. Years later, during the Second World War, after he had changed his name to Peter Cotes and was directing a production of *The Man Who Changed His Name* in Worthing, the established actor entered a pub during his lunch break. He wrote in his biography:

Every table was engaged, but at the far end of the room a petite, well-preserved, middle-aged woman, wearing a Women's Land Army badge, was lunching alone. She had practically finished her meal, so I asked if I might sit at her table. With a friendly gesture, she invited me to take the chair facing her. After I had finished my soup and she was drinking

Left: A Jean Forbes-Robertson playbill for *Peter Pan* designed by Hubert Leslie. *Right:* Jean and Mary Casson as Wendy, 1927. Casson played Wendy from 1927 through 1932.

her coffee, she ventured to ask if I was in the theatre, as I was reading *Stage*. She confessed to a certain interest in my profession and mentioned that she used to play in *Peter Pan*. I was immediately interested and rather proudly told her that I held a record in that play, having played all three parts of John, Slightly and Starkey. As she stood up to go she said, "I too, once held a record in *Peter Pan*. There was a time when I had played it more often than anyone else." I looked hard at my companion. "You're not..." I started to ask. "Yes," she smiled, "I'm Pauline Chase." By which time she had drawn on her gloves and was half-way to the cash desk to pay her bill. Peter Pan in flight![17]

Cotes wrote that Lionel Gadsden's Hook was the best as "he never transformed Hook into a funny man. He allowed the lines to speak for themselves, had a great sense of the dramatic and never played the part with his tongue in his cheek." [18]

Peter Pan turned 25 years old in 1929, so as a treat, a reunion of sorts added a nostalgic touch that Christmas. Gerald du Maurier returned for one last season as Captain Hook, which coincidently was Shelton's final season. Also back for the first time in years was the mermaids scene. One critic reported:

"Peter Pan" has become for critics what Mr. G. K. Chesterson would call a "hoy and soul-cleansing ritual."
... Sir Gerald's Mr. Darling was

Left: Sheila Moloney in the 1928–29 touring company. *Above:* Lionel Gadsden was beloved by audiences outside London for his portrayal of Captain Hook but he first appeared in the role of Panther. Gadsden played Hook on 16 tours between 1913 and 1934. This poor image from a vintage newspaper is one of the few available of Gadsden in this role (courtesy Roy Busby).

The Nursery Scene at the Great Ormond Street Children's Hospital, with Marie Lohr (Mrs. Darling), Mary Casson (Wendy), Jean Forbes-Robertson (Peter), and Gerald du Maurier (Mr. Darling) entertaining the children (courtesy Great Ormond Street Hospital Children's Charity, London).

referred to last week in "Looking Round," as he played the part before the children at the hospital in Great Ormond street. He acts with charming humour, but it is Hook who provides him with real opportunities — better opportunities, incidentally, than he has had for a very long time. The part brings out all his histrionic abilities; it is not possible to "walk through" Captain Hook. Every exponent brings some fresh ideas to the pirate, and Sir Gerald, with memories of the first performance, remains our ideal....

Miss Jean Forbes-Robertson's Peter is less elfish and more human than last year. She was an electric spark in the scene in which she exclaimed, "You do believe in fairies," but some of the famous lines are taken in a trifle too matter-of-fact a voice. There were even moments when I had the awful sinking feeling that this Peter had attended a preparatory school and he had learned the difference between a kiss and a thimble![19]

Zena Dare played Mrs. Darling in 1931, 23 years after she toured as Peter. Jean returned each year, to the delight of most critics. In 1933, a critic from *The Times* wrote:

Tall, slender, and agile, with quick turns of the head that could disconcert a whole shipload of unsusceptible pirates as easily as they bewildered poor Wendy, and with wide-set eyes that look through and beyond them all, Miss Forbes-Robertson is Puck's own Scottish cousin, in whom sentiment and heartlessness play see-saw with each other until the steely heart (which the Freudians would call the Pleasure Principle) rises in final triumph to abide in the tree-tops.[20]

There was one young lady during this period who had the distinction of being the first actress to play Wendy and Peter. Dinah Mec was born on September 17, 1920, in Hampstead, London, but she is best known for her stage name, Dinah Sheridan, and for the starring role in the 1953 film *Genevieve*, as well as her 1980s television appearances as Angela in *Don't Wait Up* and as the mother in the 1970 film *The Railway Children*. In 2005, Dinah reminisced about those years on tour in *Peter Pan*, before and during the Second World War:

> At the audition on the stage of the Palladium in London, I could hear voices discussing the young hopefuls; one of them being J.M. Barrie. Then Miss Jean Forbes-Robertson came onto the stage and stood beside me whispering: "You are a bit tall; drop onto one hip and I shall take a deep breath." It did the trick, I was chosen. I have since "lost" six inches as my spine contracted in old age and I had both hips replaced! Now I am known as Little Dinah!
>
> Every time I visit a manicurist I think of Jean Forbes-Robertson! In the little house for Wendy (as we were being wound up into the trees) I used to look at Jean's hands with the nails bitten disastrously. I swore to myself, from that first year playing opposite her, that I would stop biting my own — and did. Never again; and my hands have been praised by many a manicurist since![21]

Jean was again scheduled to play Peter for the 1935-36 season, but illness prevented this, so Elsa Lanchester and Charles Laughton, the famous husband and wife film actors, were asked by the Daniel Mayer Company to play Peter and Hook. Their busy film commitments, in turn, gave Nova Pilbeam the opportunity to play Pan. She received good notices but the next year the Laughtons were again approached about the play. "But James Barrie always had the final word on casting," wrote Elsa Lanchester, "and he

Left: An iconic image of Jean Forbes-Robertson as Peter Pan, which she first played in 1927. *Above:* Dinah Sheridan played Wendy opposite Jean Forbes-Robertson and Elsa Lanchester in 1933–1934.

wrote to us saying we weren't suitable for the parts — he didn't want us to play them."[22] She elaborated:

So off we went to Barrie's flat in Adelphi terrace, and with fear and trembling climbed the stairs. We were shown into the great man's study. Barrie at once said, "I'm afraid you will terrify the children, Mr. Laughton, and Hook must never do that." I suppose that Sir James had visions of Charles as Captain Bligh and Nero. Charles said as gently as possible that he would not. Barrie had never seen me perform and he studied me carefully. Fortunately, a few minutes after we'd arrived there, the German actress, Elizabeth Bergner, rang up Barrie. He asked her what she thought, and she told Barrie that Charles and I would be wonderful in the parts and that it would be a great mistake not to let us do it. So Barrie gave us his permission.[23]

An unlikely Peter Pan in the form of Elsa Lanchester at the London Palladium in 1936 (courtesy Nicola Biggs).

Ironically, Laughton, in part that should have fit like a glove, was mild at best. Wrote Tyrone Guthrie in his *A Life in the Theatre*:

> Hook, a heavyweight Don Quixote, became the hero of the evening. It was when Peter Pan came on that little children hid their faces in their mothers' skirts and strong men shook with fear.[24]

Noted *The Times*:

> Those who fear that Mr. Charles Laughton's Hook might be too terrifying, too macabre, may be reassured. Mr. Laughton has approached the part in a fresh and generous spirit, erring, where errs at all, on the side of the benign. This is a portly, rounded pirate with whom it would be pleasant to dine at ease after a morning's murder and a little plank — walking with afternoon tea.... Peter, too, is freshly interpreted and, whatever else may be thought of Miss Elsa Lanchester's treatment of the part, it is certainly not sticky or mawkish. What she appears to be seeking is an emphasis on Peter's fiery, Pan-like quality, and to attain this she has stylized her performance, phrasing it with a hard, clipped precision, varying her facial expression so seldom that she gives almost the effect of a mask with highly coloured cheeks and staring eyes, and regulating her movement as though she were describing the pattern of a dance.[25]

Lanchester's Pan was perhaps the most unconventional portrayal up to that point, prompting Stewart Stern to later inquire about her unorthodox approach:

> When I asked Elsa Lanchester what made her performance as Peter so scary that the audience of children looked to Hook for comfort "as she came down her wire like a black widow spider looking for meat in its web" she told me she'd wondered about Hitler as a child, and decided to play HIM — at the age of 6![26]

Lanchester elaborated in her book:

> The more I rehearsed my part, the more I saw that Peter was like a little general — ordering the children about and being very officious. In other words, enjoying power.[27]

"Back you pewling spawn. I'll show you now the road to dusky death!" Charles Laughton as Hook at the London Palladium in 1936 (courtesy Roy Busby).

Dinah Sheridan played Peter during the 1936-37 touring season while Elsa Lanchester played the role in London. Theatre programs and studio portraits show Dinah's hair darkened and in a similar pose as Jean Forbes-Robertson, but the actress also had postcards made up that showed her looking very much like herself. She recalled:

> When I had finished my engagement as Peter, Elsa Lanchester came out to join us and I was asked to remain with the company, reverting to Wendy and understudying Elsa as Peter. Whether it was a way of getting cheaper understudies I don't know but Elsa, who did not appear until the end of Act 1, seldom came to the theatre stage door until the last moment; so that I wouldn't know whether to get dressed and made-up as Wendy or Peter. Or was she often late everywhere?

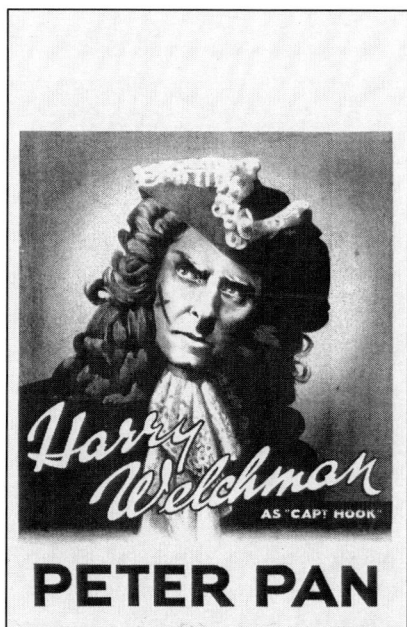

Top, left: An extremely rare poster announcing Nova Pilbeam in the 1935–36 touring company of *Peter Pan.* After playing the Palladium in the London season, she replaced Edna Moon on the tour. She would tour again in 1944. *Bottom, left:* The companion window card poster featuring Harry Welchman as Hook in the 1935–36 tour. Notice at the top there is a blank space to fill in for the name of the local theatre. *Above:* Dinah Sheridan was made up to look like Jean Forbes-Robertson's Pan. Said Dinah, "The year 1937.... I was suddenly asked to come to the Palladium to 'hover' (dressed up and made-up as Peter) in the wings as Jean was doing it again and had a good dose of bronchial pneumonia. I was told to hold — what turned out to be a bottle of scotch — and hand it to her for a strong swig whenever she came offstage for the sum of 12 pounds a week! She never gave in — but went through quite a lot of scotch!!! — and I never had to take over!!" (courtesy Nicola Biggs).

Dinah Sheridan's self-promoting postcard as Peter Pan from the 1937 tour. Elsa Lanchester later joined the tour after her London run as Peter and Dinah returned to the role of Wendy (courtesy Nicola Biggs).

I was getting good notices — in larger type than she — as I had been quite a few years appearing in *Peter Pan* around the country as Wendy and Elsa was not liked as a much more modern version of J.M. Barrie's classic character. Did she really resent me? In other ways we got on very well on stage and she introduced me to Charles Laughton when we came back to London. But he was very shy and I am sure was still smarting under his London notice as Captain Hook: "Charles Laughton as Captain Hook looked like one of the three little pigs dressed up as the big bad wolf."[28]

On June 19, 1937, Sir James M. Barrie died at age 77. Six years earlier he made his most generous gift to the Great Ormond Street Children's Hospital — perpetual rights to the books and plays of *Peter Pan*. His last play, *The Boy David*, with Elisabeth Bergner, proved a disappointment only six months before his death.

That same year Anna Neagle took a break from her busy film schedule to appear at the London Palladium. Best known for her appearances in the cinematic adaptations of such musicals as *No, No, Nanette, Sunny*, and *Irene*, Neagle had just finished filming *Victoria the Great* when she appeared in *Peter Pan*. She reminisced:

At that time it was traditional for the first performance of *Peter Pan* to be given before the lord mayor of London, in full regalia, and two thousand of London's poor children. On entering the theatre each child was given a paper bag containing an apple, an orange and some sweets. I remember so clearly the first few moments of that opening performance. The lights dimmed, soft, atmospheric music filled the stage and auditorium. As the Darling children settled down to sleep, and I flew in through their window, the smell of oranges hit me like a blow! It was a gorgeous moment![29]

Neagle also remembered how difficult it was for the actors to hear each other due to the rustling of paper bags. As much as she enjoyed playing the role, she was irritated by conductor John Crook's insistence that she play Peter just as Nina Boucicault had done in 1904.

J.M. Barrie in 1937, the year of his death (courtesy Roy Busby).

From time to time I was congratulated, or taken to task, for doing, or not doing, things the way Miss Boucicault did them. Miss Boucicault lent me the dagger she used when she created the role. In her note she had said, "This is the little dagger which fought the pirates at the first performance of *Peter*. I would love to give it to you, but I'm far too sentimental!"[30]

Nina Boucicault lent her dagger to several actresses who followed her in *Peter Pan*, making each one feel even more special. Jean Forbes-Robertson returned in 1938 for her ninth and last season, outdistancing Pauline Chase's record, but there was a last-minute substitution for the opening night.

The first thing to be said of the opening performances of this year's *Peter Pan*, which was given before a vast audience of London children on Saturday afternoon, is that, though illness had for the moment prevented Miss Jean Forbes-Robertson from appearing — and all who have seen her in a part she has made her own were disappointed — Miss Nova Pilbeam, who took her place, and who has before played Peter in her own right, enabled that personal disappointment to be forgotten. She is an imaginative and vital Peter with an openness of manner that goes far to save the part from sentimentality. She has not that flamelike conviction which can subdue even the skeptical members of the audience, but she is firm and direct, she is not a "principal boy," and those who have a natural taste for peterism are delighted by her.[31]

Top: Anna Neagle as Peter Pan at the London Palladium in 1937 (photograph: John Everard, courtesy Roy Busby). *Bottom:* Anona Winn as Peter Pan in the 1937–38 tour of England (photograph: Mme Yvonne, courtesy Great Ormond Street Hospital Children's Charity, London).

Joan Moody as the "Baby Mermaid." Quite often, minor roles, such as the mermaids, would be filled locally by youngsters from the cities on the tour. Moody played her role for two years starting in the 1936 and 1937 seasons and, during the interim, received several autographed photographs from the leading players that she held onto until her death. A few adorn this book, thanks to her granddaughter (courtesy Nicola Biggs).

And finally, Seymour Hicks played Hook, although not to the satisfaction of most critics:

> And this same year there is Sir Seymour Hicks's Hook to which to look forward.... On Saturday, Sir Seymour was not in good voice, nor could his following of the text be called slavish ... but he has hit upon little pieces of business that are new and brings to his whole treatment of the part an inventiveness that revitalizes it.[32]

Because of the dangers from the war on the home front there was no London production in 1939, but the play toured with Margaret Cooper as Peter. In 1940 most of the props and scenery were destroyed in the Blitz, thereby canceling both a London production and the touring company. However, an original cast album of sorts was recorded in London in October of that year with Jean Forbes-Robertson, preserving her last performance as *Peter Pan*. Joining her was Gordon Harker as the speaking voice of Hook, George Baker for his singing voice, Nancy Evans as Mrs. Darling, and Dinah Sheridan again as Wendy. Dinah remembered:

> In 1940 I was working in weekly Repertory in Llandudno, North Wales and received a telegram from Jean Forbes-Robertson suggesting that I should take the train to London for the records which were to be made. My mother was horrified that I should put myself in air-raid danger for three days but I was keen and begged her to let me (I was 20 after all). During that time not one bomb dropped! The company on the pier was very glad to see me back again![33]

In 2004, in honor of Peter's 100th birthday, Sepia Records reissued the 78 rpm record set for the first time on CD — a wonderful glimpse into Peter's past before other composers

Finally, after 34 years, the man Barrie first envisioned as Captain Hook, Sir Seymore Hicks, finally played the role at the Palladium in London in 1938 (courtesy Roy Busby).

and lyricists thought they could do better. And thanks to modern technology, Jean, Dinah, and company sound better than ever. I sent a copy of the CD to Julia Lockwood, who, having played Peter Pan two decades later, responded:

> I especially enjoyed listening to the great Jean FR. When I was 18 I was so in awe of her, even though I had never seen or heard her performance. Listening to her now, makes me giggle a bit, because she does sound so incredibly British and very much a Lady! However it makes no difference to my childhood imagination, thinking that she really was Peter Pan![34]

Indeed, times have changed! And Lockwood is right; Jean's Peter suffers from that proper clipped British sound we are so familiar with from old movies. Yet there is something so nostalgic about Jean's performance that even this mere audio recording at least captures a hint of that elusive stage magic. Sadly, even as her performances as Peter Pan became a theatre tradition, Jean Forbes-Robertson's health began declining significantly in the 1930s. She passed away on Christmas Eve, 1962, only 57 years old. During the decades following her last performance as Peter it appeared that one of the major considerations for choosing who was to play the part next was not necessarily based on qualifications but rather fame, on and/or off the big screen.

Jean Forbes-Robertson played her last season as Peter Pan in 1938 (courtesy Roy Busby).

10

Eva Le Gallienne:
The Civic Repertory Theatre

How Barrie would have hated my Peter Pan. It's always puzzled me that he should have written a character all boy *(the braggadocio, the cockcrows, the fear of being trapped and held—all traits which, rightly or wrongly, we associate with* boy*) and yet the performances of the part he most enjoyed were unfailingly "Girlie-Girlie"—a cross between the customary Viola of the '90s and the Principal-Boy in an English pantomime. One can scarcely imagine anything less like Peter.*

— Eva Le Gallienne, 1970[1]

When she was 13 years old, Eva Le Gallienne wrote a list of great theatrical characters that she was determined to play by her 35th birthday. Included were Juliet, Hedda Gabler, Marguerite Gautier, and Peter Pan. Amazingly, she fulfilled her aspiration! From an early exposure to the histrionics of Sarah Bernhardt the youngster realized that her life was to revolve around this art form. In her first autobiography, *At 33*, she wrote:

> One ultimate goal from which I never wavered for an instant: the Theatre — the power to spread beauty out into life.[2]

Eva was born in London on January 11, 1899, but was raised in France after her father, poet Richard Le Gallienne, and her mother, Danish journalist Julie Norregard, divorced. Her superior education was carefully planned by her resourceful mother to include six languages (which she would use later in life to translate Ibsen and Hans Christian Andersen, among others) and physical education.

Many years later, she wrote:

> I'd had a great deal of physical training in my childhood and was quite a gymnast. Since the school I went to in Paris made no provision for exercise of any sort, mother arranged that I should attend a gymnasium, the Gymnase George on the rue de Vaugirard — twice a week. Monsieur George was so pleased with my progress he asked mother to let me take a course in professional acrobatic training; he felt I had a natural aptitude for it. But the idea of her daughter becoming an acrobat had no appeal for mother and she firmly refused. However I managed to persuade Monsieur George to give me some advanced ring and trapeze work all the same. This gave me a control and flexibility invaluable to any actor. It came in very handy in *Peter Pan*.[3]

Fortunately, Eva's early interest in stretching her athletic abilities was squelched by her nanny. After seeing Pauline Chase fly in *Peter Pan*, the child went home and attempted to do the same, right out her bedroom window! "If she can do it I can,"[4] she muttered as her

Eva Le Gallienne played Peter Pan from 1928 to 1933 at her Civic Repertory Theatre. This portrait by Pinchot dates from 1929.

nurse caught her just in time. The precocious youngster was perhaps also criticizing Miss Chase's performance for "she" was just not believable to Eva as a "he." The notion would greatly influence her interpretation of the role years later.

Like many actors Eva had to pay her dues before she would be able to pick and choose her roles. Her first stage appearance was at 15, a walk-on in *Monna Vanna* that was arranged by actress Constance Collier, a close friend of the family. Eva wrote about her opening night:

> Five minutes before "Overture" was called, I rushed down to Constance Collier's room, and with the most perfect disregard of her nerves, and of the fact that after all it was she and not I that was to carry the brunt of the performance, I invaded her dressing-room and taking possession of her mirror proceeded to put a few last touches to my wig, which would not seem right to me. Instead of throwing me out, she helped me with the utmost patience, and watched me in smiling amazement. Utter thoughtlessness, utter selfishness of extreme youth![5]

After the run of the play, Julie enrolled her daughter in Beerbohm Tree's Academy. While she was appearing in a school play as a cockney, producer Lyall Swete happened to be in the audience and offered her the part of a cockney servant in *The Laughter of Fools*. Eva unintentionally left her audiences in stitches and in return received radiant reviews. When the play closed England was entering the Great War, so Eva and her mother packed up and moved to the United States.

Her first part in New York was that of a black maid. Later she lost a cockney part because she was not considered authentic. A series of disappointments and mediocre roles followed until she appeared in *Not So Long Ago*, for which her excellent notices won her the role of Julie in the Theatre Guild production of Molnar's *Liliom* (the play from which Rodgers and Hammerstein's musical *Carousel* was derived). The play was the biggest artistic and commercial success for the Guild at that time, and Eva received more than her share of laudatory reviews.

Molnar next provided Eva with another great character in *The Swan*, clearly establishing her as one of the foremost actresses of her generation. Richard Le Gallienne wrote to his ex-wife at this time:

> How often I have thought of that time when you took her to Drury Lane; and she was almost heartbroken because she couldn't be a pantomime fairy. And now her name is in big letters on the billboards of New York! I stood, one day, a full quarter of an hour, looking at it, with tears in my eyes.[6]

Her father's letter would remain with Eva for the rest of her life. But as satisfying as it was to be recognized, Eva did not relish acting in a long-running play, even one the caliber of *The Swan*. At this point she could have had her pick of roles available on Broadway, yet instead of opting for commercial success she chose to work in an area that required more of her skills and ideals. In 1926, Eva Le Gallienne, or Le G, as she liked to be called by her friends, founded the Civic Repertory Theatre and made the Fourteenth Street Theatre their home.

The purpose of the Civic Repertory was to allow the average income person the opportunity to see classic plays at affordable prices and to give the actors a chance to work in several plays each season. Orchestra and box seats went for $1.50 and the second balcony was only 50 cents. The repertoire included works by Ibsen, Shakespeare, Molière, Dumas, and Barrie, giving Le G a chance to pursue other theatrical venues in addition to acting. She believed that distinguished theatre need not be housed in a Broadway theatre. From 1926 to 1932, 34 plays were produced at the Fourteenth Street Theatre while Le G assumed the triple task of managing while also directing and acting. Wisely, she chose not to take the leading roles in every play. In her adaptation of *Alice in Wonderland*, she played the White Queen, leaving Alice's chores to Josephine Hutchinson, who also played Wendy in *Peter Pan*.

Eva Le Gallienne at the time she was playing Julie in Molnar's *Liliom* in 1921.

Josephine Hutchinson became an important member of

the company quite by chance. Her mother, Leona Roberts, a character actress best known for her screen portrayal of Dr. Meade's wife in *Gone with the Wind*, was a member of the group. Josephine, also acting for some time, was in town to see her mother in one of the plays in the repertory. Coincidently, the resident ingénue left the company rather suddenly and Roberts suggested her daughter, who had recently received excellent notices for her Broadway appearance in *A Man's Man*, as a replacement. Fate provided Josephine with a unique opportunity. More than 60 years later the actress reflected, "That was the best training you could imagine. And for me, those years in the repertory was the luckiest thing that could ever happen."[7] One week could find the company rehearsing one play while two or three were played on alternating nights.

Peter Pan was the most ambitious undertaking for the Civic Repertory, for it not only required elaborate sets and costumes, it also boasted music, dancing, and fencing, not to mention flying! In addition, Le G's version would have to live up to the memories of the Maude Adams productions.

Le G wrote:

Eva Le Gallienne as Princess Alexandria in Monar's *The Swan*. With this play she became the toast of Broadway and was considered at the same level as Helen Hayes. She would give up her commercial success to establish her beloved Civic Repertory Theatre.

I never saw her act. She left the stage shortly after I came to America; but I soon discovered that "Peter Pan" meant "Maude Adams" to most Americans.

I had been puzzled when asking various people about the Adams performance, why none of them seemed to have much recollection of Wendy; they remembered her only in the vaguest terms. Now Wendy is a tremendously important part, second only to Peter. Was the Adams magic so overwhelming that it could successfully blot out all memory of Wendy? I couldn't understand it — but I did, as soon as I studied the Adams acting version sent me by the Frohman Company from whom I leased the rights. At least two-thirds of Wendy's lines were either cut or else, incredibly enough, transferred to Peter! Even the bedtime story Wendy tells the Lost Boys, before she tucks them in, the story they loved best, the sort Peter hated (with all its typical little-English-girl Victorianisms: "Let us now take a peep into the future...," "this elegant lady of uncertain age alighting at London station...," "...and the two noble portly figures accompanying her...," etc.) — even this story was spoken by Peter Adams Pan! It's hard to believe that Barrie knew of this and condoned it, and

one wonders who thought of it in the first place: Charles Frohman? The director? Maude Adams herself? Almost certainly not the director, for directors in those days had very little importance, especially when a star of Maude Adams's brilliance was involved. Charles Frohman, who was Czar of all his enterprises, might have insisted on it as "better Box-Office"; or Miss Adams might have found the actress cast as Wendy weak in the part and decided to play most of it herself along with Peter. We shall never know.[8]

In a gesture of respect, Le G introduced herself to Maude, explaining her intentions for *Peter Pan*. The meeting ended with the older actress saying that she would attend one of the performances, which, to Le G's knowledge, she never did.

One of Le G's primary concerns was the flying:

> That flying entrance of Peter's is of the most importance. It immediately sets him apart from ordinary pedestrian folk. Most Peters simply climb in through the window — but any boy could do that, and Peter is far from being any boy; his last name being Pan.[9]

Aerial expert Fred Schultz and his family were hired to rig the machinery at the theatre and to teach the principals how to fly. At 110 feet, the grid was unusually high, perfect for flexibility in planning and executing the flying effects. The actors were taught by a daughter-in-law of the family. Before long, Josephine was able to copy every gesture of her instructor. Eva reminded the young actress that since the scene called for this to be Wendy's first attempt at flying she should be a bit clumsy during flight. At the same time, Le G herself had to resist the temptation for a graceful flight in order to maintain her vision of Peter as "all boy."

Top: Eva Le Gallienne as Peter, 1929 (photograph: Pinchot). *Bottom:* Josephine Hutchinson as Wendy, 1929 (photograph: Pinchot).

The 1931–32 Darling Family: (from left) Donald Cameron (Mr. Darling), Beatrice Terry (Mrs. Darling), Josephine Hutchinson (Wendy), Burgess Meredith (John), and Jackie Jordan (Michael) (photograph: White Studio).

During an interview over tea in her New York City penthouse apartment in 1991, it quickly became apparent that the part of Wendy had remained a favorite for Josephine Hutchinson.

We had the Schultzes. We were called on stage and Mrs. Schultz was a typical German hausfrau type and there seemed to be either her husband or son who was there, I don't remember. And

"The Wendy House," 1931. Josephine Hutchinson as Wendy at the center with Burgess Meredith and Jackie Jordan to her left. Eva Le Gallienne is at the extreme right standing on a mushroom. (photograph: White Studio [The Beinecke Rare Book and Manuscript Library, Yale University]).

Gus, who had a great mustache; he was like a character who would be cast by a casting department. And we had to have our lessons. Now the lessons ... the main thing was that it is like ballet. You must have control from here [pointing to abdomen]. And the position is arabesque, like in ballet. If you saw that show of Jerome Robbins ... a potpourri of all his work.... The girl goes by flying as Peter, she is directed, absolutely only one position ... she is flying to be beautiful. The way that we were taught to fly was to be in every position; to fly as if we were a bird because we flew all the time. This girl flies because she is showing that she can fly.

   The way they do it is with two ropes. They pull you up on one and release the other and you shoot like an arrow. Let me tell you about one of the funny things that happened.... Naturally we fly out the first time ... that's not too difficult although a danger, always a danger with her [Le G] and everybody else because that window was about that high and if Gus didn't raise you high enough you were going right into it, which was something you didn't look forward to. All right, this time they flew me quite high, too high for the proscenium, and my dress went by like that ... and a kid in the aisles yelled out, "He shot her head off," when Slightly Soiled shot his arrow — which of course blew everybody. But it was fun to fly.[10]

   The Civic Repertory productions of *Peter Pan* included flights that were labeled by many as nearly impossible, but that word was just not in Le G's vocabulary. She felt that Peter's last impression was to be even greater than his first magnificent entrance into the

Darling nursery, so important that Le G insisted that a special flight be inserted at the end of the play. Recalled Hutchinson:

> Now the fly that she loved of course was the audience fly. Eventually someone went on after Schultz and perfected it where it wasn't so dangerous. I always thought with Schultz on those wires that it was pretty tricky, that flight. But she loved doing it and the children loved it.[11]

Le G wrote:

> I took to flying like the proverbial duck to water. I'll never forget the first time I flew to the balcony and back — it was a marvelous feeling. My mother was not so happy though. She was always scared of that flight though the Schultzes repeatedly assured her that there was no danger. This was not quite true, as I discovered at a matinee a couple of years later when mother luckily was back in England. Just as I started the return from the balcony I felt the wire drop slightly and heard a gasp from the audience. Instinctively I drew my legs up as high as I could under my chin and in this way just managed to glide onto the stage; if I hadn't drawn my legs up they would have been smashed to pieces against the apron. It was the audience's warning and split-second response to it that saved me.
>
>   And how could I ever forget the look on the faces of the children sitting on the first rows of the balcony as I flew above them. Even now I quite often meet people who tell me they were one of those children, and how the memory of the thrill that "audience fly" gave them has remained vivid through the years.[12]

Le G was the first Peter Pan to fly into the audience, an innovation that recently has been the only highlight of many stock productions of the play.

   Another effective flying bit was the so-called barrel fly, a difficult piece of business that took place at the end of Act Four. After fighting Captain Hook on the ship, Peter sits on a barrel with his legs crossed, playing his pipes. Hook sneaks up and knocks the barrel from under the boy, but he remains floating in the air in the same position. Suddenly Peter turns and flies toward the captain, causing his nemesis to fall overboard to the waiting choppers of the crocodile. Le G described how this was accomplished:

> For this flight two wires were needed — the usual one from the back of the flying harness, the other fastened to a metal ring on a strap buckled around my leg. I put on this strap during the few seconds I was below in the hold [and] when I came back on deck I dashed over the rail of the ship where my Schultz attendant was concealed, and he attached both wires to me; speed and meticulous timing were needed on both our parts. Then, by putting my free leg over the leg supported by the wire, I was able to sit in the air quite comfortably.[13]

   To attain a smooth flight there were three points for the actors to remember: to stand on the designated spot — a small metal disk nailed to the stage floor; to sit down on the wire to keep it taut; and not to "help" by jumping in anticipation. Le G wrote:

> We had difficulty in persuading little Michael to feel the "mark" with his foot, instead of peering at the floor in search of it. And he also had to be deterred from jumping in the air at the moment the wire picked him up, which made for a very jerky, bumpy, "turbulent" flight![14]

Even if the actors were properly set for flight, the technicians often spoiled the smoothness. Josephine Hutchinson had an amusing flying anecdote to share:

> When we came back from flying — it didn't matter before when we didn't know how to fly — but when we came back, Gus sometimes didn't sit you on the lift. You came back and you were in the nursery and you were supposed to be yourself, yet you were far off the ground. And you have no way of getting down unless he drops you. And you had to pretend that you were meant to be there. Horrifying! And when he did drop you, you came down like that and you just had to pretend that was the right moment, but you never knew when he was going to do it.[15]

The costumes were of special concern to Le G.

Aline Bernstein who designed most of the costumes and scenery at the Civic — brilliant, dear Aline! — used to say I wore nothing but "a flying machine and a lot of Bolarminia." In fact she made me a short — a **very** short, a veritable mini-tunic, resembling the one Peter wears in the F. D. Bedford drawings. It was a mixture of delphinium blues, with a few russet leaves clinging to it, as though blown by the wind. I was ragged and faded; it didn't look like a costume. Barrie would have loathed it. Perhaps he would have been shocked by so much leg![16]

Peter's hat was made of blue/grey felt in the shape of a bluebell flower. Stewart Stern still remembers "that 'costume' as nocturnal colors of the air that fly in the moonlight picking up leaves on the way."[17]

Le G went on to write about the pirates' boots:

In studying these drawings one thing troubled me: the pirates looked like giants and Peter and the rest of the children looked tiny in comparison. I wished there were some way we could create a similar illusion. I had cast the tallest men in the company as pirates — they were all at least six feet tall — but this wasn't enough. I decided to have special boots made for them with soles literally twelve inches thick; our smallest pirate would then be seven feet tall. The boot maker assured me no actor could walk in such boots — no actor would even try to. I told him he didn't know the actors of the Civic Repertory! Our valiant actors even climbed ladders and danced a Hornpipe in them.[18]

Peter and Wendy/Eva and Josephine, 1929. They loved each other on and off stage (photograph: Pinchot).

The lavish care and large budget (for them) spent on *Pan* did not go unnoticed by the critics. The play opened on November 26, 1928. A critic from the *Morning Telegraph* wrote:

Somehow, you may feel a sort of reluctance about seeing this play in other hands than those of Maude Adams, but this idea is dispelled shortly after the rise of the curtain on the first act when Miss Le Gallienne makes her entrance, and you leave the theatre crowing with *Peter Pan*.[19]

The reviewer felt:

Miss Le Gallienne, perhaps a little more hoydenish than boyish, brings to the Barrie character an elfin charm, an eerie wistfulness, an imaginative understanding and a graceful sprightliness. It is not the Peter Pan of Maude Adams — neither is it the Peter Pan of Marilyn Miller — it is one that Miss Le Gallienne has fashioned after her own ideas, and perhaps you will find, as we did, the Barrie humor a little differently conveyed by Miss Le Gallienne's interpretation.[20]

And he concluded:

It is doubtful if a more perfect or more tasteful production has ever been given *Peter Pan*. The cast is flawless with Egon Brecher as Captain Hook, Josephine Hutchinson as Wendy and John Eldredge as Smee.[21]

The *Herald Tribune* declared the production "Brilliant!" and found:

Through it all there was evident in the production intelligent appreciation, clear understanding and tender regard for the author's fancies, and Miss Gallienne [sic] shared with him the plaudits of the audience…. Josephine Hutchinson gave to Wendy just the right sense of budding motherliness the part demanded.[22]

The critic further felt:

Lithe and graceful in every move, whether walking, running, leaping or flying, Miss Le Gallienne was an alluring picture to which her attire

A rare photograph of Walter Beck as Captain Hook at the Civic Repertory Theatre. Beck shared the role with Egon Brecker the first season but the part was his exclusively from 1929 through 1933 (courtesy Stewart Stern).

lent not a little. If, perhaps, there was not altogether that whimsical, elfish element in her characterization it must be remembered that the labor and strain involved in directing such a production makes severe demands that even the most courageous spirit and physical strength must be affected.[23]

In the *New York Times*, there was this notice:

Nothing was left undone and everything was well done, from the stage settings to the wag of Nana's tail. If Eva Le Gallienne lacked something of the sweet, keen wistfulness which Maude Adams gave the part of the boy who would not grow up, she was a gallant, buoyant, clean-cut figure, and gave Peter plenty of élan and boyish grace. She even expressed something of the aloofness of Peter — the boy who would not be mothered to the ruin of his boyhood — which was not within the compass of Miss Adams herself.[24]

And this from *The American*:

Miss Le Gallienne was splendid in her part. No doubt about it. Throughout, though, persisted the thought of those listening and watching that here was a very emotional Peter Pan, rather than the whimsical "sweet" boy of the original Barrie story. Peter Pan seemed just a bit too filled with pep and vigor. An interesting figure though.[25]

Obviously the critic never read *Peter and Wendy*, for while Peter is many things, "sweet" and "whimsical" are not his characteristics — they are the qualities that Maude Adams brought to the play.

Other critics openly compared this new Peter with their memories of old. Some were disappointed with the liberties that they mistakenly believed the Civic Repertory took. Unknowingly, they were referring to the newly published edition of the play, which was different in many ways from the acting version. For instance, in the published format Liza is no longer the writer of the play and does not introduce it. The Lagoon Scene of Act Three was omitted in the Civic version as it was in Marilyn Miller's, but the published edition included it. One critic for the *Boston Tribune* aptly appraised the situation as he wrote, "Before long, we friends of Peter and lovers of his play will be disputing over the text as scholars do when a page of Shakespeare or a speech in Sophocles is in question."[26]

The most important critics were still the children and they loved this Peter as the previous generations loved him. Josephine recalled:

> Those children that came to the matinees with their parents were one thing, but the children she [Le G] "gave a performance for" came with only a teacher. They came from various schools, various convents, and they were in groups. I could see them [from the stage]. When it got to the fights and things, I was on the upper deck and I could be above the footlights so I could see all of them. The minute the fight started the boys jumped out of their seats, came forward, and tried to get over the orchestra to get into the fight. And the poor musicians had some problems. The teachers had to grab them and get them back in their seats. But it was all very exciting.
>
> At these particular parties, some big concern gave us candy and in our costumes we went out to the lobby and when the children went out we gave them the candy. And we just felt good about that. "Oh aren't we cute and oh so nice to be giving these children candy!" So this little boy came up to me and I gave him his candy and he looked at it and said, "Hell! Hard candy!" It really blew my ego.[27]

Le G was always concerned about the response of the children to Peter's plea to save Tinker Bell. What if they didn't clap? She wrote:

> I half expected some child to shout "No!" to the famous question, but for years none of them ever did. Then — it was at a matinee in Boston, of all places — from the front row to my left it came. "Do you believe in fairies?"—"No!" I don't think anyone heard it but me — the shouts of "Yes!" were too loud and the clapping too vigorous; I stole a quick look at the child — a little girl of about eight, I judged — before carrying on with my rescue of Tinker Bell, which was successfully accomplished. But I did not forget that little girl! Now and then I went down to the footlights, stood directly above her seat and stared at her — stared right into her eyes, and gravely shook my head.
>
> Towards the end of the play I went to give her a farewell look, but her seat was empty. Then I saw that she was hiding underneath it. Peter's reproachful gaze had been too much for her![28]

During the next four seasons, the Civic Repertory's *Pan* played for 129 performances, and as in London, it became a Christmas holiday tradition for many theatre lovers in New York City. One performance was cancelled in December 1932 when after rehearsing all day for their new production of *Alice in Wonderland*, an exhausted staff and director found there was not enough time to change the elaborate sets. Eva apologized to the audience and asked them if they wouldn't mind seeing a sneak preview of their newest play. The audience responded positively and thoroughly enjoyed the substitution, which, incidentally, became the Civic's biggest money-maker.

On November 7, 1932, the *World Telegram* reviewed *Peter Pan* with an accustomed note, not knowing that this would be the last season for the Civic Repertory Theatre:

Eva Le Gallienne played many roles at the Civic Rep, including Hedda Gabler.

Miss Le Gallienne's *Peter Pan* is just about what he was, yesteryear. He is the same lovely, wistful elf that he's always been and flies about with grace. But this time, dear children, Peter flies high. Almost as high as the second balcony, to be sure, and that should be reason enough for a revisit to the play.... Heaven, Eva Le Gallienne and the Civic Repertory be praised, Sir James Barrie's whimsical tale will never grow old.[29]

In 1933, the Civic Repertory Theatre came to an end. The year before, Le G barely escaped with her life from an accidental explosion in her Connecticut home, but her hands were horribly burned. After a brief interlude she resumed her career and continued trying to find backers to help subsidize her theatre. But the Great Depression was taking its toll and they were difficult to find. A plea to Eleanor Roosevelt for government assistance looked as if it would have promising results, but the president had different ideas regarding quality and Le G wouldn't budge. She gave up her dream. The Fourteenth Street Theatre was rented out while a smaller version of her troupe toured with five plays, including *Alice in Wonderland*, *Romeo and Juliet*, and three Ibsen plays.

Coinciding with the demise of the Civic Repertory was the breakup of Le G and Josephine, who had fallen in love near the end of their first season together, despite that the fact that Josephine was married. In addition to issues such as infidelity, Josephine later confessed that she wanted her independence and had she stayed on with Le G she might have ended up very much in a lifetime role of Wendy to Le G's Pan. She went to Hollywood, where she became a respected screen actress in such films as *Oil for the Lamps of China*, *The Story of Louis Pasteur*, *Son of Frankenstein*, and others, working right into the 1980s.

For this writer, she is part of a Christmas tradition each year at home where we reunite with the Walton's Christmas story, *The Homecoming*, a 1971 teleplay in which she plays one of the Baldwin sisters, keepers of their bootlegger father's "recipe."

Le G, on the other hand, rarely allowed herself to "go commercial." She did make three screen appearances: first in 1955, in *Prince of Players* (as Gertrude in a scene from *Hamlet*), and then Shaw's *The Devil's Discipline* in 1959, and *Resurrection* in 1980, for which she was nominated for an Academy Award for best supporting actress. Every few years she was involved in some noble cause for bringing theatre to the masses. Unfortunately, much of her time on these idealistic ventures was at the expense of popularity. In 1942, Le G

Josephine Hutchinson played Alice and Wendy during the same 1932–1933 season. *Alice in Wonderland* was the Civic's most successful (financially) play and soon moved "uptown." She passed away on June 4, 1998 (photograph: Maurice Goldberg).

appeared in the highly successful *Uncle Harry* opposite Joseph Schildkraut, who had starred with her in the original *Liliom*.

In 1957 Le G played opposite Irene Worth in *Mary Stuart*, staged by Tyrone Guthrie. Eighteen years later she scored great personal success with the hit revival of *The Royal Family*. She almost lost the part, as the producers felt no one would remember her. Of course, her performance was brilliant and she proved them wrong, winning a Tony nomination and subsequently an Emmy Award when it was filmed for television. She returned to Broadway again in 1981 for *To Grandmother's House We Go* and directed and acted (as the White Queen) her third Broadway edition of *Alice in Wonderland*. Both were poorly received, although the latter was filmed and, along with *The Royal Family*, is available on DVD. Even as she appeared as a guest on the television series *St. Elsewhere*, Le G complained to Josephine, still a close friend, that "there's just not enough work." Somehow, between her many theatre projects, Le G was able to write a second autobiography, *With a Quiet Heart*, which was anything but that, revealing herself to be as feisty at "plus twenty" (her initial title) as she was two decades earlier in *At 33*. She also wrote a charming children's book, *Flossie and Bossie*, as well as a biography of Eleanor Duse, and translated many plays.

One of the great artists of the 20th century, Le G died in her Connecticut home on June 3, 1991. Despite her many roles and 60-odd years that had passed since she flew across the stage of the Fourteenth Street Theatre, a generation of children remembered her with fondness as Peter Pan.

Peter Pan remained one of Le G's favorite roles (photograph: Pinchot, 1929). *Bottom:* **The pose worked for Eva Le Gallienne, so why not for dancer Ruth Page as well in 1927?**

Eva Le Gallienne gazing in her Westport home, which she purchased in 1927.

She wrote many years later:

I once made a nostalgic visit to the old manor-house in Chiddingfold, a small village in Surrey. My father had discovered it on one of his frequent bicycle tours and rashly decided to take it. We lived there until I was nearly three and the money gave out — as it had a way of doing sooner or later! Our friends, the William Favershams, took it over from us and mother and I subsequently spent many happy summers there, so it continued to be an important part of my childhood. As I walked across the village green towards the stable gate, I heard a boy's voice declaim "Proud and insolent youth, prepare to meet thy doom!" Hearing my cue I was through the gate in a flash, crying out in Peter's voice, "Dark and sinister man, have at thee!"

"The dark and sinister man"—a small boy of about ten, dressed in a Captain Hook outfit of scarlet flannel, wearing a black cocked-hat with a skull and crossbones painted on it, his round, baby faced adorned with a beard and moustache of burned cork—gazed open-mouthed at this "lady of uncertain age" invading his stable yard.

"You ... you know the words?" he stuttered.

"Yes—I know the words."

"But those are *Peter's* words," he said severely.

"I know," I humbly answered. Then I went on to ask his permission to look over the old garden—his parents were away for the day it seemed.

A great lady of the theatre, Miss Le G, in 1983 (Photofest).

Every now and then as I wandered through the well-remembered paths, stroked the old sun dial, stood under the Monkey-puzzle tree, or peered under the yew hedges where the Faversham boys and I used to hide, I caught sight of a flash of scarlet in the distance. The "dark and sinister man" was keeping an eye on me. He was evidently puzzled. How *could* that lady say Peter's words and *sound* like Peter, too?

I naturally didn't tell him I had been Peter. He would never have believed it. How could he? There are times when I find it hard to believe too![30]

11

Jean Arthur: A Touch of Bernstein

Real maturity comes only when you have learned to hang on to your youth.
If you can hang on to your individuality, hold tight to your freedom, and
not get squiggled out as you grow older, then and only then are you mature.
Years have nothing to do with it.

— Jean Arthur, 1950[1]

For movie fans the name Jean Arthur immediately evokes a bubbly yet sharp sophisticate. Her distinct crackly voice and infectious laugh, combined with a stunningly well-groomed appearance, personified the emerging confidence of the American woman in the work force of the 1930s. Films such as *Mr. Deeds Goes to Town, Mr. Smith Goes to Washington, You Can't Take It with You, The Devil and Miss Jones,* and *The More the Merrier,* for which she was nominated for an Oscar, made her one of the most familiar faces on the silver screen in the 1930s and 1940s. Yet, next to Garbo, Jean Arthur was probably the most reclusive star in Hollywood. She honestly believed that audiences were more interested in her movies than her life. "How can anyone in an interview, really understand your thoughts, your ideas, when even people who know each other often can't really tell?"[2] she asked a reporter in 1950.

Jean Arthur was born Gladys Georgianna Greene in Plattsburg, New York, on October 17, 1900. Her family moved to Manhattan, where she attended George Washington High School and worked as a model. Inevitably, she signed a contract for films and moved to California, appearing in many two-reel silent film comedies. But Jean was determined to become a good actress, so she returned to New York to work on the stage. Although most of the plays she appeared in had very short runs, the experience strengthened her skills and she signed with Columbia Pictures, where she made many of her classic films.

When the relatively reticent Jean read about Peter Lawrence's plan to produce *Peter Pan* on Broadway, she called him: "Hello, this is Jean Arthur — you want to speak to me?"[3] She had been looking for a show to take to Broadway and had a particular affinity for *Peter Pan.* In fact, Jean and her good friend, Mary Martin, often discussed their mutual desires to play Peter, keeping track of whose turn it was to dress as the character at Hollywood masquerade parties. As far back as the late 1920s Jean had dressed as Pan at costume parties and in the 1930s she commissioned a series of portraits taken of her in a Pan outfit.

Opposite, top: A 1930s portrait of Jean Arthur as Peter Pan, a role she had coveted for many years before finally playing the part on Broadway in 1950. *Bottom:* Jean Arthur and James Stewart in a scene from the 1938 film, *You Can't Take It with You.* Arthur was director Frank Capra's favorite leading lady and, for most critics, the best "screwball comedy" actress in films.

That Lawrence opted to star Jean Arthur in his production is interesting, for although a great talent, she was also a quiet, moody woman who was sometimes unreliable when she let her emotions take over. In fact, she left the cast of *Born Yesterday* after a much-publicized feud with writer/director Garson Kanin, who had written the part of Billie Dawn specifically for the actress. Judy Holliday replaced Jean and in the process not only aided the play in becoming a huge hit, but also won an Oscar for best actress in the film adaptation.

According to John Oller's biography, *Jean Arthur: The Actress Nobody Knew*, Lawrence had originally planned on *Peter Pan* as a vehicle for Joan Fontaine. When that casting coup collapsed, he desperately toyed

Left: Margaret Sullivan as Peter very early in her career before her work in films (courtesy Stewart Stern). *Right:* Jean Arthur dressed as Peter Pan at a costume party with her good friend, Mary Martin, long before they ever thought they would both eventually play the part. This photograph is probably from the early forties while Mary was working in Hollywood.

with using such varied choices as Margaret Sullivan, comedian Beatrice Lillie (!), and musical comedy star Mary Martin (who let it be known that she was dying to do it). However, with *South Pacific* a new smash hit, there was no way that Rodgers and Hammerstein would allow Martin to be free for such a lark. Margaret Sullivan would have been an excellent choice; the beloved film actress had recently re-established her reputation on the stage in the 1943 hit *The Voice of the Turtle*, her sentimental yet piquant charm similar to that of Maude Adams. Yet, surprisingly, it was dancer Vera Zorina who was signed for the part with husband Goddard Lieberson, head of Columbia Records, promising financial backing. Fortunately, Zorina's difficult temperament quickly dissolved the union, although Columbia Records eventually recorded the original Broadway cast album of the play. In fact, two albums were recorded, one for adults and another for children. Time was running out on Lawrence's option of the play when Jean let it be known she wanted to play Peter.

> I had to ask myself, "can I play a little boy — or is it too late?" I hired a theater, got into costume and got on the stage and tried out a few lines for some people whose judgment I respect. It felt wonderful.... I was at home on the stage for the first time in my life. Peter is my maturity.[4]

Once hired, Jean was instrumental in aiding Lawrence in acquiring financial backing to get the play on Broadway, including investing in the show herself.

Initially, Peter Lawrence wanted *Peter Pan* to be a musical. He called upon his friend, Leonard Bernstein, to write the score. Bernstein was quick to accept. "First time in five years someone hasn't called me to say he has a wonderful show for me to do — all about subways, skyscrapers, and New York's crowds," he said, referring no doubt to his success with the musical comedy *On the Town.* "I'm very flattered to be thought of for this kind of play."[5]

Ironically, Bernstein's lasting contribution to the American stage is best exemplified by three musicals that indeed utilize New York City as an important setting. *Wonderful Town*, a 1953 musical version of *My Sister Eileen*, with lyrics by Betty Comden and Adolph Green, is a glorious glimpse of Manhattan's Greenwich Village scene in the 1930s. Its older cousin, *On the Town*, created with the same lyricists, was a bubbly salute to the virtues of the Big Apple. His third work about life in New York was an extreme departure from the other two. *West Side Story* was a landmark musical depicting the rivalry of two street gangs and its effect on the lives of two young lovers. Bernstein's

Beatrice Lillie as Peter Pan? This is a 1935 photograph of the incomparable funny lady, Lady Lillie.

music, Stephen Sondheim's lyrics, and a compelling script by Arthur Laurents were just as exciting in their 2009 revival as they were in 1957 when the show opened.

One of Bernstein's least successful musicals is also now recognized as one of his most brilliant works — *Candide*. Transforming the satirical Voltaire novel into a musical was described by him as "three years of agony, trying to make an impossible situation possible." Although it lasted for only 73 performances initially, it was totally revised 17 years later by Harold Prince and played Broadway for 740 performances.

Peter Lawrence also asked Bernstein's friend and colleague, Jerome Robbins, to direct his production. On December 25, 1949, an announcement was made that Jean Arthur would star in *Peter Pan*, "a fantasy with music"[6] and not a full-blown musical.

A lot had transpired since Lawrence's initial plans to make a musical of the play. Jean was at first attracted to the idea of appearing in a musical treatment and Bernstein had already written several new songs and revised a few of his other tunes that were taken out of past shows. One in particular, "Dream with Me," which he penned with Comden and

A rehearsal for *On the Town* in 1944 with Leonard Bernstein at the piano, choreographer Jerome Robbins to his left, and writers Betty Comden and Adolph Green in the foreground. Each would become a major player on the Broadway scene and eventually contribute to American versions of *Peter Pan* (Photofest).

Green, is a beautiful ballad that speaks of unrequited love that could be shared between two people worlds or oceans apart. The song was written for *On the Town*, but could easily be sung by Peter to Wendy at the end of the play. There was just one problem: Jean Arthur was no singer!

Jean was no dummy either; to appear in a musical where the star would not be singing would have been theatrical suicide. It was decided that *Peter Pan* would not be a musical after all, but it would retain some of Leonard Bernstein's songs and suites. Therefore, Jerome Robbins's specialized skills were no longer necessary and Jean asked for English director John Burrell to be given the task of staging the production. Choreographer Wendy Toye was assigned as his associate director. Another song omitted from the score was "Hallapalooza," a reworked tune dropped from another play. The six songs that remained were "Who Am I?," "My House," and "Peter, Peter," all sung by Wendy; "Never Land," sung by two mermaids; and two songs for Hook and his pirates, "Pirate Song," and "Plank Round."

The part of Wendy was given to Marcia Henderson, a young ingénue from Massachusetts who was advised at the age of 15 by Sinclair Lewis to seek a career on the stage. Marcia followed his advice and enrolled in the American Academy of Dramatic Arts, where she graduated in 1949. There were several seasons of summer stock during her formal education, but *Peter Pan* marked her New York debut. Marcia later appeared in a few films, including *All I Desire* and *The Glass Web*.

Left: Jean cropped off her hair for the 1950 Broadway production of *Peter Pan.* *Right:* A stunning portrait of Jean Arthur from the late thirties. Ironically, the actress had a great inferiority complex, which included her looks (photograph: A.L. Schafer). *Bottom:* Marcia Henderson (Wendy) learns her songs from Leonard Bernstein (Photofest).

The most interesting piece of casting was veteran Boris Karloff as Captain Hook. Karloff, equally comfortable on stage and screen, left his native England, where he was educated for the British diplomatic service, and spent 20 years with various acting companies in the United States and Canada. He appeared in several silent films but it was not until *Frankenstein* in 1931 that audiences became aware of the actor. Other horror films followed, including *The Mummy, The Black Cat,* and *The Bride of Frankenstein* in 1935 with Elsa Lanchester, who would play Peter in 1936. On stage, Karloff enjoyed the delicious irony of playing Cousin Jonathan, a character in *Arsenic and Old Lace* who has his face altered to resemble Boris Karloff.

Mrs. Darling was played by Peg Hillias and Joe E. Marks

A conference with (from left) choreographer Wendy Toye, director John Burrell, producer Peter Lawrence, Boris Karloff, and Leonard Bernstein.

played Smee. Marks, an excellent character actor, previously appeared in *The Man Who Came to Dinner* with Alexander Woolcott and in the musical *Bloomer Girl.*

Norman Shelly, who was cast as Nana and the crocodile, shared the amusing details of his audition:

> I knew the producer, I knew the stage manager. I did not know the director, so I came to the audition and they gave me a script to read. The description was kind of charming. The stage manager came out, Mortimer Halpern, who is now considered the dean of stage managers, and I said, "Where's the dialogue?" And he said, "No dialogue."
>
> I kept reading ... "dog comes in with a child on his back, puts him in bed, tucks him in, comes out..." Again I said, "Where's the song? Any songs?"
>
> "No songs."
>
> So then they asked me to come in, they wanted to know if I was in good shape and physical condition. I said yes.
>
> "Do you think you could play the dog?"
>
> "Yes."
>
> Then they said, "Can you bark?"
>
> "I don't know, but I'll try." I barked and that was it.... I did not audition for the crocodile.[7]

During the opening-night curtain Jean received thunderous applause for her performance.

> And all the time, Miss Arthur, her hands locked behind her back, looking very much like the urchin who's just been trapped with a handful of cookies by the corner merchant, stood there bewildered, overwhelmed and uncomfortable.
>
> Finally, she got down on her knees and took off Nana's head so that Norman Shelly ... could share in the tumult too.[8]

Jean explained:

> I just didn't know how to act, I didn't know what to do."[9]

Joe E. Marks as Smee with Boris Karloff as Hook in *Peter Pan*, 1950. Marks would reprise his role four years later in the musical version (Photofest).

Shelly was grateful for her acknowledgement, but he was satisfied to remain in his costume during the future curtain calls. He did not want the illusion of the show to be broken for the children. Jean would also adopt the same practice, leaving the theatre still dressed as Peter.

Peter Pan was one of the most eagerly awaited entries of the 1949-50 Broadway season. Except for a charity benefit of six performances in 1946, it had been almost 17 years since Broadway offered Peter's flight to Never Never Land, and while Le G's Peter was a critical and commercial success, the budget allocated for this Broadway venture, $110,000, promised a sumptuous production. There are many who consider it to be the best *Peter Pan* ever done on Broadway, with Jean's performance as a prime factor. Her passion for the role, the fencing instructions and work with ballet masters Edward Caton and Margaret Crasque on how to move like a boy, paid off. Oddly, Jean's bio in the program must be one of the shortest ever written for a star of her stature:

> Miss Arthur is one of the best-known actresses on the American screen. Her present contract with Paramount Studios permits her to do plays and pictures independently of this studio. Her favorite picture of all time is *Mr. Smith Goes to Washington*. She feels the same way about *Peter Pan*, the play.[10]

The play opened on April 24, 1950. John Chapman of the *Daily News* wrote:

> To a time and town which badly needed it, J.M. Barrie's *Peter Pan* has brought the sweet, sentimental and complete enchantment of Never Never Land. This whimsical comedy about the only boy who ever licked the world — he licks it by simply refusing to grow up — has been given a lovely production at the Imperial Theatre, and last evening it cast its unworldly spell over one of the most worldly of groups, the regular first nighters.
>
> I'm an old Maude Adams man — or was until last night, now I'm an old Jean Arthur man and I felt much younger than I did three hours ago. Miss Arthur's *Peter Pan* is in all ways splendid — boyish and cocky, yet one to tug at the heartstrings. And Boris Karloff's dual roles of Mr. Darling and Captain Hook are a triumph of comedy — a performance of high style and sly humor.[11]

Chapman went on to observe:

> But it may come as a surprise to many modern theatergoers, as it does to me, that *Peter Pan* is still a thoroughly disarming stage entertainment, even for adults who imagine they have no time for anything except important things. Since it was a genuinely imaginative creation when it was new — as genuine in its way as *Alice in Wonderland* — it is still fresh and enchanting today.[12]

From *Theatre Arts*:

> As Peter, Jean Arthur is thoroughly winning. She is funny, heroic, beguiling, and at times pathetic, taking the different hurdle of transvestitism in her delicate stride. Her Peter is unconventional in that he is a real boy, not just an attractive woman with a feather in her cap. Boris Karloff alternates between quiet malice and unbridled savagery in the dual role of Mr. Darling and Captain Hook. His piracy should satiate the blood-lust of even the most imaginative child. As Wendy, Marcia Henderson is attractive but mechanical, and the little boys overdo everything in a manner traditional to child actors. Norman Shelly doubles as the crocodile and Nana, a tremendously beguiling St. Bernard dog; both performances seem authentic.
>
> Leonard Bernstein has composed good incidental music and a few pleasant songs which are not sung particularly well and do not stand out.[13]

Like his fellow critics, the *Herald Tribune*'s Howard Barnes raved about Jean Arthur:

> It is a bravura performance, but that is exactly what the Barrie script called for. That she manages to give the piece a great deal of feelings as well as fairy tale high jinks is the greatest index to the quality of this first revival of *Peter Pan* in some twenty-two years.... Karloff, in the doubly bombastic role of Mr. Darling ... and the evil Captain Hook ... is captivating. And Marcia Henderson, Peg Hillias and Joe E. Marks add to the excitement and make-believe.[14]

Barnes also felt that

> Leonard Bernstein has written an excellent musical accompaniment for the action. It heightens the fantastical mood of the drama at every point and contributes such enchanting songs as "Who Am I," "My House," and "The Plank."[15]

Jean Arthur (Peter) watches Marcia Henderson (Wendy) and the Lost Boys in the 1950 production of *Peter Pan* (Photofest).

New York Times critic Brooks Atkinson echoed Barnes, stating, "Leonard Bernstein, a modern composer, is doubtless more passionately involved in other thoughts and problems. But he has enthusiastically written songs and music for 'Peter Pan' in an affectionate and suitably old-fashioned style, the orchestrations by Hershy Kay being more modern than the themes."[16] Not a bad review for a composer who wrote much of the score on train journeys between other professional engagements.

In 2005, Daniel Felsenberg reevaluated the score for the CD liner notes of the first issue of Bernstein's complete score.

> In the songs Bernstein provided we can hear not only that composer of the frisky *On the Town* at his exercise, but the man who, in years to come, would change the face of the Broadway show as it was known. The lovely, lilting "Who Am I" suggest the composer who would come to write "A Little Bit in Love" in his next show *Wonderful Town*, and establishes well the searching, beyond-her-years intelligent character of Wendy, the show's other (non-eponymous) lead. Both the "Pirate's Song" and "Plank Round" are scurrilous, bouncy numbers, ideally suited to the scurvy lot on Barrie's fictional island, as is the "Captain Hook Soliloquy" whose cantankerous, uppity jazz-like sound clearly foreshadows the Sharks and the Jets to come. "Build My House" is a sweet tune, an innocent hortatory number Wendy sings to the Lost Boys as she lands in Neverland, which, in its scope and build, forecasts the composer of "Make Our Garden Grow" from Bernstein's other mostly-forgotten show *Candide*. "Dream With Me" shows the composer at his Broadway best, with smooth, fluent harmonies, and a gorgeous, arching melody, setting spare, potent lyrics. "Peter Peter," in its ribald bounciness, is in the same space as the composer's hilarious masterwork "What's the Use," also from *Candide*.[17]

Not every critic was entirely won over by Jean's portrayal of Peter or Bernstein's music. Richard Watts, Jr., of the *New York Post* wrote:

As a production, it has considerable charm and beauty. Mr. Bernstein's music doesn't seem to me to have much to it.... In the title role, Jean Arthur, looking and sounding pleasantly like Mary Martin, is boyish and engaging, even though she hardly makes the part as impressive as theatrical legend makes it out to be.... But the most charming performance is contributed by young Marcia Henderson, who is fresh and delightful as Wendy. She and the manipulators of the wires for the flying children are the triumphs of *Peter Pan*.[18]

Eva Le Gallienne attended one of the performances but did not share Watts's enthusiasm for Henderson nor was she impressed with Burrell's direction, which she thought was too stiff. She was, however, very pleased with Jean Arthur in the title role and told her so after the performance when she also made a few suggestions to Jean about loosening up and adding a bit more of the magical Pan to her successfully boyish Peter. Le G later lamented in her diary that she had not been asked to direct the new production, which also had the flying effects supervised by Kirby's Flying Ballet specialist, Peter Foy. A few years later, after his success with the Mary Martin production of *Peter Pan*, Foy would corner the market on most American productions of the play with his "Flying by Foy" trademark.

Perhaps the best review for *Peter Pan*, and indeed, specifically for Jean Arthur, we must hear again from Brooks Atkinson, who exclaimed that Arthur was perfect as Peter.

> To a pleasant personality she has added the pleasantest kind of acting. When you think of how arch and maudlin the part might be in less scrupulous hands, you can appreciate the ease and simplicity of her performance. She is smiling without being coy and friendly without being patronizing. If there seems to be no acting at all in her performance it is because she is acting it superbly and has mastered the spirit and technique of the theater's most wining fairy story.[19]

Finally, what did the children think? Robert Garland of the *Journal American* wrote:

> They tell me I saw Maude Adams as Peter Pan. Could be, although I remember nothing of it. I do remember Marilyn

A record advertisement for the original cast album of *Peter Pan* in 1950. There was another version recorded that same year just for children, minus the songs.

Mermaids Stephanie Augustine and Eleanor Winter in *Peter Pan*. After this 1950 production, the mermaid scene would be cut from other Broadway productions.

Miller, who was sadly out of element. And Eva Le Gallienne, who was Eva Le Gallienne on or off the ground. Beyond a doubt, Jean Arthur's is the biggest of the three, the most mature.... But happily in my vicinity, Dorothy Kilgallen's young son, Dickie, found last night's doings "keen." If a direct, desirable quotation for "Peter Pan" is needed, Richard Kollmar Jr. "loved it." He surely, knows more about such things than I do.[20]

During the run, the play moved to the St. James Theatre with Miss Jackson Perkins taking over the role of Mrs. Darling. The play was so well received that an extra matinee performance had to be added weekly for school children off for the summer, making this "modern" version the longest run yet for "The Boy Who Wouldn't Grow Old," at 320 performances. Inexplicably, this high point in Arthur's career was soon stained with her artistic temperament and the stubbornness of all concerned.

Jean Arthur and Marcia Henderson in *Peter Pan* at the Imperial Theatre in 1950.

According to Norman Shelly, Jean Arthur was painfully shy and particularly preoccupied near the end of the run. On August 11, late Friday afternoon in the theatre, she received a telephone call before curtain time and abruptly left the theatre. He remembered that her understudy, Anne Jackson, had to cover the role that evening, although by this time Jackson was no longer in the company and it was Barbara Baxley who actually went on that night, literally learning to fence and fly a few hours before the evening's performance and rehearsing the final scene for the first time during intermission. John Oller reported the chaos:

> "If you don't hit those marks you can break a rib," Foy cautioned. "As long as you put it that way, Peter, I'll hit the marks," she responded. Just before going on, she reminded stage manager Halpern that she had never rehearsed the climactic scene. "We'll learn it at intermission," he said, and she did.[21]

Unbeknownst to Shelly and most of the cast, Jean had requested a four-week vacation just a few days earlier but the request was denied by producer Lawrence, reasoning that the play had only been running for four months. But push came to shove with Lawrence looking for a replacement in case Arthur actually went AWOL. Oddly, his choice was Shirley Temple, who flew in from the west coast with her mother to meet with the producer. Lawrence tactfully told Jean that he had someone who could take her place, hoping that it would change her mind. No one likes involuntarily handing over a leading role to another performer, and Jean was no exception. Shirley Temple recounted about the night she went to see the show, noting that Jean's

> eyes kept sweeping the audience from the stage in a purposeful manner.... My phone was jangling as I reentered the hotel room.
> "Don't take Peter Pan away from me, please!" cried the voice, without introduction.
> "Stop. Who is this?" I interjected, guessing full well the identity.
> "You know who I am," the voice cried. "I'm Jean Arthur. I'm Peter Pan."
> Then she hung up.[22]

The situation became more complicated when Jean missed a performance, setting the legal mechanism of show business in motion. Lawrence contacted Actors' Equity to end Jean's contract if she was indeed going to stay out for a month and he also lined up Betty Field to take over the role of Peter. However, a compromise was met with Jean that allowed her one week's vacation.

In retrospect, understudy Barbara Baxley remembered Jean as not only tired but also genuinely physically sick. Norman Shelly recalled to author Oller that Jean's ex-husband, producer Frank Ross, was "trying to take her for a lot of dough,"[23] for which the author gives evidence in that Ross needed the money for a $1.8 million lawsuit for not finishing his ambitious film, *The Robe*, on time. He also provides one more story where a young actress rejected Arthur's advances, thereby setting the stage for disaster. In any case, Jean returned to the play and finished the run, which ended on January 27, 1951.

The tour moved out with most of the original cast (Jennifer Bunker replaced Henderson and two actors took over for Shelly), but Jean left the tour prematurely when called back to Paramount for her starring role in *Shane*. Joan McCracken was called in to replace her but it was apparent that it was Jean's box-office appeal that turned this *Pan* into a hit. While McCracken was certainly a reasonable choice in terms of talent — a saucy little comedian and dancer, who, incidentally, was later married to Bob Fosse — she did not possess the necessary box office appeal. Famous for her small role in the stage version of *Oklahoma!* as the girl who falls during the "Many a New Day" number, she brightened up the stage in several Broadway shows in supporting roles, including *Bloomer Girl*, *Me and Juliet*, and *Billion Dollar Baby*, which brought her to the attention of M.G.M. In fact, the Hollywood studio showcased her in Comden and Green's 1947 screen adaptation of *Good News*. Her dance number with Ray

Joan McCracken as Peter in the 1951 tour (courtesy Roy Busby).

MacDonald, "Pass That Peace Pipe," was one of the film's highlights as well as serving as one of the highpoints for *That's Entertainment— Part III* over 40 years later.

Another touring company was formed, this time with Veronica Lake and Boris Karloff, who was later replaced by Lawrence Tibbett. The former Paramount leading lady with the peek-a-boo bangs had fallen on hard times since her studio exit in 1948. While she caused quite a sensation in her early films for the studio, it was "the look" more than anything else that fascinated her audiences. So it came as something of a surprise that she was selected to tour in *Peter Pan*, although her co-star Lawrence Tibbett certainly made more sense. Yet her personal reviews were quite generous from the various critics of the cities she toured. "Veronica Lake captivated first-nighters. So did Lawrence Tibbett,"[24] boasted the *Baltimore Sun*. *Variety* concurred, stating that Veronica gave "a boyish quality and engaging matter-of-fact reading to the whimsical lead character that projects to the entire audience, young and old."[25]

"Everything about this 'Peter Pan' is good," agreed the *Pittsburgh Post-Gazette*. "Veronica Lake is more than a pleasant surprise. She has an affection for the part that comes through on the stage. Lawrence Tibbett's Captain Hook has an expansive humor, and his baritone voice is well worth listening to."[26] The production, directed by Frank Corsaro but based on John Burrell's staging, was moderately successful.

English Pan historian, Roger Lancelyn Green, was not able to see the Jean Arthur production but he vocalized his displeasure of the musical changes. He wrote in *Fifty Years of Peter Pan*:

> By this time the craze for "musicals" had fallen like a blight upon the American stage, and therefore *Peter Pan* must be shorn of Crook's music, Leonard Bernstein must write a new score and interpolate five songs, while a ballet sequence must be devised for the Redskins, and the pirates become a chorus.[27]

Wendy Toye wrote him a most reassuring letter:

> I truly don't think you could have been appalled with the New York production; it was done with great, great respect and love. For my part, I love the play so and am such an admirer of Barrie, that if anyone was going to be shocked by it, then it would have been me. I must say I have been shocked sometimes going to London productions — there seemed little enough love or money spent on it.
>
> We hardly altered a word of the script, and the music came in exactly the same places as always — the Indian ballet is always in, and I did the whole of the fight very musically, although extremely realistically: the music had great youth and joy about it. There were two extra songs for Wendy, and that's a matter of opinion if it was an improvement or not. All I can say is that America loved it — and it introduced Barrie's *Peter* before Disney's arrived on the scene.[28]

The respect for the original script was indeed displayed in this production. In fact, no new script was needed as the director and cast hand-wrote the musical additions in Barrie's script.

Nothing was heard of again of a production of the play with the Bernstein score until 2006 when the King's Head, London's first "pub theatre," took a chance. The small theatre, while garnering such review headlines as "Little Room to Grow Up or Sideways" and "Neverland Never Looked So Cramped," produced a production where the staging was better received than Leonard Bernstein's score. Paul Taylor of *The Independent* proclaimed, "Bernstein score takes flight at last":

> Though Peter Pan and the Darling children create the illusion of flight merely by standing on hydraulically rising pedestals and stretching out their arms, Stephanie Sinclaire's delightful

production — of her own adaptation synthesized from JM Barrie's various versions of his self-invented myth — is uplifting in other ways....

Hook — brilliantly played with a flamboyant, nervous energy and drolly self-guying swagger by the hilarious Peter Land (who doubles as the neurotically sly and cowardly Mr. Darling) — enjoins his comrades to "Eat blood!/Drink blood! ... in the cod blood-curdling "Pirate Song," while in his furious mock-operatic solo, he bewails the fact that, though he'd always fancied making a big, showy

Veronica Lake and Peggy O'Hara in second touring company of *Peter Pan* in 1951 (courtesy Roy Busby).

dying speech, now that he's actually confronting death, there's just no time for it. With shells for bosom-covers, the delicious mermaids sing solipsistically of the lazy, hazy sea and sand delights.[29]

Wrote Dominic Cavendish for the *Daily Telegraph*:

We've had to wait until now to be treated to a "fully staged theatrical production," featuring a total of nine [Bernstein] songs. But, when you're talking about a show at the tiny King's Head theatre in Islington, the phrase "fully staged" needs to be taken with a pinch of salt.

This is a space that's barely big enough to swing a cat in, let alone a crocodile. Not that this has deterred director Stephanie Sinclaire from cramming more than 20 actors on to the stage.

Mildly ingenious as it is that Pan (perky Katherine Kastin) and the little Darlings are able to rise a few feet up off the ground on pedestals operated from behind the backcloth, or that the lagoon is represented by a gently flapped bit of blue sheeting, or that Hook's nemesis is evoked with a few sharp tick-tocks on a wooden xylophone, this can hardly be the staging that Bernstein had in mind.[30]

Critic Fiona Mountford of the *Evening Standard* wrote:

Apart from the thrill of seeing this Islington venue become a producing house once more, the major draw is the chance to witness the stage premiere of Leonard Bernstein's nine songs and full score, which didn't all make it to Broadway in 1950. Unfortunately, after this hearing, it's easy to see why no one has bothered to exhume them in the intervening 56 years.[31]

However, Paul Taylor wrote:

The tunes are lovely; the wit (Bernstein was his own lyricist) is deft and mischievous; and the new arrangements written by Mike Dixon, which orchestrate the music for piano, cello, clarinet and flute, combine breadth and crisp clarity, managing to project everything from dreamy sensuality to the tongue-in-cheek attack of Tiger Lily's Indian Dance with Braves.[32]

"Dream with Me" was cited by Taylor as "a dramatic fudge that pretends that, in dreams, the two of them [Peter and Wendy] will be able to enjoy the kiss never taken, the love never acted upon. Listening to this false consolation, I was reminded how, in the celebrated Trevor Nunn/John Caird version of the myth, Barrie was himself a character who pointed out, at the end, that Peter had 'ecstasies innumerable that other children can never know; but he was looking through the window at the one joy from which he must be forever barred.'"[33]

One reviewer, Robert Shore of *Time Out London*, not only captured the spirit of Sinclaire's production in his critique but also expressed the state of affairs of *Peter Pan* in Great Britain.

If you're looking for a conventional family panto to seduce, amuse and amaze this Christmas, avoid the King's Head: this "Peter Pan" contains few special effects (though a fair amount of dry ice) and little in the way of audience participation (clapping to revive an expiring Tinkerbell). If, on the other hand, it's a high-culture version of traditional seasonal entertainment you're after, director Stephanie Sinclaire's adaptation of JM Barrie's children classic, featuring a rarely performed score by Leonard Bernstein may just prove the ticket.... Katherine Kastin's Peter has impressive, almost alarming, emotional depth. This is a "Pan" that doesn't seek to conceal the darkness at the heart of Barrie's tale.[34]

Katherine Kastin as Peter with Talia Mehmet as Tinkerbell in a King's Head Theatre production in London, 2006 (photograph: Alastair Muir, courtesy Alastair Muir).

A few years ago, when this writer expressed his desire to direct *Peter Pan* at the high school where he was teaching, complete with its darker implications, his administrator laughingly commented, "The next thing you're going to tell me is that Peter Pan kills!" "As a matter fact," I started.... Instead I was "allowed" to direct *The Wizard of Oz*.

Upon leaving *Peter Pan*, Jean Arthur gave one of the finest performances of her screen career as the wife of Van Heflin in *Shane*, an adult western in which Alan Ladd, Jack Palance, and little Brandon De Wilde rounded out the excellent cast. Oddly, not only was it Jean's last film, it was also her last major work. Despite earlier psychoanalysis with famed Dr. Erich Fromm, to whom she remarked in 1972 — "I guess I became an actress because I didn't want to be myself"[35] — Jean continued to be her own worst enemy. In 1954, she again withdrew from a play, the highly anticipated *Saint Joan* by George Bernard Shaw during the tour and just prior to its New York opening. Like Peter Pan, it was a role she had coveted for but this time there was no film role waiting. She retired to her home, "Driftwood," on the beautifully scenic Monterey Bay, where she became close friends with her neighbor,

Jean Arthur as Peter Pan, 1950, her favorite stage role.

Ellen Mastroianni. While she was not tempted to return to film, she finally allowed herself to revisit Shaw's *Saint Joan* in a staged reading at the University of California at Berkeley. The play was reviewed by several papers, all with glowing words for Jean, who at 63, was still able to convey a young girl.

In 1964 Lucille Ball beckoned Jean to come out of retirement to do a guest stint on her popular television series, *The Lucy Show*. While nothing came of it, Jean's appetite for television was whetted and she let her agent know she was available. Wasting no time, her agent booked her on the long-running western television series *Gunsmoke*, in an episode modeled specifically for her talents. Director Joe Lewis thought that her work was "delightful, harmonious, with a sense of professionalism that he hadn't experienced since "the days of the great, great luminaries."[36] Again, Jean received outstanding reviews, which in turn interested her in developing her own series. But *The Jean Arthur Show*, which cast the actress as a lawyer, was poorly conceived and was cancelled after only 12 episodes.

While it is heartbreaking to read of Jean's attempts to continue any sort of stage career, it is downright inconceivable to think that with her record for leaving shows any producer would take a chance on her again. Yet that is exactly what Cheryl Crawford did when she cast her in *The Freaking Out of Stephanie Black* on Broadway. The play itself was a disaster, but once again, Jean left the show before it officially opened at the cost of her own $25,000 investment. Eight years later, in 1975, Jean was cast for the last time in a play, *First Monday in October* by Jerome Lawrence and Robert E. Lee, the team who had earlier written the hugely successful and yet controversial play, *Inherit the Wind*. Slated for an opening in Toledo, Ohio, Jean once more dropped out, although she made it through a few performances.

Jean finally retreated to the privacy of her Carmel home, "Driftwood." Once, when a reporter tried to interview her in 1959, he was told, "I don't mean to be impolite to you personally, but I'm out of the business and all I want to do is read and be let alone."[37] She died in a Carmel nursing home on January 19, 1991, at the age of 90, perhaps never really knowing that her talent was the summation of her experiences and her personality. Her stage fright, her lack of confidence, her unique talent and longing for perfection, prevented Jean Arthur from appreciating what she had to offer. Perhaps it is best to end with Mary Martin's praise of Jean's performance in *Peter Pan*:

> Jean did it first, on Broadway in 1950. She was absolutely wonderful. I hate to admit it, but she is Peter Pan. She is youth, joy, freedom, all the things Peter tells Captain Hook when Hook asks, "Pan, who and what are you?"[38]

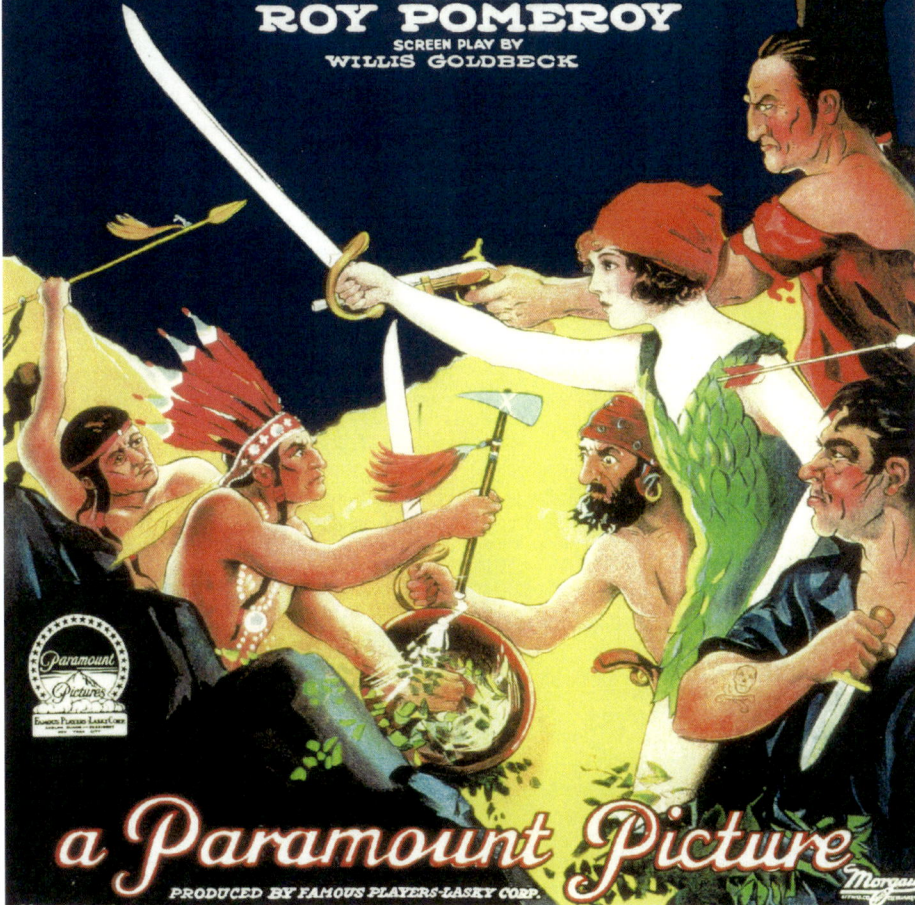

A stunning lithograph window card advertising the 1924 silent film, starring Betty Bronson, produced by the Morgan Litho Co. in Cleveland. Although advertising a motion picture, early film posters often emulated a theatrical quality.

C-1

Top: The first "original cast" record album of *Peter Pan* was released in 1940 as wartime conditions prevented any London productions for two years. Although the cover for this tri-fold record set is in vibrant colors, most of the albums were housed in plain brown folders, making this set even more of a rarity. The cover is a replica of the Peter Pan Club certificate. Each member also received an official Peter Pan pin. *Bottom:* Jeremy Sumpter as Peter, Rachel Hurd-Wood as Wendy, Harry Newell as John, and Freddie Popplewell as Michael peer from the clouds far above Never Never Land. The film, almost a year in production, was released in 2003 (Universal Pictures/Photofest).

Top: "The Fight with the Pirates," Strobridge Litho Co. 1907 (private collector). *Bottom:* This is the most famous Peter Pan poster, which, designed by Charles Buchel, advertised the first production at the Duke of York's Theatre in 1904. Color lithograph (courtesy Beinecke Library at Yale University).

Mary Martin is playing shadow puppets in the number "I've Gotta Crow," from the first full musical adaptation of *Peter Pan*. 1954 (Photofest).

A poster of the irrepressible Sandy Duncan as Pan in 1979. That production was the longest single run of *Peter Pan* ever to appear on Broadway.

Issued Monthly
$3.00 a Year.

FEBRUARY 1906

Vol. VI. No. 60.
25 c. a Copy.

THE THEATRE

ILLUSTRATED MAGAZINE
OF DRAMATIC AND MUSICAL ART.

The Theatre Magazine Co., 26 W. 33d St. N. Y.

MISS MAUDE ADAMS "Peter Pan."

PHOTO OTTO SARONY

C-6

Maude Adams as Peter Pan, February 1906.

For several years this poster was used in London and on tour. There was no need to state the name of the actress as most everyone knew her by sight: Pauline Chase. Poster by Frank Harreland.

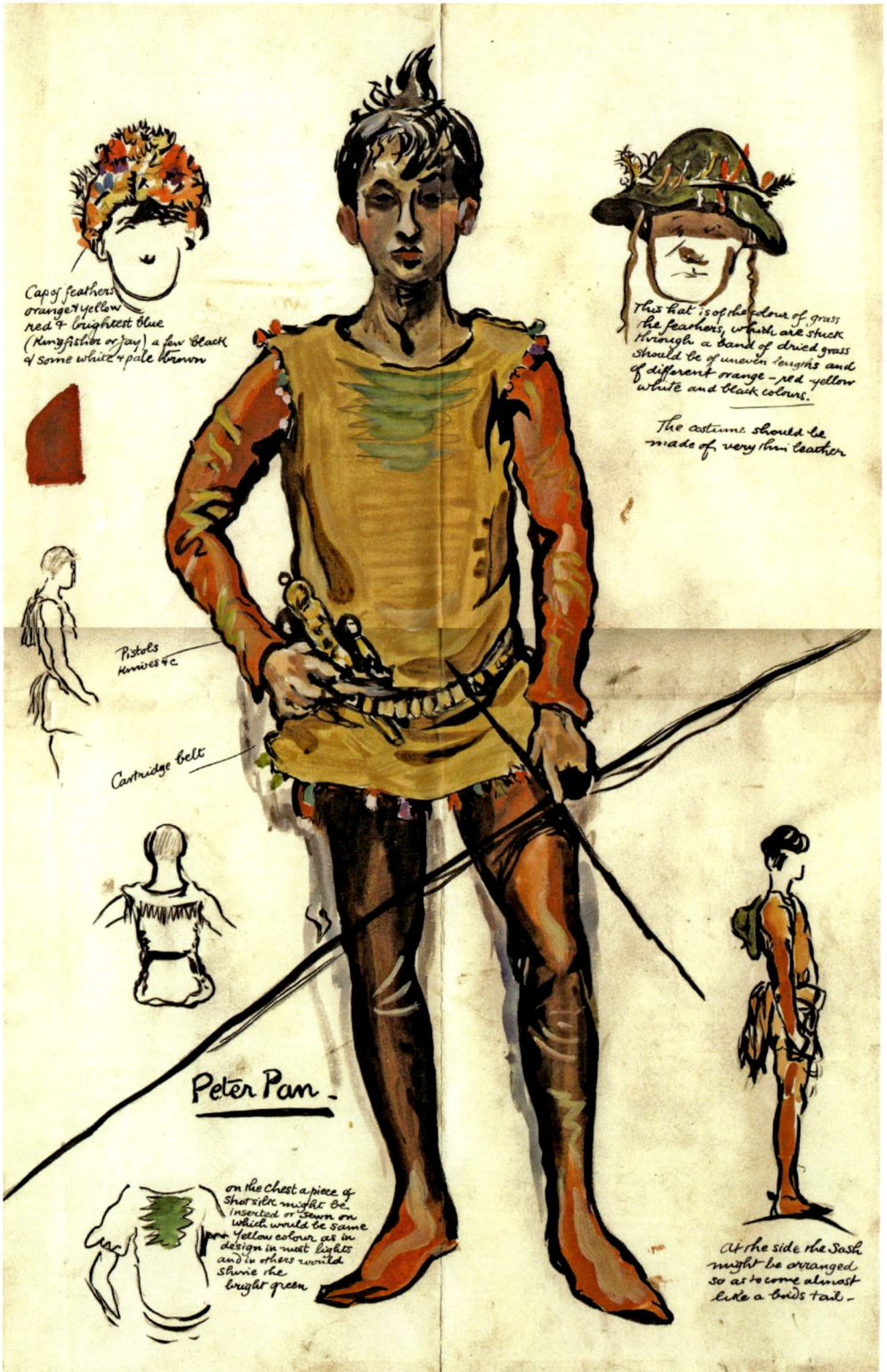

The original 1904 Peter Pan costume design by William Nicholson for Nina Boucicault (courtesy Karpeles Manuscript Library Museum).

C-8

Peter Pan

As Betty Bronson plays the part, and Wendy as played by Mary Brian
The third page in the Companion's series of motion-picture paper dolls

THESE fairy-tale people have been in the movies and on the stage and you can also read about them in a delightful book by Sir James Barrie.

Tinker Bell, the fairy

Peter Pan's redskin cap

Peter's knapsack

Peter Pan's everyday cap

Wendy's Never-Never-Land cap

Peter Pan

Wendy

THE picture above shows how Peter Pan's shadow looks when he wears it. In cutting out Peter Pan himself, omit the shadow.

IN Never-Never-Land Wendy wore the frock at the left and on the pirate ship she was all wrapped in this cape.

Attach Peter Pan's shadow with little bits of beeswax

BEFORE cutting out these paper dolls, paste the page to a sheet of heavy paper and press flat; cut slits on dotted lines.

Peter Pan paper dolls from the 1924 silent film.

Tarnished
Gold Lace

Wig should be made
of Black Chenille or blackest possible
stuff so as to catch no light whatever

Hair Curls
uncurled

soiled shirt

Brown Leather Patches to hold 3 pistols
each side in sort of wide
braces

Coat is to be a
dusty Blue Black
with pale blue
lining

Pistols to be
at this angle

Soiled Lace

Pistol
— very
sharp

Sash to be colour
of dry blood

Pocket

Rusty Buckles

S 694.

Captain Hook.

Captain Hook's costume for Gerald du Maurier designed by William Nicholson, 1904 (courtesy Karpeles Manuscript Library Museum).

The legendary beauty of Marilyn Miller is captured in this extremely rare color flyer from 1924. The red streak to the right is the feather in her cap.

Peter Pan returned to Kensington Gardens in the summer of 2009 with Ciaran Kellgren in the leading role. Photograph: Simon Annand (courtesy Simon Annand).

12

The Disney Touch

The greatest challenge I have ever faced is the task—the very pleasurable task—of bringing Peter Pan to life in a dream world which only he and his friends can see—and only the animated cartoon can reveal to us in all its magic.

—Walt Disney, 1953[1]

The Walt Disney film of *Peter Pan* might not seem to belong in a book that traces the history of an entertainment performed by live actors but then neither does the 1924 film nor the 1991 *Hook*. Yet how can an art form that has been responsible for introducing this famous literary character to so many children be ignored? The 1953 feature-length animated film with depictions of Peter, Wendy, John, Michael, Captain Hook, and even Smee is recognizable to children all over the world. The only name on the film more famous than Peter is Disney, a name that immediately suggests magic, music, color, and fun.

Born in Chicago in 1901, Walt Disney was one of five children. He was always interested in art and enrolled in an art school at the age of 14. He formed his own commercial art studio four years later. But Disney was intrigued by animation and gave up his firm to work at the Kansas City Film Ad Company. He was moonlighting cartoons on his own and soon was able to finance his own company, Laugh-O-Gram, which moved to Los Angeles. There he created 57 "Alice" films, a successful series of shorts that featured a live child actress in animated adventures.

His next creation was a cartoon character named "Oswald," a rabbit. This too became popular, but Disney lost his rights to the character during a contract dispute with Universal Pictures. It was then that he decided to first create the product and then offer it for distribution, keeping the titles in his name. His first creation under these new conditions is still his most famous, Mickey Mouse. In 1928 Mickey made his debut in a silent cartoon, "Plane Crazy," but didn't really make news until his third film, "Steamboat Willie," which had a musical soundtrack. The cartoon premiered on November 18, 1928.

In 1929, Disney began creating a series of shorts called "The Silly Symphonies." One of the most successful entries was "The Three Little Pigs," with Frank Churchill's deceivingly simple nursery-rhyme tune providing the structure for the plot and the dialogue as well as the lyrics of Pinto Colvig. When Hal Roach asked Disney a few years later if he could use the now-standard song for his own classic film, *Babes in Toyland*, with Laurel and Hardy, Disney consented. He recognized the musical content of any film as an important asset. Despite the critical acclaim for his work, these cartoon shorts were prohibitively expensive and did not make much of a profit. Disney needed to create a full-length animated film

It will live in your heart forever!

Walt Disney's PETER PAN

COLOR BY TECHNICOLOR

Top: "The Greatest in Showmanship History," boasted the Disney Studio (copyright Walt Disney Productions). *Bottom:* Walt Disney.

that would cure his financial troubles while fulfilling his artistic dreams.

Even before he completed the landmark film *Snow White and the Seven Dwarfs,* Disney hoped to animate *Peter Pan.* He bought the film rights in 1939, but with films like *Pinocchio, Fantasia, Dumbo,* and *Bambi* (all four considered masterpieces of animation) in production, he was not able to begin work on *Pan* until 1949. Four years and $4 million later, the film was released. While not quite in the same league as the other films mentioned, it, too, is recognized as a Disney classic.

Amazingly, the general structure of the screenplay does not deviate much from the book, *Peter and Wendy.* What is added — slapstick humor and a mad chase between the crocodile and Captain Hook — leaves children in stitches. A new ending unnecessarily reveals that Wendy has been dreaming about the adventures in Never Never Land. While a dramatic switch from the real world to a dream world aided a live-action film like *The Wizard of Oz,* the animated *Pan* did not need to remind audiences that this was not the real world. The very nature of the genre succeeds in that area.

The original songs by Sammy Cahn and Sammy Fain are delightfully integrated into the dialogue. One of the most exciting numbers is "You Can Fly, You Can Fly, You Can Fly," which begins in the nursery, continues over London, and finishes as the children near Never Never Land.

"The Second Star to the Right" is a beautiful song (just listen to Barbara Cook's rendition for proof) sung over the opening credits by a heavenly chorus to an arrangement by Jud Conlon. Other Cahn-Fain songs include "The Elegant Captain Hook," "What Makes the Red Man Red?," and a sweet lullaby for Wendy, "Your Mother and Mine." Oliver Wallace and Erdmann Penner, two Disney staff composers, wrote "A Pirate's Life," and Wallace penned "Following the Leader" ("Tee-Dum Tee-Dee") with Ted Sears and Winston Hibler. Frank Churchill, who also wrote the Snow White songs with Larry Morey, contributed the humorous "Never Smile at a Crocodile" with Jack Lawrence, but the song was deleted from the release print.

Disney child star Bobby Driscoll's voice was perfectly matched to the artists' renderings of Peter, whose movements were copied from the studio-made live-action test film that featured dancer Roland Dupree as Peter. Driscoll also posed for the artists for the more impish qualities of the character. Bobby was Disney's first actor under contract but before that association the lad made his first film appearance in *Lost Angel* with Margaret O'Brien. Though it was only a bit part, he was noticed and cast as the younger version of Al Sullivan in 20th Century–Fox's *The Five Sullivans* in 1944. Two years and five films later he was cast by Disney in *Song of the South*, then in *So Dear to My Heart* and Disney's remake of *Treasure Island*, as well as a film noir thriller, *The Window*, in which he was loaned out to RKO, Disney's distributor. At first RKO owner Howard Hughes did not want to release the film, as he did not think Bobby's performance very good. However, Bobby received excellent reviews, especially from the *New York Times*:

> The striking force and terrifying impact of this RKO melodrama is chiefly due to Bobby's brilliant acting, for the whole effect would have been lost were there any suspicion of doubt about the credibility of this pivotal character.... "The Window" is Bobby Driscoll's picture, make no mistake about it."[2]

Bobby won an Academy Award for 1949 as the "outstanding juvenile." Like many child actors, as Driscoll matured, his film offers grew fewer. Disney saw the boy's looks growing into what he would have cast as a bully but either way he was typecast as "Disney's boy." After high school and an unsuccessful marriage with three children, drug addiction, and fewer and fewer film appearances, Bobby joined Andy Warhol's Factory, producing collages that were briefly exhibited. Tragically, he died on March 30, 1968, and was buried in Potter's Field in NYC as a pauper. It was only through the Disney company that he did not remain a John Doe.

Bobby Driscoll in the 1949 thriller *The Window*, which helped to win him an Academy Award for best juvenile performance.

Bobby Driscoll, in London in 1949 to film *Treasure Island,* surrounded by pigeons in Trafalgar Square. The filming had to be rushed as it was discovered that Bobby had no passport and therefore could only stay in London for six weeks.

Opposite, top: Bobby Driscoll dressed as Peter Pan in 1952 for the live-action film used as a model for the animators (copyright Walt Disney Productions) (Photofest). *Bottom:* Bobby Driscoll as Peter Pan performing live action to guide the animation. Two of the mermaids are Margaret Kerry and June Foray. Circa 1952 (Photofest).

Kathryn Beaumont, who provided the voice of Wendy in Walt Disney's *Peter Pan*, is seen with one of the film's composers, Oliver Wallace, in 1953 (Photofest).

His father was dying and his mother was desperately searching for her son to be there in his final moments. She contacted Disney for help. The public, however, did not learn about Bobby's death until two years later when *Song of the South* was rereleased, as the reporters were looking for cast members with a "where are they now?" angle.

The voice of Wendy was supplied by Kathryn Beaumont, who three years earlier did the same for *Alice in Wonderland*. The dialogue written for her in *Pan* is especially humorous as she never seems to stop talking.

For Captain Hook, the studio decided to use Hans Conried as a model in their live film and his voice in the animated film. In Leonard Maltin's *The Disney Films*, Conried remembered his work on the film:

> Usually they had pantomimists and/or dancers, but they felt that I could play the part. Now when I say I worked two and a half years, I don't say that I worked constantly, but over that period they would say, "Have you got two weeks?" "Have you got four days?" "Have you got a week?" I was in costume, and they had an elemental set, and I would go through the business making my physical action coincide with the soundtrack, which was already finished. Usually, in dubbing, which I've done a lot of for foreign actors, you have to make your sound coincident with his latent action, but here you make your physical action coincident with the soundtrack. That was lots of fun; it was a very friendly, familiar surroundings at Disney, particularly in those days.[3]

Another big change in this *Peter Pan* was the new look for Tinker Bell. The fairy was presented as a sexy little nymph hopelessly in love with Peter. The cartoon character had so much appeal that she became a trademark for the popular Disney show on television.

The critics apprehensively approached this new version of the stage play. In the *New York Times*, Bosley Crowther suggested that the characters were not too original, with Wendy being a close cousin to Snow White, Smee akin to the dwarf Happy, and Michael derived from Dopey. Crowther wrote in his review:

> Mr. Disney's picture ... has the story but not the spirit of Peter Pan as it was plainly conceived by its author and is usually played on the stage. However, that's not to say it isn't a wholly amusing and engaging piece of work within the defined limitations of the aforementioned "Disney style." The Disney inventions are as skillful and clever as they have ever been — perhaps even more so, in some cases, as in the encounter of Captain Hook with the Crocodile. This episode in the story has been worked out in a burst of violent farce, with Hook struggling frantically to stay out of the ferocious old Crocodile's pink maw. The colors, too, are more exciting and the technical features of the job, such as the synchronomization of lips, are very good.[4]

Top: Live action reference model Margaret Kerry as Tinker Bell, 1952 (Photofest). *Bottom:* Tinker Bell, jealous of Wendy, listens to a scheme proposed by Captain Hook in *Peter Pan*, 1953 (Photofest).

Barrie biographer Roger Lancelyn Green observed:

> There is, of necessity, no place in this kind of film for the delicacy of the play and the story. The magic must be purely visual and rather heavily underlined — just as the sentiment tends to be, and the excitement also.[5]

The film has been reissued many times, on many formats, and in several editions. There have also been sequels and prequels, including *Return to Never Land* and a couple of tales featuring Tinker Bell. An interesting review appeared in *Entertainment Weekly* in 1990:

> The sad thing is the finished product doesn't quite stand with the best in the Disney canon. The stage version starring Mary Martin, taped for TV in 1960 and newly released on video, is the clearly superior fantasy. The problem is not so much the

Top: The Lost Boys led by John Darling as they sing "Following the Leader" in the 1953 animated film by Disney. *Middle:* The success of Disney's *Peter Pan* in 1953 spawned many commercial items for the kiddies. Pictured here is "Walt Disney's *Peter Pan* Toy Balloon Toss-Up" from the Oak Rubber Company in Ravenna Oregon. *Bottom:* "Walt Disney's Peter Pan String Marionettes," Peter Puppet Playthings Inc., Long Island City, N.Y., 1953.

liberties the animated version takes with James M. Barrie's original play as it is the Disney team's inability to get a grip on the story. It comes off as a series of disconnected bits, not a magical meditation on the melancholy fate of growing up.[6]

The critic, who saw the film 11 hours after experiencing a reunion by the rock group The Who, went on to explain the durability of its appeal.

One is that the talents of Captain Hook (and to some extent, the crocodile) hold up almost as well as Pete Townshend's and Roger Daltrey's. Another is that Tinker Bell shakes her booty with all the pizza-joint vigor of a notorious high school tart. Another is that, by contrast, Wendy is ooooh so straight. Is it possible that Uncle Walt's universe too conveniently divided girls into "fast" and insipid? ... Besides, this Hook is super, and the songs aren't bad — even if "Never Smile at a Crocodile," a mild-or-more hit in '53, is inexplicably used only as background music.... Yet how many tunes — now or then — offer advice upon which to construct a life?[7]

Top: "Walt Disney's Peter Pan School Bag," National Leather Mfg. Co., Brooklyn, N.Y., 1953. *Bottom:* Peter, Wendy, John, and Michael fly by Big Ben on their way to Never Never Land (copyright Walt Disney Productions) (Photofest).

13

Mary Martin:
A Musical Peter Pan

Peter Pan is perhaps the most important thing, to me, that I have ever done in the theater.

— Mary Martin, 1976[1]

When Mary Martin first agreed to Edwin Lester's proposed musical version of *Peter Pan* she had no idea that the generations of children in the country who had never seen the play would be watching it together — all on the same night! And then again, and again....

Even if Mary never appeared in the musical *Peter Pan*, she would still be regarded as the consummate musical star, one of the best ever to grace the Broadway stage. Her portrayals of Nellie Forbush, Maria Von Trapp, Venus (as in *One Touch of...*), and even Dolly Levi granted her "legend in her own time" status. Most of the Martin roles were real, likable women. The characters in *Annie Get Your Gun* and *The Sound of Music* actually existed, while the heroines of *South Pacific* and *I Do! I Do!* are very much like the women we might encounter. Yet, with all of the accolades and awards she received during her long career, it was television that brought her immortality.

The native Texan's first Broadway appearance was little more than a featured solo in the 1938 Cole Porter musical *Leave It to Me*, yet when she introduced "My Heart Belongs to Daddy" while warming up some native Eskimos (including an unknown Gene Kelly) with a mock striptease, Mary Martin became a sensation. Her picture was put on the cover of *Life* and before long, Paramount Pictures took notice of this saucy new Broadway star and offered her a contract despite the fact that just a few years earlier Mary had failed at trying to break into pictures. But try again she did. However, before she left for Hollywood, Mary did one more show, probably her least known, *Nice Goin'*, with a score by Ralph Rainger and Leo Robin. It closed out of town, but what did that matter — Mary Martin was about to become a movie star.

Ironically, the lackluster film roles offered by Paramount reflected none of the qualities that first brought the actress to Hollywood's attention. Although she was teamed with some of the studio's top stars, from Bing Crosby on down, it was clear that, as with Ethel Merman earlier, Paramount was not quite sure what to do with the Texas bombshell even though Mary appeared perfectly natural before the cameras, something that eluded the great Merm. Each picture had her being groomed into the image of someone else. In her autobiography, *My Heart Belongs*, Martin remembers that "for months the makeup men had a field day. Using my same face they made me up to look exactly like Jean Parker ... and Jean Arthur

210

... Claudette Colbert ... and Rosalind Russell ... kinda. They even tried to make me look sexy. But most of the time, I just looked sick."[2]

Despite Mary Martin's lack of screen identity and the so-so parts in *Rhythm on the Range*, *The Great Victor Herbert*, and *Star-Spangled Rhythm*, a story editor for Paramount named Richard Halliday recognized great talent in the musical star.

When Halliday was first introduced to Mary, she had no idea of the impact that he would have on her career. Their relationship transformed into one of those rare show-business phenomena — a marriage of mutual love and respect. Soon, Halliday gave up editing to manage his young wife's career. Under his nurturing and guidance, a new Mary Martin emerged: confident, beautifully coiffured, handsomely dressed, and, of course, still brimming with talent, the actress was treated like a queen by her new husband. He chose her wardrobe, her hairstyles, and roles she was to play. Her arrivals and departures from the theatre were always to be in grand fashion with a limousine. As dresser, hairstylist, confidant, and husband, Halliday was the perfect manager because his wife was his only client. With her new partner she accepted a role in a Broadway show that she never before would have considered — Venus!

Mary thought that audiences would never buy her as the beautiful goddess of love, a role originally intended for Marlene Dietrich! Little did she realize that her ability to handle this exciting role was actually helped by Hollywood's indecisiveness. There was no problem with typecasting as Mary Martin was not identified as any type. With a score by Kurt Weill and libretto by Ogden Nash and S.J. Perelman, *One Touch of Venus* was directed by Elia Kazan and choreographed by Agnes de Mille, and became a hit of the 1943 season, putting Mary Martin on her second *Life* cover.

After her next show, the lovely *Lute Song*, Mary had clearly established herself as a notable Broadway musical-comedy actress. The following year marked a personal disappointment when she appeared in the eagerly anticipated London production of Noël Coward's *Pacific 1860*. Its failure created a rift between the star and writer that would take years to mend. Upon seeing Ethel Merman in *Annie Get Your Gun* on Broadway, Mary knew she had to play the role of Annie, yet she had to prove to producers Rodgers and Hammerstein that she could handle the lead. It is interesting that she would take a chance on a part so closely associated with Merman, but Mary was not intimidated. An impromptu audition at Richard Rodgers's home proved that she could belt a song when needed and she was given the role in the national touring company. This eventually led to Mary being cast as Nellie Forbush in *South Pacific*.

Mary charmed audiences and critics with her lovely voice and down-to-earth characterization of a small-town Arkansas nurse in love with a worldly older man in the South Pacific during World War II. She gave her hair a permanent so that it could withstand the nightly onstage shampooing in the delightful "I'm Gonna Wash That Man Right Out of My Hair" number. With her picture on yet another *Life* cover, Mary had clearly established herself as the toast of Broadway. Yet she was soon to attain a celestial level in show business seldom reached by actors.

Mary always wanted to play Peter but after Jean Arthur played the part in 1950, Martin assumed that she would never get a crack at it. Edwin Lester, director of the San Francisco and Los Angeles Light Opera Company, approached her with the idea.

Lester wrote in the program for the show:

My first invitation was extended in 1951 in the hope that she would do *Peter Pan* for us between the close of her *South Pacific* engagement in New York and her London opening of the same play.

Mary Martin as Peter Pan, 1954.

It could not be arranged at that time. But neither of us forgot. And in the fall of 1953, knowing that her commitment to *Kind Sir* was limited to that season only, I proposed again that she come to California and that we make *Peter Pan* a festive event of our 1954 Civic Light Opera season.[3]

When he assured Mary that they could create a wonderful musical version of the play with her choice of director and composer, she immediately accepted, telling Lester that she wanted Peter to fly further than he had ever flown before in a musical number and that the children should share a flying song with him. Leland Hayward and Richard Halliday, who eventually replaced a convalescing Hayward as co-producer, carefully laid out their plans for the new musical. The director-choreographer who had first been asked to direct *Peter Pan* with Jean Arthur was again beckoned to create a new version for Mary Martin.

"Jerome Robbins was our director," Martin wrote. "And actually as far as I was concerned, he was another Peter Pan. Working with him was one of the most exciting experiences I have ever known in the theatre."[4] Robbins first made a splash in theatre with his choreography of *On the Town* in 1944. Prior to this he had astounded the dance world as well with his ballet "Fancy Free." He also was responsible for staging the memorable 12-minute Mary Martin–Ethel Merman duet on the Ford fiftieth anniversary television show in 1953, with the two stars merely sitting on a couple of chairs as they belted out one song after

Mary in Rodgers and Hammerstein's *South Pacific*, 1949.

another. This type of staging seems conventional now but in 1953 it was new and intimate. This convinced the Hallidays that Robbins should direct their play. The following decades would find him as one of the major creative forces in ballet and musical theatre, making dance an integral part of the story of several Broadway musicals such as *Billion Dollar Baby*, *West Side Story* and *Fiddler on the Roof*. To that distinguished list we must add *Peter Pan*, which he not only directed with the assistance of Mary Hunter but also adapted from the original play.

The flying sequences have always been the most memorable aspect of Barrie's play and there was a real challenge to bring a fresh approach to it. Just as necessary, however, was a specialist who could fly Peter further than he'd ever flown. Once again, Peter Foy was called in.

An important and immediate concern was to commission a score that would serve the book in a memorable way. The text of *Peter Pan* had proven the test of time, but could a

Director Jerome Robbins and Mary Martin flying during a rehearsal for the 1954 musical, *Peter Pan*.

musical score live up to the expectations generated by such a venture? Martin recalled that one night she and her husband heard Carolyn Leigh's "Young At Heart'" on the radio while driving home in their car and immediately agreed that whoever wrote that song should work on the score for *Peter Pan*. While Johnny Richards actually composed the music, it was the optimistic lyrics of Carolyn Leigh that most interested the Hallidays. Through ASCAP, Halliday located Leigh, who was under contract to write lyrics for a music publisher. During the two decades following *Peter Pan*, she would become one of the busiest lyricists in the business, with many of her songs now recognized as standards. "Witchcraft," "Pass Me By," and "Hey, Look Me Over" are just a few of her hits, written with Cy Coleman. Not all of the shows she wrote for were overwhelming successes, yet popular songs from the likes of *Wildcat* and *How Now Dow Jones* were able to live beyond the run of the plays. Despite her untimely death in 1983, Carolyn Leigh is remembered as one of the most talented lyric writers of the Broadway musical.

A year before her death, Leigh spoke to an audience at the Society of Stage Directors and Choreographers symposium on *Peter Pan*:

It might interest you to know that, very briefly, Leonard Bernstein was supposed to have done the music. Leonard at that time was busy with about five other things, and he and Mary didn't quite see eye to eye about which should take place first.... Also, he wanted to incorporate a score he had done for *Peter Pan* a few years earlier, which had starred Jean Arthur, and Mary felt she couldn't sing that; so that all passed in a hurry.[5]

By the time she signed with the Hallidays, Leigh was working with a young composer, Morris (a.k.a. Mark) Charlap, or, as he was affectionately called, "Moose." Moose was only five foot two, considerably shorter than the more statuesque Leigh. In fact, the nickname "Moose" was self-delegated during childhood to suggest an imposing figure. It worked! Overwhelming in his openness, Moose enjoyed meeting people and he would think nothing of walking up to strangers to initiate conversation. Yet he was also troubled by diabetes and a weak heart. His widow, singer Sandy Stewart, summed up his presence. "Moose was like a low-yield atomic weapon, ready to go off. He was fresh, young, and new! He did not sleep much. He knew that he wouldn't live to be an old man."[6]

Like Leigh, Moose approached life idealistically, but more important, he was able to convey innocence in his music. He was quite capable of composing sophisticated symphonies and jazz pieces but he loved writing material for children. Sadly, Moose Charlap did not attain the status in the music world that he so richly deserved. A 1958 musical, *Whoop-Up*, closed after only 56 performances but fortunately the cast album was recorded, revealing a humorous and upbeat score that provides guilty pleasures for many musical comedy aficionados. Another musical, *Clown Around*, closed before reaching Broadway, despite the direction of Gene Kelly. It too was recorded but it remains one of the rarest of Broadway recordings. During rehearsals for *Clown Around* Moose suffered three heart attacks, yet he continued to work on that as well other projects. At his death at 45 in 1974, he was composing a score for a musical based on the life of Paul Gauguin.

In 1953, when Mary Martin was first introduced to Moose Charlap, he was the youngest member of ASCAP. She immediately liked the brash young man and the feeling was mutual. Despite the fact that established teams such as Rodgers and Hammerstein were interested in writing the score, Martin committed herself to her new discoveries. Sandy Stewart told me that "later, during one of the *Pan* rehearsals, Richard Rodgers sat behind Moose and quipped, 'My boy, you have not written a show, you've written an annuity!'"[7]

The team's first three songs, "I've Gotta Crow," "I'm

Mark "Moose" Charlap and Carolyn Leigh taking a break to pose for photographer Bob Willoughby while working on their score of *Peter Pan* in Los Angeles in 1954. Willoughby was hired to trace the development of the musical through photos from early rehearsals in LA right through to opening night on Broadway (photograph: Bob Willoughby, courtesy Christopher Willoughby).

Flying," and "I Won't Grow Up," were characteristic of the innocence and magic that Robbins sought. "I remember playing some things in my stocking feet for Mr. Robbins," said Leigh. "It was my very, very first venture. I had only been to see a musical once in my life prior to that. I was frightened out of my wits. Moose had no idea of what was happening either, although I think that he was braver than I was." Leigh went on, "I remember singing a line to Jerry, 'If I can lead a life of crime, and still be home by dinnertime,' and we got a nod of approval from him.... We had no idea what we were doing; we were only praying to get through it alive, and I didn't quite know what my function was. I wrote lyrics quite blindly, quite desperately."[8]

Leigh also admitted that in 1954 she had "too much awe"[9] for Jerome Robbins, a director who could be quite intimidating. She recalled her difficulty in writing an Indian song for the show: "Robbins explained that the song should show that while noisy Indians are usually at peace, when they turn quiet they go on the warpath. I couldn't make any sense of the idea as it related to the show, so I wrote a song that was simply pleasant nonsense. Later it finally occurred to me that Robbins was making a metaphor about children, that when children become quiet you have trouble. But our communication problem was so bad that I missed the point completely."[10] This is clearly reflected in the lyrics to "Wild Indians," which was removed from the show.

> Wild Indians Home in Wigwam
> Heap Noisy, Beat on the Tom-Tom
> But When We're Out on the War-Path
> Wild Indians Make Big Hush-Hush
>
> When All Is Still in the Bushes
> When Come No Sound of a Foot-Fall
> You'll Know, That's Us, Take Care
>
> When All Is Still in the Bushes
> When All Is Calm in the Forest
> We Come, Get You, Be-Ware

During this creative process Robbins began to recruit actors for the play. Actually, besides Mary Martin, there was one other performer cast from the conception of the project. "Long before we went in rehearsal for the show here on the coast [L.A.] I was preparing for my part at home in Norwalk," wrote Heller Halliday, Mary's daughter. "I learned the part of Wendy because at the time I thought I was going to play Wendy. But we all decided it would be a big responsibility for me and I am very happy with my part of Liza. Some day I would like to play the part of Wendy."[11] Heller Halliday, Martin's daughter, was 12 years old when she wrote this passage for a magazine article. Mary explained:

> My daughter Heller playing Wendy was something we always talked about, but she was only twelve or thirteen. She did play the part of the little maid and performed a toe dance in the second act. Later on, when I was doing *Peter Pan* for the last time on television and Heller was away at college, we called and asked if she'd like to come back and finally play Wendy. But she thought it best that she stay in school.[12]

The decision not to cast Heller as Wendy did not come easily. Mary Martin was the star of the show and the star wanted her daughter in the play! That was that. Robbins argued that the audience did not need to be reminded that Mary was a mother. A compromise to cast Heller as Liza didn't meet with Robbins's approval either. This was the one time during this production that his associate director disagreed with him. "We need to do

Mary Martin as Peter with Liza, played by Heller Halliday, her daughter, during a rehearsal in LA in 1954. An early conception of the musical found Heller cast as Wendy (photograph: Bob Willoughby, courtesy Christopher Willoughby).

this to have a happy company,"[13] reasoned Mary Hunter. Robbins conceded and Hunter was assigned to direct the scenes with Heller, which would be written to include a duet with her mother and a ballet. However, Robbins relented and choreographed the ballet.

Unconscious of the backstage politics until she read the first edition of this book, Heller wrote:

> In reading your account of our *Peter Pan* I was interested in all the flack about my being part of the production. I am glad I was unaware of it because I don't think it would have helped my ego.... I can't tell you the thrill I had every night to be able to sing with my mother. Also, not everyone I know had a ballet created for them at the age of 13 by the famous and wonderful Jerry Robbins, something I know he would not have been involved in if he hadn't thought it was right. It was a fun learning experience in my life.[14]

Heller Halliday at her dressing table backstage at the Winter Garden in 1954 (from the collection of the Doss Heritage and Culture Center, Weatherford, Texas).

The part of Mrs. Darling was assigned to veteran Margalo Gillmore, actress and author. Gillmore's prestigious appearance with Katharine Cornell's *No Time for Comedy* and a series of grande dame roles in films would bring certain legitimacy to a musical version of *Peter Pan*. "For the villainous Captain Hook, Peter's sworn enemy, we had only one choice — the great Australian actor, Cyril Ritchard." In her autobiography, Mary Martin recalled, "I had seen him perform only once, in a Restoration comedy with his wife, Madge Elliot, and with John Gielgud, who also directed, but I had never forgotten his perfect timing, his presence. He would be the ultimate Hook, and he was."[15]

Ritchard's career was quite diversified. He began as a chorus boy in Australia, coming to the United States to appear in a musical revue, *Puzzles of 1925*, as a song-and-dance juvenile. While usually thought to be associated with Restoration classics, he had appeared in many contemporary musicals and comedies, including *Daddy Long Legs* and later *Visit to a Small Planet*. Ironically, the San Francisco program on *Peter Pan*'s 1954 premiere treated the actor as a newcomer with the billing, "introducing Cyril Ritchard."

Off stage, Cyril Ritchard was nothing like Captain Hook. A loving father whose infant son's death made him sensitive to the needs of other children, Ritchard later became the mentor for David Bean, the boy who portrayed Slightly. The youngster's father was Ritchard's dresser.

The casting of *Peter Pan* was now official ... almost.

May 15, 1954

To New York Times
Sam Zolotow
Dear Sam:

   You can now make official the announcement that Cyril Ritchard will play the roles of Captain Hook and Mr. Darling with Mary Martin in my production of Peter Pan. Please include in the announcement that Jerome Robbins is staging, also Margalo Gillmore as Mrs. Darling. No final decision yet on Heller's role so would prefer that you do not mention her in this story. Will give you that within a few days.

Best Regards,
Edwin Lester[16]

Mrs. Darling (Margalo Gillmore) and Nana, 1954 (Photofest).

On June 21, Kathleen Nolan, then known professionally as "Kathy," the actress who was to play Wendy, entered her first rehearsal. She had won the role after several auditions and much competition. She started her acting career at only 13 months old, spending most of her early childhood on the stage with her family, including a stint on a Mississippi riverboat. After graduating high school in 1951, she moved to New York City to attend the Neighborhood Playhouse School of the Drama. She paid for her classes by working as an usherette at the Palace Theatre, where Judy Garland was making her first legendary comeback.

Kathleen, who possesses a beautiful singing voice, learned Garland's entire act and performed it to the amazement of the other usherettes. Well, it was only a matter of time before word reached the headliner about this talented young lady. One evening after the show, Garland asked Nolan if she could remain at the theatre for a while and perform her (Garland's) entire act. As Nolan performed the "Palace Medley" and other songs, Garland situated herself in different locations of the theatre so she could see how effective the staging was to all parts of the audience. "You can imagine how I felt," mused Kathleen, "singing 'Over the Rainbow' to Judy Garland."[17] Apparently, Garland was impressed enough to introduce Kathleen to Richard Rodgers, who a few years later was instrumental in arranging Nolan's audition for Wendy at the old Theatre Guild. Meanwhile, the young actress was busy in "live" television dramas and a series entitled *Jamie*.

Ironically, Kathleen Nolan was the first actress to try out for the part of Wendy and impressed the producers so much that they could not believe their luck. In fact, they brought in other actresses for the part with the belief that if they were this fortunate on the first audition there must be other prospects. "They kept bringing me back," remembered Nolan. "They would audition somebody else and then they would bring me back.

"On one occasion Barbara Cook auditioned before I did. I heard Barbara sing and I left. I never heard a beautiful sound like that. How could I possibly compete? And the stage manager ... Bob Linden, came running after me. And I said, 'I'm not going to follow her!' And he said, 'It's not about just what your voice is. You don't have to hit that high C.' So I went in and I auditioned again."[18]

Kathleen continued, "There were some of us that were hired in New York ... Billy Summer and Sondra Lee, I think that there were about five

Top: Cyril Ritchard won the Tony Award for his performance as Mr. Darling and Captain Hook in 1955 (courtesy Roy Busby). *Bottom:* Kathleen Nolan as Wendy in 1954. The young actress, then known as "Kathy," would later find television success on *The Real McCoys* (Photofest).

dancers ... Bobby Tucker, Jerome Robbins's assistant, auditioned the rest of the dancers in Los Angeles. We started rehearsing at the Union Hall on Vine Street. So being the energetic young lady that I was I wanted to do the bar with the dancers. I wanted to get right in there. So Jerry came in and Bobby Tucker was sitting next to him. The dancers were doing their morning bar and I was at the bar. Obviously I wasn't hired as a dancer although I could dance, but not very well. Jerry was always trying to get me to point my toes in the flying. So Bobby was sitting on a chair and finally he fell off the chair laughing. We found out later that Jerry said, 'Did you hire her? Did I hire her?' I had my hair

Kathleen Nolan as Wendy poses for a publicity still with Mary Martin as Peter, 1954.

pulled back and he didn't recognize me as the girl he hired for Wendy even though he had seen me fifteen times."[19]

Playing Wendy is one of Kathleen Nolan's most cherished experiences. A few years later she became Kate on the long-running television series, *The Real McCoys*. Ironically, the success of that program cost her the opportunity to reprise the role of Wendy in the 1960 videotape of *Peter Pan*. Nolan continued to act on many television shows, including her own series, *Broadside*, as well as on the stage, and has had the distinction of being the first woman to become national president of the Screen Actor's Guild.

Some of the casting required no search at all. From the Jean Arthur revival, Joe E. Marks was to repeat his role of the lovable Smee, while Norman Shelly would be on all fours again as Nana and the crocodile. "There was nothing deep here," Shelly pointed out. "I needed the job."[20] Tiger Lily was not immediately cast, as there was no conception of her character, but as time went on one of the Lost Boys took the part. This boy was played by the only female of the group, dancer Sondra Lee. Jerome Robbins had directed her in

High Button Shoes and brought her along for *Peter Pan* even though he was not sure at the time how he was going to use her. The small pert blonde has since graced other Broadway musicals such as *Hello, Dolly!* while she also danced with Les Ballets de Paris and Robbins's Ballets U.S.A. Years later, Sondra Lee is still best remembered for her captivating performance as Tiger Lily.

Robbins was trying to convey the innocence of childhood by directing the actors to portray children, who, in turn, pretend to be Indians, pirates, and, of course, Peter Pan. Like real children, Sondra Lee recalled that their games were quite serious. "When you're playing fantasy you have to believe it every second. Children play to win. They play it total. When they are a cowboy, they *are* a cowboy. And the bad guys *are* bad guys! You have to play with that kind of conviction. When Tiger Lily says that Peter Pan is the sun, the moon, and the stars, she means it!"[21]

Lee's philosophy about acting in a fantasy play is very close to Barrie's own thoughts on how to produce a Fairy Play. Barrie wrote:

> The difference between a Fairy Play and a realistic one is that in the former all the characters are really children with a child's outlook on life. This applies to the so-called adults of the story as well as to the young people. Pull the beard off the fairy king, and you would find the face of a child.

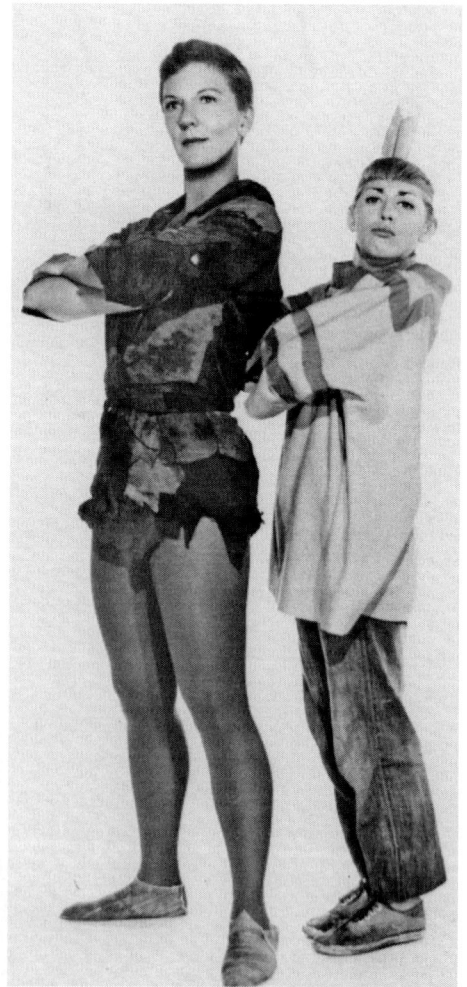

Left: Peter and Nana, played by Mary Martin and Norman Shelly. Shelly, later a successful psychiatrist in NYC, passed away in 2005 (photograph: John Engstead). *Right:* Mary Martin as Peter with Sondra Lee as Tiger Lily in 1954. Lee's autobiography was published in 2009.

> The actors in a fairy play should feel that it is written by a child in deadly earnestness and that they are children playing it in the same spirit. The scenic artist is another child in league with them.[22]

Robbins had the difficult task of maintaining the innocence of the source while also creating a production that was a proper vehicle for his star. Audiences would not buy just another *Peter Pan* so soon after the Jean Arthur success. Rather, they would be paying to see Mary Martin as a singing Peter Pan. Contrary to popular belief, the vehicle was always to be a full-scale musical. Below is an outline of the scenes of *Peter Pan* prior to its opening in San Francisco.

ACT ONE

Scene One
> Dressing Up — Wendy and John (Introduction and Pantomime)
> Lazy Shepherd [*sic*] — Mrs. Darling, Wendy, John, and Michael
> I've Got to Crow [*sic*] — Peter (Shadow Dance)
> I'm Flying — Peter, Wendy, John, and Michael

Scene Two
> I'm Flying (Development) — Peter, Wendy, John, and Michael

Scene Three
> Introduction to Never Land — Animals and Lost Boys
> Indians Are About — Tiger Lily and Indians
> Pirate Song — Hook and Pirates
> Princely Scheme #1 — Hook and Musicians
> Be Our Parents — The Lost Boys to Wendy and Peter
> Princely Scheme #2 — Hook and Musicians

ACT TWO

Scene One
> Adventuring — Peter and Children
> When I Went Home — Peter
> The Battle (Pantomime) — Indians and Pirates
> Capturing the Boys and Wendy — Pirates and Children
> Poisoning Peter's Medicine — Hook and Peter
> Death of Tinker Bell — Peter

Scene Two
> Now It's Hook or Me — Peter, Animals, and Indians

Scene Three
> Soliloquy and Song — Hook and Musicians
> The Big Battle — Company

Scene Four
> Reprise: I've Got to Crow — Peter and Liza

Scene Five
> Reprise: Lazy Shepherd — Wendy, John, and Michael

Scene Six
> Remember Me — Peter

During the rehearsals it was decided that the production would be featured on NBC's *Producers' Showcase*. However, Martin reserved the right to cancel this, as well as any plans for a Broadway run, if she felt the musical was not up to snuff.

Los Angeles Civic Light Opera Association Philharmonic Auditorium 1954

Program cover for the Curran Theatre from the summer of the 1954 Los Angeles Civic Light Opera Association production. A similar design would later be used for Mary Martin's 1958 Disney album, *Hi-Ho*.

By the time the new musical of *Peter Pan* opened at the Curran Theatre in San Francisco on July 19, 1954, scenes were cut and reshuffled and new songs were added. The five acts were condensed into two with eight scene changes — five in the first and three in the second. Essentially the original play was abridged to allow time for the musical numbers. One of Robbins's regrets was the loss of Peter's "To die would be an awfully big adventure" scene, but material had to be deleted to make room for the songs.

The basic text of the play remains in the first act with but a few alterations. This time, Michael walks into the nursery rather than riding on Nana, which saved some wear and tear on Norman Shelly. There was also some extended dialogue for Liza, who cannot be much older than the Darling children. They bid her to take part in their playacting of being Mother and Father, but Liza remains adamant that she has more important housekeeping duties to keep her busy. While Mrs. Darling tucks the children into their beds, they sing "Lazy Shepherd," a rather insecure lullaby about a shepherd who loses his sheep. By the time the show was moved to New York, the title was changed to "Tender Shepherd."

Later, after Wendy has successfully attached Peter's shadow to him, he sings "I've Got to Crow." Here is a fine example of the songwriters' ability to write a song that is an extension of the dialogue. In the original book, Peter announces his cleverness after Wendy accomplishes the task of attaching his shadow. It should be noted here that the title and lyrics of this song eventually were altered to "I've Gotta Crow," which is used in this passage.

PETER: Wendy, look, look; oh the cleverness of me!

WENDY: You conceit, of course I did nothing!

Peter: You did a little.

WENDY: A little! If I am no use I can at least withdraw.

PETER: Wendy, don't withdraw. I can't help crowing, Wendy, when I'm pleased with myself. Wendy, one girl is worth more than twenty boys.[23]

The dialogue was revised a bit so that it reads as follows:

PETER: Look, Wendy, look! My very own shadow. Oh, I'm clever. Oh, the cleverness of me.

WENDY: Of course I did nothing. You're conceited.

PETER: Conceited? Not me.

It's just that I am what I am and I'm me.
When I look at myself and I see in myself
All the wonderful things that I see
If I'm pleased with myself
I have every good reason to be...
I've gotta crow
I'm just the cleverest fellow
'Twas ever my fortune to know.
I taught a trick
To my shadow to stick
To the tip of my toe
I've gotta crow.

Charlap and Leigh wrote a buoyant number that not only served to show Peter's conceit but also gave the audience a taste of Mary Martin's total abandonment. The performance of this song had to be a key

"I've Gotta Crow." A publicity shot of Mary Martin taken in California in 1954 and eventually incorporated as part of the design for the cover of the R.C.A. original cast album of *Peter Pan*.

moment as Peter must convince Wendy and the audience of what a wonderful time he has in store for them.

The biggest change in scene one and certainly the most exciting is the flying ballet, whose clever lyrics and joyful sequence of ascending notes was beautifully wed to Robbins's exciting and at times humorous choreography. Peter rapturously soars and sings "I'm Flying" as the children are entranced to a near frenzy. Soon, they join Peter in flight all about the nursery, and the excitement is expanded with a new scene, En Route to the Never Land. Liza is sprinkled with some fairy dust by a departing Michael and as she spins about the nursery, suggesting her eventual flight, the set moves apart, displaying a starlit sky for Peter and the Darling children to frolic through. Even John Crook's excellent flying music paled by comparison to this exhilarating experience. For the first time, the sheer joy of watching

The original 1954 cast of (from left) Kathleen Nolan (Wendy), Joseph Stafford (Michael), and Robert Harrington (John) fly to Never Never Land with Mary Martin (Peter Pan) (Photofest).

Mary Martin as Peter has his shadow sewn on by Wendy, played by Kathleen Nolan.

the flying performers was enhanced by Peter's song. An unforgettable piece of musical theatre, it is a small wonder that Jerome Robbins included it as a part of an ensemble of key musical moments that he choreographed in *Jerome Robbins's Broadway* in 1989. After 35 years the number had lost none of its magic.

Scene three takes us to Never Land and included the soon-to-be-aborted "Wild Indians." (This song was also titled "Indians Are About" and "Beware.") Then Captain Hook and the pirates plan a "Princely Scheme" for the death of Peter Pan and all of the Lost Boys. Hook was also to sing a song entitled "The Croc."

> And then to my horror and wild alarm,
> It swallowed my hand and my strong right arm
> And it liked the taste; so it started to look
> To find the remainder of Captain Hook!

Wendy is shot down by the Lost Boys and remains semiconscious until Peter pulls the arrow from her "kiss," the acorn he gave her earlier in the nursery scene. When it is announced that she will be staying with the Lost Boys to tell them stories and act as their mother alongside Peter's pretense of being their father, they all perform "Be Our Parents." This song also went through several title changes ("Be Our Mother" and "Happy Is the Boy").

> *Boys:* Happy is the boy who has a mother
> *All:* Happy we would be with one like you
> Wendy Lady, say you'll be our mother
> Do, please do

> *Boys:*   But don't be one who dear-oh-dears
> *(Big Boys):* Dreadful manners, dirty ears
>   Don't be one who interferes, but be our mother
>   Do, please do

WENDY *(Spoken)*: All right! (Boys cheer) Provided Peter will be father.
BOYS *(Spoken)*: Peter, please be our father, please.
PETER *(Spoken)*: All right.

> *Boys:*   Happy is the boy who has a father
>   Happy we would be with one like you
>   Peter, say that you will be our father
>   Do, please do
>   But don't be one who'll make us each
>   Practice all the things you preach
>   Never make an angry speech, but be our father
>   Do, please do
> *Peter:*   Happy I would be to be your father
>   Even though I'm just pretending to
> *Wendy:*   Now do I agree to be your mother
>   Yes I do
> *Boys:*   Be our parents
>   Loving parents
>   What happy family
>   We'd be
>   And once we are a family
>   Perfect children we will be
>   Peter, Wendy Please agree to
>   Be our parents (P & W: Be your parents)
>   Say you love us (P & W: We love you)
>   Do, please do

Scene three ends with another "Princely Scheme." "I Won't Grow Up" is featured in scene four as Peter's lesson for the children. This is a particularly effective song, one that most children remember and enjoy with the same nursery-rhyme quality as "Following the Leader" from the Disney film, but infinitely more interesting and memorable.

Scene four contains the essence of Act Three from the original play when Peter rescues Tiger Lily, although it takes place in the woods rather than Marooners' Rock, which does not appear in the musical. Upon his return to his crew, Hook realizes that someone has been impersonating his voice in order to save the Indian princess. This leads to "Spirited Conversation" or "Who Are You?" as Hook asks and finally emerges with the title, "I'm Hook." The music for Carolyn Leigh's short duet between Peter and Captain Hook was written by another composer, Roger Adams.

Later, when the boys and Indians are safely home in the underground hideout, they share a peace pipe and perform "The Pow Wow." After this large production number, Wendy, pretending to be the Lost Boys' mother, asks their father if he knows a lullaby. In a most pensive moment Peter sings:

> When I went home I thought that certainly
> Someone would leave the door or window open wide for me
> And surely there would be a welcome light.
>
> When I went home I counted so upon
> Somebody waiting up to ask me questions on and on

> To ask me where I'd gone
> Was I alright.
>
> But the door was barred
> And the windows barred
> And I knew with an awful dread
> That somebody else
> Was sleeping in my bed.
>
> When I went home I found that sad to say,
> You must expect to be forgotten
> Once you've gone away.
>
> And so I couldn't stay that lonely night
> When I went home.

Act Two opens on the pirate ship with "The Old Gavotte" a grotesque soliloquy by Captain Hook. Written by Nancy Hamilton to the music of William Morgan Lewis, Jr., it explains the origin of the pirate captain with lyrics full of gore.

> *Hook:* A gently born mother, she could have been mine
> *Pirates:* Or mine or mine ...
> *Hook:* Not quite. Was sitting at dinner, the flowers, the wine, the children,
>   the cloth all white.
>   She glanced at her first born. It could have been me....
> *Pirates:* Or me or me ...
> *Hook:* You think. His jacket was velvet, her lace filigree
>   His collar and cuffs were mink.
>   Her thoughts were most sad for this delicate lad
>   The world would distress him no doubt
>   When in came a footman with duck on a tree
>   And the lad began to shout:
>   Rip up his anchor and down his hatch
>   And nip his nibs in the bud
>   Then pass the fingerbowl Charlie
>   We'll all dip our hands in the blood.

Interestingly, when interviewed, nobody remembered that song — not Mary Martin, Mary Hunter, or Jerome Robbins, who did not even remember Hamilton or Lewis working on the show. Hamilton was a good friend of Mary Martin's, so it's possible that she or her husband asked her to write the song, as a favor. Hamilton and Lewis had been working in the business for many years. One of the many songs that they co-wrote was "How High the Moon."

The scene ends with the reprise of "I've Got to Crow" sung by Peter and Liza.

"Lazy Shepherd" is reprised in scene two, the Nursery, by the Darling children when they are greeting their mourning mother. Once Mr. Darling has agreed to adopt all the Lost Boys, the family sings "Happy Is the Boy." Here begins the major departure from Barrie's play, and as Mary Martin told this writer, one of her favorite moments. "It's when Peter returns from Never Land to fetch Wendy. Peter discovers that Wendy now has a daughter named Jane who has been waiting for Peter to teach her 'how to fly' and take her with him to Never Land. Wendy asks if she can come too and Peter answers, 'No, you see, Wendy, you're too grown up.' I think, for me, that's the most touching dialogue in the show."[24] When interviewed in 1989, Mary Martin was asked if Peter was being a little cruel in his statement to the now grown-up Wendy. She pointed out that Peter can be cruel, but this is part of his character as well as that of any child. Children can be brutally honest, not necessarily to hurt anyone but just because they say things as they see them.

A prerequisite for a conventional musical comedy is a happy ending, which could have been problematic as there are so many tragic overtones in *Peter Pan*. Furthermore, Peter's adventures with Wendy have a decidedly unhappy ending when the audience realizes that there will be tragic encounters in the future as Peter comes to bring Wendy back to Never Land for spring cleaning. The girl must age!

Fortunately, Barrie himself supplied the alternate ending in *An Afterthought*, which was also incorporated into *Peter and Wendy*, the novelization of the play. In the last scene Peter flies into the Darling nursery many years later only to discover that Wendy (without an aged Nana) has grown up. She is now too old to fly. But she has a daughter, Jane, who begs her mother to let her do his spring cleaning. The text of the novel states:

> Of course in the end Wendy lets them fly away together. Our last glimpse of her shows her at the window, watching them receding into the sky until they were as small as stars.[25]

The act ends here with a subtle understanding that this sort of thing will continue so that Peter will never be too lonely. The book is more blatant.

> As you look at Wendy you may see her hair becoming white, and her figure little again, for all this happened long ago. Jane is now a common grown-up, with a daughter called Margaret; and every spring-cleaning time, except when he forgets, Peter comes for Margaret and takes her to the Neverland, where she tells him stories about himself, to which he listens eagerly. When Margaret grows up she will have a daughter, who is to be Peter's mother in turn; and thus it will go on, so long as children are gay and innocent and heartless.[26]

The tragedy of Peter's future is just as powerful as in the original. In fact, it seems almost more tragic than Peter's first meeting with Wendy as the grown-up version of the character reminds the boy of what he is missing. Jane does not realize the tragedy and irony in her line to her mother, "He wants me always to do his spring cleaning."[27] The innocence of childhood blinds her to the fact that she, like all children, will grow up.

The musical was to end with another song for Peter, "Remember Me." Early rehearsals found Kathleen Nolan playing the grown-up Wendy. She was very excited over the prospect of aging in a play. Unfortunately, it soon became apparent that there was not enough time for a costume change, so the part was given to Sally Brophie.

While the initial prospects for the show seemed to be promising, the critics were polite at best and the general consensus was that the show was in trouble. In its review of August 25, 1954, *Variety* said:

> *Peter Pan*, in a musical version, got away to a flying social start tonight at the Curran Theatre, San Francisco, thanks to the presence of Mary Martin in the title role and the enthusiasm of the Civic Light Opera subscribers. But whether it will be material for New York is debatable.
> Miss Martin, as Peter, is in one of her best moods, charming, lively, lithe and understanding. Cyril Ritchard is excellent as the troubled father and ominous Captain Hook. Sondra Lee is delightful as the whimsical Tiger Lily and Joe E. Marks is very amusing as the pirate Smee.[28]

Variety's critic went on to criticize Jerome Robbins's direction, citing that he spent more time in the staging of musical numbers at the expense of the story. "In its present form it would be a little difficult for anyone unfamiliar with the Barrie story to understand just what it is all about."[29] The reviewer labeled the music simply "indifference," although "When I Went Home" was recognized as "the second act socko number ... a plaintive refrain."[30] Ritchard's rendition of "The Old Gavotte" was applauded.

Ironically, the most damning comments by *Variety* were those stating the excellence of Sondra Lee and Cyril Ritchard.

> The entertainment lies chiefly in the handling of the ensembles and choruses and the occasional ballets. As a consequence, the point of interest is Captain Hook, rather than Peter Pan, and Miss Martin is in the rather curious position of functioning as a subordinate player, while Ritchard emerges as the star of the performance.... In the dance department, Miss Lee has no difficulty establishing herself as an important factor. She has a keen sense of timing and a shrewd method of establishing audience relationships.[31]

According to Kathleen Nolan, the problem was easy to identify. The show was in trouble "because the role of Peter Pan was not as clearly defined or wasn't working. If you have a vehicle for Mary Martin and Mary Martin is not getting all the reviews, then something is wrong and it has to be fixed."[32]

Each day a song was substituted and restaged. Among the several numbers dropped were "Happy Is the Boy," "I'm Hook," "When I Went Home," Sondra Lee's "Wild Indians," and Ritchard's "Gavotte." Lee was devastated when she arrived at the theatre after an open-

ing night of glowing personal reviews only to be informed by Robbins that her number was cut. "The number was struck because it stopped the show. I thought that you were rewarded for that." Yet Lee wisely reflected, "The show revolves around a star. You have to face the nitty gritty. And the nitty gritty has to do with reality. It may be tipping the show. Unfortunately for me, the show is about Peter Pan. On the other hand, fortunately for me, a wonderful character emerged unscathed finally, in the end. Is it a matter of creating a character that is memorable or getting another number?"[33]

Often it was Richard Halliday who would inform members of the cast that a piece of their material or stage business was being cut. The tension was further heightened

Mary Martin looking delightfully impish as Peter Pan, 1954 (Photofest).

when the next rehearsal required the star to perform the song that had just been taken from another. Yet how could they be angry with Mary, who was so sympathetic to their loss? The character of Wendy, in particular, lost important lines and songs. "It was very painful at the time." remembered Kathleen Nolan. "I was very young and it was my first Broadway show.... In retrospect now I can be a little bit more gracious about it, but I'm afraid I wasn't as gracious as I would have liked to have been at the time ... but now having had the experience of carrying a show, I guess I have a little bit more understanding."[34] In spite of her dwindling part, Nolan continued to be singled out by critics for her treatment of Wendy.

Only Cyril Ritchard seemed to be calm throughout all the deletions and additions as his contract specified that he was to sing a set amount of songs in the show. During all of these cuts the cast not only managed to continue performing, but they were also able to maintain a sense of humor as well. Nolan shared an amusing anecdote:

> It became so prevalent in San Francisco of things being taken from other people that the little boy (David Bean)

Kathleen Nolan as Wendy singing "Distant Melody" to Peter during a 1954 rehearsal in LA (photograph: Bob Willoughby, courtesy Christopher Willoughby). *Bottom:* Photographer Bob Willoughby caught a chagrined Kathleen Nolan (on the rocking chair) at an LA rehearsal in the summer of 1954, when Kathleen's solo, "Distant Melody," was given to Mary Martin to sing. The Lost Boy with glasses lying on the floor is Ian "Inky" Tucker, who played Tootles. He is also the son of assistant choreographer Bobby Tucker (photograph: Bob Willoughby, courtesy Christopher Willoughby).

who had the lines, "Slightly Soiled, that's my name," kept hearing all of the adults talking about what was being taken away and he was learning all of this show-business jargon.... [At a rehearsal] I remember Jerry saying "Aren't you going to say your line?" He said, "I'm holding back 'til opening night!"[35]

Interestingly, one number that was cut was one of the few that the critics really liked. The beautiful yet simple lyrics of "When I Went Home" and its lovely melody paired with Mary's caressing voice produced a haunting effect on its listeners that was greeted with a deafening silence. It was a tender, moving moment that caught the audience off guard. Sondra Lee remembered "When I Went Home" as "one of the most beautiful songs I have ever heard in my life. The reason that it was withdrawn was that they [the audience] didn't even applaud. They didn't applaud for the Gettysburg Address either. I believe that it was so deeply wounding that people would not want to applaud. It is the story of *Peter Pan*."[36] Norman Shelly echoed Lee's adulation for the song. Jerome Robbins remembered the song and liked it, but he did not recall why it was removed. Kathleen Nolan stated, "It's a wonderful song. I remember hearing ['When I Went Home'] for the first time in the lobby of the Curran Theatre when Mary sang the song with Moose Charlap when they were down in the bowels of the theatre, mysteriously working away. And it was just incredible. It was so right for her voice.... I remember all of the words!"[37]

Surprisingly, most of the performers interviewed for this book not only remembered the words, but they sang them too. Mary Martin told Moose Charlap that the song was just too sad. It fits the story of *The Boy Who Wouldn't Grow Up* so well that one would think that Barrie had written all of it, but Mary's point remains valid. For a musical of the 1950s that was being aimed specifically for children at an age when their chief anxiety is over separation from their parents, the song was not appropriate. It was removed before the play went to Los Angeles, and remained in oblivion until a recording was made a few years ago so finally others could hear what Sandy Stewart called "a perfect marriage of music and lyrics. It is what *Peter Pan* is all about!"[38]

Carolyn Leigh and Moose Charlap had attempted to create a score that was close to the heart of Barrie's *Pan*, but it was not working as a musical comedy. Furthermore, Mary Hunter remembered the great pressure placed on the inexperienced Leigh and Charlap. "It is very difficult to write and produce fast enough late at nights in a hotel room with a stranger at your elbows and someone to write copy."[39] As if things were not tense enough, Robbins had to leave for a few days when his mother died, and Mary Martin was under tremendous pressure from Rodgers and Hammerstein to abort the show to star in something that they were working on. This period was described by Mary Hunter as "very difficult and very painful."[40] At the *Peter Pan* symposium, she related to the audience what followed:

> There was a change in the middle of the production in regard to the music and the kind of help needed for the design of the show. But what I remember so well is that at no point was there any question that there were great songs done by Mark Charlap and Carolyn Leigh that set in the public imagination the character for Mary as Peter, songs that were right for her voice, and also a springboard for the whole play. It's valuable to think about that because there was a consensus among all the people who worked on the play that that was the case.[41]

What remained unknown to most of the creative staff, however, was that Halliday and Lester were toying with the possibility of having a completely new score written by a different team.

Recalled Betty Comden in 1989, "We were working in Hollywood on a movie, *It's Always Fair Weather*, when we got a call from San Francisco, from Jerry Robbins and Leland

Hayward. The show was in trouble and they thought that they were going to close it. They asked if we would come up with Jule Styne and take a look at the show."[42] The "we" that Miss Comden was referring to was, of course, her lifelong writing partner, Adolph Green.

Green remembered, "They wanted to see if we had any ideas and we all told Jerry afterward that the show could be saved. He got very excited and so did Mary Martin and we went to work on it."

"And actually at that point, we could have had the whole score," continued Comden. "I mean we would have said we will start from scratch with the whole score, but Carolyn Leigh and Moose Charlap had written some very nice things and they were young people with their first show. We certainly didn't want to come in and push them out. But what they had was a play with some songs; they didn't have a musical yet. I remember we talked to Jerry and he said we'll go back and tell Mary, and we told her that this could be the greatest role of your life. She got very excited."

"Before this she was desolate," said Green. "The show wasn't working ... they were playing already, the show looked weak and they thought they would close it. That's why they called us."[43]

Composer Jule Styne was also asked to look at the ailing musical. "I produced *Anything Goes* for Leland on television and he liked my kind of thinking and working so he came to me with Comden and Green."[44] Styne was a producer's dream. If there was a song needed,

The turmoil in the development of the musical version of *Peter Pan* is reflected in this 1954 candid photograph of conferences between (from left) Adolph Green, Betty Comden and Jerome Robbins; and Mary Martin and Jule Styne (photograph: Bob Willoughby, courtesy Christopher Willoughby).

he would have it the next day and if that song was no good, no problem; he would write another just as quickly. Yet speed was not at the expense of quality. Built with a strong, confident personality, the man worked with the best to create the best.

Styne elaborated, "Mary Martin wanted to leave the show because she felt she needed more material and Cyril Ritchard the same. So we went up there and saw the show. We weren't going to do it because there was so much to do. We only had eight days to do it because she was going to L.A. from San Francisco."[45]

"We had a free hand in whatever we felt should stay and what should go," remembered Green.[46]

Styne recalled, "We were good friends with Carolyn Leigh and Moose Charlap. We didn't want to destroy everything. I told Mary that we can't improve on 'I'm Flying.' It's damn good.... We didn't have the time to finish ... we did eight songs in eight days. That's about as much as we could have done."[47]

Theatre historian Stanley Green called Styne "one of the most successful musical comedy composers of all time."[48] His music is known around the world. At eight he was playing with symphonies and later, as a young man, he worked with a dance band, eventually drifting to Hollywood as a vocal coach and songwriter. He wrote "Three Coins in the Fountain," "It's Magic," and "Let It Snow, Let It Snow, Let It Snow." As successful as he was in films, he was even better on Broadway, writing the music for the likes of *Gentlemen Prefer Blondes*, *Bells Are Ringing*, *Funny Girl*, and *Gypsy*.

Comden and Green met at New York University in the late 1930s and soon began writing a series of skits for themselves. Then, with young Judy Holliday, Alvin Hammer, and John Frank, they formed an act called the Revuers and performed material satirizing current events. Betty's piano talents were limited to a few notes, yet those notes were incorporated into the songs they wrote. Their act caught on at the Village Vanguard and soon they became "the act" to see. The group moved uptown to the Rainbow Room, and even made a film where the Revuers appeared as themselves, but their footage ended up on the cutting-room floor, leaving Betty with one line and Adolph in the background reading a book.

One of their friends was Leonard Bernstein, who enjoyed being a member of their audience and, on occasion, part of the show. A bond developed among the three that professionally and personally spanned nearly five decades. When Bernstein was asked to derive a musical comedy after his success with his 1944 *Fancy Free* ballet score, he immediately suggested Comden and Green as the writers and lyricists. *On the Town*, the adventures of three sailors on a 24-hour leave in New York, was packed with youthful freshness, fast dialogue and action, and a beautiful score. It was the perfect entertainment for 1944 wartime audiences. There were so many good songs — "A Lonely Town," "New York, New York," "I Can Cook Too," "I Get Carried Away," and "Some Other Time" — all from one show! Another show, *Billion Dollar Baby*, followed in 1945 (written with Morton Gould), and before long, Hollywood was calling.

Under the tutelage of producer Arthur Freed at Metro-Goldwyn-Mayer, Comden and Green quickly became the screenwriters for some of his best musicals, musicals that still show up on someone's "ten best" list. Their screenplays include *Singin' in the Rain*, *On the Town*, and *The Band Wagon*, while their stage credits are just as impressive with *Wonderful Town*, *Bells Are Ringing*, *On the Twentieth Century*, and *The Will Rogers Follies*. Their satirical sharp wit and understanding of human nature, combined with their ability to reflect changing attitudes of the times, kept them working into their sixth decade, when, in 1991, they were among the recipients of the Kennedy Center Awards.

Although 18 years have passed, speaking with the lyricists was a truly memorable experience for this writer as they conversed "in harmony," interjecting and completing each other's thoughts throughout the interview.

Betty Comden explained how they began to "doctor" the play. "We approached this thing on an overall basis to try to make a musical out of it, and the first thing we said was it needs an overall theme, a big song that expresses Barrie and expresses the feeling of *Peter Pan*..."

"And," added Green, "expresses Mary Martin, the star in Peter Pan."

Comden continued, "So we wrote "Never Never Land" and that was the kind of thing that pulled the whole thing together..."[49]

Indeed, "Never Never Land" not only provided Mary with a song that expressed just why Peter refuses to grow up, but the song has also survived as an anthem for hope and beauty.

> I know a place where dreams are born
> And time is never planned.
> It's not on any chart,
> You must find it with your heart,
> Never Never Land.
>
> It might be miles beyond the moon
> Or right there where you stand.
> Just have an open mind,
> And then suddenly you'll find
> Never Never Land.

"When she got 'Never Never Land,' she decided that she was in good shape," stated Styne nonchalantly. "And then she gave the okay to do New York when she had the eight songs."[50]

Comden said that "Cyril was a terrific musical performer and we wanted to combine those elements with his character of Captain Hook."

"So we wrote 'Captain Hook's Waltz,' a crazy musical comedy." Green continued, "The [songs] that we took out were all wrong. We had to write a whole new thought, a whole new character and a whole new theme."

"We had to go back to L.A. where we were working on the film," Comden continued, "so we spent some time there and we also went over the book with Jerry and we had some suggestions for condensing and putting it together and organizing it. Then they came to the play in L.A...."

"And we got permission from the studio," interjected Green.

"Oh yes, we got permission to take some time and work on it."

"We were almost finished with the picture."

"Deadlines are wonderful," said Comden, who was used to writing under pressure. A few years later the team would come to the rescue of producer George Abbott when his songwriters backed out of the show *Wonderful Town*. The musical was to star Rosalind Russell, but her contract stipulated an opening that was then only six weeks away. In just four weeks an entirely new score was written by Bernstein, Comden, and Green!

"Yes, it moves along and it's either gonna happen or it isn't but there it is," Green concluded. "That's a good way to work!"[51]

In addition to the lyrics, Comden and Green wrote additional dialogue to lighten up the play. "The book was there but Jerry was quite worried about the book being too long or too wordy. So we did some work with it, more or less cutting, trimming, or rearranging it.... There's a speech when Wendy is telling the story that Hamlet and everybody gets killed and we don't know if that's in the original play or if we made it up,"[52] mused Comden about their changes. The dialogue she referred to is typical of their delicious wit.

CURLY: Tell us the end of Cinderella.

WENDY: Well, the Prince found her, and ...

BOYS: And?

WENDY: And they all lived happily ever after. (Boys cheer)

#2 TWIN: Tell us the end of Sleeping Beauty.

WENDY: Well, the Prince woke her up, and ...

BOYS: And?

WENDY: And they all lived happily ever after! (Boys cheer)

TOOTLES: Tell us the end of Hamlet!

WENDY: Hamlet! Well the Prince Hamlet died, and the king died, and the queen died, and Ophelia died, and Laertes died, and ...

BOYS: And?

WENDY: Well the rest of them lived happily ever after![53]

Barrie's text was perfect for the kind of humor that Comden and Green instilled in the musical.

Perhaps the most controversial change was the addition of a new song, "Oh My Mysterious Lady." Styne reflected, "They [Leigh and Charlap] missed the boat, you know. They didn't have a duet for the two stars or a number for 'Hook's Waltz.' We did our own thing."[54] Early rehearsal scripts and programs indicate there was a song for Mary Martin to share with Cyril Ritchard, "I'm Hook," but it is probable that this song was deleted in San Francisco long before Styne ever had a chance to see it.

"Oh My Mysterious Lady" extends naturally from Barrie's dialogue. Disguising his voice as Hook's, Peter tricks the pirate crew into freeing the captured Tiger Lily. Hook arrives moments later only to be fooled by the boy as well. The forest appears to be bewitched with the unknown voice of Peter.

HOOK: Have you another name?

PETER: Ay, ay.

HOOK: Vegetable?

PETER: No.

HOOK: Mineral?

PETER: No.

HOOK: Animal?

PETER: Yes.

HOOK: Man?

PETER: No.

HOOK: Boy?

PETER: Yes.

HOOK: Ordinary boy?

PETER: No.

HOOK: Wonderful boy?

PETER: Yes.

Mary Martin and Cyril Ritchard as Peter and Hook. This photograph was taken in San Francisco in 1954.

> HOOK: Do you have another voice?
> PETER: Yes. (Peter sings a few high notes.)
> HOOK: A lady![55]

At this point, Peter sings in a beautiful soprano voice as he tricks Hook into believing that he is a mysterious lady. The staging is every bit as clever as the lyrics, and children still roar with laughter during revivals of the play. Betty Comden remembered, "That was a risky thing. She plays a boy and we took a chance having her play this role, singing in her coloratura voice. It worked and it was very exciting."[56]

"I liked the additional songs very much," said Carolyn Leigh many years later, "but I felt a little nervous around Betty and Adolph for some time. What finally set me at ease was a sight gag that Betty performed while Robbins was complaining about having one too many Indians on stage. Suddenly Betty pointed at one of the Indians and said, 'Bang.' That broke the ice."[57]

While Comden, Green, and Styne were writing new material for the play, Charlap and Leigh continued with their own revisions as well. Added was their version of "Never Land" in Act One, a change in title from "Happy Is the Boy" to "Be Our Mother," and "Saturday Night Polka" in Act Two, which deleted "The Pow Wow." This last change reminds one of the scene in the Maude Adams production where Peter and the boys are curious about what their parents would be doing on a Saturday night. It could be possible that Charlap and Leigh made this change in an attempt to emulate "Sally in Our Alley." "Never Land" was also reprised at the end of the play, taking out the reprise of "I'm Flying." Another reprise, "Lazy Shepherd," replaced "When I Went Home." Charlap and Leigh's new material was included during the first few Los Angeles performances at the Philharmonic Auditorium.

"Moose Charlap was just such a wonderful human being," recalled Kathy Nolan. "And he had this incredible vitality, a little fireball. I suppose there was an initial resentment at the time ... you are kind of on the road and you want to give them a chance. I'm not sure that Moose Charlap and Carolyn Leigh ever got the real credit that they deserved for *Peter Pan*."[58]

Each night during the Los Angeles run the cast performed a variation of the show. With all the changes, it was sometimes quite hectic. Yet, Mary Martin said, "We just did it. Everyone helped each other. We were all having such a good time."[59]

When the play opened in Los Angeles the new reviews were certainly better than those of San Francisco; the star was finally emerging as the focal point of the show. According to *Los Angeles Times* critic Milton Luban, the high points of the show were

> ... a direct tribute to the magic of Mary Martin, whose versatile and exuberant talents override a mediocre score by Carolyn Leigh and Mark Charlap and a second act that sags woefully, although it is soon forgotten through the spell of a moving and entrancing final act that holds one enthralled.... Miss Martin's *Peter Pan* is one of the great events of theatredom and, as such, should be seen. She creates an elfin atmosphere of childlike gaiety that is contagious and is almost certain to make a box office hit of the show both here and in New York.[60]

Kathleen Nolan, Sondra Lee, Cyril Ritchard, Norman Shelly, and Heller Halliday were also significantly praised for their support. With the score still in trouble, Comden, Green, and Styne exercised their right to remove material by eliminating all of Charlap and Leigh's new songs. Five of Moose and Carolyn's original songs were to remain, but their "Never Land" would be replaced by Comden and Green's "Never Never Land."

Comden and Green were not familiar with the original John Crook score, but they placed several of their new songs in the same spots as he did and as Leonard Bernstein also did in 1950, as well as Charlap and Leigh four years later. For instance, "Wendy" replaced "Be Our Mother." Bernstein's "Build My House," also in the same spot, merely replaced Barrie's original "I Wish I Had a House."

"Wendy" is a delightful piece of fluff that could quite conceivably be sung by children. It was cleverly choreographed with Peter and the Lost Boys building and painting a small house around their new mother.

> *Peter:* Bring lots of wood
>   Bring lots of leaves
>   Bring lots of paint
>   But hush, hush, hush, hush, hush.
>   Let's be quiet as a mouse
>   And build a lovely little house
>   For Wendy, all for Wendy
>   She's come to stay,
> *Boys:*   And be our mother,
>   At last we have a mother
> *Peter:* Home sweet home upon the wall,
>   A welcome mat down in the hall
>   For Wendy, so that Wendy won't go away,
> *Boys:*   We have a mother,
>   At last we have a mother.

When construction was finished, Wendy emerged and sang:

> I'll be your mother
> Gentle and sweet
> I'll fill your pockets with good things to eat
> Tell you of Cinderella too
> *Boys:* Do, please do, do, please do.

Mary Martin painting the Wendy house while singing "Wendy" with two of the children in Never Never Land in 1954 (Photofest).

Traditionally, Wendy always sang the song about the house she wanted. In this version Wendy did have a small vocal part, but it was eventually taken away so that only Peter is singing it with the Lost Boys. Jule Styne told me, "We did that on purpose because Mary Martin is the star and you don't want anything to interfere with it."[61]

An important substitution was the lullaby replacing "When I Went Home." An early draft shows the development of this song:

> I can hear a distant melody
> Somewhere from the past it comes to me
> Faintly as the whisper of a sigh
> I can hear this tender lullaby
> My child, my very own ...

In a short time, "Distant Melody" emerged as a lullaby within a lullaby with a nostalgic sweetness suggesting a song with a history, one that was sung to all of us when we were children. Comden and Green's ability to create diverse styles aided them in writing lyrics that were very much in keeping with Barrie's own genius at creating familiarity with original material.

> Once upon a time and long ago
> I heard someone singing soft and low.
> Now when day is done and night is near
> I recall this song I used to hear.

Mary Martin and the cast of Lost Boys singing "I Won't Grow Up." 1954 (Photofest).

> My child my very own
> Don't be afraid you're not alone
> Sleep until the dawn for all is well
>
> Long ago this song was sung to me
> Now it's just a distant melody.
> Somewhere from the past I used to know
> Once upon a time and long ago.

In a noble gesture, the veteran songwriters refused equal credit, delegating themselves instead to the status of "additional music and lyrics by" Jule Styne, Betty Comden, and Adolph Green. Their contribution included six wonderful songs and numerous changes in the script that gave a new comic flavor to the proceedings.

Mary Martin finally gave the approval needed to move the musical to New York, where it opened on October 20, 1954. Under the headline "Peter Pan Plain Wonderful; Martin, Ritchard Are Superb," critic Whitney Bolton of the *Morning Telegraph* led the praise.

Miss Martin is a smashing Peter Pan, boyish, eager, touching, her hair blonde as gold and short as caterpillar fur. She swings through the air with a pleased grin, plays her scenes with Wendy with a charm that is enormous and at times and under all conditions may be put down in theatre history as one of the truly great Peter Pans of all time. She has the voice, the figure, the air and the spirit.[62]

The reviewer felt that

whatever troubles may have beset the production in California, and it was only hearsay that there were such troubles, have all vanished now and from first curtain to last, Peter Pan at the Winter Garden is a show of tremendous and hypnotic magic.

Mary Martin as Peter Pan, pleading with the audience to applaud in order to save Tinker Bell's life (Photofest).

There is no place in which it is weak or faltering, there is no moment but what it is a thoroughly lovely moment.[63]

Variety wrote:

With Mary Martin as the personification of perennial boyhood, and a brilliantly inspired production, Peter seems the perfect vehicle for musicalization. How could it have been overlooked so long?

Miss Martin is so completely right, so believable and infectious as the eternal boy that it seems incredible that Barrie didn't write the original play for her. From her first, electrifying entrance through the Darling children's bedroom window to the curtain, when Peter and the three kids fly away to Neverland, soaring breathtakingly back and forth across the stage, it is one of the thrilling first acts in memory.[64]

Other critics echoed these accolades. In the *New York Times*, Brooks Atkinson called it "A vastly amusing show." He found:

Miss Martin is the liveliest *Peter Pan* in the record book.... She has more appetite for flying and swinging than any of her more demure predecessors, and she performs as actor, dancer and singer with skill and enjoyment. Peter Pan may have been a proper Victorian originally. Hers is a healthy, fun-loving American now.

As the bloodthirsty Captain Hook, Cyril Ritchard gives a superb performance in the grand manner, with just a touch of burlesque. Among the other stars of the production, put Jerome Robbins' name high on the list ... he has directed this phantasmagoria with inventiveness and delight....

The taste in performance is impeccable. Kathy Nolan's round-faced beaming Wendy is perfect — girlish without sentimentality. As the mother of the Darling children, Margalo Gillmore gives a beautiful performance. Sondra Lee, as Tiger Lily, the Indian Maid, is uproarious. She dances and acts a sort of gutter Indian with a city accent that is mocking and comical. Altogether it is a bountiful, good-natured show.[65]

In the *Herald-Tribune*, Walter Kerr said of Mary Martin:

She has tumbled into the role, like an eight-year-old hurling himself over and over in the best mud he can find, and as she darts, skips, and soars, she is the happiest truant in New York.[66]

John Chapman of the *Daily News* found:

The musical version of this most endearing of all theatrical fantasies is a captivating show.... Mary Martin and Cyril Ritchard win over another audience.[67]

Wrote the *Post*'s Richard Watts:

A gay, lavish and colorful musical extravaganza.... A resounding hit.[68]

Strangely, the score was generally not credited as an element for the success of the musical. *Variety* reported the songs as "generally undistinguished"[69] and Atkinson agreed, adding that the score "has no audible fondness for Barrie."[70] Yet the most disturbing criticism was that the tunes were not memorable, or as one reviewer put it, the writers had not "come up with the type of songs that can be hummed at will from the recording of one's memory."[71] While Stephen Sondheim has proved that a well-integrated score need not be "hit parade" material, most of the songs in *Peter Pan* are direct outgrowths of the dialogue and are indeed impressive. It is inconceivable that one cannot hum the beautiful "Never, Never Land" or even be able to sing a line or two of "I Won't Grow Up" after a first hearing. In fact, in the U.S., this musical version of the play is performed more often than Barrie's published version, making it, for many people, the quintessential *Peter Pan*. The new material by Styne, Com-

Top: Peter Pan (Mary Martin) flies above the Lost Boys and Captain Hook (middle) to save Wendy and the boys, 1954 (Photofest). *Bottom:* Sitting in the audience on opening night, Bob Willoughby captured the exhilaration of Sondra Lee's dancing in "Indians" at the Winter Garden, October 20, 1954 (photograph: Bob Willoughby, courtesy Christopher Willoughby).

den, and Green is so well woven into the fabric of the play that it remains difficult to label each songwriting team's efforts. What started on shaky ground was transformed into a sturdy musical comedy.

Peter Pan was scheduled for a limited Broadway engagement from the start as NBC bought the rights to broadcast the musical on *Producers' Showcase* for $500,000, entire cast intact. It is most probable that the play would have had no problem playing to packed houses, but it would have taken a considerable amount of time to pay back its investors and net a profit. The television deal was extremely lucrative for its time and quickly brought the play out of the red.

After 152 performances at the Winter Garden Theatre, the five sets were transported to a studio in Brooklyn, where they were adapted for the camera by NBC's set builders. Although there were only 15,000 color television sets in the United States at the time, the program was broadcast live and in color on March 7, 1955. On that single evening, more

Top, left: Mary Martin's favorite photograph with her husband, producer Richard Halliday, as he congratulates her on the opening night of *Peter Pan*, October 20, 1954 (from the collection of the Doss Heritage and Culture Center, Weatherford, Texas). *Above:* While in later years writers have often stated that the Broadway run of *Peter Pan* was short lived and unsuccessful, the musical, from the beginning, was scheduled for only a 16-week engagement before being performed "live" on television.

people experienced Barrie's play than all the previous performances in its impressive history. Audiences and critics were charmed as the actors moved from set to set in the stadium-sized studio. Larry Elikann, later a prolific TV director, was technical director of this live television production. "It was opening night," he remembered, "flowers and telegrams. When the clock went straight up, you went straight through, and you didn't stop, except for commercial breaks. It was a tremendous strain on everybody, but it was wonderfully satisfying when things went right."[72]

Since Walt Disney controlled the motion picture rights to the play, the production could not be filmed. Luckily, a record of this performance was preserved in the crude form of a black-and-white kinescope. Among the deleted portions were the "Hamlet" story, a dance, and some dialogue from "Never Never Land," which was incorporated into an introduction for each act narrated by Patricia Wheel. Otherwise, what remains is recorded document of a legendary Broadway show.

Most of the coverage of the show concentrated on the mother-and-daughter aspect of casting, which understandably hurt Kathleen Nolan. Here she was, Wendy to Peter, and had received glowing reviews. "And I would constantly be having to tell people, 'No, I'm playing Wendy,' because there was so much press of Mary and Heller."[73]

What is strange is that Peter and Wendy never shared a song. The few times that Wendy was to sing alone or with Peter were taken away. "Distant Melody" was originally sung by Wendy. From a dramatic point of view, it makes sense. The song tells of a yearning for home and ultimately convinces Wendy that she must return to her parents.

A duet for Peter and Wendy would also have suited the structure of the play. Unfortunately, the most obvious place for a duet was lost when Heller Halliday was given the "Crow" reprise with her mother. While the part of Wendy was not as complete as it should have been, Nolan played it for all it was worth. Author Ken Mandelbaum reviewed the kinescope in 1991 for *Show Music* magazine and concluded that "the original Wendy, Kathleen Nolan, is quite marvelous and definitely superior to her 1960 counterpart, Maureen Bailey."[74]

Nolan reminisced, "Years ago, I guess it was in 1979 or whenever [Mary] was doing *Legends* or maybe before that when I was at the Screen Actors Guild ... I was driving down Wilshire Boulevard in Los Angeles and I saw this big, huge window filled with a picture of Mary Martin flying. It was a promotion for the sale of linens of which she had designed patterns. There was supposed to be a reception for Miss Martin, so I pulled into the parking lot and I called the Screen Actors Guild and I said, 'Just cancel my appointments. I'll be there in a couple of hours.'"

Nolan continued, "I went in and I got in the middle of one of the big beds with her sheets and towels on it and she was out to lunch. When she came back from lunch she screamed across the J. Robinson, 'Wendy!' And there I was sitting crossed-legged on the bed and sheets."[75] Whenever Nolan would see Martin in a new show she would give her a "kiss" with a symbolic thimble.

Although the part of Liza is superfluous, Heller Halliday had an opportunity to show her dancing talent in a very charming ballet with the animals.

Despite the major changes in Tiger Lily's part, Sondra Lee still managed to be as animated and humorous as those early California reviews indicated. Her dancing, her delightful mugging, indeed, her very look seems to belong to a bygone era that was taken for granted.

A beautifully controlled comic portrayal came from Joe E. Marks as the lovable Smee. His reactions to Hook's antics are priceless. In fact, all the performers are so good in their parts and at creating a true ensemble, it is difficult to pick individual accomplishments.

Peter Pan also succeeds from the ingenious casting of Cyril Ritchard and the revisions to the text to suit his style. The script indicates that Hook asks Wendy to say a few last words to her "sons" before they walk the plank. Her speech is long and noble. Yet, in the actual performances, Hook cuts her speech — "These are my last words..." — with a simple "Thank you!" His Captain Hook was unlike anything done before. He was hilariously theatrical in his operatic approach to the villain, and his solo moments in song were truly funny. "Oh My Mysterious Lady" and "Hook's Waltz" were exuberantly performed, as were the tidbits of the song "Princely Scheme," which presents Hook finding any excuse to perform in front of an audience.

The actors who were interviewed for this book were all quick to identify Jerome Robbins as the major force behind the success of the show. But like all good theatre, it's teamwork. "Everyone in the cast was perfect,"[76] stated Mary.

At the end of the two-hour program, RCA, one of the sponsors, presented a commercial for the original cast album of Peter Pan. Peter and Captain Hook were represented in the form of marionettes moving to the music of the show. Finally, in full costume, Mary Martin came back on to bid farewell to the children. "Thank you, all you grown-up children, all you little children, and all you middle-sized children for being with us tonight and believing with us in Never Land," she said. "I can't tell you how happy we are to share this lovely land with you. And I can't think how to say thank you to the Ford Motor Company, RCA, and NBC for making it possible for us to be with you. And remember this: always keep youth and joy and freedom of spirit within you. Think lovely, wonderful thoughts and don't forget to learn to crow a little ... with fairy dust on you. Good night."[77]

As she rose to fly behind the credits, the overture swept in for the finale. And a television tradition was born.

Dear Mary Martin. I am wirteing you because I like your Peter Pan show so much. I would like to see it again if you are not too busy. If you can not show it again please write and tell me. If you can show it again please wirte me anyhow. I will be 10 July the nineth and all I want is to see you in Peter Pan again. Please do not tell anyone about this.

Love,
Doris MacDonald

P.S. I ware glass's now and have short hare.[78]

Despite her spelling errors, the little girl who wrote this letter was voicing the opinion of thousands. NBC was overwhelmed with mail requesting that *Peter Pan* be shown again, and they immediately announced plans for a repeat presentation the following year. On January 9, 1956, most of the original cast gathered for an even rarer television event — an encore performance. It is still incredible to believe that musicals of such proportions were telecast "live" at all but a second time is astonishing. As was the first, the encore show was treated with great enthusiasm.

Four years were to pass before television audiences would be treated to the musical again. In the meantime, Mary won a Tony Award as best actress in a musical, with a supporting actor Tony going to Cyril Ritchard. They also won the Donaldson Awards. Mary continued to visit the small screen on several other occasions, each time with outstanding success. Between the telecasts of the first two *Pans* she joined Noël Coward for an hour and a half of "live" entertainment, *Together with Music*, that won unanimous praise from the

Flying back into
your homes
and your hearts

Monday, January 9, 7:30 to 9:30 p. m. N. B. C. TV
Channel ❹ on Producers' Showcase

MARY MARTIN as "PETER PAN"

with

CYRIL RITCHARD

Adapted, staged and choreographed by

JEROME ROBBINS

A presentation of Showcase Productions, Inc.
Brought to you live in color and black-and-white

RCA Victor and Ford Motor Company

TV advertisement for *Peter Pan* during its second telecast in 1956.

critics as a "tour de force accomplishment." Another successful tour of *Annie Get Your Gun* in 1957 also culminated with a special television production. She then spent 1958 touring 47 cities with a concert that was transformed into two "live" television specials on the same day, Easter Sunday! The afternoon program was entitled *Magic with Mary Martin*, a show created for children. The evening show was called *Music with Mary Martin*, which was highlighted by a retrospective revue of songs from her career, ending with "I'm Flying." As she swayed across the stage, you could hear her exclaiming, "I love it!" This was not Peter flying on the stage, it was Mary Martin expressing her love for the part. These brilliant concerts and television specials were merely meant to be fillers in her professional life as *The Sound of Music* was being prepared for Broadway. Sometime during these projects the idea of another television production of *Peter Pan* was germinating.

In a *New York Times* interview in 1960 Mary said, "Since we last did *Peter Pan* on television in 1956, the mail has never stopped coming in asking that we do it again. Now that it is being put on tape, it will be a permanent treasure and I hope it will be shown every year."[79]

"The talk around NBC is that they intend to put this Pan in a vault," said director Vincent J. Donehue, "and it will last for years and years. Magnetic tape, they tell me, will stand the test of time better than film."[80] It is interesting that for this permanent recording, Mary chose a director other than Robbins to stage it, yet Donehue was no stranger to Mary Martin showcases. He directed her in the West Coast revival of *Annie Get Your Gun* as well as *The Skin of Our Teeth*, *Music with Mary Martin*, *Magic with Mary Martin*, and Broadway's *The Sound of Music*. It was during the run of the latter that *Peter Pan* was taped. For convenience, Richard Halliday rented the Helen Hayes Theatre across the street from where *The Sound of Music* was playing for early rehearsals.

Due to the matinee performances of *The Sound of Music*, the two weeks of rehearsal days were limited to Mondays, Tuesdays, and Fridays. During the taping at the NBC studio in Brooklyn, the Hallidays took a nearby apartment. Taping began very early in the morning, yet the actress was able to give stunning performances as both Peter Pan and Maria von

Trapp. "This role for some strange reason doesn't make me tired," she insisted. "It's mostly fun when I'm doing the most physically taxing part — the flying."[81]

A flying accident almost ended the production when Mary suffered a serious injury to her elbow upon hitting a wall during a practice routine. "I nearly killed myself," she recalled in an interview many years later. "I started really fast and suddenly I'm out of sight, and I don't feel anything pulling me back. I'm heading for the wall, and like a shot, hit it. The man who was supposed to pull me back was new, and he got so thrilled he forgot. I said, 'I have to fly again, or those children never will.' The next time out, there was a mattress at the top of the theatre with a sign, 'Mary Martin Crashed Here.'"[82] (For our British readers, crash is a slang word for sleep.) Equally funny is Mary's other version:

> Later, when we went back to do the show, they had a huge mattress up there where I'd hit the wall and they had spray painted it, saying. "Mary Martin Slapped Here." Isn't that heaven?[83]

Not only did rehearsals continue, but she also performed nightly in *The Sound of Music* with her arm in a cast!

Mary wanted the same supporting cast as in the previous productions. Of course, the children had outgrown their parts, but NBC was able to get Sondra Lee, Joe Marks, and Norman Shelly without too much difficulty. Cyril Ritchards, though, was another story. He had to be bought out of his contract with an Australian touring company of *The Pleasure of His Company* and, in addition, NBC had to pay any losses to the theatre company incurred by the absence of the actor. Ritchard resumed that tour after finishing the taping.

The videotape was aired again in 1963 and 1966. In September 1968, Mary wrote to Robert W. Sarnoff inquiring if the videotape would be shown again. Sarnoff wrote back:

> Everyone, myself certainly included, shares your enthusiasm for "Peter Pan." It is truly a classic.
>
> The problem NBC management and program people faced was how to maintain the NBC rights from the Hospital (which expired [sic] in November, 1968 unless two more telecasts were committed) and at the same time rest the property for presentation at a later date. Research had convinced them that the too frequent scheduling of the program in the past — approximately every other year — is what was responsible for the audience decline and conmitment [sic] sales problems with each telecast. NBC is convinced that "Peter Pan" itself is as strong as ever but needs the protection that must be accorded a special to have it remain a "special event" in the public eye.

Mary Martin as Peter with her new Wendy, Maureen Bailey. Bailey went on to write songs and coproduce records for Motown Records, later becoming a vocal coach. She passed away in 2010.

Top: Sprinkling the Magic Fairy Dust on the 1960 Darling Brothers — Kent Fletcher (Michael) and Joey Trent (John). Kent Fletcher starred as Percival in the 1963 film adaptation of *Lord of the Flies.* Joey Trent, a close friend of Patty Duke's, disappeared from the entertainment scene (from the collection of the Doss Heritage and Culture Center, Weatherford, Texas). *Bottom:* Maureen Bailey, Kent Fletcher, and Joey Trent rehearsing a quintessential moment in Jerome Robbins's flying choreography: when Michael slips between his flying siblings. Mary's stand-in watches the 1960 rehearsal where the play was filmed in Brooklyn (from the collection of the Doss Heritage and Culture Center, Weatherford, Texas).

"Just think lovely thoughts and up you go!" Mary Martin as Peter is off to Never Never Land with her new 1960 television cast: (from left) Maureen Bailey, little Kent Fletcher, and Joey Trent (Photofest).

Accordingly, when NBC learned that a motion picture studio was interested in making a feature they were able to work out with the Hospital and the picture company an arrangement whereby NBC's option on "Peter Pan" as a television property could be extended from November, 1968 to November, 1972 with NBC's agreement not to present the television program during this period. It was also their feelings that the feature might be helpful rather than harmful to a future revival of the television special.[84]

The special was televised again in 1973 and then what seemed to be an annual event ended. The original cast album was taken away to college by many students along with their Beatles and Rolling Stones records, but by the 1980s Mary Martin's *Peter Pan* was added to the collection of childhood memories.

Of course, by now, *Peter Pan* was popular with regional theatre and summer stock. Some of the artists to play Peter included Jane Powell and Bonnie Franklin. At the University of Wisconsin, a production of the play made the news for its unorthodox staging. The pirates were brutal policemen, six coeds danced in the nude, Tinker Bell died, and Peter Pan left Never Never Land and became an adult. An Off-Broadway review, *Forbidden Broadway*, good-naturedly poked fun at the reverence many feel about the play, and in particular, Mary Martin as its star.

Mary did not exactly sit back and rest on her laurels. Following *The Sound of Music* she starred in *Jenny* with a Howard Dietz–Arthur Schwartz score. Not the success as anticipated, Mary "played it safe" with her next show in 1965 by touring the world with an established hit, *Hello, Dolly*— that is, if you consider performing for the soldiers in Vietnam safe! In 1966 *Dolly* producer David Merrick starred her in a Broadway musical that boasted a cast of two — Mary and Robert Preston. *I Do! I Do!* was a lively adaptation of *The Fourposter* by Jan de Hartog, a narrative covering 50 years of marriage. With only one set — a bedroom — it earned another Tony nomination for Mary for her portrayal of Agnes in the musical written by Tom Jones and Harvey Schmidt, creators of *The Fantasticks*. However, the 560 performances began to take their toll and the tour was cut short due to the poor health of both stars. The Hallidays retired to Brazil to property that they had purchased some years earlier to be near their good friends, the legendary designer Adrian, who had since passed away, and his wife, Janet Gaynor, who remarried and moved away. When Richard Halliday died in 1973, Mary moved to California and began to act again.

Mary Martin played London and entertained the American troops in Vietnam as Dolly Levi in *Hello Dolly* in 1965.

During the next few years she tried new plays such as *Do You Turn Somersaults?* (a failure) and her own talk show (a moderate success), but it was her son Larry Hagman who provided her with professional and personal joy. Hagman had already established himself in the long-running television series *I Dream of Jeannie,* but it was his portrayal of dastardly J.R. Ewing on *Dallas* that made him a household name.

In 1982, Mary was badly hurt in a San Francisco car accident that immediately killed her manager, Ben Washer, and later claimed the life of Janet Gaynor. A punctured lung, a broken pelvis, and two fractured ribs caused concern over whether Mary would walk again. Yet a year later she was flying through San

Mary Mary and Robert Preston in the 1966 Broadway hit, *I Do, I Do* (Photofest).

Francisco's Symphony Hall for a charity benefit wearing her original Peter Pan costume, which was borrowed from the Museum of the City of New York.

In 1985, anxious to act in a play again, Mary and Carol Channing were ill advised to accept the leads in *Legends!*— a great title in need of a great play. Playwright James Kirkwood, who had already won praise and prizes for his novels and plays, which included *P.S. Your Cat Is Dead, Some Kind of Hero,* and *A Chorus Line,* literally begged Mary to costar. It became apparent on the road that *Legends!* would never reach the status of his other work, but the real shame arrived in 1989 when Kirkwood's *Diary of a Mad Playwright* was posthumously published. With chapters like "Chasing Peter Pan," "Meeting Peter Pan," and "Hello, Dolly," Kirkwood's book, valid or not, was bent on humiliating his stars.

Suddenly, in 1989, Mary Martin and *Peter Pan* were making news again. "The clapping worked," read the cover of *People* in 1989. "Peter Pan Is Back!"[85] It was hard to believe, but the perennial favorite had not been telecast in 16 years! On March 24, NBC telecast its property but it was not that easy to get Peter back on television. For years rumors persisted that the original tapes were lost, destroyed by a warehouse fire, or accidentally erased. Then, to everyone's surprise, on June 13, 1988, a refurbished tape of the show was presented at the Museum of Broadcasting in New York. The initial screening was introduced by Mary and just her appearance alone caused cheers from the audience. Sondra Lee was there and remembered, "What was thrilling was sitting in the audience, seeing this show with Danny DeVito and his kids. The audience went crazy screaming! They called me up from the audience.... You would have thought I was a baseball player coming home from a great game or something!"[86]

Sondra Lee was not the only person impressed by the reception of this long-lost gem. "I had always loved the property," Richard Riesenberg later told reporters when he took his wife and son, they came out exhilarated. He said there were "a lot of men in suits who looked like they sneaked in."[87] Riesenberg was a director of program development for an advertising firm. One of its clients was the Campbell Soup Company and he suggested that Campbell sponsor the return of *Peter Pan*. When NBC learned of a potential buyer, the network's West Coast vice president, Carl Meyer, was asked to see if the tapes from its "New Jersey mystery warehouse" were usable. Meanwhile, Riesenberg began negotiating with the many parties responsible for the musical, including the songwriters, the director, the star, and the estate of Richard Halliday. The Children's Hospital in London was also involved, for even though NBC owned the tape, it did not own the rights to televise it again.

Technician Edward Ancona found many problems with the condition of the tapes. A master tape no longer existed and the first-generation tapes had a lot of scratches, not to mention that they were shedding iron oxide. Two of the best copies were brought to Image Transform, a videotape post-production house, so that they could be edited onto one tape. The new tape then went to another company to digitize the optical signal and reduce the visual noise, which appears as snow in a weak picture. Color quality also had to be improved for the original had bluish shadows instead of neutral. Then the improved picture was matched to the original sound recordings from a two-inch tape.

Ancona credited NBC for taking the time to do it, noting that there was no pressure as there was no air date at that point. He insisted that *Peter Pan* was saved in the nick of time! When the new tape was completed, the network was still reluctant to offer it to a sponsor, their concern being that the production values would not meet contemporary standards. Sandy Duncan's successful Broadway run was another reason why the television special could not be aired, but the main concern was public interest. Brandon Tartikoff stated that the 1970s Mia Farrow production had not done very well so there was no impetus to show *Peter Pan* again at that time. By the end of the eighties, though, they realized what a nugget they had in the Mary Martin production. Miraculously, all the legalities were worked out, and an Easter weekend date was set. In January 1989, Brandon Tartikoff told reporters that *Peter Pan* would again be shown on television. The special had become the pet project for the peacock network, and everyone held their breath. If this beloved relic did not command respectable ratings, it was unlikely that it would be aired again, much less made available on video.

The announcement of the airing was greeted with unexpected enthusiasm by the press and public, with almost every paper and magazine featuring the story. Across the country parties were organized at private residences to watch the show, and countless VCRs were set to record the musical for keeps. "And it is my thinking that Yuppies will station their puppies in front of the tube to enjoy the magic they remember,"[88] wrote critic Steve Sonsky of the *Miami Herald.* The ratings were the best that NBC had seen in several months. A few minutes of the tape were omitted for commercial time, including Liza's entrance to Never Never Land and her dance, making it a bit strange to see her later sing "I've Gotta Crow" with Peter.

The uncut version was released on home video in 1990 by Good Times Video, at about the same time Disney

Top: Sondra Lee (front) and her Indians in another memorable dance moment. *Bottom:* Mary and the 1960 cast reprise "I've Gotta Crow" (Photofest).

was marketing its animated version. The only problem with the tape was the packaging, which falsely labeled the classic as "live" television. In any case, the tape sold very well. A few years later the program was released on the new emerging format, DVD, which quickly sold its initial units, thus becoming a collector's item. This writer has seen the DVD being sold on Ebay at $200 and up. (There are even bootleg copies being offered complete with the Good Times Video graphics!)

RCA tried to cash in on the video's success by changing the cover of its initial CD release of the Broadway cast recording to the same package design as the videotape. When I first spotted the disc, I thought that the television soundtrack had been released, but further inspection revealed it to be the Broadway version.

Tragically, as *Peter Pan* was being welcomed back, Mary Martin left us, dying of cancer on November 3, 1990. Just a year before, Mary had been planning to star in *Grover's Corners*, the Tom Jones and Harvey Schmidt musical adaptation of Thornton Wilder's *Our Town*. Renowned for having trouble remembering lines this late in her career, Mary was to have played the stage-manager, who, according to the original stage directions, would be holding the script. Robert Goulet later played the role but the musical never made it to Broadway. It's a shame that Mary was not considered to repeat her stage successes in the film versions of *South Pacific* or *One Touch of Venus*. Ironically, the stars of these film adaptations are unmemorable while Mary's performance as Peter Pan remains a gem.

"The very important aspect of that production of *Peter Pan* was her presence, her absolute belief in the show, and her insistence that she was going to do it," reflected Mary Hunter at the *Peter Pan* symposium. "I remember very well indeed when a New York delegation made up of her very dear friends, each of whom had a special project that he or she wanted Mary to do, came out to visit the show in San Francisco. She and Richard suffered their presence, while each of that group, one after the other, said 'This is terrible. It'll ruin your career. What are you doing in this?'" Hunter continued, "It was one of the most extraordinary and devastating experiences that could happen to a person who is responsible, as a star must be, to the success and final result of the show. Mary and Richard smiled sweetly, took those people out to dinner, got them plastered, and put them back on the train. And that was that."[89]

Hunter summed up, "Mary's contribution, as a creative person and as a performer, at a point in her career when she was subject to all kinds of pressures, was that she never wavered. She even survived being dropped from the wire in a terrible, horrible accident, which could have been fatal. And it never stopped her from performing."[90]

Mary Martin with her Peter Pan portrait in 1989, celebrating the return of the television classic.

14

Margaret Lockwood and Toots:
A Family Affair

My obsession with Peter Pan began when I was eight years old. My mother, Margaret Lockwood was invited to play "The Immortal Boy" (as we called him) at the Scala theatre in 1949. I used to sit in the wings transfixed, longing to be up on the stage with her and the lost boys, flying through the air and fighting the pirates.

— Julia Lockwood, 2009[1]

While the years following the Second World War saw changing styles and attitudes, instant or concentrated food products, and atomic weapons, *Peter Pan* flew back to London for its yearly visit, each season welcomed with anticipation as to which actress was gong to play the boy who wouldn't grow up. Among those were Glynis Johns, Phyllis Calvert, and Joan Hopkins. Welcome as it was, the play was merely being dusted off rather than given fresh interpretations.

Peter Cotes wrote:

The version of *Peter Pan* which we see to-day is based on this admirable original production at the Duke of York's, but it is in sad need of "re-production." It has lost so much during the forty-odd years of its life. Each year it has been based on the production of the previous Christmas, and each year it has lost something. Little appears to have been brought to the play during its lifetime. The original Boucicault version should be used as the traditional foundation for a new production which could easily draw the town, without the names of popular film stars on the posters.[2]

Despite the staleness in the production there were still occasional moments of freshness, especially when Alastair Sim donned the Hook costume in 1946. "For sheer skill no one could rival Alastair Sim," wrote Roger Lancelyn Green, "getting every possibility out of every line, gesture, facial expression with that command of timing and balance which signalizes the really great actor. Undoubtedly the humour of the part made him play for comedy a little more than Barrie had intended, and indeed it was his avowed opinion that the children must on no account be frightened by Hook."[3]

Julia Lockwood remembered Sim giving a very frightening interpretation during the matinees almost two decades later opposite her Peter Pan. "However, he really 'camped' it up for the adults during the evening performances."

One piece of "business" enjoyed by Sim was explained by Green in 1954:

At the beginning of the ship scene, according to another scrap of traditional which has since disappeared, the orchestra fails to complete the final bars of the hornpipe as Hook pauses to dance

Top, left: Ann Todd as Peter at the Winter Garden Theatre in London, 1942. *Right:* Julia Lockwood as Peter Pan in 1960. *Bottom:* A hard to find photograph of Glynis Johns playing Peter at the Cambridge Theatre in 1943 (photograph: Fred Daniels, courtesy Roy Busby).

it during his soliloquy. Alastair Sim would always make much of this: he came down to the footlights, shook his head menacingly at the conductor, and growled an imprecation. The whole orchestra immediately growled back at him and he retreated in mock fear; at this the children in the audience would laugh, Hook would growl at them, shaking his claw, they would shriek back defiance at him, and his exaggerated terror would bring a roar of delight from the house.[4]

In 1949, Margaret Lockwood, one of England's most beloved film actresses, was signed to play Peter. Margaret was a beloved institution of the British film industry and equally acknowledged for her stage acting so it comes as a bit of a surprise that she is not better known in the States. Surely her performance in Alfred Hitchcock's *The Lady Vanishes* should bring a nod of recognition from

film buffs, yet this does not seem to be the case.

Born on September 15, 1916, young Margaret showed an early interest in theatre and, much to her father's chagrin, was encouraged by her independently minded mother. She made her professional stage debut in a short-lived play, *House on Fire*, in 1934. That same year she was cast in a minor role in the film *Lorna Doone*, but when the second lead actress suddenly left the production, Margaret was moved to her place. On October 17, 1937, Margaret married her childhood sweetheart, Rupert Leon. However, afraid of her mother's reaction to the marriage, the couple did not live together until March of 1938, after her mother discovered the secret from a reporter. By this time, Margaret was already quite popular with the public but even her fame could not ease the tension between her husband and her mother, who refused to allow her son-in-law in her home.

Margaret's real breakthrough as an actress occurred with the release of a film based on a novel, *The Wheel Spins*, by Ethel Lina White. Initially adapted and re-tooled for the screen as *Lost Lady*, Alfred Hitchcock took on this production to fill his last commitment with Gainsborough Films before leaving for the States to

In addition to his classic turn as Scrooge in the 1951 film version of *A Christmas Carol*, Alastair Sim played Captain Hook in Peter Pan for five seasons between 1941 and 1964 (courtesy Roy Busby).

work under David O. Selznick. Completed in only five weeks and with a very small budget, the film, now titled *The Lady Vanishes*, was received enthusiastically by critics and audiences, making Hitchcock an international sensation and Margaret a star. Next she was loaned to 20th Century–Fox in the U.S. for *Susannah of the Mounties* but the excitement of filming in Hollywood soon paled as the film was really a vehicle for Shirley Temple with Margaret relegated to a co-starring role. Despite a couple of other films, her stay in Hollywood was unmemorable, what with her husband still in England, and the looming war with Germany almost a certainty. Rupert joined her for the remainder of her stay, which brightened her

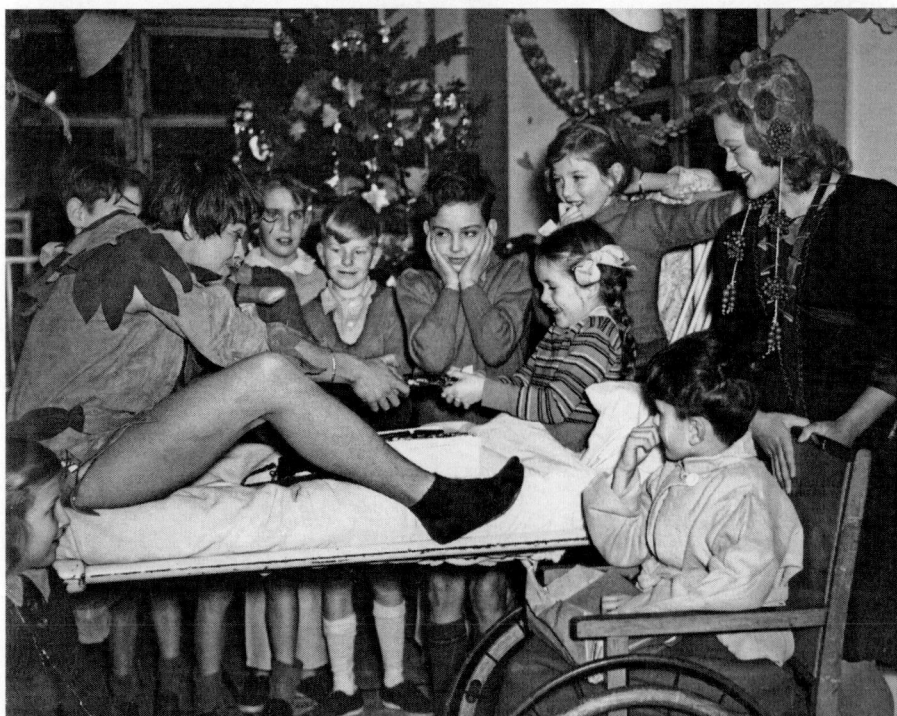

Top: (from left) Walter Fitzgerald, dressed as Mr. Darling, and Francis Day as Peter Pan meet the Duchess and the young Duke of Kent at the Great Ormond Street Hospital in 1944 (courtesy Roy Busby). *Bottom:* Mary Morris as Peter (sitting on the gurney) and Diana Calderwood as Wendy (far right) visit the Great Ormond Street Hospital in 1946 (photograph: Reuters, courtesy Great Ormond Street Hospital Children's Charity, London).

outlook on the experience, but it would prove to be her last dealing with the film capital. Back in England, the outbreak of the war didn't seem to affect the steady flow of motion pictures starring Margaret Lockwood. While still not warmed up to her daughter's husband, Margaret's mother adored her new grandchild, Margaret Julia Leon, who was born on August 23, 1941. Nicknamed "Toots," the newborn child was the best thing about the marriage, for with Rupert serving his country in the army, his relationship with his wife became even more estranged.

Margaret continued making films while her mother took charge of the upbringing of young Toots in the country. For a while, with the absence of Rupert and the mutual love for Toots, relations between mother and daughter improved. And her career in films was progressing smoothly as audiences fell in love with Margaret's sweet screen persona. However, in 1945 Margaret was cast in a role quite different from those for which she was known: the seductive and beautiful villainess of *The Wicked Lady*, who made Scarlett O'Hara look like milquetoast. While the critics slammed the film for being immoral and too daring, it was Queen Mary's opinion that concerned the producers the most as her royal stamp of approval would affect her ticket-buying subjects. Margaret described the events in her autobiography, *Lucky Star*:

That evening was tense. There were enormous crowds outside the Gaumont in the Haymarket, waiting for the Queen and the other celebrities to arrive. Inside the cinema, there was a journalist at every vantage point; watching and waiting for one flicker of displeasure to cross Queen Mary's face....

Her Majesty stopped by the end of the aisle where I was standing. She turned to me, and for a second I wondered if she was going to tell me that this was a reprehensible film.

Not a bit of it. With one of the most gracious smiles I have ever received from anyone she said: "You were *very* good. I enjoyed it all very much. An excellent picture."[5]

Although Rupert returned from the war relatively unscathed, it was obvious to Margaret that their marriage was over, as she had fallen in love and hoped to obtain a divorce from Rupert so she

Phyllis Calvert as Peter Pan at the Scala Theatre in 1947 (photograph: James Swarbrick, courtesy Beinecke Library at Yale University).

could marry the man. Perhaps in retaliation for her losing interest in him, Rupert refused. Fearful of losing custody of Toots in a fierce battle that had her own mother testifying against her (upset herself at not being allowed to care for her grandchild any longer), Margaret broke all ties with her lover. From now on she would concentrate on motherhood and acting — period. She decided to return to the stage in 1949 with a play she hoped would be brought to London, Noël Coward's *Private Lives*. Despite reviews in her favor (except for Coward's), this was not to be. However, a few months later she was offered to play another leading role for a play in London.

Top, left: Margaret Lockwood, the immensely popular British film actress, in the mid–1940s. *Right:* Margaret Lockwood as Peter at the Scala Theater in 1949 (photograph: Wilfred Newton, courtesy Roy Busby). *Bottom:* Margaret Lockwood as Peter Pan to the rescue. The mustached pirate in the center is Cecco, who was played by William Luff for 45 seasons between 1906 and 1953 (photograph: Houston Rogers).

Susan Shaw replaced Margaret Lockwood as Peter Pan at the end of the 1951 tour (photograph: Wilfred Newton).

I was asked to play "Peter Pan."

I asked Herbert de Leon to say "Yes" in one breath, and the next summoned my hairdresser, Norah, to come round straight away and cut off all my hair. "I want to look like a boy."

"Peter Pan" was at the Scala theatre. The Scala, where, twenty-six years ago, my photographs had hung for six hours, proclaiming "Margie Day" as one of the "Babes in the Wood" ... and then the leading girl had returned and I was reduced to being a broken-hearted fairy. I had not been to that theatre since those days, when they paid me thirty shillings a week.[6]

Although not coming back to the Scala as a fairy, Margaret was going to be appearing in the most popular fairy play of all time. The reviews were mostly positive, with some better than others. "There is also a new Peter, as there nearly always is," ran *The Times*. "Miss Margaret Lockwood does not get out of the part what some actresses have got out of it (perhaps after planting it there first) but she strikes us as being the kind of Peter with whom, when we were eight or nine and really sophisticated, we should instantly have fallen in love; so we may say Miss Lockwood does very well."[7]

"She played Peter with utter enjoyment," exclaimed the *Derby Telegraph*, "all arms and legs and youthfulness, wistful, worried, merry, masterful, flamboyant and flummoxed — a typical boy who wouldn't grow up."[8]

As excited as she was about this opportunity, Margaret was even more delighted with Toots's reaction.

I knew then that Toots would be an actress, too.

At first she was like any other girl, fascinated as she watched them fix the complicated harness to my costume so that the wires could lift me and make me "fly" across the stage.

Then I saw myself in her all over again.

She begged to be taken to the theatre every day. All through the rehearsals she stayed entranced. At home in the evenings, Toots acted the whole of "Peter Pan" for me, just as I used to do

Top: Joan Greenwood played Peter Pan in 1951 (courtesy Roy Busby). *Bottom:* (from left) Peter (Brenda Bruce), Nana, and Wendy (Hilary Rennie) entertain some children and their nurse at the Great Ormond Street Hospital in 1952 (courtesy Roy Busby).

By the time we opened she was word-perfect for the entire play, and she was only eight and a half.[9]

It was only a matter of time before young Julia expressed her aspiration:

"I'd like to play Wendy; I could you know, Mummy," she had said to me once wistfully, when she had watched "Peter Pan" for quite the twentieth time. Indeed, Angus Mcleod, of the Daniel Mayer Co., had already thought of this, and suggested it would be a good idea if Lockwood mother and Lockwood daughter could be the Peter and the Wendy one year.

"I'll make you a promise, Toots," I said suddenly. "As soon as you are old enough you shall if we can arrange it. And I'll be your Peter."[10]

Top left: Barbara Kelly as Peter Pan in 1955. *Right:* Donald Wolfit as Captain Hook threatens Peter Pan (Pat Kirkwood) (photograph: John Watt Associates, courtesy Great Ormond Street Hospital Children's Charity, London). *Bottom:* Nana and Peter (Peggy Cummings) visit a sick child in the hospital (courtesy Great Ormond Street Hospital Children's Charity, London).

"And I'll make that promise come true for her,"[11] Margaret finished.

"My prayers were answered in 1957," declared Julia Lockwood. "When I played Wendy to my Mother's Peter.... We were thrilled to be working together; we were gigglers. Once, when she flew she started to spin and then unwound so fast the other way that we were roaring with laughter. The audience applauded us both."[12]

The critics applauded too, if perhaps without great enthusiasm: "Miss Margaret Lockwood plays Peter for the third time," wrote *The Times* critic. "It is a thoroughly friendly performance which smilingly hustles out of court the criticism that there is too much of the Principal Boy in it. She has a tall, graceful, motherly Wendy in her daughter, Miss Julia Lockwood."[13]

Although this was to be Margaret's last official association with the play, Julia was just beginning.

The following year I again played Wendy to Sarah Churchill's Peter. This was a memorable production, mainly because, on a couple of occasions, Peter flew in through the nursery window, drunk in charge of his Kirby wire! Apart from that, she was a joy to

Top: Margaret Lockwood as Peter Pan — a different look, a different year, 1957 (photograph: Vivienne). *Bottom:* Making good on her promise: Margaret played Peter Pan opposite her daughter, Julia "Toots" Lockwood, as Wendy in 1957 (courtesy Roy Busby).

work with and we became close friends. Her father, Sir Winston, came to a matinee at the Scala Theatre and a very nervous little "Wendy" was taken into the Royal box to meet him. I hadn't realised he was such a huge man, as he sat with a rug over his knees, surrounded by his grandchildren. Looking back I suppose it was his incredible persona — his aura — that seemed to swamp every inch of that box.[14]

David Drummond, the owner of Pleasures Past, a theatrical ephemera shop in London, played Jukes during the 1957 season with Margaret and Julia Lockwood. However, his interest in *Pan* continued and he remembered that on one particular occasion the following year, Sarah Churchill was so intoxicated that she was denied the right to perform by being locked in her dressing room. With some gentle prodding, Julia Lockwood elaborated on his story of the frantic backstage shenanigans:

She [Sarah Churchill] came in blind drunk and she was indeed locked in her dressing room. Her understudy, "Meg" [Margaret Riley] couldn't be found so the floating understudy was put into Peter's costume and harness. However, she was shivering and shaking with pleurisy and she loathed flying. She was to carry a script but she was afraid of flying. "Bity" [Elsie Watson], a wonderful wardrobe mistress, told me that I would have to play Peter as I practically knew all of the lines from my experiences of playing Wendy with my mother. "Now look at this poor girl," she told me. "She's terrified of flying! She can't fly. I know that you know all of the parts."

"No, no, I can't!" I cried. She slapped me and said, "Stop it! You're a professional! You can do it!" So, now we had two Peter Pans floating about — the floating understudy and me.

A few minutes before curtain the front manager came flying back and said, "Look who I've found!" Margaret Riley had been spotted in the audience ready to watch the play, unaware of what was going on backstage. So she was dragged backstage and put into a costume. For a moment there were three Peter Pans! I changed back in my Wendy nightgown.

Top: Julia Lockwood and Sarah Churchill in a publicity shot announcing the 1958 cast for *Peter Pan* on October 29, 1958. Their prop is Roger Lancelyn Green's book, *Fifty Years of Peter Pan* (courtesy Roy Busby). *Bottom:* The volatile Sarah Churchill poses as Peter Pan in 1958. She played the role at the Scala Theatre (photograph: Vivienne).

For the opening scene the floating understudy did the flash at the window while Meg was being readied. Because it was only a moment and dimly lit, the audience wouldn't know the difference when Meg would enter later in the scene. But from the stage we could hear all this screaming and shouting in Sarah's dressing room. When I got into bed I heard Bity say, "It's all right, it's all right! Meg's getting in her wire now!" But Sarah got out of her dressing room and pushed the understudy out of the way. "Put that wire on me!" she demanded. I was lying in bed, terrified and shaking, wondering which Peter was coming in.[15]

Sarah made the next entrance but she was not on stage for long. As Peter and the Darling children hid behind the curtains to get their wires attached, Sarah left the stage shouting, "Get my agent! I need to speak to Hal Parker!"[16] Meanwhile, Julia was calling to the crew backstage:

The Churchill family visits Peter Pan backstage in 1958: (from left) Sir Winston Churchill, his daughter Sarah dressed as Peter, Mrs. Churchill, Julia Lockwood in her Wendy costume, and two Churchill grandchildren sitting on the floor.

"What's happening, what's happening" I cried. They threw me through the bathroom exit back on stage to cover. "Where are you Peter?" I cried desperately, "Where are you?" Finally, Sarah returned to the stage to fly only to miss her mark on the fireplace mantel. "Fuck!" she said.[17]

Somehow Julia remained calm as the play continued. During the Lagoon scene David Drummond remembered Sarah removing the pillow from under her knees that was used for gliding across the stage through the dry ice lagoon; she was trying to instigate a pillow fight with Julia. While Julia doesn't recall the pillow incident she does remember the audience getting upset with Sarah, who in turn flicked them off with a "V" sign. "Luckily, they thought she was using her father's 'V for Victory' rather than saying 'fuck you.'"[18] The play was almost over but Julia remembered that Sarah still had one more antic left:

When it was time for Peter to answer Hook's question, "Pan, who and what art thou?" with "I'm youth, I'm joy, I'm a little bird that has broken out of the egg," Sarah shouted, "I'm youth, I'm joy, I'm an omelette!" Lady Churchill later called my mother to apologize for her daughter.[19]

Only a few actresses (Dinah Sheridan and Sandy Duncan come to mind), have had the opportunity to first play Wendy and then Peter Pan; Julia is among that elite group.

A year later, my love affair with the play really began. I was over the moon to be upgraded from "Wendy" to Peter (the second youngest actress to play the part) and was lucky enough to work with some really splendid "Hooks": Richard Wordsworth (the nearest thing to Barrie's Hook); Donald Sinden; Alastair Sim, my favourite; and Ron Moody.[20]

Wrote Patrick Gibbs for the *Daily Telegraph* of Julia in 1959:

There is much to be said for a youthful Peter Pan. It was said very eloquently by Julia Lockwood in the annual revival of Barrie's play at the Scala last night.... It is a part in which appearance is half the battle, and this Miss Lockwood won immediately and easily by looking with her cropped hair and clean-cut features very much the boy of phantasy.[21]

Gibbs continued:

To this impression her grace of movement contributed much — no Peter that I recall has flown so gracefully or with less apparent anxiety. I only hope, though, that her operator steers her more accurately in future through the nursery window in her first act exit — it's no part of the magic to have Peter fly through the wall![22]

Margaret Lockwood celebrates her daughter Julia's birthday backstage at the Scala Theatre. Another reason to celebrate was that Toots was playing Peter Pan for the first time during that 1959-1960 season (courtesy Roy Busby).

Anna Neagle, who had seen many actresses play Peter, including Jean Forbes-Robertson and Margaret Lockwood, thought "that Julia caught the spirit of this unique character most completely. She not only had the long-legged appearance of a real boy, but that spine-tingling other-worldliness which for me at least gives this strange personality a haunting, disturbing, quality."[23]

Julia remembered:

My most treasured memory of playing Peter came during my first production. One day after the matinee, dear old "Gaddie" [Lionel Gadsden] poked his nose 'round my door and said, could he bring someone in to meet me. I was still in my costume and said, "Yes, of course." In walked Jean Forbes-Robertson! I nearly fainted! My jaw dropped and I tried to speak, but the words wouldn't come out. I think I even dropped a curtsey, for this was royalty to me. She was quite an old lady by now [actually only fifty-four years old but poor health aged her beyond her years] and as Gaddie had told me, she hardly ever came to see the play and if she did, it was always when the lights went down, so that she could sneak in and out and not be seen. She had never asked to meet anyone and never went back stage. Although I had never seen her, Jean Forbes Robertson was my heroine and I had photos of her all round my dressing room. Lionel Gadsden, who had played the pirate Cecco in one of my productions, had been Jean's Captain Hook in a touring production of the play in 1935. He told me she was the epitome of Peter Pan. In total she played the part nine times [years] and rumour had it that she wore the costume at home. I found that completely understandable. I felt exactly the same way about Peter. He really got under my skin. So you can imagine how thunder struck I was.

She had a small brown paper parcel in her hand, which she pushed towards me. She said, "You were very good and I would like you to wear this." She muttered a shy goodbye and was gone. I opened the parcel and inside was a thin belt made of suede in the design of autumn leaves. I recognized it immediately as the belt she had worn over her tunic as Peter. I was amazed, delighted and honored. I kept it until a few years ago when I attended a *Peter Pan* celebration at the Duke of York's Theatre. There I handed it over, along with my leafy leather jerkin to the Theatre Museum.[24]

On April 5, 1960, tragedy struck the Llewelyn Davies family once again when Peter Davies, now a 63-year-old publisher, committed suicide by throwing himself in front of a train. Always moody, he had been even more troubled for some time, no doubt by the death of Jack the year before, and perhaps even more so by the depressing self-appointed task of compiling letters of correspondence between his brothers and J.M. Barrie. The disheartening project he called "The Morgue" finally became too much for Davies, who stopped and burned many of the documents. While Barrie's creation of *Pan* delighted millions, Peter Davies always referred to it as "that terrible masterpiece,"[25] something from which he could not escape. Even his death was reported as "The Boy Who Never Grew Up Is Dead," "Peter Pan's Death Leap," and "Peter Pan Commits Suicide."[26]

Meanwhile, *Peter Pan* continued its yearly visits to the West End. During the 1960 season, John Inman, better known to television audiences as the flamboyant sales clerk, Mr. Humphries, on the long-running series *Are You Being Served*, was one of the deputy stage managers whose responsibilities included hiding inside one of the trees while ringing the bells for Tinker Bell. Julia recalled that when children came backstage to visit her, Inman would arrange for the meeting to take place near a prop tree in which he would hide. Of course, the children wanted to talk to Tinker Bell as well as Peter so Inman and Lockwood worked out a system where Tink could answer their questions: Inman would ring a bell once for yes and twice for no from inside the tree.

Despite the excellent reviews received by Lockwood, it was decided the next year to go with another actress, thus reinstituting the annual question of who would play Peter.

"Anne Heywood Leaping into Pantomime" in 1960. Each year theatregoers eagerly anticipated the announcement of who would play Peter in the upcoming holiday season. And each actress would jump off a couch or chair to show off their flying abilities for publicity.

"After playing two seasons, I found that in 1961 Anne Heywood had been cast in the role," explained Julia. "I was terribly jealous. That Christmas, I didn't know what to do with myself and pined horribly."[27]

In 1962, for the first time since World War II, there was no West End production of *Peter Pan* although there was an adaptation on ice. The next year, however, Julia was "back in harness" and was welcomed with open arms from the critics and the public. Like Pan, she had now become a Christmas tradition.

Wrote Eric Shorter of the *Daily Telegraph*:

> Having been on ice at Wembley last year, "Peter Pan" is back at the Scala home and dry. This is a relief.... This year is probably a vintage one, with Julia Lockwood repeating her pretty performances of three and four years ago, and Alastair Sim coming to terms again with Hook after 17 years.
>
> Miss Lockwood is as charming as ever both in the air and on the ground; and she also adds a psychological touch by wondering if, rather than asserting that, to die will be an awfully big adventure.
>
> Mr. Sim plays the captain with a semi-detached glee: a sort of Sim's own alienation effect. And the Hook itself is a thing of latter-day beauty which do credit to any cloakroom.
>
> The performance has the extra distinction of not being doubled with Mr. Darling. To historians this is no doubt theatrical heresy but enough after all is enough.[28]

Mr. Shorter continued:

> Franny Taylor has redesigned the settings, which was a thing they stood in need of. And Zena Keller threatens to stop the show with her perky little Liza.[29]

Like most long-running plays, *Peter Pan* had its share of backstage romances. "Mrs. Darling would inevitably hook-up with Hook," Julia jested during our interview. "And one Wendy; well she went through every Lost Boy and then moved on through the pirates!"

Ron Moody, famous for his Fagin in the stage musical *Oliver*, and only two years away from his Academy Award–win-

Above: Julia Lockwood played Peter Pan for her last Christmas season in 1966. *Right:* Sylvia Syms as Peter Pan in 1965 (photograph: Tom Hustler, courtesy Great Ormond Street Hospital Children's Charity, London).

ning performance of the same role on screen, joined Julia in 1966.

Peter's 58th season "was to be my last encounter with the Immortal Boy," lamented Julia. "But, like Jean Forbes-Robertson, it took years for me to go and see anyone else play what I considered to be MY part."[30] Movies such as *Please Turn Over* and *No Kidding* as well as several stage plays kept Julia busy professionally but she longed to stay at home and raise her children. Finally, she retired from the business in 1976 with the birth of her third child and allowed her husband, Ernest Clark, an actor best known for his role as Professor Geoffrey Loftus in the comedy series *Doctor in the House*, to be sole bread-winner. Clark passed away in 1994. As for Julia, she is happily living in the country in England, a doting mother of her four children and their children.

The sixties was a turbulent era with many traditions thrown by the wayside as students protested the war in Vietnam, morals

Ron Moody as Captain Hook in 1966 (courtesy Roy Busby)

were seemingly loosened, and the music scene exploded with the introduction of the Beatles, one of the finest English exports to the U.S. since, well, since *Peter Pan*. Yet Peter continued in his yearly visits to the London stage with a range of such assorted actresses as Millicent Martin (1967) and Wendy Craig (1968). Donald Elliott and Neil Feiling contributed to the Crook-Abbott score, which would remain a constant until 1971 when Grant Foster supplied a whole new score.

A young actress who practically grew up on the large screen courtesy of Walt Disney with such films as the classic *Pollyanna*, *The Parent Trap*, and *That Darn Cat*, not to mention the non–Disney screen adaptation of *The Chalk Garden*, Hayley Mills was a natural to portray Peter. Although (regrettably) Hayley did not play Peter in the States, her theatre programs continue to be the most coveted of *Peter Pan* collectible ephemera. Interestingly, that year the play moved to the New Victoria Cinema in Westminster, a controversial move as the theatre was huge compared to the Scala, which was demolished after a fire. The governors of the Great Ormond Street Hospital strongly objected to the cinema house but the High Court, while agreeing that it was not a "first class London Theatre" as specified within the terms of the agreement governing the play, explained that if their objection had been approved, there would have been no *Peter Pan* that Christmas.

The reviews were mixed. Wrote *The Times*, "Haley Mills, pencil-slim and suitably boyish, but so vulnerable — looking as to seem in need of a child welfare officer."[31]

The *Daily Telegraph* wrote that it was a "charming creation" but the voices were drowned out by the orchestra and distorted by clumsy microphoning, and that "ice creams are sold after the curtain has gone up."[32]

Still, despite the flaws with the venue, there was praise for the star. From the *Evening Star*: "For being able to surmount this new environment so successfully, credit must first of

all go to Haley Mills, whose Peter is the most boyishly athletic and positively uncomplicated I have seen in many years."[33]

That delightful actress for all seasons, Maggie Smith, took the challenge in 1973, but *Peter Pan* was not to be her cup of tea as her tongue-in-cheek performances were not appreciated by critics or audiences. "She seems to be having a private chuckle at the expense of Peter's melodramatic style," wrote Irving Wardle of *The Times*, "and she presents him with no sense of danger or sexual empathy."[34]

Michael Billington of the *Guardian* agreed, writing that "she rescues a role from robust thigh slapping archness and presents us with a complex manic-depressive trying to ward off internal demons by surrounding herself with young people ... at the end, her Peter becomes a potentially tragic Tennessee Williams hero living off memories and music in a warm climate."[35]

Top: Mia Martin as Wendy sews on Millicent Martin's shadow, 1969, Scala Theatre (photograph: Tom Hustler, courtesy Roy Busby). *Bottom:* Wendy Craig with her Pan pipes in 1968 (photograph: Tom Hustler, courtesy Great Ormond Street Hospital Children's Charity, London).

Anthony Thomas wrote a letter to the editor of the *Daily Telegraph*:

> Sir — The time of year is approaching when we read announcements of Christmas theatre productions and the news that some eminent actress is to appear as Peter Pan. These ladies generally disclose the astonishing fact that in doing so they will be achieving a lifetime ambition. Too often, alas, this satisfaction is not reached until middle age![36]

Thomas went on to ask, why not use a boy? "Is it too much to hope that one day the controlling management and an enterprising director may make the experiment?"[37]

Singing sensation LuLu, best known by American audiences for her wonderful performance in the film *To Sir, with Love*, played the part in 1975, followed by Susannah York, Jane Asher, and Gayle Hunnicut.

A national tour of *Peter Pan* was sold out all over Great Britain, primarily because it starred Anita Harris, a popular television star of *Jumbleland*. So successful was the 1974-75 tour that a record album, *Anita is Peter*,

Peter was panned when the annual production moved to the huge New Victoria Cinema at Westminster in 1969. But Hayley Mills received good notices despite the controversy (photograph: Tom Hustler, courtesy Great Ormond Street Hospital Children's Charity, London).

was recorded, featuring two songs written by John Taylor for Anita to sing. And sing them she did, with a powerful, Streisand-like voice just perfect for musical comedy. "Building the House for Wendy" is a fast-paced "pitter-patter" song with a contemporary sound.

The incomparable Maggie Smith as Peter Pan? Indeed, at the London Coliseum in 1973 (courtesy Great Ormond Street Hospital Children's Charity, London).

The other song, a ballad, "Nobody," is found at the end of the program when Peter realizes that he will be alone. While both songs work on their own, they do not fit stylistically with the other music by Grant Foster and John Crook. In any case, J.M. Barrie's play was quickly becoming a hybrid creation to bolster its current star. Looking at the program for this production it is obvious that no one else was needed for such a task. The cover has a photo of Anita flying over London followed by the first page, where we are confronted with a large

Anita Harris toured as Peter for a year, breaking all sorts of attendance records (photograph: John Watt, courtesy Great Ormond Street Hospital Children's Charity, London).

head-shot of the performer with the bold headline, "Anita News." The following page has "Anita Harris as J.M. Barrie's Immortal Peter Pan," along with the other credits for the production. Then there is a full page ad for "Anita Is Peter, an Album of Magical Songs from Anita Harris, Star of the Record Breaking National Tour." Her half page bio is opposite the ad and two pages later there is another full page ad for "Anita's Jumble Trick Book," where the actress "presents a whole lot of exciting things to make from all sorts of odds and ends around the house. This book which will keep children happily occupied for hours and

Bonnie Langford starred in the London premiere of the Mary Martin musical in 1985, receiving outstanding notices.

hours." Finally, on the last page in the booklet, is, yes, another full page ad, where Anita Harris says, "There's no magic—*Sweetex* helps me stay slim. It saves me 3,150 Calories a week."[38] Pauline Chase certainly had nothing compared to the enterprising Harris.

One of the reasons for the success of the first London presentation of the Mary Martin version of *Peter Pan* in 1985 was the performance by Bonnie Langford, who received excellent reviews from critics who, seemingly, were not familiar with the American musical. In 1988,

Lulu! That "To Sir with Love" lass played it straight as Peter Pan at the Palladium in 1975 but critics liked her better in the musical version at the Cambridge Theatre in 1987 (courtesy Great Ormond Street Hospital Children's Charity, London).

LuLu bridged the gap between the old and the new, being the only actress to have played Peter in the traditional London revival and then, over a decade later, returning to the West End in the musical. She also was warmly received for this adaptation but the production marked the end of an era as Peter's traditional yearly Christmas flight to London was to be no more.

15

Mia Farrow and Another Musical

Flying has come into my dreams ever since I can remember. No wings or anything like that. In the dream I find myself flying completely naturally but the extraordinary thing is that I so often find I can't put the brakes on and I go faster and faster. This seems to wake me up without my ever having landed.
— Mia Farrow, 1976[1]

On December 12, 1976, NBC telecast a new musical version of *Peter Pan* as one of *Hallmark Hall of Fame*'s prestigious specials. There was quite a bit of excitement on the part of the baby boomers as it had been three years since the Mary Martin version was last broadcast. Armed with all sorts of goodies to snack on, another generation was about to be introduced to a time-honored tradition.

As Julie Andrews sang a beautiful song, "Once Upon a Bedtime," over the opening credits, no one realized that they were witnessing the highlight of the evening. Within the next half hour television channels were switched while other viewers fell asleep. This was a shame as there were some encouraging aspects of the program. The teleplay, produced by Gary Smith and directed by Dwight Hemion, was beautiful to look at with its handsome sets and its cast made up of distinguished performers. There was just one problem — the songs! For reasons unknown, an intelligent script by Jack Burns (with a little doctoring help from Andrew Birkin) was allowed to be cluttered with an undistinguished score that just got in the way. The song-writing team of Leslie Bricusse and Anthony Newly may not have been Rodgers and Hammerstein or a Steven Sondheim, but they were no slouches either. Together they had written the music, lyrics, and books for *Stop the World — I Want to Get Off* and *The Roar of the Greasepaint — The Smell of the Crowd*, in both of which Newly starred. With Henry Mancini, Bricusse created the excellent score for the film version of *Victor, Victoria*, and alone he wrote the songs for the films *Goodbye, Mr. Chips* and *Doctor Doolittle*, including the charming "Talk to the Animals."

With syrupy songs like "Love Is a House," "If I Could Build a World of My Own," "Mothers," and "Friendly Light, Burning," is was no wonder that this *Peter Pan* was never shown again. Only Danny Kaye's performance saved "By Hook or by Crook" and "The Rotter's Hall of Fame," which strongly resembled the delightful tongue-twisting specialty numbers that Kaye's wife, Sylvia Fine, wrote for him, and this definitely was not the musical performer at his best. Danny Kaye stopped the show in *Lady in the Dark* with "Tchaikovsky (and Other Russians)" by Ira Gershwin and Kurt Weill, in fact almost upstaging the great Gertrude Lawrence, for whom the musical was written. He went even further with his double-talk antics in *Let's Face It* when he sang Cole Porter's "Let's Not Talk About Love" and

Mia Farrow as Peter Pan. The television special was screened in the UK on Feb. 29, 1976, and in the U.S. on December 12, 1976 (courtesy Roy Busby).

Sylvia's "Melody in Four F." The musical was quite successful but it was obvious that it was Kaye's genius that sold tickets. While the dismal film version was made without Kaye in 1943, he went on to higher acclaim in such classic films as *Hans Christian Andersen, The Inspector General, The Court Jester,* and that perennial favorite, *White Christmas.* Adored by children, teenagers and adults, it seemed as if there was nothing Kaye could not do. Captain

Hook should have capped an outstanding career, but instead it remains an uninspired performance.

Despite her vocal limitations, Mia Farrow played and sang a dark and melancholy Peter with a conviction that resembled the English critics' early-day descriptions of Nina Boucicault and Jean Forbes-Robertson. The several songs given to Mia, though, are not worth the bother. "I'm Better with You," a song Peter sings once he has regained his shadow, was fun but only because of the animated shadow that would not stay attached. The other songs were simply boring and only prolonged the action. It is interesting that just a few years later Farrow's untrained voice sounded terrific when she sang for *The Last Unicorn*, an animated film with songs by Jimmy Webb.

Mia Farrow is remembered warmly by television audiences for her role as Alison MacKenzie in *Peyton Place*, the first prime-time soap series based on the motion picture, which in turn was based on the best-selling novel by Grace Metalious. It's hard to believe today, but Farrow made news in the 60s when she cut her beautiful "Alice in Wonderland" hair during the run of the show. She is the daughter of actress Maureen O'Sullivan, best known for her role as Jane in the M.G.M. series *Tarzan*, and director John Farrow, who, although receiving no credit, directed most of the scenes in *Tarzan Escapes* in 1936. The couple was married that same year. A Hollywood child whose childhood friends included Liza Minnelli and Candice Bergman, Farrow's own challenge to grow up was perhaps finally met when she confronted her demons in her sensitively frank 1997 autobiography, *What Falls Away*. Her fragile, almost fawn-like beauty and innocence were used to great advantage in the screen adaptation of Ira Levin's best-selling novel, *Rosemary's Baby*, which brought her international acclaim. A list of other films indicates her diversity: *The Great Gatsby*, Robert Altman's *A Wedding*, and *Death on the Nile*.

In 1981 the actress began a professional and personal association with Woody Allen, which, artistically, brought her to even greater heights as an actress. Among the films she appeared in under his direction were *Zelig*, *Hannah and Her Sisters*, *Broadway Danny Rose*, *The Purple Rose of Cairo*, *Alice*, and one of the most hysterically funny performances ever as an aspiring radio star in

Danny Kaye as Captain Hook (courtesy Roy Busby).

Radio Days. Farrow's stage credits are also quite impressive: *The Three Sisters, The Seagull,* and *Twelfth Night.* Sadly, off stage, headlines of Farrow's personal life often eclipsed the contributions she made as an actress. While her marriages to Frank Sinatra and André Previn ended noisily, it was her relationship with Woody Allen that shocked many. Allen's purported sexual abuse of Farrow's adopted daughter was just one of a series of alleged abuses he inflicted on his family. Perhaps the sensational news was unsubstantiated and Farrow's allegations were treated by many with a grain of salt, but it can't be denied that the actress is a relentless and strong advocate for children's rights around the world and, in particular, Africa. She has been a UNICEF Goodwill Ambassador, and has traveled to Darfur three times to plead for aid for Darfuri refuges. With 15 children (three with Previn, one with Allen, and eleven adopted), this is one lady who literally acts from her heart.

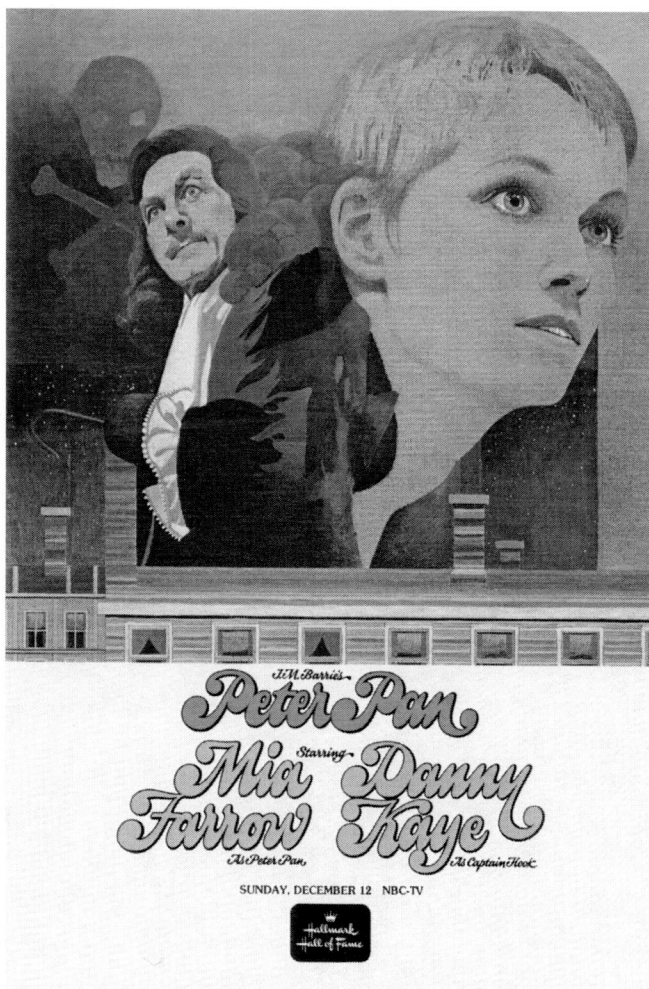

A Hallmark Moment — The poster advertising Mia Farrow and Danny Kaye in the 1976 Hallmark Television production of *Peter Pan.*

In view of her love of children, one could understand the attraction that the role of *Peter Pan* might have for Mia Farrow. As a matter of fact the actress came very close to portraying Peter in a film project that never came to fruition. "I was relieved," she stated in 1976, "because I still hadn't brought myself around completely to thinking of Peter Pan as a girl."[2]

The actors playing the Lost Boys in the 1976 special were excellent, but they were also too old and, as costumed by Sue Lucash, they looked as if they belonged at a casting call for *Hair.* And their collective overt masculinity only added to Farrow's femininity.

Talented Paula Kelly's dancing was, as always, excellent, but as Tiger Lily she was far too sexy and merely in the way.

Other performers included John Gielgud as the Narrator and Virginia McKenna as Mrs. Darling. It's unclear whether McKenna did her own singing, but the entire show was dubbed, and poorly at that, which is inexcusable for a musical. Briony McRoberts played Wendy competently, if without any panache. On the other hand, the play had a definite

Mia Farrow and Danny Kaye screened in the UK on Feb. 29, 1976, and in the U.S. on December 12 of the same year (courtesy Roy Busby).

English atmosphere and it even included an opening scene at the site of the Peter Pan statue in Kensington Gardens. It also restored Peter's "To die..." speech.

My favorite bit takes place in the nursery when Mr. Darling cannot fix his tie. In a moment of frustration he loudly commands Nana to sit down, which of course she ignores. While helping with his tie, Mrs. Darling softly tells her husband to sit, and he obeys like a well-trained dog. Such light moments were surprisingly few and far between in a production filled with so much talent and effort. Watching the program over 30 years later I have softened, as I do not find it as bad as I first thought, but it still remains one of the weakest versions of Barrie's play. Too bad; it would have been a much better play if the creators had cut the songs.

The lack of audience response to the new musical fogged any interest by NBC of repeating this version as well as the Mary Martin video. However, Andrew Birkin must have learned a thing or two, for just a few years later the Royal Shakespeare Company would benefit from his contribution to their version of *Peter Pan*. As for Mia Farrow, she has only blossomed as an actress, with each project a showcase of her versatility and living up to a statement she made at the beginning of her career: "I'm a kaleidoscope, a thousand different colors, a thousand different moods."[3]

16

Sandy Duncan: Back on Broadway

When I was doing it there was a lot of encouragement to be Sandy Duncan doing Peter Pan. I said if I'm going to do it I'd like to do it as much as possible like a boy.

— Sandy Duncan, 1991[1]

In the theatre it is always difficult for an actor to play a part that another created and received universal recognition for, and while too many years have passed for comparisons to Maude Adams's performances, the perseverance of Mary Martin's *Peter Pan* on video continues to allow critics and audiences to indulge. Not since Marilyn Miller bravely fought and lost her battle against the memory of Adams has there been a more difficult challenge for an actress playing Peter. In 1978, Sandy Duncan decided to take the plunge in a production that was specifically planned as her first starring vehicle on Broadway.

"I was doing a nightclub act when I first met with producer Zev Bufman," explained Sandy. When asked if there was a musical that she would like to star in on Broadway she responded, "There is really nothing that I want to revive."

"Why don't you do *Peter Pan*?"[2] he suggested.

Now Sandy had enjoyed playing Peter in summer stock in Dallas and Ohio and she even played Wendy opposite Betsy Palmer in the musical in 1966 that Bufman produced, but she confessed that his suggestion did not generate much enthusiasm with her. "Oh, the rights were so complicated. Someone always held on to them. Michael Bennet had them at one point. He was going to do a new musical version of it. They just went from hands to hands to hands in those days. So Zev said, 'Well, let me get on it and see if we can get them.' So Michael released them to him."[3]

No one could have predicted that this new *Pan* would meet with success, but Sandy was used to such challenges. In fact her career seems to consist of excellent performances in roles created by other actresses. Born on February 20, 1946, in Henderson, Texas, Sandy made her first stage appearance in a stock company of *The King and I* in Dallas at the age of 12 and since she has continued to impress audiences and critics with her acting, singing, and dancing talents. At New York's City Center she appeared in several shows, including *The Music Man*, *Carousel*, and *Finian's Rainbow*. An appearance in the Off-Broadway musical *Your Own Thing* led to Broadway's *Canterbury Tales*, for which she was nominated for a Tony Award. This was followed by another Off-Broadway show and then back to Broadway again for a second Tony nomination for her work in *The Boy Friend* in 1970. The musical might have been revived as a showcase for Judy Carnes, a featured star of the popular television show *Rowan and Martin's Laugh In*, but it was Sandy who stole the show.

Sandy Duncan as the longest-running Peter Pan on Broadway (courtesy Roy Busby).

Fred Silverman, then an executive with CBS, spotted her in *The Boy Friend* and offered her a television series to be built on her talents — *Funny Face*, whose bubbly title was borrowed from the Audrey Hepburn–Fred Astaire film, which in turn was based on a 1927 Broadway musical featuring songs by George and Ira Gershwin. The success of her new television series was dampened with a divorce from her first husband, singer-actor Bruce Scott, whom she had met while performing in *Your Own Thing*, and severe headaches and dizziness. X-rays showed nothing, but in fact a tumor was growing inside her brain, pressed against the optic nerve of an eye. The operation to remove it was successful, but it cost her sight

in that eye. "It was an ordeal, but I refused to deal with it," she told *TV Guide*. "There I was, eighty-six pounds with my head in a big white bandage — I looked like a Q-Tip — running up and down the hospital halls checking on everyone else and signing autographs and being cheerful. I was locked into that perky, cheerful persona I had created for myself over the years." She went on, "I remember a psychologist saying to me, and 'You think you're being brave, but you really haven't dealt with this at all.' He was right. It took me years — until after I married Don [Correia]. One month

Top, left: This is Sandy's headshot when she played Wendy in 1966 but in those days she was "Sandee" Duncan. The change in spelling was a good idea. *Above:* Sandy played Wendy to Betsy Palmer's Pan in 1966. This is the program cover.

after the operation, still bald, I was guesting on *The Sonny and Cher Show*."[4]

Following the operation, Sandy married Dr. Thomas Calcaterra, whom she had met during her stay in the hospital. He tried to convince her to give up her career and settle down as a doctor's wife but her blood was too infected with greasepaint and the marriage eventually ended. In 1977 she had one of her best roles in one of the most important miniseries ever made for television, *Roots*. Critics were impressed with another facet of her talents as she aged from 20 to 70 years in a startling performance, which earned her an Emmy nomination.

On September 6, 1979, Sandy Duncan stepped into the shoes of Broadway legend Mary Martin when she opened in *Peter Pan* at the Lunt-Fontanne Theatre in NYC. Wrote Marilyn Stasio of the *New York Post*:

From the moment she flies into the darling nursery and throws a tantrum because she can't get her wayward shadow back on, Duncan alerts us that her Peter will be all boy. An adorable boy, to be sure, with her grin-cracked face and graceful bounds in mid-air; but a boy, for all that, with ants in his pants and a nose that runs and a downright willful disdain for authority. Without losing any of the fun of the role, she avoids even the most tempting moments to be cute, or to signal a flash of grownup femininity. Her Peter is, at all times, a tough little guy who literally dances with the itchy joy of boyhood.[5]

WCBS-TV (New York) critic Dennis Cunningham raved:

Sandy Duncan is the complete Peter Pan, which is to say Sandy Duncan is delightful perfection.

Reported ABC's Joel Siegel:

Yes she flies. All that energy from all those Wheat Thins [referring to a product she was endorsing on national commercials] ... I've never been a fan of Sandy Duncan's. She's always come across so sugary, I was afraid if I watched her I'd get cavities. But she is absolutely perfect. At *least* Mary Martin's equal.

The show was directed and choreographed by Rob Iscove, who guided her nightclub act. He was replaced near the end of the rehearsal period by Ron Fields. In addition to the exciting new orchestrations by Ralph Burns, "I've Gotta Crow" was also improved with a clever bit of magic. The shadow took on a life of its own thanks to another dancer behind a scrim. The idea may (or may not) have been lifted from the Mia Farrow television version, but the execution was far better, not the least due to a superior song.

Another song, "Happily Ever After," written by Jule Styne, Betty Comden and Adolph Green, was added to replace the reprise of "I've Gotta Crow," but it really wasn't needed, and besides, the staging left something to be desired. Sandy remembered the one time she performed it: "We had some weird song that I did one night. They sort of just threw it in the show during previews. It had nothing to do with the character of Peter Pan. It was a real kind of vaudeville thing. I was hysterical with embarrassment and I came off the stage and said, 'That's it! I'm never singing that again! I'm sorry!'"[6]

Sandy Duncan as Peter and Marsha Kramer as Wendy in 1979 at the Lunt-Fontaine Theatre.

"I'm Flying" with Sandy, Jonathon Ward (Michael) and Marsha Kramer (Wendy) in 1979 (photograph: Martha Swope).

There were two very important changes that affected the characters of Liza and Wendy. "In our version Liza doesn't get to Never Land," Sandy explained. "There's no reason for her to be there, so we leave her home."[7] The other adjustment was that Wendy now sang "Distant Melody." "I just felt it was more appropriate and more poignant for Peter to be excluded from that," Sandy said. "I thought it made more of a statement of his loneliness. It was an important step in Wendy's character."[8]

Bright-eyed Marsha Kramer was given additional material and offered an effective performance as Wendy, but Sandy exerted so much verve and energy as Peter that almost everyone in the cast paled by comparison.

Walter Kerr of the *New York Times* wrote:

Sandy Duncan has convinced me of one thing at least. Flying is the only way to go. From the time of her moonburst entrance through the suddenly parted rooftop windows of the darling nursery right through to her second curtain call — in which she soars rather far than most performers care to chance — Miss Duncan is a Peter Pan who is at her most exhilarating when dizzying airborne.

Peter Pan, for all that Mary Martin and television were able to make of it, was never a landmark musical in Broadway history. It was a patch job — be nice and call it a patchwork quilt — originally put together by Mark Charlap and Carolyn Leigh, then hurriedly supplied with seven new songs on the road by Jule Styne, Betty Comden and Adolph Green.[9]

Douglas Watt wrote in the *Daily News*:

Though some of the songs — "Neverland" [*sic*] and "I've Got to Crow" [*sic*], to cite two of the best — are enjoyable, this is hardly a topnotch musical effort, a fact attested to by the realization, 25 years ago, that a second team, was needed to bolster the show's musical elements.[10]

Countered *Newsweek*'s Jack Kroll:

The 1954 score holds up surprisingly well. It's an amiable potpourri of songs by Mark Charlap and Carolyn Leigh like the exultant "I'm Flying" and Peter's anthem of eternal infantilism, "I Won't Grow Up," with additional numbers by Jule Styne with Betty Comden and Adolph Green.[11]

Kroll continued:

Barrie's sentimentality is notorious, but it's the desperation that's really interesting. Sandy Duncan catches more of this than most Peter Pans (including, if memory serves, the sainted Mary Martin).... One of the charms of her performance is its hint that Peter's refusal to grow up is a predicament as well as a blessing. Not that this is a "Peter Pan" inspired by Peter Brook. It's a well-produced revival of a well-loved show that's high on energy and color. Director Rob Iscove seems to understand that there's an interesting and perverse sensibility lurking behind Barrie's whimsy.[12]

George Rose's Captain Hook and "Oh My Mysterious Lady" were not generally praised. Wrote Walter Kerr:

Miss Duncan, with her slight, lithe build and her close-cropped hair, is much more nearly a boy than Mary Martin was, which makes it rather preposterous for her to drape herself in a veil, waggle a rose above her head, and prove instantly enticing to Captain Hook ("Mysterious Lady"). And dear old Hook, in this case George Rose, fares rather more poorly. Mr. Rose is a master of understatement, an exemplary deadpan farceur; the need to contort his evil countenance, complete with penciled-in-mustache, in the broad Restoration-Comedy style of his predecessor is enough of a strain to push him over into camp.[13]

Other critics, including Howard Kissel of *Women's Wear Daily*, agreed that Rose was too campy in the role. He wrote:

Most of the supporting cast is colorless. George Rose, one of my favorite actors, does not seem completely at ease as Captain Hook — though he too is occasionally given bits that make the role more campy than necessary. Arnold Soboloff seems embarrassingly uncomfortable as Smee. Maria Pogee, who has a thick Latin accent, makes a very puzzling Tiger Lily.[14]

Audiences flocked to the theatre with their children to share Sandy Duncan's *Peter Pan*, which ran for 551 performances, making it the longest-running *Pan* ever to fly on a Broadway.

The only negative criticism the star received was for her participation in the duet with Hook. Wrote Kissel:

Sandy Duncan, an immensely winning performer, really plays Peter as a little boy — impish, energetic, and peevish. She does not mess with the Grand Tradition of alternating between boyishness and femininity, so the "Mysterious Lady" number, a focal point of the original production, just seems silly and dumb.[15]

Peter Pan was nominated for a Tony Award for Best Reproduction (an odd choice of words at that) of a play or musical, as was Sandy for Best Actress in a Musical but she lost to Patti Lupone for her portrayal as *Evita*. It was Sandy's third time being nominated for a Tony.

One of the disappointments for Sandy was that the show was never videotaped. "I've always wanted to do it," she lamented. "And the other thing that's been a real heartbreaker

George Rose looking very much like the Demon King in a Victorian Pantomime, 1979 (courtesy Roy Busby).

for me is never having our production and the arrangements that we did recorded. And the reason that's never happened is once again, there are so many people with a piece of the pie."[16] Sandy confessed in 1991 that her *Pan* almost made it to NBC. "About two years ago Brandon Tartikoff [then head of NBC's Entertainment Division] called and asked if I would do that production as a television special for Easter. I said, 'I would love to. I can just make it — energy-wise. Another year goes by and I don't think that I will have the stamina to do it. I'll be too old and too tired. I'd be happy to do it.'"[17]

Sandy continued, "At that point in time a man named Jerry Winthrop owned the rights and he said [to Tartikoff], 'I want to do a big expensive film of the musical and I would

Maria Pogee as Tiger Lily with Sandy Duncan as Peter and the Crocodile. What is going here? (courtesy Roy Busby).

ask as a personal favor that you wouldn't do this as it would hurt my production.' So Brandon called me and said, 'I'm really sorry we can't get the rights together.' That was the Easter they ran Mary's version."[18] Ironically, no musical version of the play ever reached the screen and we were deprived of a permanent record of Sandy's *Pan*.

During the Broadway run, Mary Martin attended one of Sandy's performances as Peter, an event that scared the new Peter more than opening night. Mary was delighted with Sandy, as were the thousands of children who will always think of Sandy Duncan as Peter Pan.

In 1980, she married Don Correia, a talented song-and-dance man, who starred in the Broadway adaptation of *Singin' in the Rain*. He and Sandy succeeded Tommy Tune and Twiggy in *My One and Only*, proving themselves to be just as good as (if not better than) the original stars.

In 1987 Sandy was asked to replace Valerie Harper in the television series *Valerie* when, after its second season, legal entanglements caused Harper to withdraw as its star. Based on a recent pilot that featured Sandy, it was agreed that she would be perfect as the aunt of the three boys on the show. Her warmth and natural comic abilities were ideal for the program, which was first re-titled *Valerie's Family* and finally became *The Hogan Family*.

Mary Martin and Sandy Duncan. Mary introduced Sandy singing "Never Never Land" on the 1982 TV special *Night of 100 Stars* (from the collection of the Doss Heritage and Culture Center, Weatherford, Texas).

In 1997 she and Tommy Tune did a workshop for a Broadway-bound version of *Easter Parade*, which unfortunately did not reach fruition. However, during the last decade Sandy has continued to broaden her skills and take risks in a variety of genres, including the one-woman show, *Belle of Amhurst*, as well as *Chicago*, *The King and I*, and most recently, *The Glass Menagerie*, with her son, Jeffrey Correia. Perhaps Fergus McGillicuddy's review of Sandy in *Chicago* best exemplifies the payback for such risks.

Sandy Duncan brings a fresh and genuinely heartbreaking vulnerability to Roxie Hart, the ageing chorine who attempts to parlay a murder into one last shot at her dream of the big time. Those who can only picture Duncan as Peter Pan or a wholesome TV mom are in for a shock. Duncan's Roxie is a trashy loser with a Southern accent who never gives up because she's not quite smart enough to realize she'll never win. This is a performance that at any moment could descend into cheap pathos, but never does. Duncan always was a superb singer and dancer, but here we are forcibly reminded what an uncompromising and accomplished actress she is.[19]

17

Cathy Rigby: Peter Pan —
A Record Breaker

It is show that is just magical. I always wanted to go back and do it. I didn't think about it for a long time, and then I was offered the part in 1986 and jumped at the chance to do it. It's one of those shows when you know a part is so right for you.

— Cathy Rigby, 1990[1]

Among the performers seemingly born to play Peter Pan, Cathy Rigby must be considered as the top contender. Yes, arguably, longevity alone would certainly aid her in winning this distinctive title but longevity does not sell tickets. Cathy Rigby as Pan does. I recently asked Keith Stava (co-producer of Cathy's first Broadway appearance as Peter Pan) why she keeps coming back to the role. Why not venture further in developing herself as an "actress"? Noting that the inflection of my question was oozing with sarcasm, Stava quickly cut me down to size while defending Cathy: "Why are you revisiting Peter Pan with another book?"[2] Touché! I immediately got off my high horse.

Since 1990, Cathy has been playing the role, off and on, to sold-out houses across the country and on Broadway, where she was nominated for a Tony award in 1991. Even before this extraordinary run Cathy played the role in 1973 for the NBC Arena Touring Production and in 1986 for a West Coast production where she received the DramaLogue award (she received another in 1988 for her role as Dorothy in *The Wizard of Oz*). When it was announced that she would be making her farewell tour in the production of 1999, tickets were selling on Ebay for astronomical prices. And, just as this book goes into print, there's talk of Cathy returning to the role for an international tour, evoking anticipation akin to that which audiences experienced 100 years ago when awaiting the return of Maude Adams as Peter Pan each year. Not bad for a kid from Long Beach, California.

When Cathy first came to Broadway as Pan, one would have thought that prospective audiences were up to their ears with the boy who wouldn't grow up. Not only were the Disney and Mary Martin versions available on videotapes and discs, another adaptation was brought to the small screen by Fox television via *Peter Pan and the Pirates*, presented to afterschool kiddies every weekday. The wonderfully executed drawings and dazzling colors became a delightful diversion from the run-of-the-mill animated cartoons offered during the early nineties. Yet, on December 13, 1990, amid the videos, television series, and even comic books, *Peter Pan* once more flew on Broadway to the delight of children and their parents.

Cathy Rigby as Peter Pan in 1990. Cathy first played the role in 1975.

Producers Thomas P. McCoy and Keith Stava booked a cross-country tour that did fantastic business since its beginning nearly a year before. Though the Broadway run was limited to only six weeks, it generated an enthusiasm for children's theatre that had become rare at that time of year. Perhaps what surprised the critics most were the performances given by a little waif named Cathy Rigby.

Cathy Rigby was already a household name thanks to her spectacular acrobatics as a gymnast in the Summer Olympics of 1968 and 1972. Her position as sports commentator for ABC furthered her appeal to mass audiences. In 1973 Cathy was offered the part of Peter in the NBC Arena Touring Production. The physical combination of Cathy's natural athleticism and *Peter Pan* seemed a natural as her gymnastic experience would enhance the character's bravado. The voices for this show, however, were all prerecorded and did not necessarily belong to the performers seen on the stage. Tom Adair joined Jule Styne to create two new songs, "Hook's Hook" and "Youth, Joy, and Freedom," the latter sung by Yvonne Green as Peter. A souvenir 45-rpm record of "Youth, Joy, and Freedom" was paired with "I've Gotta Crow" and was sold at performances (see Appendix A). Green also assisted director Tom Hansen with choreography. Despite the dubbed voice, this production hooked Cathy on acting.

    Aided by her strict sense of discipline ("She's a pro," Stava offered; "that's what makes her so good!"[3]), Cathy began acting and singing lessons, and in 1981 she appeared as Dorothy in *The Wizard of Oz*, for which she received excellent reviews. From there she went on to *Meet Me in St. Louis*, *Paint Your Wagon*, and *They're Playing My Song*. Then, in 1986, she got the lead in the legitimate version of the musical, *Peter Pan*. During our interview in 1991, Cathy presented an analogy between herself and Peter: "I grew up very much like him. On one hand I was full of adventure and taking risks, being very daring and throwing caution to the wind with my gymnastics. There was another part of my situation [where] I had a coach who wanted to keep me a child, didn't want me to grow up, didn't want me to take responsibility. I didn't deal with feelings very well."

    She continued, "I was very much like Peter.... I'd put my fingers in my ears if I couldn't deal with something ... a lot of bravado, toughening-everything act. And that's exactly what [he] does. I also grew up very tomboyish. There were many parallels in my life to that of Peter Pan. I felt like I was at home with the part."[4]

    This writer felt like Scrooge as he shelled out $97 for two tickets to see a December 26, 1990, performance of the musical. I had never seen Cathy Rigby in a play and I wasn't too keen on spending that kind of money for an introduction. Furthermore, this was to be a special evening as I was introducing my six-year-old son, Drew, to Broadway. While it seemed apropos that *Peter Pan* was being offered

Peter Pan to the rescue. A young Cathy Rigby in 1975 in the NBC Touring Production.

during the Christmas season as it had been in London for so many years, I wanted Drew's first Broadway experience to be a memorable one. For my part, I merely expected a serviceable performance by a gymnast.

Surprise! Cathy Rigby gave an enchanting and poignant portrayal that instantly captured the hearts of the audience and, more importantly for me at the time, Drew. Rather than saturate the character with her renowned acrobatic talents, she was beautifully restrained. Her Peter had the physical ability to do what he wanted, but only when he wanted. Her natural athletic prowess was seen to great advantage in "I've Gotta Crow," where Peter can actually impress Wendy in ways that a real little boy might try. No more theatricality in a finger-shadow puppet show or a trick shadow

Cathy Rigby's 1986 *Peter Pan* program from Long Beach, California.

with a life of its own — just a little boy running about showing all of his special tricks. But wait a minute! Cathy Rigby could also sing! Her voice was strong, clear, with just enough huskiness to provide another asset to Peter.

"I think one of the things that we tried to do in this particular version is to go back and make it as much of the straight play as we could," Cathy reflected. "The show has been so commercialized over the years that it lost some of the integrity of the story." Hmm, I wonder if Cathy has seen any of the English pantomime versions of the play. Director Fran Soeder omitted the "Oh My Mysterious Lady" number and reverted to Barrie's original "Marooners' Rock," which, according to Rigby, "is crucial to the show."[5]

Since Cathy has played the musical with and without "Oh My Mysterious Lady," it was interesting to hear her comments about that number. "It totally took away from the fact that this is a boy. All of a sudden he becomes this woman singing this aria, it becomes about slapstick and shtick. I think as a vehicle for Mary and Cyril Ritchard, it worked! It was lovely and funny. It fit the style of the show they were doing. But I felt it would really not fit." She explained further, "If we were going to make this play with music and go back

The Long Beach *Peter Pan* production in 1986. John Schuck as Captain Hook and Cathy Rigby as Peter Pan (Photofest).

to the book, we needed to take it out. The writing is clever enough. It's funny, it's endearing; you don't need to add that stuff to it. It holds itself without it and we want people to get lost in the story."[6]

The addition of Marooners' Rock allowed audiences to experience the vulnerability of Peter as well as hear a classic line in literature, "To die will be an awfully big adventure."

It also provided Rigby with an opportunity to show her range as an actress. This segment is the most touching in the play and a welcome addition for audiences who have never witnessed what is regarded as a classic scene in theatre.

Stephen Hanan brought a sinister quality to Hook that generations of audiences had not encountered. Even his makeup resembled that of early portrayals in England. When he threatened to blow up the ship, creating a holocaust of children, you better believe that he would do it. Hanan combined his excellent voice and poise to create a villain straight out of an operetta, reminiscent at times of Barnaby from *Babes in Toyland*, yet devoid of camp. He was fully capable of torturing his victims before murdering them, but not before he entertained them with a song. Altogether, this Hook was a demented character who could easily scare young children who were accustomed to such villains from films and television. He scared me!

Cindy Robinson was delightful and humorous as Wendy with her sharp delivery in that odd little voice. Lauren Thompson brought a fresh interpretation to Mrs. Darling, a woman who now tolerates her husband's behavior. Finally, Don Potter was as memorable as Smee as any before him, only his costume was quite more ornate.

So how did the critics react? Linda Winer of *New York Newsday* was impressed with Rigby's gymnastic abilities but

> more important, she creates a character — believably boyish, a little gruff, a little fragile — who knows his way around Neverland [sic] like a long term resident.... When someone comes too close to touching Peter's heart, she hunches her shoulders and stiffens up like a scared tough kid. With her solid little body and her round face, she has the pug quality of the young James Cagney.[7]

Daily News critic Howard Kissel said:

> When Cathy Rigby, who plays Peter in this revival, whooshes in through the window of the Darling's London townhouse, flying with an abandon, a carefree spirit few have equaled, the musical seems utterly fresh and enchanting.... Chunky, tomboyish, uncomplicated, Rigby is youthful energy itself. She crows jubilantly. She has a hearty singing voice, fine for most of the music, not agile or high enough for the operatic duet written for Peter and Hook, which has been cut.[8]

Kissel also felt that Rigby

> acts with great conviction, especially when she makes her impassioned plea for us to clap to save Tinker Bell's life. She is most persuasive when she's in the air: No one has made flying look more exhilarating.[9]

Edwin Wilson of the *Wall Street Journal* was equally impressed with the flying scenes. He went on to write:

> But Ms. Rigby has other assets. She is a true tomboy, which is just right for Peter, and she has quite an acceptable singing voice — certainly good enough for the score of *Peter Pan*. All in all, this remains an ideal introduction for the youngsters to the joys of theatre. The older folk who take them won't have a bad time either.[10]

Among the unimpressed was Clive Barnes of the *New York Post*, who wrote that

> this musical version of *Peter Pan* ... has only two things wrong with it: the play upon which it is based and the music which has been added to it.[11]

Bah! Humbug!

He found the production mediocre at best. "Which brings us to Cathy Rigby," he continued. "Who flies through the air with no-nonsense athleticism and, in this vastly over

Cathy Rigby as Peter and Cindy Robinson as Wendy.

amplified production, sings boldly, accurately and with a touch of that trace of charming huskiness which was a Mary Martin trademark."[12]

Huskiness? Mary Martin's voice? Perhaps during her last years performing but certainly not when she was in her prime. As a matter of fact, while I very much enjoy listening to Mary Martin's recordings of the songs on CD, Cathy Rigby sings the songs as extensions of her dialogue and character. Mary sounded like a child while acting but when she sang, what we heard was the beautiful voice of a woman. Cathy manages to be a child, even when singing. Her character is never split.

Still, there were others who were not as impressed: "So far so moderately good, but unfortunately Rigby, while engaging in her enthusiasm, is charmless in her personality. She also lacks that androgynous grace (neither masculine, feminine, nor neuter) which Barrie stole like a shadow from the 'principal boys,' always played by women, of English traditional pantomime, and was once admirably displayed by Martin and Duncan."[13]

But let's end on a high note! Mel Gussow of the *New York Times* praised Rigby's "stage presence and a pleasant singing voice and, as one might expect, her physical capacity in flight exceeds that of her predecessors."[14] He was not, however, impressed with the production as a whole. Almost all of the critics agreed the sound system was overamplified, giving the feeling that occasionally the singing was not "live," although co-producer Stava assured me that this was not the case.

Following the Broadway run, Cathy took the show back on the road, returning to the Great White Way in 1991 just in time for Christmas for the so-called *Thirty-Fifth Anniversary Production*, which this time was solely produced by McCoy/Rigby Entertainment, a company formed by Cathy and her husband, producer Tom McCoy. Together they package musical plays to showcase Cathy's talents. In 1992, she appeared in *Annie Get Your Gun*. By 1998 she was touring as Peter again and even taped a video version of the play for A & E that was also available on VHS and DVD formats. And I'm telling you folks, honestly, she keeps getting better and better. On tape she has added a bit of a cockney accent and she even looks more like a boy now. (OK, there is an overblown "Ugg-A-Wugg" number that emulates something from *Stomp*. But audiences eat it up.)

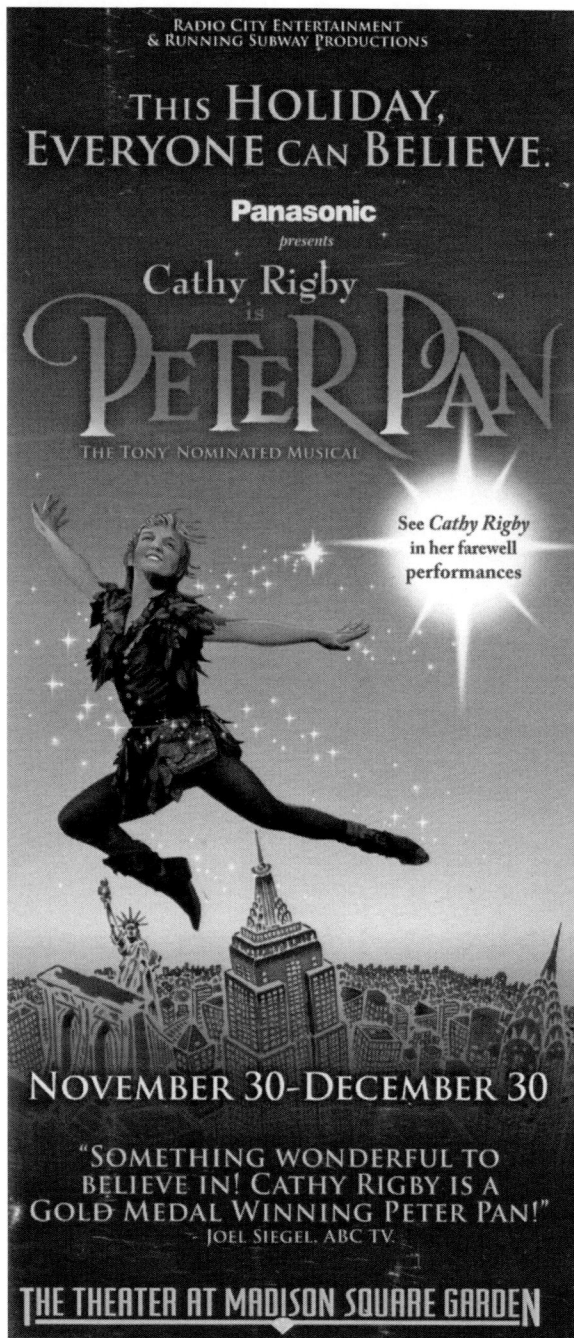

RADIO CITY ENTERTAINMENT & RUNNING SUBWAY PRODUCTIONS

THIS HOLIDAY, EVERYONE CAN BELIEVE.

Panasonic *presents*

Cathy Rigby is PETER PAN

THE TONY-NOMINATED MUSICAL

See *Cathy Rigby* in her farewell performances

NOVEMBER 30–DECEMBER 30

"SOMETHING WONDERFUL TO BELIEVE IN! CATHY RIGBY IS A GOLD MEDAL WINNING PETER PAN!"
— JOEL SIEGEL, ABC TV.

THE THEATER AT MADISON SQUARE GARDEN

Cathy Rigby's farewell performance flyer.

Cathy continued flying as Pan in 2005, gave a farewell tour that ended in 2009 and plans on still another tour — world-wide. If you have not done so already, I urge you to catch her act so that you may someday tell your grandchildren, "I saw Cathy Rigby in *Peter Pan*." Because it's not just that she has been flying longer than anyone else; no, it's that she continues to add layers of depth and nuance worthy of, well, worthy of J.M. Barrie's original play. Cathy has joined with *Peter Pan* to become a theatrical tradition. And perhaps, someday, when the McCoy/Rigby club has run its course with *Peter Pan*, and vehicles tailor-made for her musical talents, Cathy will be able to really spread her wings as an actress and fly. Not for any world records, and not for oodles of more money, but rather because, above all, she is an actress; she makes her audiences believe that she is Peter Pan. Meanwhile, like *Peter Pan*, Cathy Rigby never grows up ... I mean old.

18

A Change of Gender:
Peter Pan as a Real Boy

Why does it always have to be a peterless Pan?
— Silent film actor Gareth Hughes, 1924[1]

On December 16, 1982, British audiences were buzzing as they once again flocked to treat themselves to Barrie's Christmas treat. The cause of the excitement was that Peter Pan would be performed at the Barbican Theatre by the Royal Shakespeare Company and Peter would be played for the first time by a man. As previously seen, the tradition of Barrie's time mandated that an actress play the role of the principal boy in pantomime. Barrie had no idea that his play was beyond the level of that kind of theatre. This is not to say that he never wanted a boy to play Peter, for one of his letters reveals that he was more than interested.

---

29 September [ʼ20]

Ainley has found a boy whom he thinks highly of a possible Peter. I have sometimes hankered after that, and as the photographs he sent me are promising I've agreed to wait a fortnight until I can see the boy. Of course if he is decided on, it would affect Wendy and the other boys — mean their being children, so nothing definitive can be done as present about such parts. Ainley also says he would like to play Mr. Darling as well as Hook — as du Maurier used to do.[2]

In 1920 Henry Ainley temporarily restored the tradition of one actor doubling in the parts of Hook and Mr. Darling, but the part of Peter was again played by an actress, this time Edna Best.

Barrie also expressed interest in silent film star Charlie Chaplin playing the part and it has been suggested that he wrote his film scenario with that thought. Yet by 1924, he was insisting that a girl must play Peter in the Famous Players' silent film, causing Gareth Hughes, an excellent Tommy in the film version of Barrie's *Sentimental Tommy*, to lament publicly his displeasure of the casting of a female Peter.

Not counting the Davies boys, the first male Pan was probably played by Herbert Hollom in a special performance by the juvenile members of the *Peter Pan* company at the Duke of York's Theatre in London. This merry masquerade became something of a tradition since the first 1906 performance when Winifred Geoghegan traded her part of Michael for

Peter that day and was performed at different times by the various children who were then in the production. Young Herbert Hollom followed his older brother Ernest's footsteps into the part of Michael when Ernest left the company at the end of the 1906-07 season. For three years Herbert played the part, and when he outgrew it in 1909, he simply went on to play John. In between his transition he was able to play Peter for that one performance on February 8, 1910 (two years later he played Captain Hook).

Child actor Jimmy Hanley was thought of for the leading role after play-

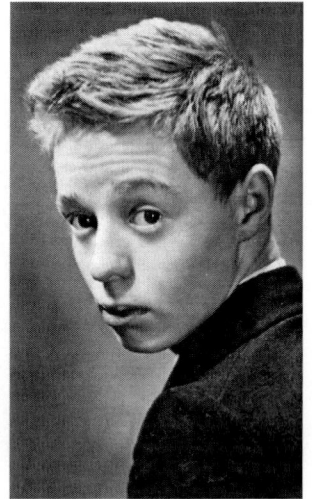

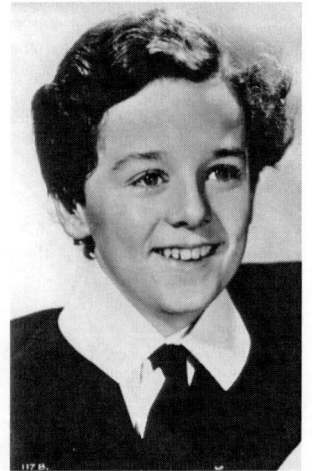

Above, left: Jeremy Sumpter as Peter Pan from the 2003 film (Universal Pictures/Photofest). *Top right:* Jimmy Hanley was the perfect juvenile lead in the late thirties. According to theatre historian, Roy Busby, many thought he would have made the perfect Pan. He played Slightly in the 1937 and 1938 seasons. A few years later he would have a moderately successful career in films and marry Dinah Sheridan (courtesy Roy Busby). *Bottom right:* Freddie Bartholomew as Peter Pan? The child actor, famous for the title role in the film *Little Lord Fauntleroy*, would have been a good bet. But he only played the part on the radio in 1936.

ing John at the Palladium. Hanley, a student of the Italia Conti Academy, which in the 1920s and 1930s was one of the main sources for finding youngsters for Peter Pan, was a handsome youth who went on to specialize in juvenile roles by the Rank Studio. He was married to Dinah Sheridan for ten years, producing two children.

The first commercial venture that saw Peter finally being played by a boy was not on the stage or, for that matter, in England. On February 24, 1936, Freddie Bartholomew took the part on a radio program. The British-born Bartholomew was at the height of his career as a child movie star in *David Copperfield*, *Little Lord Fauntleroy*, and *Captains Courageous*. Although usually cast as the ideal English youngster, this attractive, curly-headed child demonstrated that he could also play a real rough-and-tumble boy, but his performance as Peter never went beyond radio, and for that he was only mildly received for his pleasant vocal performance. Aaron Stein for the *New York Post* wrote:

> Unfortunately, the production can boast the dubious distinction of being that very rare thing, a *Peter Pan* with a masculine star. The all important illusion faltered and died.[3]

Two year later the Clare Tree Majors Children's Theatre of New York presented the first major production of the play since the demise of the Civic Repertory Company. John Ireland played Captain Hook with Jewel Morse as Wendy, and Leslie C. Gorall, an 18-year-old boy from New Haven, Connecticut, was Peter. Sturdily built with dark curly hair, Leslie was one of 50 young men who auditioned for the role. He began his acting career at the age of six, appearing in a stage version of *The Wizard of Oz*. On Broadway he was featured in *Daughters of Atreus* and *High Tor*. Audiences must have liked him, as the play toured the United States for a year!

Eighteen-year-old Leslie Gorall toured in *Peter Pan* with the Clare Tree Major Children's Theatre Production from 1938 through 1939 (photograph: Stadler).

John Ireland as Hook, Clare Tree Major Children's Theatre Productions, Chappaque, New York, 1939 (photograph: Stadler).

Except for Bobby Driscoll's voice in the Disney film, Peter would not be played by a boy again until the Royal Shakespeare Company decided to add *Peter Pan* to its 1982 season.

The RSC has the reputation as one of the best theatre companies in the world. The classical training of the actors and their dedication to Shakespearean drama is combined with repertory experience that adds to the distinction of each play, even those not by the Bard himself. The company's origins trace back to 1875 in Stratford when it was incorporated as the Shakespeare Memorial Theatre. A fire destroyed the building in 1826 and the company was housed in a cinema house for six years. In 1932, a new Royal Shakespeare Theatre was built. In addition to that one, the Aldwych in London was used from 1960 until 1982, when the company, under the artistic direction of Trevor Nunn, moved to the Barbican. It is here *Peter Pan* was blessed with its finest production in many years.

The core of the creative talent responsible for the look of the new production was the same group that created *Nicholas Nickleby*—directors Nunn and John Caird, designer John Napier, and composer Stephen Oliver. For *Nickleby* the directors used Charles Dickens's narrative as part of Nicholas's dialogue. They decided to approach *Peter Pan* in a similar way. Andrew Birkin, author, film director, and an authority on Barrie, was asked to help create a version of the play that was as close to the author's intentions as possible. The sources for the revised script included the 1904 version, the novel, the silent-film scenario, and original unpublished manuscripts. During the meshing of this material, new elements were also added to give a "Barriesque" touch. Much of the charm of the 1928 published play is in the insightful stage directions, the only way the author could include himself as part of the text. The dialogue may belong to the characters, but the comments belong to Barrie. Normally, when a company chooses this script, Barrie's thoughts are left unheard. The creative team cleverly allowed Barrie to take his rightful place as one of the characters. A delightful narration was added for the Story Teller, not Liza, but an actor dressed to look like Barrie. This loving and respectful tribute allowed the audience to see the author deeply entrenched in his Never Never Land.

From the original manuscript was added the ending of the Lost Boys grown up to be stockbrokers and judges, while an adult Wendy was incorporated from *An Afterthought*. Peter, no longer the wholesome boy he had become in recent productions, regained his original selfish character, the one Nina Boucicault had written about, culminating with a threat to stab Jane when he bitterly discovers that she is Wendy's daughter.

With so many wonderful innovations added to the play, the casting of an adult male as Peter did not become a gimmicky attraction of the play or an issue with the critics when the curtain first rose on December 16, 1982.

David Roper wrote in the *Daily Express*:

> Whether or not the Royal Shakespeare Company had chosen to defy tradition by casting a full-grown man as the boy who never grew up, their Peter Pan would be a noteworthy production. Wendy herself is infinitely more fascinating now as Jane Carr is playing her as a purse-lipped, clever little madam determined to get her man, Tinker Bell or no damned Tinker Bell.
>
> Sadly, the 35-year-old Miles Anderson as Peter is not the revelation everybody expected. Despite some spectacular flying and antics in the magic lagoon created from billowing blue satin,

Miles Anderson as Peter in the Royal Shakespeare Company's 1982 production (photograph: Sophie Baker, courtesy Sophie Baker).

he makes a stubborn and sulky child, though doubtless closer to the unlikeable monster Barrie intended.[4]

In the *Guardian* review, Michael Billington echoed the raves for Jane Carr's Wendy but also admired Anderson's performance.

> Miles Anderson also treats Peter as a tough, rough, cocky, tattered urchin whose pathos comes from his plight rather than from any signaled winsomeness. And there is a gem of a Wendy from Jane Carr, full of precocious maternal briskness and a genuine sexual jealousy towards the possessive Tinkerbell [*sic*].[5]

The revision in text was also approved by Billington:

> Just occasionally, the narrative-line gets a little clogged by the spectacle. But this is my only cavil against a production that gets right to the heart of what Peter Llewelyn Davies called this "terrible masterpiece."[6]

The *Daily Telegraph*'s John Barber thought that the grown-ups playing the children were weak but

> Joss Ackland's Captain Hook is as dastardly as his Mr. Darling is Pompous — a splendid double.... Jane Carr's bossy little Wendy is a triumph.
> Miles Anderson, both adult and male, is an intelligent young actor, and he touches in both cockiness, the self-containment and even the tragedy of the fairy boy. But he does not seem to be of a different flesh from the others. Perhaps Peter should be the only genuine child in the cast.[7]

Jane Carr was able to revitalize the character of Wendy, elevating her to her former status enjoyed during the early years at the Duke of York's Theatre. An extremely versatile actress, Carr was born Ellen Jane Carr on August 13, 1950. At age 16 she played a student in *The Prime of Miss Jean Brodie*, aging from 11 to 18. A few years after appearing as Wendy on the London stage she appeared in RSC's production of *The Life and Adventures of Nicholas Nickleby* and toured with the production in the United States, where she decided to stay, marrying actor Mark Arnott and working on television and stage. Although known more these days for providing the voice role of "Pud'n" on the animated series *The Grim Adventures of Billy and Mandy*, she also has appeared as "Mrs. Brill" in the Broadway production of *Mary Poppins*.

While the role of Peter was not Miles Anderson's best effort, he is nonetheless a respected actor who has won the London Critic's Circle Drama Theatre Award. Anderson, who was born on October 23, 1947, lives in Los Angeles, but works regularly on television in his native England and has appeared in such series as *Midsomer Murders* and *Waking the Dead* and played Major Marchbanks in the BBC production of Philip Pullman's *The Ruby in the Smoke*.

Along with Anderson, *Peter Pan* was criticized as a fascinating enigma of antiquity. Robert Cushman of the *Observer* wrote:

> The traditional dilapidated productions have left Peter Pan looking like a relic. Now the Barbican takes it over, in a careful and occasionally brilliant production ... and it still looks like a relic; a fascinating one, but appealing more as a guide to the author's psyche than as a play or adventure story in its own right.[8]

Cushman goes on to say

> But the middle episodes are diminished! The fact of the children's escaping to Never-land is more important than what happens to them there.... The flying is thrillingly done, up to the full height

of the monstrous stage; though if ever a play cried out to be turned into a musical it is this one at the moment of lift-off.[9]

On December 22, 1983, the RSC repeated its success with Stephen Moore swapping his part of the Story Teller for the more challenging Captain Hook, a new Wendy in Katy Behean, and a replacement for Peter, too. Moore and Behean received good notices, but it was Peter whom the critics really noticed. John Barber in the *Daily Telegraph* wrote:

A too-mature Miles Anderson turned in a decent professional job as Peter before. But Mark Rylance with his faun-like face is a capering sprite — young, slim, lithe and, as Barrie wanted, more impish. There is a devil in him. Dancing with Wendy, he almost whirls her into perdition. Something of a mystery and melancholy of the actor's Ariel still clings to him.[10]

Despite the change in gender for the title role, Jane Carr stole the show as Wendy in the 1982 RSC's revival (photograph: Sophie Baker, courtesy Sophie Baker).

In the *Tribune* Barney Bardsley agreed:

I must congratulate Mark Rylance on a beautiful performance — one of the best all year. His mixture of clench-fisted petulance and surefooted grace suited Pan's character exactly. No sweet-faced boychild this, but an angry Puck who damn well would not grow up — or do as he was told.[11]

Mark Rylance is perhaps one of the best actors in the business today. By the time he played Peter Pan, the 23-year-old was already a theatre veteran. He was born one David Mark Rylance Waters in Ashford, Kent, on January 18, 1960, but his parents moved to the

United States two years later, where Mark later attended the prep school, University School of Milwaukee, where his father taught. By the age of 16 he played Hamlet, followed by Puck the next semester. In 1978 he auditioned for and won a scholarship to the Royal Academy of Dramatic Arts in London. A few years later he began his association with the RSC, appearing as Ariel in *The Tempest*, and the title roles in *Hamlet* and *Romeo and Juliet*. In between stage roles Rylance has appeared in films and television in such diverse roles as Leonardo da Vinci, Henry V, Richard II, and most recently, as Thomas Boleyn in *The Other Boleyn Girl*. He received excellent notices in the controversial film *Intimacy*, and won a Tony award for best leading actor in *Boeing Boeing* in 2008. In addition to his busy acting schedule, Rylance also was the Artistic Director of Shakespeare's Globe Theatre from 1995 until 2005, where he acted and directed. Along with Derek Jacobi (as well as Mark Twain, John Gielgud, Charlie Chaplin, and Orson Welles before them), Rylance publicly questioned the authorship of William Shakespeare's works in a "Declaration of Reasonable Doubt." It's too bad that he only portrayed Peter for one season but Rylance is responsible for bringing a sense of dignity back to the children's play.

In 1984, the RSC once more presented Barrie's classic play, this time with John McAndrew as Peter. McAndrew, who appeared as Michael the year before, received good reviews such as the following from Keith Nurse of the *Daily Telegraph*, who wrote that McAndrew's Pan

is as healthy and refreshing as they come: athletic, spring-heeled and displaying all the giddy talents of an airborne gymnast.[12]

Carole Woddis of the *City Limits* used just a few words to describe this special episode in the life of the RSC.

Katy Behean as Wendy with Mark Rylance as Peter in the 1983 Royal Shakespeare Company's production of *Peter Pan*. This time Peter reclaimed the show and the notices (photograph: Sophie Baker, courtesy Sophie Baker).

Wonderfully realized by designer John Napier and Andreanne Neofitou ... the Nunn/Caird partnerships have done for Barrie what they did for *Nickleby*. It's the kind of experience of which legends are made.[13]

Finally, from *Punch*:

The flying is spectacular (but can't technology do something to disguise the always visible wire?). Stephen Oliver's piercing, melancholy music conjures all our lost domains. The acting has more

The Darling family in the RSC's third year revival in 1983. From left: John, kneeling (David Parfitt), Mrs. Darling (Frances Tomelty), Michael, seated (John McAndrew), Mr. Darling (Stephen Moore), and Wendy (Katy Behean). In 1984 John McAndrew played Peter (photograph: Sophie Baker, courtesy Sophie Baker).

integrity down the line than we're used to these days, in RSC productions of the house dramatist. Philip Franks must be the best John ever: a humourless, pompous, snobbish, dangerously superior, blinkered young man.... Two things must be asserted. Firstly, the RSC must mount its production on a suitable West End stage next Christmas, with John Caird directing. Secondly, let us never see a gal as Peter again.[14]

Despite its success, it would be 12 years before the RSC staged the play again, this time with Ian McKellen as Hook, Alec McCowen as the Storyteller, and Daniel Evans as Peter. The *Express* declared McKellen to be hilarious, "stuttering and waggling his chrome sickle, he's drawlingly foppish.... But it's the dark interior of this fantasy which grabs you. Wendy betrays Pan by growing up and you can feel the deep yearning and undertow of regret. One niggle: it's too long at just over three hours, but the co-directors John Caird and Fiona Laird have created a haunting night out which a child might well remember for life."[15]

According the *Financial Times*, the following year the RSC surpassed its success:

David Troughton is a better Mr. Darling and Captain Hook than Ian McKellen was: more menacing, weighty, *and* absurdly funny. Susannah Fellows sings so naturally to the Darling children that she casts maternal magic on us all, and makes the Olivier Theatre her nursery. As Wendy, Rebecca Johnson starts with such utterly innocent childishness that it is wonderful, as the story progresses, to see her gradually disclose the inner wife and mother that Wendy becomes. Justin Salinger is an even more perfect Peter Pan than Daniel Evans was; you see in him the adult man he refuses to let out, and yet his childishness has no hint of affectation about it.[16]

England wasn't the only place where a change of gender in the casting of Peter Pan was of interest. In the U.S. a few years before, Howard Kissel ended a 1979 *Women's Wear Daily* review of the latest *Peter Pan* with the following thought:

Some time ago Michael Bennett wanted to rethink *Peter Pan* completely — with Peter as a boy really faced with the problem of growing up. Bennett said he gave up the idea because he resolved the issue the play presented to him in analysis. Seeing this enjoyable but not really satisfying revival made me wish he had a less skillful analyst.[17]

Twelve years later Steven Spielberg filmed a variation of the same theme.

Actually, the idea of a live-action film of *Peter Pan* had occurred to more than one producer since Disney invaded Never Never Land with his animated adaptation. In 1962, Leonard Key, president of Berkely Films, purchased the rights for 35,714 pounds for a projected movie starring Audrey Hepburn as Peter, Hayley Mills as Wendy, and Peter Sellers as Hook. Two years later, it was announced that George Cukor would direct a film version of *Pan* following *My Fair Lady*, and again Hepburn's name was mentioned for Peter.

In 1967, Mel Ferrer planned on making the film with Mia Farrow, but he sold the rights to Universal in 1968. With a new script that he had written, Ferrer again bought the film rights from the Great Ormond Street Hospital for Sick Children with hopes of producing the film at Pinewood Studios in England. Nothing materialized.

For several years in the eighties it was rumored that rock star Michael Jackson was going to star in a Steven Spielberg film, but the producer-director denied this in 1984, telling *Variety* that while Michael was a very close friend he never was and never would be Peter Pan. The director hoped to have the film ready for a 1986 Easter release, however, plans fell through, and by 1989 he was stating that he would never film the play.

Dustin Hoffman's name also began surfacing in the late eighties as a leading contender for the part of Captain Hook, even though no definite film was in the works. In 1987, Jerry Weintraub Entertainment said that Hoffman would be in their version, which was to be directed by Lasse Hallstom, and Hoffman's name came up again in 1990 for a film to be produced by Dodi Fayed. For a while it looked as if Hoffman wouldn't have any better luck with the material than Michael Jackson.

In 1989, TriStar bought the rights to an original screenplay entitled *Hook*. Developed by screenwriter Jim Hart, it was initially presented as a package by producers Gary Adelson and Craig Baumgaren. The script was shown to Steven Spielberg, who became very excited over the prospects only to find out that Nick Castle was included as part of the package as director. At this point, TriStar chairman Mike Medavoy decided that such an expensive venture could only succeed under Spielberg's direction. Castle was disappointed, but he was promised another TriStar film and a handsome settlement for his contribution to the story. Finally, Steven Spielberg was going to work on the film that he seemed destined to create.

For years Spielberg's imagination and love of filmmaking was obvious to all, it seemed, except to his own industry. Everyone wanted to work with him or be involved in one of his projects, but it took years to be recognized by other filmmakers as one of the major "artistic" directors of our time. This brings us to *Hook*, an ambitious film that succeeds and fails on many different levels.

Hook must not be considered a sequel to *Peter Pan*, for Barrie made it clear that Peter would not grow up. Screenwriter Jim Hart derived the idea from a dinner game with his son, a series of what ifs such as "What if Peter Pan grew up?" Together with Hart and screenwriter Malia Scotch Marmo, Spielberg envisioned a fantasy film with very important message to the materialistic "yuppie" generation: don't forget your priority — the family!

The writers respected the premise of Peter's continued visits to the Darling nursery — until he gazes on the beauty of Wendy Moira Angela Darling's granddaughter, Moira. He falls in love with her and will not leave. The film opens with Peter "Banning," now an adult, married to Moira with two children! More shocking, he has become a pirate of the 1990s, a lawyer! He hardly has any time for his family, and he is warned by his wife to spend time with his children now while they want to be with him, because in a few years he will be chasing them to spend time with him.

A visit to London opens his eyes when his children are kidnapped by Captain Hook, who managed to escape that crocodile after all. What happens is an adventure fantasy as Tinker Bell aids Peter in returning to Never Land to rescue them. Slowly, Peter is able to recapture the spirit of his youth, and eventually he relearns how to fly.

The tale is subtly sprinkled with authentic lines and characters from Barrie's original works. Wendy, played by Maggie Smith, herself a *Peter Pan* graduate, is a woman of about 90, just the age Wendy would be if the story originates from Barrie's 1911 novel instead of the play. Living in her home is one of the last survivors of the original Lost Boys, Tootles (veteran actor Arthur Malet), who symbolically lost his youth when he "lost his marbles," toy marbles. There is also a housekeeper named Liza, but she is much too young to be the same servant employed by Wendy's parents, unless she enjoyed quite a few extended holidays in Never Land!

Robin Williams is the stuffy Peter Banning, who transfers back to Peter Pan with all of the impish qualities of "Mork," a character he made popular on television in the 1970s. Even his ears become Spock-like, closer to Disney's conception.

Jack Mathews of *Newsday* found that "ultimately, *Hook* is Robin Williams's film and it's at its best when he's being Robin Williams, tossing out lines that only he could have conjured up."[18] Critic David Ansen of *Newsweek* also enjoyed Williams's performance, stating that "he gives us just enough hint of the lost waif in Peter Banning to redeem this

'90s cliché of the soulless corporate grind, and his transition to Pan is built with lovely comic steps."[19]

As for Dustin Hoffman's Hook, the critics felt that it was not one of his best perform-ances. "He's perfectly amusing," wrote Kathleen Carroll of the *Daily News*, "but not terri-fying enough to have the reputation as 'the sleaziest sleaze of the high seas.'"[20] David Ansen found his portrayal agreeable but added that Hoffman "never becomes the dominating figure the title promises."[21]

Good performances also came from 13-year-old Charlie Korsmo as Peter's son and Bob Hoskins as Smee. However, Carroll found the Lost Boys' antics monotonous and the boys themselves as "'Our Gang' look-alikes, the multiracial band of rambunctious urchins."[22]

Julia Roberts plays Tinker Bell, who, despite all the hype, could have easily been replaced by the traditional flickering stage light. Not that Roberts was bad, her role just was not interesting.

The film's most satisfying aspects were the stunning sets by John Napier, who also greatly enhanced Broadway's *Miss Saigon* with his helicopter scene and was also responsible for the highly praised décor of the RSC's production of *Peter Pan* a decade earlier. Never Land cost some $8 million and looked it. Napier designed a magnificent 70-foot *Jolly Roger* pirate ship docked at a fantastic wharf made of other vessels that Captain Hook had blown out of the sea. Unfortunately, when all you hear about are the sets of a film and how much it all costs, the final product has to compete with its own publicity. The film reportedly ran between $60 to $70 million, although when compared with the costs of fantasy films of just over a decade later (such as any one in the *Harry Potter* series or *Iron Man*) this is peanuts.

Dustin Hoffman in the title role of the 1991 film *Hook* (copyright 1991 TriStar Pictures, Inc.).

Robin Williams, with the Lost Boys — as Peter Pan Banning in *Hook*; a rebel with a cause (copyright 1991 TriStar Pictures, Inc.).

The originality of *Hook* and what was borrowed from Barrie was a clever concept never totally realized. The major problem is that it is not a great film. It settles for blandness in small areas that together harm the film as a whole. Why would Spielberg hire Leslie Bricusse to write the lyrics for the quasi–"I Won't Grow Up" tune, "We Don't Wanna Grow Up"? Perhaps the rights to the original song were impossible to obtain, but was the lyricist paid to create a mediocre version of a recognized anthem of youth? Even the old Toys "R" Us commercial song was better, yet salaries paid for such ineffectiveness are partly responsible for the ever-soaring costs of making a film. "When You're Alone" is the other non-distinguished contribution offered by Bricusse, which, amazingly, was nominated for an Oscar! Is this the same man who wrote the wonderful song lyrics for *Victor/Victoria* a decade earlier?

John Williams composed another of his soaring Spielbergian scores, making the music of *Hook* sound like his work for *E.T.*, *Superman*, and *Close Encounters of the Third Kind*. Too bad he couldn't have delved a little deeper to create something a bit more unique as he certainly did with his beautiful score from *Goodbye, Mr. Chips*, the 1969 film musical with Peter O'Toole and Petulia Clark.

In his review in the *New York Times*, Vincent Canby found *Hook* to be

> overwhelmed by a screenplay heavy with complicated exposition, but what are, in effect, big busy non-singing, non-dancing production numbers and some contemporary cant about rearing children and the high price paid for success. The acute difficulty of having it all may be of greater urgency to Mr. Spielberg than to most of the people who will see the movie.[23]

Julia Roberts, Steven Spielberg, and Robin Williams watch the daily rushes from *Hook* (copyright 1991 TriStar Pictures, Inc.).

Canby also considered that

> it's probably not the writers' fault that one keeps hearing what sounds like song cues, if only because the 1954 *Peter Pan* remains so fresh.... Perhaps one day Mr. Hoffman will get a chance to sing that show's classic "Captain Hook's Waltz."... In the meantime he does very well just acting the role with brilliance, a cappella.[24]

Interestingly, the last line in the film is most appropriate for a period in our recent history of increased teenaged suicides. As a boy Peter declares, "To die will be an awfully big adventure." As a man he reflects, "To live will be an awfully big adventure." With *Hook*, Steven Spielberg attempted to illustrate an important message to parents and children. Unfortunately, the medium in which he chose to sell it fell short of expectations from the master filmmaker. "After seeing what he and $70 million can do with sets and flying cameras," wrote Jack Mathews, "we recognize that the film almost certainly would have become the *Peter Pan* for generations to come — all over the world.

"But Spielberg chose to make *Hook* instead," concluded Mathews, "and the match made in heaven turned out to be just another deal made in Hollywood."[25]

In 2003, *Peter Pan*, the motion picture, was released with all of the hoopla, bells and whistles associated with blockbuster films the likes of *Stars Wars*, *Batman*, and *Lord of the Rings*. The beautiful poster with Peter flying in front of the pirate ship with the caption, "This Time It's Hook or Die," set the tone for an adventure film of a grand nature and for something new. Yet, somehow, audiences were not attracted to the film spectacular in the masses usually expected of such blockbuster films.

A.O. Scott of the *New York Times* wrote:

While Peter, played by 14-year-old Jeremy Sumpter, is appropriately dashing and adventurous, and Tink (Ludivine Sagnier) is as cute and naughty as anyone could wish, the movie belongs to Rachel Hurd-Wood's Wendy Darling.

   Ms. Hurd-Wood, a 13-year-old British actress making her professional debut, was born for the role, which calls on her to be a precocious child, an action heroine, the surrogate mother of a tribe of Lost Boys and the romantic lead. Her soft, sensitive features display her childlike eagerness and her incipient wisdom without overdoing either trait, and she and Mr. Sumpter remind us that "Peter Pan," beyond all the swashbuckling and fantasy, is a love story, which ends on a poignant Jamesian note of renunciation.[26]

And from critic Roger Ebert:

The movie has been directed by P.J. Hogan, best known for the Julia Roberts comedy "My Best Friend's Wedding." Here he stays closer to the J.M. Barrie book, which is about to celebrate its centenary, and also closer to the book's buried themes, which are sidestepped by most versions of "Peter Pan." When a muscular and bare-chested gamin appears on the windowsill of the prettiest 12½-year-old in London and asks her to fly away from home and family to join with the Lost Boys in Neverland, he is exactly the kind of strange man her mother should have warned her about. When the other major player in Neverland is the one-armed Capt. Hook, who takes an uncomfortably acute interest in both Peter and Wendy, there's enough inspiration here to have Freud gnawing on his cigar.[27]

Ebert continued:

It's not that the movie is overtly sexual; it's just that the sensuality is *there*, and the other versions have pretended that it was not. The live action contributes to the new focus; Peter Pan is played by Jeremy Sumpter, who was so effective in Bill Paxton's "Frailty," and Wendy Darling is played by Rachel Hurd-Wood, who was selected at an open casting call and is delightful in her first role. They're attractive young people in roles that in the past have been played by such actors as Robin Williams and Mary Martin, and there is chemistry on the screen.[28]

He concluded:

But to never grow up is unspeakably sad, and this is the first "Peter Pan" where Peter's final flight seems not like a victory but an escape.[29]

   In the U.S. Cathy Rigby was flying from city to city with the Mary Martin musical of *Peter Pan* while in London, as well as the provinces of England, *Peter Pan* was being adapted for the stage in the form of pantomimes. In 2004, while in England celebrating Peter's one hundreth anniversary, my two friends took me to see one such production. One of the two, a great fan of Pan himself, kept complaining how we Americans ruin the play with music and dancing. Then, as we watched the play; as Mr. Darling was introduced drunk with his buddies (who eventually became Smee and Starkey); as he arrived home late and was scolded by Mrs. Darling; as five acrobats were introduced as pirates, who in the middle of the show and with nothing to do with the script, arbitrarily displayed their acrobatic act; as the audience was given gray sponges to throw at Hook and his pirates; as children in the audience were flashing Tinker Bell flashlights while eating popcorn and cotton candy, my friend turned to me with an apologetic smile and asked, "What do you think?" I smiled back and answered, "It's quite fun."

   Indeed, it was fun: a lark, a circus, a pantomime. But it was not *Peter Pan*—at least not the *Peter Pan* written by J.M. Barrie.

   "Pantomime is very specific (and British) art form," wrote my friend Simon Moss, "which relies on certain key characteristics, only two of which Peter Pan shares [flying and a girl dressed as a boy]. *Peter Pan* ... certainly had links with panto, but I'm not sure that Barrie would ever have called PP a pantomime, and to do so now is a little denigrating (though many do). Panto in 2004 is something very bawdy, an excuse for B-grade TV stars to lark it up in silly costumes at Xmas, with lots of audience participation and ad-libbing. Very different to Edwardian Pantomime, which was built on the Victorian tradition with magical transformation effects. PP has BECOME a panto, but I don't think it was in 1904. It's a debatable point."[30]

Five years later, while visiting London again, another of my English friends gave me a promotional 2-CD set from the 2001 *Peter Pan, A Musical Adventure*. A concert version of this new work was presented at the Royal Festival Hall with the BBC Concert Orchestra. Directed by Julia McKenzie and Jonathan Butterell, it was presented as "a work in progress." The reviews were not very kind, citing that the producers didn't know what to do with it. "What is it to be," asked *The Times* critic, Rodney Milnes. "A play with incidental music, or a full-blown musical? On Thursday last it was definitely the former, inviting invidious comparisons with the famous John Caird-Trevor Nunn RSC version, which had memorable music by Stephen Oliver."[31] Really? I liked Oliver's score but I would hardly consider it more memorable than this stunning score by George Stiles and Anthony Drewe. I listened to the CDs again with all of the songs and complete dialogue being wildly cheered by the audience. Was I hearing something different? Of course a live performance can never be duplicated on record, as exemplified in Milnes's final words:

> There was one moment of pure magic, right at the end: [Sheila] Hancock, a great actress, stopped narrating and became the mature Wendy, and her brief exchange with Pan suggested, heart-stoppingly, what the show could be. Yes, a lot of work to be done.[32]

The old saying goes: when it rains, it pours, which is exactly what happened during the last few years of the first decade of the twenty-first century. Apparently, writer Willis Hall, along with Stiles and Drewe, read the reviews of their 2001 concert quite carefully, for their play was finally produced at the Birmingham Repertory Theatre in November 2007 and again two years later when it opened on November 21, 2008, at the West Yorkshire Playhouse to great acclaim. "The tunes escalate the magic," raved the *Yorkshire Evening Post*, "and make the already brilliant J.M. Barrie story all the more sublime."[33] "An absolute joy!"[34] agreed the *Express and Star*. The *Independent* wrote that "the contemporary score is timeless and tuneful" and that the musical was "surprisingly emotional."[35]

The songs, finely crafted, are soundboards with the emotional impact necessary to move the story along while also being entertaining in their own right. The opening song, "There's Something in the Air Tonight," is sung by the whole company as if their collective voices are transformed into a gentle evening breeze that slowly builds up, revealing danger. The fear that Mrs. Darling fears when preparing her children for bed is shared with the audience. It's a delicious fear, the kind that when you were a child, you would cover your eyes but peer through your fingers so as not to miss anything.

When Peter tries to seduce the Darling children to fly away with him, he is at an extreme advantage due to the exciting melody and lyrics of "Never Land," an unexpected play on words:

Peter Pan: YOU MUST THINK OF SOMETHING WONDERFUL
A SIGHT, A SMELL, A SOUND
A SHAKE OR TWO OF FAIRY DUST

```
                  AND YOU'LL BE SKYWARD BOUND
                  THERE IS JUST ONE RULE WHEN FLYING
                  WHICH IS NOT TOO HARD TO UNDERSTAND
                  WHATEVER YOU DO
                  NEVER LAND
                  NEVER LAND
                  THAT'S THE SECRET OF FLYING
                  NEVER LAND
                  NOTHING EQUALS THE THRILL
                  TAKE HER HAND
                  THERE IS NO HARM IN TRYING
                  JUST BELIEVE THAT YOU CAN AND YOU WILL
                  NEVER LAND
                  FEEL THE WIND THROUGH YOUR FINGERS
                  NEVER LAND
                  LET THE CLOUDS BRUSH YOUR HAIR
                  AND TO STAY ON THE WING
                  JUST REMEMBER ONE THING
                  NEVER LAND
```

The three children tentatively rise from the bedroom floor.

THE THREE: Look at me, look at me, look at me!

JOHN: I say! Why shouldn't we go outside?

PETER PAN: There are pirates.

JOHN: Pirates? (He grabs his Sunday top hat) We must go at once!

PETER PAN: And Indian braves — mermaids too.

WENDY: (Slipping on a distinctive hooded cape) Mermaids! How spectacular!

PETER PAN: Follow me ...

	NEVER LAND
Michael & John:	WHY JUST SIT AROUND TALKING?
All:	NEVER LAND
Wendy:	WE CAN SOAR THROUGH THE SKY
John:	WHO CAN STAND
	RUNNING, JUMPING OR WALKING
	WHEN IT'S SO MUCH MORE FUN IF YOU FLY?
All:	NEVER LAND
Peter:	KEEP STRAIGHT ON UNTIL MORNING
All:	NEVER LAND
Peter:	SECOND STAR TO THE RIGHT
All:	NO-ONE CARES WHERE YOU ROAM
	WHEN THE SKIES ARE YOUR HOME
	NEVER LAND
	NEVER LAND

Big orchestral swell as the children fly out of the nursery — the walls of which seem to almost blow apart. PETER and the DARLING CHILDREN fly through the night-sky above London.

Wendy:	ALL OF LONDON LOOKS SO MINIATURE
John:	BIG BEN IS NOT SO TALL
Michael:	AND WHO WOULD THINK THAT KENSINGTON
	COULD EVER SEEM SO SMALL?
Wendy:	THERE'S LORD NELSON ON A MATCHSTICK
	AND THOSE TINY PEOPLE IN THE STRAND

All:	IF ONLY THEY KNEW
	THEY'D WANT TO FLY TOO
	AND ...
	NEVER LAND
Wendy:	SEE HOW TINKER BELL TEASES
All:	NEVER LAND
Peter:	TRY TO FOLLOW HER LIGHT
Wendy:	IT'S SO GRAND
	FLOATING OFF ON THE BREEZES
Michael:	THOUGH I FEEL I'VE BEEN FLYING ALL NIGHT
All:	NEVER LAND
Peter:	NOT TILL WE'RE ON MY ISLAND
All:	NEVER LAND
Peter:	NOT MUCH FURTHER TO GO
	THERE'S THE BEAR THERE'S THE PLOUGH
	WE SHOULD SOON BE THERE NOW
All:	NEVER LAND
	NO ONE CARES WHERE YOU ROAM
	WHEN THE SKIES ARE YOUR HOME
Peter & Wendy:	NEVER NEVER LAND
John:	There it is!
All:	NEVER LAND
	NEVER LAND
	NEVER LAND

"The Lost Boys Gang" is as lively and tuneful a song ever sung by Peter's gang. Other songs include the rousing "Good Old Captain Hook," "One Big Adventure," and the gorgeous "Just Beyond the Stars," sung by Wendy as she realizes that she will miss her own childhood if she continues taking care of Peter and the Lost Boys. In the song, home becomes as idyllic as Never Never Land and the song itself matches the timeless beauty of the central song created by Styne, Comden and Green in the Mary Martin musical:

> Close your eyes and imagine,
> Close them tight and pretend
> There's a place where prayers are answered
> And dreams never end.

"When I Kill Peter Pan" is performed with gusto by David Birrell as Hook after he witnesses Peter escaping Marooners' Rock with Wendy by kite. Smee bids his captain to consider the cleverness of the escape and to perhaps "let Peter off the 'hook.'" David Birrell was cited by the *Birmingham Mail* as "the runaway star of the show."[36] Even cleverer is Peter's song, "The Cleverness of Me," sung by James Gillan, whom the *Yorkshire Evening Post* called "brilliant as the flippant, mischievous Peter Pan." Finally, "There's Always Tomorrow," a gentle and lovely ballad sung by Peter as he contemplates life alone. Like Scarlet O'Hara, for Peter "tomorrow is another day"; everything—adulthood and its implied responsibilities—tragically, can wait for another day. Gillan makes the most of his vocals, adding the vulnerability of a child, soft yet masculine.

Lynn Walker of the *Independent* elaborated about Gillan:

The Scottish novelist would have appreciated James Gillan's ambivalent Scottish Peter Pan, conveying a chameleon nature and decidedly chauvinistic egotism ("The Cleverness of Me"). He's captivating, whether daringly leading his band of Lost Boys or mischievously frightening the

James Gillian as Peter singing the beautiful closing song, "There's Always Tomorrow," in *Peter Pan, A New Musical Adventure* in 2008 (courtesy George Styles and Anthony Drewe).

living daylights out of Captain Hook. It's an awkward role to get right, but Gillan carries it off nimbly.[37]

While *Peter Pan, A Musical Adventure* was still wowing English audiences early in 2009, a spectacular new adaptation of Barrie's play was already in the works at a venue that even he would have approved: *Peter Pan in Kensington Gardens*.

It was such an obvious place to produce *Peter Pan* that one wonders why no one ever thought of it before. Perhaps because of the technology required to create an environment in the park that would logistically have to be set up and removed after the season. For this production would not only require a theatre, it would need to keep audiences dry if it should rain (which is likely in an English summer) and keep them warm should the temperature drop (which is likely in an English summer).

"For too long now, Peter Pan has been siphoned off into the strange theatrical Neverland of pantomime, always starring, to my mind at least, Bonnie Langford," wrote Fiona Mountford of the *Evening Standard*. "Here though, it's come home, both as a straight play and by, literally, pitching a tent in Kensington Gardens, the location that inspired JM Barrie more than 100 years ago."

"This swanky 1,000-seater rainproof big top provides an appealing in-the-round setting not only for the action itself but also for a 360-degree cyclorama of CGI designs, expertly created by William Dudley." The flight to Never Never Land was absolutely exhilarating, as the actors "flew" through and around the upper cityscape of London, giving the audience a feeling of flying themselves too.[38]

Mountford found the non-flying scenes lacking the charm of Barrie. That appeared to be the consensus of most of the critics. "This new Peter Pan has everything," wrote Charles Spencer of the *Daily Telegraph*, "except a soul."[39]

Wrote Benedict Nightingale of *The Times*:

The plot is pretty much as Barrie wanted it, but the dialogue has been so rejigged by Tanya Ronder, you are startled when an authentic line surfaces, like Pan's "to die will be an awfully big adventure." Never mind the new ending, which makes kind of sense.[40]

Generally, the actors were accorded positive, though cautious, reviews. The *Guardian*'s Michael Billington wrote:

David Birrel as Captain Hook with James Byng as John Darling in the new Styles and Drewe musical. Birrel almost ran away with the show (courtesy George Styles and Anthony Drewe).

Ciaran Kellgren also plays Peter effectively enough as an aggressive meddler who incites the lost boys into angry dances. But the burden of acting falls on Jonathan Hyde who doubles as a subdued Mr. Darling and a closeted, campy Etonian Captain Hook who gives Smee a loving kiss on the forehead. This is an evening, however, where the play's poignant humanity is swamped by the technical dazzle.[41]

At one point in the play, Peter is treated to what can only be referred to as a lap dance by Tiger Lily. Wendy responds that the Indian princess is no lady but this brief moment

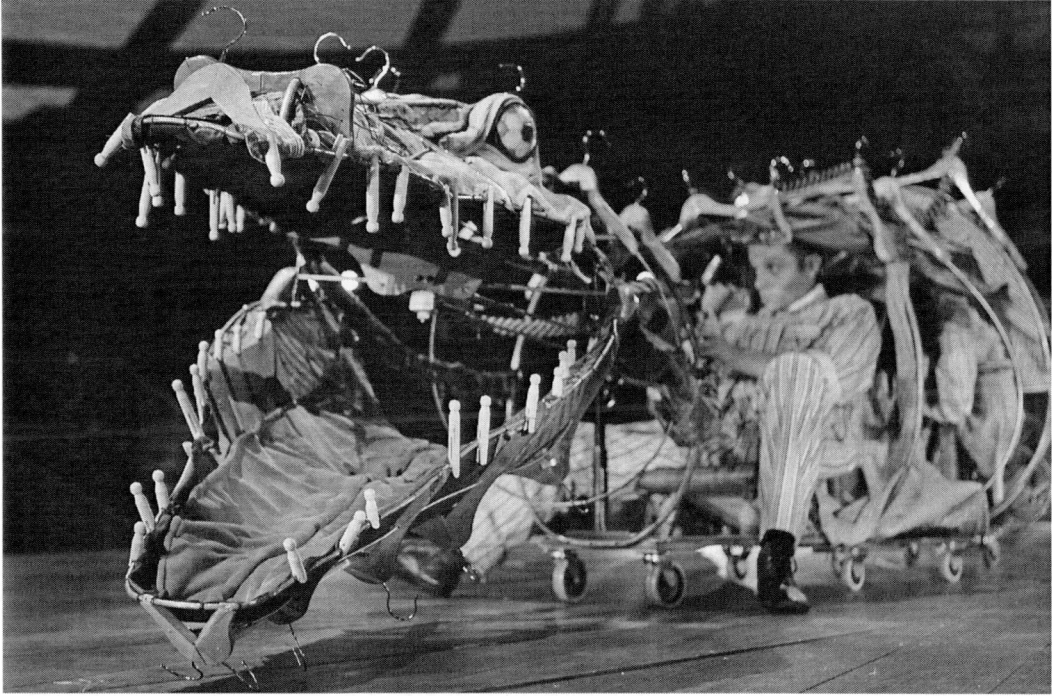

The Croc! A puppet on wheels from *Peter Pan in Kensington Gardens*, 2009 (photograph: Simon Annand, courtesy Simon Annand).

reminds the audience that actor Ciaran Kellgren is really a man and not a boy at all. *Variety's* Karen Fricker remarked that the play was "unapologetically, a story about the dawning of sexual desire: Tinker Bell, here depicted amusingly by Sandra Maturana as a punky elf in pink tutu and workboots, and Abby Ford's touchingly tomboyish Wendy are engaged in an ongoing, low-level catfight over Peter, whose feelings for Wendy are intriguingly Oedipal."[42]

Fricker continued:

> This is enhanced by the choice to have child characters played by young adult actors. While Kellgren over exaggerates the impish/puckish side of his character, there's something productively disconcerting about his exposed and well-toned physique.[43]

Near the end of the nursery scene, as Mr. Darling agrees to adopt the Lost Boys, they leave the stage singing a few bars of "Following the Leader," an homage to Disney that was not only unnecessary but also a bit tacky. For whatever its drawbacks, the rest of *Peter Pan in Kensington Gardens* was anything but tacky. And what just two decades before seemed so innovative and fresh — a boy playing Peter Pan on the London stage (or in the park) — is now accepted without reservation.

The massive production (minus Kensington Gardens) began touring the States in 2010, where it was praised with even more enthusiasm than at home. "Trust the Brits to cut through the layers of Disney dross," wrote a critic for the *Orange County Register* in California. "A new travelling production of 'Peter Pan' presented in a tent in Costa Meesa ... celebrates the magic and the message of the story in a way that's true to Barrie's vision yet still ultimately joyous, playful and uplifting. Above all, this 'Peter Pan' is grandly and unabashedly theatrical — an appropriate homage, since Barrie's creation began more than a century ago as a play."[44] Even as this fresh and innovative approach to *Peter Pan* was touring the States, the popularity of the now traditional pantomime approach to the play continued with David Hasselhoff, television's *Knight Rider* and *Baywatch* hero, playing Captain Hook in England at the New Wimbledon Theatre from December 2010 through January 2011. While Peter was played by actor Robert Rees, the publicity focused mostly on Hasselhoff and Louie Spence, the artistic director of the hit English show *Pineapple Dance Studio*. Spence played the "Cabin Boy," a role not featured in the original play. Still, Peter Pan, whether played by a man or a woman, a school-aged child or an animated figure, continues to entertain and engage his audiences on a higher level, "so long as children are gay and innocent and heartless."[45]

Back where we started —*Peter Pan in Kensington Gardens,* 2009 — only this time with Peter *and* Wendy. Ciaran Kellgren and Abby Ford managed to create full and nuanced characters despite the extravagant flying effects (photograph: Simon Annand, courtesy Simon Annand).

Afterword: The Lasting Appeal of Peter Pan

It has been over 60 years since Broadway audiences have seen a "straight" version of *Peter Pan*. When I interviewed the late Betty Comden and Adolph Green they took great pleasure in relating to me that their musical treatment of J.M. Barrie's play remains for most Americans the definitive *Pan*. Ironically, like the original score they shared with Moose Charlap, Carolyn Leigh and Jule Styne, there have been several changes with each new production of the musical. Songs are removed or added, while the libretto moves unconsciously between the additions, the original play, *Peter Pan, or the Boy Who Wouldn't Grow Up*, and the book, *Peter and Wendy*. Producers make changes in the musical as vehicles for their stars while publicly stating that they are trying to get back the integrity of Barrie's play and not be so commercial. Nonsense! The very act of these changes is commercial in itself. If they truly want to retain their so-called "integrity" then why not simply produce the straight play as Barrie had written it? Or as Robbins, Comden and Green had written their musical for that matter. If the star can't reach the notes of the "Mysterious Lady" song don't state that it has been omitted for artistic reasons or the integrity of the play. The purpose of a musical version of *Peter Pan*, any musical version, is to entertain in a different manner than the original play. It is part of theatre, it is part of entertainment, and it is part of something called *show business*, which by its very nature lacks pure integrity.

In England, despite some rather dreadful pantomime versions, a newly resurrected version using mostly Barrie's words shows up every now and then, making us once again appreciate one of the stage's most enigmatic characters. But there is no "pure" *Peter Pan* and there never was.

What is the secret of Peter Pan's longevity? J. A. Hammerton wrote of a debate that took place at the Cambridge Union in 1927 regarding eternal youth. Said one Mitchell Banks, K. C., M. P.:

> The reason why older people are happier than young people is because they are more conscious of happiness. It is in memory that thorough pleasure lies. The wish to be always a child, always a youth, is a coward's wish. It is not the wish of a man.[1]

"This appealed to me as the truest thing said in the report of the debate that came under my notice," wrote Hammerton. "There is no real happiness that is divorced from memory. Youth has nothing to do with the number of years: it is a quality of the mind."[2] He continued:

I submit, therefore, that the secret of *Peter Pan* is not to be found in the idea conveyed by the sub-title of the play. Nor is it the purely fairy element of the play that anything of its secrets abides.... I would incline to attribute the hold the play has upon old and young alike to the amazing skills with which a group of the most universal of human experiences is assembled and presented to the material eye with a naturalness that implies both faith and knowledge.[3]

How did Charles Frohman explain the success of *Peter Pan*?

Life in the big cities where huge buildings shut off from the child's contemplation of the open sky, and where dull grey streets have replaced green fields, where the lesson of the day is "getting on in the world" rather than being a child and enjoying the dream — while of pirates, fairies, and Indians — all these are pointed out as tendencies towards early self-consciousness and the stagnation of the imagination. We are reminded that the whistling boy and the little girl singing her own improvised airs — those mirthful little Peters and Wendys of yesterday — are no longer with us. Today they are bent rather upon aping their elders. And it is asserted that with their disappearance will go that imaginative impulse which creates for a nation its great songs and lyrics.

As against these facts we know that men, women, and children have sincerely appreciated *Peter Pan*—a play which appeals to them because they come of a people possessed of a healthy imagination. At every performance old hearts and old brains live over again the thrills and sensations of romantic youth. Its appeal is universal.

There is joy in it for all classes and all ages. It is simply a matter of light attracting light. The pleasure taken by the audiences at *Peter Pan* has come, I think, from the fact that whatever is human and healthful in thought or feeling in them has been touched by Barrie's humanity. Everybody who has been gripped by the charm of *Peter Pan* has only to thank himself that he has within him that to which the author has successfully appealed.... It has fallen to Barrie to evolve what, in all my experience, the American stage has only now accorded — namely, an entertainment creative of pure fancy in the city-bred child, and quickening to the imagination of the little people whose natural Fairyland we grown-ups have possessed — an illusion of a night during which the mother or father and child find abundant delights in common and realize new joys in being complete chums.[4]

I read Frohman's assessment of Pan's appeal several times in expectation of allowing his voice from 100 years ago to be the final word on the subject, at least in this volume. Yet, I couldn't help but feel that something was still missing; something so dear, so precious, and so ethereal —*a constant*. Perhaps that is it! *Peter Pan* symbolizes the elusive constant that we work, study and strive for. Whether through our love of a husband, wife, partner, children or friends, we desperately try to maintain some sort of regularity in our lives with this constant, which in turn is maintained by traditions. Just the simple tradition of having a story read to us by our parents or guardians not only displays an act of love, it enriches our lives with literature and theatre, for even the worst readers attempt to "act out" the parts of the book they are reading aloud. In these extraordinary times as tools for communication become more and more sophisticated, thereby making contact between humans more convenient, more casual, and less tactile, nothing can replace the immediacy and love conveyed in reading a story or presenting it live on the stage. That is precious. And toward that end *Peter Pan* still maintains its peculiar position. "His is the only story of recent centuries to escape from literature into folklore," wrote Roger Lancelyn Green. "For every one person who has seen the play or read the story, there are hundreds who know perfectly well who and what Peter Pan is. Besides being a fairy-tale character, he is also a symbol — of what, precisely, even Barrie could not find the words to describe: 'I'm youth, I'm joy! I'm a little bird that has broken out of the egg!'"[5] Like folklore, Peter Pan is a constant that belongs temporarily to the teller, the listener, the actor, and the audience. I'd like to think that Barrie must have prided himself on knowing that Peter was here to stay even as the play evolved through his own revisions. A musical Pan, a Pan on ice, a movie Pan, or even a "Pananimated" television series — the boy who wouldn't grow up is here to stay (or at least for the next 100 years).

Appendix A: A Selected Discography

In addition to the various musical adaptations created from *Peter Pan, or the Boy Wouldn't Grow Up*, there are many recorded readings as well as musical versions created specifically as sound recordings. All recordings released in the U.S. unless otherwise indicated.

The J.M. Barrie/John Crook Score

Columbia 9768 (12 inch 78 rpm) \ Peter Pan — Selections \ Released: 1928, England
J.H. Squire Celeste Octet

His Master's Voice #10 (3 78 rpm record set in tri-folder) \ Released: 1939, England
Scenes, Songs, and Music from Peter Pan. Music and lyrics by James Crook and J.M. Barrie. Jean Forbes-Robertson (Peter), Dinah Sheridan (Wendy), Gordon Harker (Captain Hook), George Baker (Hook's Songs), Nancy Evans (Mrs. Darling), Orchestra conducted by Clifford Greenwood.
> B. 9117
>> Excerpts from Act I — The Nursery Scene
>> Excerpts from Act I — The Nursery Scene — Part Two
> B 9118
>> Scene: The Home Underground
>> Captain Hook's Song — George Baker; "Lullaby" — Nancy Evans; Song of the Lost Boys, "We'll Build a House for Wendy" — The Italia Conti Children
> B 9119
>> Jolly Tunes from the Incidental Music
>> "Hook's Monologue" — Gordon Harker; "The Pirate's Song" — George Baker

Sepia Records 1037 (Compact disc) \ Released: October 4, 2004, England
100 Years of Peter Pan. A compilation commemorating centenary featuring 27 tracks from the various productions and features the complete Jean Forbes-Robertson album plus all of the songs from the 1950 Broadway production; the complete children's version of the 1950 show; Disney selections sung by Doris Day, Jean Carson, Gilbert Harding, the Sandpipers, Anne Lloyd, Mitchell Miler and Orchestra, etc.

Columbia 2693 (12 inch 78 rpm) \ Peter Pan Selections Part 1 and 2 — Released: unknown date, England
London Palladium Orchestra conducted by Richard Crean.

B.B.C. Radio Collection ZBBC (2 cassettes) \ Released: 1989, England
Peter Pan: The Original Play and Music. With the BBC concert Orchestra. Music by John Crook. Graham McGrath (Peter), Lucinda Bateson (Wendy), and Robert Lang (Captain Hook). Adapted and directed by Glyn Dearman.

Marilyn Miller Version

The only recordings were 78 rpm records of a song dedicated to the actress by songwriters Robert King and Ray Henderson. It should be noted that in other countries this song was also dedicated to Betty Bronson as her film reached a wider audience than the play with Miller.

Cameo 630 \ Released: 1924
    "Peter Pan (I Love You)"—Bob Haring and his Orchestra
    "Oh! Flo"—Dixie Daisies

Edison 51462 \ Released: 1924
    "Peter Pan (I Love You)"—Billy Wynne's Greenwich Village Inn Orchestra
    "Not Now—Not Yet—But Soon"—Billy Wynne's

Emerson 10835 \ Released: 1924
    "Peter Pan, I Love You"—Lenox Orchestra
    "I'll See You in My Dreams"—Lenox Orchestra

Gennett 5609 \ Released: 1924
    "Peter Pan (from *Peter Pan*)"—Westchester Biltmore Country Club Orchestra
    "Nobody Loves You Like I Do"—Willie Creager's Orchestra

Okeh 40278 \ Released: 1924
    "Peter Pan (from *Peter Pan*)"—The Yellow Jackets
    "Because They All Love You"—The Yellow Jackets

Oriole 367 \ Released: 1924
    "Peter Pan (I Love You)"—Irving Post

Perfect 14331 \ Released: 1924
    "Dear One"—Mike Speciale and His Carton Terrace Orchestra
    "Peter Pan (I Love You)"—Max Terr and His Orchestra

Resona \ Released: 1924
    "I'll See You In My Dreams"—Tom Moore (Tenor)
    "Peter Pan, I Love You"—Tom Moore

Victor \ Released: 1924
    19570
    "All Alone"—International Novelty Orchestra
    "Peter Pan (I Love You)"—Waring's Pennsylvanians
    19651
    "Peter Pan (I Love You)"—Henry Burr
    "West of the Great Divide"—Henry Burr

Vocalion \ Released: 1924
    "Peter Pan—Fox Trot"—Ben Selvin and His Orchestra
    "Does My Sweetie Do—And How"—Ben Selvin

Glynis Johns

Caedmon CAE (CS) CPN-1395 (stereo LP) \ Released: 1970
    Peter Pan. This is not a cast recording but rather a reading by the actress who appeared as Pan in 1943. The music for this recoding was composed by Dick Hyman.

Jean Arthur Version

Columbia ML/OL-4312 LP (mono LP) \ Released: 1950
    Peter Pan. Broadway Cast. Songs and lyrics by Leonard Bernstein. (This recording omits the incidental music by Trude Rittman and substitutes the music of Alec Wilder.) Jean Arthur, Boris Karloff, Marcia Henderson, Peg Hillias, Joe E. Marks, Orchestra conducted by Ben Steinberg.
    Columbia A-931 (4 45 rpm EP record set)
    Columbia AOL-4312 LP (mono LP) 1973 reissue
    Columbia CK 4312 (Compact disc) 1988 reissue
    Also included on Sepia Records 1037 *100 Years of Peter Pan* sans the dialogue.

Columbia MJV-92 (2 78 rpm records) \ Released: 1950
    Peter Pan. In this special recording for children by members of the 1950 Broadway cast, the Bernstein songs have been omitted. Jean Arthur, Boris Karloff, Marcia Henderson, Peg Hillias, Joe E. Marks, Narration by Miriam Wolfe as Nana. Orchestra conducted by Ben Steinberg. Includes attached illustrated booklet.
    Also included on Sepia Records 1037 *100 Years of Peter Pan*.

Painted Smiles PS-1377 (stereo LP)
Ben Bagley's Leonard Bernstein Revisited. Jo Sullivan sings "Dream with Me," which was cut from the production.

Etcetera ETC-1037 (stereo LP)
Roberta Alexander Sings Bernstein. Includes "Never-land."

Koch 7596 (Compact disc) \ Released: 2005
Leonard Bernstein's Peter Pan. All of the songs and incidental music Bernstein created for the 1950 Broadway play. Linda Eder, Daniel Narducci, Orchestra conducted by Alexander Frey.

Disney Version

RCA 10" LPM-3101 (mono LP) \ Released: 1953
Peter Pan. Songs from the film. Conducted by Hugo Winterhalter. Vocals: Stuart Foster and Judy Valentine. Includes "Never Smile at a Crocodile," which was eliminated from the film.

RCA Victor WY-4001, Little Nipper Series (2 45 rpm EP record set spiral-bound with book) \ Released: 1952
Walt Disney's Peter Pan. Songs by Sammy Cahn and Sammy Fain, Oliver Wallace, Ed Penner, Ted Sears, and Winston Hibler. Bobby Driscoll, Kathryn Beaumont, Hans Conreid, Bill Thompson, and Verne Smith as the "Disney Story Teller."

RCA Camden CAL 1009 (mono LP)
Walt Disney's Peter Pan and Alice in Wonderland. Same as above minus references to changing pages as Story Teller narrates.

Disneyland 1206 (mono LP) \ Released: 1963
Peter Pan. Film soundtrack. Songs by Sammy Cahn and Sammy Fain, Oliver Wallace, Ed Penner, Ted Sears, and Winston Hibler. Bobby Driscoll, Kathryn Beaumont, Hans Conreid, Bill Thompson, and Candy Candido.

Music for Pleasure mfp 1284 (mono LP) \ Released: 1968, England
Walt Disney's Peter Pan. Film soundtrack. Same as above plus three selections of music by Gilkyson.

Disneyland 304 (mono 33 ⅓ rpm 7 inch record) \ Released: 1977
Walt Disney's Story of Peter Pan (book and record). Same cast as above.

Ovation 5000 (stereo LP) \ Released: 1978
The Magical Music of Walt Disney. A four-record set and book that includes five songs from the film soundtrack.

Columbia (EP) B-1590 \ Released: 1953
Peter Pan— Doris Day. "The Second Star to the Right" and "Your Mother and Mine."

Capitol CAS-3163 (78 rpm) \ Released: 1953
Jerry Lewis Sings Never Smile at a Crocodile. Conducted by Dave Cavanaugh. Also includes "Following the Leader" conducted by Van Alexander.

Philips P.B. 130 (78 rpm) \ Released: 1953, England
Peter Pan. Songs from the Disney film sung by Gilbert Harding, Jean Carson, Hermione Gingold, The Rita Williams Singers. Narrated by Jean Metcalfe with orchestra conducted by Wally Stott.

Conquest CE 1029 (45 rpm EP) \ Released: unknown date, England
Peter and Wendy. Dialogue with songs from the Disney film with Nicolette Roeg (Peter), Belinda Sinclair (Wendy), Michael Sammes (Captain Hook), and Joy Leman (Tinker Bell). Narrated by Rex Graham with the Michael Sammes Singers and the Westminster Festival Orchestra conducted by Burt Rhodes.

Summer County (45 rpm record set) \ Released: 1965, England
Walt Disney's Peter Pan. Includes "Never Smile at a Crocodile" sung by Rita Williams & The Babits. "Second Star to the Right" sung by Kathie Kay. Both with Billy Cotton & His Band.

Golden Record RD 35 (78 rpm) \ Released: 1952
"Peter Pan Theme Song"— The Sandpipers, Anne Lloyd, Dan Ocko, Mitch Miller and Orchestra.
"You Can Fly"— The Sandpipers, Anne Lloyd, Dan Ocko, David Anderson, Mitch Miller and Orchestra.

Golden Record RD36 (78 rpm) \ Released: 1952
> "Second Star to the Right" — The Sandpipers, Anne Lloyd, Dan Ocko, Mitch Miller and Orchestra.
> "March of the Lost Boys" — The Sandpipers, Anne Lloyd, Dan Ocko, David Anderson, Mitch Miller and Orchestra.

Golden Record RD37 (78 rpm) \ Released: 1952
> "What Made the Red Man Red" — The Sandpipers, Anne Lloyd, Dan Ocko, David Anderson, Mitch Miller and Orchestra.
> "Your Mother and Mine" — The Sandpipers, Anne Lloyd, Dan Ocko, Mitch Miller and Orchestra.

Golden Record RD38 (78 rpm) \ Released: 1952
> "A Pirate's Life" — The Sandpipers, Anne Lloyd, Dan Ocko, Mitch Miller and Orchestra.
> "Elegant Captain Hook" — The Sandpipers, Anne Lloyd, Dan Ocko, Mitch Miller and Orchestra.

Golden Record RD40 (78 rpm) \ Released: 1952
> "Peter Pan's Song" — The Sandpipers, Mitch Miller and Orchestra.
> "Never Smile at a Crocodile" — The Sandpipers, Mitch Miller and Orchestra.

Children's Records

Cricket Records C 765 (78 rpm) \ Released: 1953
Peter Pan: A Complete Story. Sung by The Cricketones, conducted by Warren Vincent (on the record label the group is referred to as The Overtones).
Re-released as C 65

Peter Pan Records 335 (78 rpm) \ Released: 1954
Peter Pan. Sung and played by Toby Deane, narrated by Victor Kasen and directed by Vicky Kasen.

Robin Hood Records RHLP 1000 (Mono LP) \ Released: circa 1955
Complete Story of Peter Pan. The Robin Hood Players, an "all star" TV cast. Directed by Catherine Faulconer.

Twinkle Tunes KD \ Released: ?
The Story of Peter Pan. No credits given.

Mary Martin Version

RCA LOC-1019-LP (mono LP)
EOC- 1019 (2 45 rpm EP record set) \ Released: 1954
Peter Pan. Broadway cast. Songs by Mark Charlap, Carolyn Leigh, Jule Styne, Betty Comden, and Adolph Green. Incidental music by Trude Rittman and Elmer Bernstein. "Tinker Bell" by Jaye Rubanoff. Orchestra conducted by Louis Adrian.
EYA-48 (45 rpm EP) Mary Martin as Peter Pan sings with her daughter plus members of the original cast.
RCA LSO-1019- LP (Rechanneled stereo) 1959 reissue.
RCA PR-136 (45 rpm EP) "6 Enchanting Tunes from the Original Cast Recording," 1962.
RCA AYL1-3762e (Rechanneled stereo) 1981 reissue.
RCA 3762-2-RG Compact Disc (mono) Issued with two different covers.

Dolphin I 10" (mono LP) \ Released: 1955
Cyril Ritchard: Odd Songs and a Poem. Includes "The Old Gavotte" by Nancy Hamilton and Morgan Lewis. Accompanied by Stuart Ross at the piano.
Reissued in 1999 by DRG Records 19009 (Compact disc) John *Muray Anderson's Almanac and Other Broadway-London Revues.*

Heritage 0057 LP (mono) \ Released: 1955
Comden and Green. The songwriters perform their own material that includes "Distant Melody," "Hook's Waltz," "Never Never Land," and "Oh My Mysterious Lady."
Reissued in 1998 by DRG Records 5247 (Compact disc).

Capitol WAO 1197 LP (mono), SWAO 1197 (stereo LP) \ Released: 1958
A Party with Betty Comden and Adolph Green. A live performance of the Theatre Guild production that includes "Oh My Mysterious Lady."
Reissued in 1993 by Angel Records. ZDM 0777 7 64773 2 9 (Compact disc)

Stet S2L-5177 LP (stereo LP) \ Released: 1977
A Party with Betty Comden and Adolph Green. A new production of their revue recorded live on May 1, 1977, in Washington, D.C. Includes "Hook's Waltz," "Never Never Land," and "Oh My Mysterious Lady."

N.B.C. Entertainment (45 rpm stereo record) \ Released: 1973
    "Youth, Joy, and Freedom"— a song by Jule Styne and Tom Adair that was added to the 1954 score for the 1973 NBC Arena Touring production of *Peter Pan*, sung by Yvonne Green. Orchestra conducted by Paul Weston.
    "I've Gotta Crow"— Yvonne Green.

A Parody

Private Label (mono LP) \ Released: 1969
Peter Pandemic or There's a Lot About. Westminster Medical School. Written by John Lee. Musical director Anthony Seddon.

Compilations

Varése Sarabande VSD-5475 (Compact disc) \ Released: 1994
Lost in Boston. Songs cut from various Broadway shows including "When I Went Home"— Michelle Nicastro.

Varése Sarabande VSD-5722 (Compact disc) \ Released: 1996
The Musical Adventures of Peter Pan. A wonderful recording featuring selections from various productions from 1904 through Hook in 1991. Includes "Once Upon a Bedtime Story," "When You're Alone," and "Dream with Me."

Delos DE 3201 (Compact disc) \ Released: 1996
An Awfully Big Adventure: The Best of Peter Pan, 1904–1996. Grant Gershon conducts beautiful arrangements by Donald Fraser. Includes instrumental versions of "Went I Went Home," John Crook's "The Arrival of Wendy," etc.

Anita Harris

Golden Hour GH-590 LP (stereo LP) \ Released: 1974
Anita Harris is Peter. Includes "Nobody" and "Build a House" by John Taylor. The rest of the album contains songs that are not from this production.

Hong Kong Version

Crown CST-12-24 \ Released: 1976 Hong Kong
Peter Pan. Songs by Mark Charlap, Carolyn Leigh, Jule Styne, Betty Comden, and Adolph Green. Sung in Cantonese by Betty Chung (Peter), James Wong (Captain Hook), Alice Lau (Wendy), etc.
    Reissued on Compact Disc in 1995 on HMI-103.

"Casino de Paris" Version

Carrere Music (A Time Warner Company) (Compact disc) \ Released: 1991, France
Peter Pan. Songs by Mark Charlap, Carolyn Leigh, Jule Styne, Betty Comden, and Adolph Green. Incidental music by Trude Rittman and Elmer Bernstein. In French, with Fabienne Guyon (Peter), Nathalie Lhermitte (Wendy), Sophie Tellier (Tiger Lily), and Bernard Alane (Captain Hook).

Sandy Duncan

Dove Books (Cassette tape) \ Released: 1989
Sandy Duncan Reads Peter Pan. Not the Broadway musical but a straight reading of the play. Several songs from the musical were recorded by Duncan and cast for promotional use and are in private collections.

Cathy Rigby

Jay CDJAY 1280 (Compact disc) \ Released: 1997
Cathy Rigby Is Peter Pan. Songs by Mark Charlap, Carolyn Leigh, Jule Styne, Betty Comden, and Adolph Green. Incidental music by Trude Rittman and Elmer Bernstein. With Elisa Sagardia (Wendy) and Paul Schoeffler (Captain Hook). Also: Jay CDJAY 1352 / Released: 2000

Hook

Epic 48888 (Compact disc) \ Released: 1991
Soundtrack. Music composed and conducted by John Williams. Includes "We Don't Wanna Grow Up" and "When You're Alone" with lyrics by Leslie Bricusse.

An Israeli Musical

Hed Arzi Records 15947 (Compact disc) \ Released: 1993
Peter Pan. Sung in Hebrew.

The British Musical

EMI 7243 8 31946 2 9 (Compact disc) \ Released: 1994
Peter Pan: The British Musical. Music and Lyrics by Piers Chater-Robinson. With Ron Moody (Captain Hook), Nicola Stapleton (Peter Pan) and Debbie Wall (Wendy).

The Mabou Mines Adaptation

Alula Records ALU-1006 (Compact disc) \ Released: 1997
Peter and Wendy. Music written and arranged by Johnny Cunningham.

A New Millennium Production

Chicken Shed Theatre Company (Compact disc) \ Released: 2000, England
Peter Pan. Music by Jo Collins and David Carey. Lyrics by Paul Morrall, Paula Rees, and MC Tommy Doyle. Special performances by Sam Fuster-Burnett and Julian Marc Stringle.

A New British Musical

Imagination Entertainment Ltd. (Compact disc) \ Released: 2001, England
Peter Pan: A Musical Adventure. A two-disc set for demonstration purposes of the World Premiere concert performance with the BBC Concert Orchestra, Royal Festival Hall, April 26, 2001. Music by George Stiles, lyrics by Anthony Drewe, and book by Willis Hall. Conducted by Rebecca Turner. Joe McFadden (Peter), Laura-Michel Kelly (Wendy), Jenna Russell (Mrs. Darling), John Thaw (Hook), Sheila Hancock (The Woman)

Argentina

PELO 7243 8 66115 2 9 (Compact disc) \ Released: 2004, Argentina
Peter Pan—Todos Podemos Volar. Music by Patricia Sosa. Diego Reinhold (Peter) and Ivanna Rossi (Wendy).

A Grand New Musical

Speckulation Entertainment SPECKCD002 (Compact disc) \ Released: 2009, England
Peter Pan: A Musical Adventure. West Yorkshire Playhouse production. Music by George Stiles, lyrics by Anthony Drewe, and book by Willis Hall. James Gillan (Peter), Amy Lennox (Wendy), and David Birrell (Hook). Musical director — Stephen Ridley.

Film

Varése Sarabande B000011D190 (Compacty disc) \ Released: 2003
Peter Pan. Soundtrack. James Newton Howard.

Royal Shakespeare Company

Dakota Records Ltd. RSP1 (stereo 45 rpm mini L.P.) \ Released: 1983, England
Peter Pan or The Boy Who Wouldn't Grow Up. Music and lyrics by Stephen Oliver. Sheila Hancock (Mrs. Darling) and Jane Carr (Wendy). Musical director — Nigel Hess.

Appendix B: Casts of *Peter Pan*

All cast lists were derived from original vintage programs or playbills, with Roger Lancelyn Green's *Fifty Years of Peter Pan* used as a secondary source. In several cases the spelling of actors' names were altered from one year to another while a few performers changed their actual names, presumably as a career move — the new name looking better on a marquee. However, I have chosen to use the playbills as the ultimate source. Also, due to limited space, minor roles (e.g., wolves, extra unnamed pirates, chorus, etc.) have been omitted. Early programs list Miss Jane Wren as Tinker Bell. Miss Wren did not exist.

London Productions

1904–05

Duke of York's Theatre

Peter Pan	Nina Boucicault
Captain Hook	Gerald du Maurier
Mr. Darling	Gerald du Maurier
Mrs. Darling	Dorothea Baird
Wendy	Hilda Trevelyan
John	George Hersee
Michael	Winifred Geoghegan
Nana	Arthur Lupino
Tootles	Joan Burnett
Nibs	Christine Silver
Slightly	A. W. Baskcomb
Curly	Alice Dubarry
First Twin	Pauline Chase
Second Twin	Phyllis Beadon
Smee	George Shelton
Starkey	Sydney Harcourt
Cookson	Charles Trevor
Mullins	Hubert Willis
Cecco	Frederick Annerley
Jukes	James English
Noodler	John Kelt
First Pirate	Gerald Malvern
Second Pirate	J. Grahme
Black Pirate	S. Spencer
Panther	Philip Darwin
Tiger Lily	Miriam Nesbitt
Liza	Ela Q. May
Crocodile	A. Ganker & C. Lawton
Ostrich	G. Henson

1905–06

Duke of York's Theatre

Peter Pan	Cecilia Loftus
Captain Hook	Gerald du Maurier
Mr. Darling	Gerald du Maurier
Mrs. Darling	Enid Spencer-Brunton
Wendy	Hilda Trevelyan
John	George Hersee
Michael	Harry Edwin Duff
Nana	Arthur Lupino
Tootles	Joan Burnett
Nibs	Christine Silver
Slightly	A. W. Baskcomb
Curly	Winifred Geoghegan
First Twin	Pauline Chase
Second Twin	Phyllis Beadon
Smee	George Shelton
Starkey	Ben Field
Cookson	Charles Medwin
Mullins	Chris Walker
Cecco	Frederick Annerley
Jukes	James English
Noodler	John Kelt
First Pirate	Gerald Malvern
Second Pirate	J. Grahme
Black Pirate	S. Spencer
Panther	Benson Kleve
Tiger Lily	Mary Mayfren
Mermaid	Rosamund Bury
Baby Mermaid	Geraldine Wilson
Liza	Ela Q. May

Crocodile .... S. Grata & A. Ganker
Ostrich .... G. Henson

1906–07

Duke of York's Theatre

Peter Pan .... Pauline Chase
Captain Hook .... Gerald du Maurier
Mr. Darling .... Marsh Allen
Mrs. Darling .... Sybil Carlisle
Wendy .... Hilda Trevelyan
John .... George Hersee
Michael .... Ernest Hollom
Nana .... E. Sillward
Tootles .... Joan Burnett
Nibs .... Nellie Bowman
Slightly .... A. W. Baskcomb
Curly .... Winifred Geoghegan
First Twin .... Maie Ash
Second Twin .... Phyllis Embury
Smee .... George Shelton
Starkey .... Charles Trevor
Cookson .... Charles Medwin
Mullins .... Chris Walker
Cecco .... Frederick Annerley
Jukes .... James English
Noodler .... John Kelt
First Pirate .... Gerald Malvern
Second Pirate .... Rodney Barry
Black Pirate .... S. Spencer
Panther .... Douglas Vigors
Tiger Lily .... Mary Mayfren
Mermaid .... Gladys Herries
Baby Mermaid .... Winifred Delevanti
Liza .... Dorothy Le Marchand
Crocodile .... A. Hall & B. Rose
Ostrich .... Ernest Marini

1907–08

Duke of York's Theatre

Peter Pan .... Pauline Chase
Captain Hook .... Robb Harwood
Mr. Darling .... A. E. Matthews
Mrs. Darling .... Sybil Carlisle
Wendy .... Hilda Trevelyan
John .... George Hersee
Michael .... Herbert Hollom
Nana .... Edward Sillward
Tootles .... Faith Celli
Nibs .... Nellie Bowman
Slightly .... A. W. Baskcomb
Curly .... Winifred Geoghegan
First Twin .... Violet Hollom
Second Twin .... Phyllis Embury
Smee .... George Shelton
Starkey .... Charles Trevor
Cookson .... Charles Medwin
Mullins .... Chris Walker
Cecco .... William Luff
Jukes .... James English
Noodler .... John Kelt

First Pirate .... Gerald Malvern
Second Pirate .... Rodney Barry
Black Pirate .... S. Spencer
Panther .... Humphrey Warden
Tiger Lily .... Mary Mayfren
Mermaid .... Norah Dwyer
Baby Mermaid .... Tessie Parke
Liza .... Dorothy Lemarchand
Crocodile .... B. Rose & A. Hall
Ostrich .... Ernest Marini

1908–09

Duke of York's Theatre

Peter Pan .... Pauline Chase
Captain Hook .... Robb Harwood
Mr. Darling .... Reginald Owen
Mrs. Darling .... Sybil Carlisle
Wendy .... Gertrude Lang
John .... George Hersee
Michael .... Herbert Hollom
Nana .... Edward Sillward
Tootles .... Dorothy Minto
Nibs .... Nellie Bowman
Slightly .... A. W. Baskcomb
Curly .... Irene Clarke
First Twin .... May Kinder
Second Twin .... Ivy Knight
Smee .... George Shelton
Starkey .... Charles Trevor
Cookson .... Charles Medwin
Mullins .... Chris Walker
Cecco .... William Luff
Jukes .... James English
Noodler .... John Kelt
First Pirate .... Gerald Malvern
Second Pirate .... Frank Saker
Black Pirate .... S. Spencer
Panther .... Humphrey Warden
Tiger Lily .... Margaret Fraser
Mermaid .... Marjorie Moore
Baby Mermaid .... Beryl St. Leger
Liza .... Tessie Parke
Crocodile .... B. Rose & W. Child
Ostrich .... Marini (Ernest)

1909–10

Duke of York's Theatre

Peter Pan .... Pauline Chase
Captain Hook .... Robb Harwood
Mr. Darling .... Walter Pearce
Mrs. Darling .... Sybil Carlisle
Wendy .... Hilda Trevelyan
John .... Harry Duff
Michael .... Herbert Hollom
Nana .... Edward Sillward
Tootles .... Dorothy Minto
Nibs .... Nellie Bowman
Slightly .... A. W. Baskcomb
Curly .... Gertude Lang
First Twin .... Dagmar Wieche

Second Twin .... Bertha Stewart
Smee .... George Shelton
Starkey .... Charles Trevor
Cookson .... Charles Medwin
Mullins .... Chris Walker
Cecco .... Frederick Annerley
Jukes .... James English
Noodler .... John Kelt
First Pirate .... Frank Saker
Second Pirate .... Bell
Black Pirate .... S. Spencer
Panther .... Humphrey Warden
Tiger Lily .... Margaret Fraser
Mermaid .... Alice Robinson
Baby Mermaid .... Tessie Parke
Liza .... Tessie Parke
Crocodile .... D. Searle & W. Child
Ostrich .... E. Marini (Ernest)

1910–11

Duke of York's Theatre

Peter Pan .... Pauline Chase
Captain Hook .... E. Holman Clark
Mr. Darling .... Donald Calthrop
Mrs. Darling .... Viva Birkett
Wendy .... Gertrude Lang
John .... Herbert Hollom
Michael .... Charles Thomas
Nana .... Edward Sillward
Tootles .... Dorothy Minto
Nibs .... Francis Kapstowne
Slightly .... A. W. Baskcomb
Curly .... Mary Glynne
First Twin .... Gwendoline Brogden
Second Twin .... Doris MacIntyre
Smee .... George Shelton
Starkey .... Charles Trevor
Cookson .... Charles Medwin
Mullins .... Chris Walker
Cecco .... Frederick Annerley
Jukes .... James English
Noodler .... John Kelt
First Pirate .... Ernest Young
Second Pirate .... A. Wade
Black Pirate .... S. Spencer
Panther .... Humphrey Warden
Tiger Lily .... Margaret Fraser
Mermaid .... Florence Piggott
Baby Mermaid .... Stephanie Bell
Liza .... Stephanie Bell
Crocodile .... D. Searle & P. S. Nagle
Ostrich .... E. Marini (Ernest)

1911–12

Duke of York's Theatre

Peter Pan .... Pauline Chase
Captain Hook .... E. Holman Clark
Mr. Darling .... Donald Calthrop
Mrs. Darling .... Viva Birkett
Wendy .... Hilda Trevelyan

John .... Stephen Thomas
Michael .... Alfred Willmore
Nana .... Edward Sillward
Tootles .... Gertrude Lang
Nibs .... Stephanie Bell
Slightly .... W. West
Curly .... Marjorie Graham
First Twin .... Doris MacIntyre
Second Twin .... Rosemary Craig
Smee .... George Shelton
Starkey .... Charles Trevor
Cookson .... Charles Medwin
Mullins .... Chris Walker
Cecco .... William Luff
Jukes .... James English
Noodler .... John Kelt
First Pirate .... A. Grand
Second Pirate .... D. Darrell
Black Pirate .... S. Spencer
Panther .... Humphrey Warden
Tiger Lily .... Margaret Fraser
Mermaid .... Evangeline Hilliard
Baby Mermaid .... Moya Nugent
Liza .... Moya Nugent
Crocodile .... D. Searle & P.S. Nagle
Ostrich .... Ernest Marini

1912–13

Duke of York's Theatre

Peter Pan .... Pauline Chase
Captain Hook .... E. Holman Clark
Mr. Darling .... Lawrence Robbins
Mrs. Darling .... Viva Birkett
Wendy .... Mary Glynne
John .... Alfred Willmore
Michael .... Reggie Sheffield
Nana .... Edward Sillward
Tootles .... Gertrude Lang
Nibs .... Marjorie Graham
Slightly .... Charles Thomas
Curly .... Prudence Bourchier
                     (matinees), Joan Caroll
                     (evenings)
First Twin .... Anna Langley
Second Twin .... Sybil Hook
Smee .... George Shelton
Starkey .... Charles Trevor
Cookson .... Charles Medwin
Mullins .... James Prior
Cecco .... William Luff
Jukes .... James English
Noodler .... John Kelt
First Pirate .... Charles Calvert
Second Pirate .... A. Stevenson
Black Pirate .... S. Spencer
Panther .... Humphrey Warden
Tiger Lily .... Margaret Fraser
Mermaid .... Dora Sevening
Baby Mermaid .... Moya Nugent
Liza .... Moya Nugent
Crocodile .... S. Nagle & M. Rose
Ostrich .... W. Child

1913–14

Duke of York's Theatre

Peter Pan . . . . Pauline Chase
Captain Hook . . . . Godfrey Tearle
Mr. Darling . . . . Basil Foster
Mrs. Darling . . . . Nina Sevening
Wendy . . . . Mary Glynne
John . . . . Alfred Willmore
Michael . . . . Donald Buckley
Nana . . . . Edward Sillward
Tootles . . . . Gertrude Lang
Nibs . . . . Marjorie Graham
Slightly . . . . Noël Coward
Curly . . . . Prudence Bourchier
First Twin . . . . Doris McIntyre
Second Twin . . . . Joan Coulthurst
Smee . . . . George Shelton
Starkey . . . . Charles Trevor
Cookson . . . . Charles Medwin
Mullins . . . . James Prior
Cecco . . . . William Luff
Jukes . . . . James English
Noodler . . . . John Kelt
First Pirate . . . . William Harberd
Second Pirate . . . . A. Stevenson
Black Pirate . . . . S. Spencer
Panther . . . . Humphrey Warden
Tiger Lily . . . . Margaret Fraser
Mermaid . . . . Dora Sevening
Baby Mermaid . . . . Moya Nugent
Liza . . . . Moya Nugent
Crocodile . . . . D. Buckley & F. W. Cecil
Ostrich . . . . Gordon Carr

1914–15

Duke of York's Theatre

Peter Pan . . . . Madge Titheradge
Captain Hook . . . . E. Holman Clark
Mr. Darling . . . . Donald Calthrop
Mrs. Darling . . . . Madge Murray
Wendy . . . . Hilda Trevelyan
John . . . . Roy Royston
Michael . . . . Elyot Hawkins
Nana . . . . Edgar Pleon
Tootles . . . . Gertrude Lang
Nibs . . . . Marjorie Graham
Slightly . . . . A. W. Baskcomb
Curly . . . . Prudence Bourchier
First Twin . . . . Doris McIntyre
Second Twin . . . . Nancy Pawley
Smee . . . . George Shelton
Starkey . . . . Ben Field
Cookson . . . . Charles Medwin
Mullins . . . . William Harberd
Cecco . . . . William Luff
Jukes . . . . James English
Noodler . . . . Frederick Leister
First Pirate . . . . Dick Cooper
Second Pirate . . . . Gordon Carr
Black Pirate . . . . George Welch
Panther . . . . Humphrey Warden

Tiger Lily . . . . Margaret Fraser
Mermaid . . . . Dora Sevening
Baby Mermaid . . . . Moya Nugent
Liza . . . . Moya Nugent
Crocodile . . . . F. W. Cecil & D. Rose
Ostrich . . . . Gordon Carr

1915–16

New Theatre

Peter Pan . . . . Unity More
Captain Hook . . . . Arthur Wontner
Mr. Darling . . . . Martin Lewis
Mrs. Darling . . . . Madge Murray
Wendy . . . . Dot Temple
John . . . . Patrick Ludlow
Michael . . . . Eric Stuart
Nana . . . . Edgar Pleon
Tootles . . . . Nancy Pawley
Nibs . . . . Jane Graham
Slightly . . . . Arthur Cleave
Curly . . . . Elyot Hawkins
First Twin . . . . Doris MacIntyre
Second Twin . . . . Hilda Blake
Smee . . . . George Shelton
Starkey . . . . A. G. Poulton
Cookson . . . . Charles Medwin
Mullins . . . . Chris Walker
Cecco . . . . William Luff
Jukes . . . . James English
Noodler . . . . Cecil Belcher
First Pirate . . . . Dick Cooper
Second Pirate . . . . Donald Searle
Black Pirate . . . . George Welch
Panther . . . . Frederick Leister
Tiger Lily . . . . Tonie Edgar Bruce
Liza . . . . Babs Farren
Crocodile . . . . D. Rose & W. Barbour
Ostrich . . . . Donald Searle

1916–17

New Theatre

Peter Pan . . . . Unity More
Captain Hook . . . . E. Holman Clark
Mr. Darling . . . . Martin Lewis
Mrs. Darling . . . . Stella Mervyn Campbell
Wendy . . . . Dot Temple
John . . . . John Williams
Michael . . . . Terri Storri
Nana . . . . Edgar Pleon
Tootles . . . . Sybil Hook
Nibs . . . . Jane Graham
Slightly . . . . Arthur Cleave
Curly . . . . Marjory Holman
First Twin . . . . Doris MacIntyre
Second Twin . . . . Dorrie Russell
Smee . . . . George Shelton
Starkey . . . . Sam Lysons
Cookson . . . . Charles Medwin
Mullins . . . . Rawson Buckley
Cecco . . . . William Luff
Jukes . . . . James English

Noodler . . . . Alfred Lugg
First Pirate . . . . Edgar Wood
Black Pirate . . . . Enest Trimingham
Panther . . . . Arthur Hambling
Tiger Lily . . . . Margaret Fraser
Mermaid . . . . Dora Sevening
Baby Mermaid . . . . Babs Farren
Liza . . . . Babs Farren
Crocodile . . . . F. Alexander & L. Lewis
Ostrich . . . . Alfred Thompson

1917–18

New Theatre

Peter Pan . . . . Fay Compton
Captain Hook . . . . E. Holman Clark
Mr. Darling . . . . Martin Lewis
Mrs. Darling . . . . Stella Mervyn Campbell
Wendy . . . . Isobel Elsom
John . . . . Pat Kay (Anton Dolin)
Michael . . . . Vesta Sylva
Nana . . . . Pauline Prim
Tootles . . . . Betty Faire
Nibs . . . . Phyllis Pinson
Slightly . . . . Arthur Cleave
Curly . . . . Cherrie Carver
First Twin . . . . Doris MacIntyre
Second Twin . . . . Noreen O'Connor
Smee . . . . George Shelton
Starkey . . . . Hugh E. Wright
Cookson . . . . Walter Lake
Mullins . . . . Rawson Buckley
Cecco . . . . William Luff
Jukes . . . . James English
Noodler . . . . John Kelt
First Pirate . . . . A. Thompson
Second Pirate . . . . Greenville Darling
Black Pirate . . . . J. Wilson
Panther . . . . Garrett Hollick
Tiger Lily . . . . Netta Wescott
Mermaid . . . . Dora Sevening
Baby Mermaid . . . . Babs Farren
Liza . . . . Babs Farren
Crocodile . . . . F. Alexander & L. Lewis
Ostrich . . . . Alfred Thompson

1918–19

New Theatre

Peter Pan . . . . Faith Celli
Captain Hook . . . . Julian Royce
Mr. Darling . . . . Wilfred Fletcher
Mrs. Darling . . . . Stella Campbell
Wendy . . . . Isobel Elsom
John . . . . Patrick Kay (Anton Dolin)
Michael . . . . Vesta Sylva
Nana . . . . Edward Batley
Tootles . . . . Sybil Hook
Nibs . . . . Jane Graham
Slightly . . . . Arthur Cleave
Curly . . . . Lois Carruthers
First Twin . . . . Doris MacIntyre
Second Twin . . . . Sybil Faye
Smee . . . . G. W. Anson

Starkey . . . . Hugh E. Wright
Cookson . . . . Walter Lake
Mullins . . . . Rawson Buckley
Cecco . . . . William Luff
Jukes . . . . Basil Dyne
Noodler . . . . John Kelt
First Pirate . . . . A. Carlaw Grand
Second Pirate . . . . Dudley S. Crewe
Black Pirate . . . . J. Wilson (listed as Third
                              Pirate)
Panther . . . . Garrett Hollick
Tiger Lily . . . . Margaret Fraser
Mermaid . . . . Ethel Wellesley
Baby Mermaid . . . . Babs Farren
Liza . . . . Babs Farren
Crocodile . . . . Joseph Owen & Percy Buss
Ostrich . . . . Dudley S. Crewe

1919–1920

New Theatre

Peter Pan . . . . Georgette Cohan
Captain Hook . . . . Allan Jeaves
Mr. Darling . . . . Philip Easton
Mrs. Darling . . . . Phyllis Joyce
Wendy . . . . Renee Mayer
John . . . . Patrick Kay
Michael . . . . Vesta Sylva
Nana . . . . Edgar Pleon
Tootles . . . . Sybil Hook
Nibs . . . . Ena Best (Edna Best)
Slightly . . . . Arthur Cleave
Curly . . . . Lois Carruthers
First Twin . . . . Doris MacIntyre
Second Twin . . . . Terri Storri
Smee . . . . G. W. Anson
Starkey . . . . Charles Trevor
Cookson . . . . Walter Lake
Mullins . . . . Rawson Buckley
Cecco . . . . William Luff
Jukes . . . . James English
Noodler . . . . John Kelt
First Pirate . . . . Dudley S. Crewe
Second Pirate . . . . A. Carlaw Grand
Black Pirate . . . . Donald Walcott
Panther . . . . Garrett Hollick
Tiger Lily . . . . Nancy Pawley
Mermaid . . . . Ethel Wellesley
Baby Mermaid . . . . Babs Farren
Liza . . . . Babs Farren
Crocodile . . . . Joseph Owen & Cyril
                              Holland
Ostrich . . . . Dudley S. Crewe

1920–21

New Theatre

Peter Pan . . . . Edna Best
Captain Hook . . . . Henry Ainley
Mr. Darling . . . . Henry Ainley
Mrs. Darling . . . . Sybil Carlisle
Wendy . . . . Freda Godfrey
John . . . . Val Pragnall

Michael . . . . Ivy Pike
Nana . . . . Gordon Carr
Tootles . . . . Carmen Woods
Nibs . . . . Delina O'Sullivan
Slightly . . . . Donald Searle (evenings)
                      Arthur Cleve (matinees)
Curly . . . . Noreen Hamilton
First Twin . . . . Doris MacIntyre
Second Twin . . . . Terri Storri
Smee . . . . George Shelton
Starkey . . . . Fotheringham Lysons
Cookson . . . . Walter Lake
Mullins . . . . Rawson Buckley
Cecco . . . . William Luff
Jukes . . . . James English
Noodler . . . . John Kelt
First Pirate . . . . S. Grenville Darling
Second Pirate . . . . William D'Arcy
Black Pirate . . . . Donald Walcott
Panther . . . . Garrett Hollick
Tiger Lily . . . . Nancy Pawley
Liza . . . . Rosemonde de Perrinello
Crocodile . . . . William Darbourne &
                      George Boyle
Ostrich . . . . William D'Arcy

1921–22

St. Jame's Theatre

Peter Pan . . . . Joan Maclean
Captain Hook . . . . Ernest Thesiger
Mr. Darling . . . . John Williams
Mrs. Darling . . . . Sybil Carlisle
Wendy . . . . Sylvia Oakley
John . . . . Keith Hudson
Michael . . . . Monica Disney
Nana . . . . Gordon Carr
Tootles . . . . Esta Pendair
Nibs . . . . Blossom Churan
Slightly . . . . Donald Searle
Curly . . . . Norah Westbury-Jones
First Twin . . . . Doris MacIntyre
Second Twin . . . . Pamela Williams
Smee . . . . George Shelton
Starkey . . . . Charles Trevor
Cookson . . . . Walter Lake
Mullins . . . . Rawson Buckley
Cecco . . . . William Luff
Jukes . . . . James English
Noodler . . . . John Kelt
First Pirate . . . . A. Carlaw Grand
Second Pirate . . . . William D'Arcy
Black Pirate . . . . Donald Walcott
Panther . . . . Garrett Hollick
Tiger Lily . . . . Nancy Pawley
Liza . . . . Gabrielle Casartelli
Crocodile . . . . Jack Lee & George Boyle
Ostrich . . . . William D'Arcy

1922–23

St. James Theatre

Peter Pan . . . . Edna Best
Captain Hook . . . . Lyn Harding

Mr. Darling . . . . C. Stafford Dickens
Mrs. Darling . . . . Prudence Vanburgh
Wendy . . . . Sylvia Oakley
John . . . . Leonard Hibbs
Michael . . . . Marie Vinten
Nana . . . . Gordon Carr
Tootles . . . . Joan Maude-Price
Nibs . . . . Jill Esmond-Moore
Slightly . . . . Donald Searle
Curly . . . . Stella Freeman
First Twin . . . . Ursula Moreton
Second Twin . . . . Dorothy Lynne
Smee . . . . George Shelton
Starkey . . . . Charles Trevor
Cookson . . . . Walter C. Lake
Mullins . . . . F. Rawson Buckley
Cecco . . . . William Luff
Jukes . . . . James English
Noodler . . . . John Kelt
First Pirate . . . . S. Grenville Darling
Second Pirate . . . . William D'Arcy
Black Pirate . . . . Donald Walcott
Panther . . . . Garrett Hollick
Tiger Lily . . . . Nancy Pawley
Liza . . . . Violet Aubert
Crocodile . . . . Edgar Webb & Victor
                      Tunwell
Ostrich . . . . William D'Arcy

1923–24

Adelphi Theatre

Peter Pan . . . . Gladys Cooper
Captain Hook . . . . Franklyn Dyall
Mr. Darling . . . . Jack Raine
Mrs. Darling . . . . Stella Patrick Campbell
Wendy . . . . Lila Maravan
John . . . . Patrick Harvey
Michael . . . . John Secker
Nana . . . . Gordon Carr
Tootles . . . . Joan Maude
Nibs . . . . Jill Esmond-Moore
Slightly . . . . Donald Searle
Curly . . . . Diana Beaumont
First Twin . . . . Sunday Wilshin
Second Twin . . . . Nancy Burt
Smee . . . . George Shelton
Starkey . . . . Charles Trevor
Cookson . . . . Arthur Pond
Mullins . . . . F. Rawson Buckley
Cecco . . . . William Luff
Jukes . . . . James English
Noodler . . . . John Kelt
First Pirate . . . . S. Granville [sic] Darling
Second Pirate . . . . Joseph Owen
Black Pirate . . . . Donald Walcott
Panther . . . . Walter C. Lake
Tiger Lily . . . . Nancy Pawley
Liza . . . . Violet Aubert
Crocodile . . . . Norman Phillips &
                      James Gilbert
Ostrich . . . . Joseph Owen

1924-25

Adelphi Theatre

Peter Pan . . . . Gladys Cooper
Captain Hook . . . . Ian Hunter (replaced by
William Luff in early
January)
Mr. Darling . . . . Ian Hunter (replaced by
Anthony Bushell in early
January)
Mrs. Darling . . . . Stella Patrick Campbell
Wendy . . . . Angela du Maurier
John . . . . Gerald Anderson
Michael . . . . Brian Glennie
Nana . . . . Gordon Carr
Tootles . . . . Audrey Lucas
Nibs . . . . Jill Esmond-Moore
Slightly . . . . Harold Scott
Curly . . . . Diana Beaumont
First Twin . . . . Phil Buchanan
Second Twin . . . . Agatha Kentish
Smee . . . . George Shelton
Starkey . . . . Charles Trevor
Cookson . . . . Walter Lake
Mullins . . . . F. Rawson Buckley
Cecco . . . . William Luff
Jukes . . . . James English
Noodler . . . . John Kelt
First Pirate . . . . Allan Whittaker
Second Pirate . . . . Joseph Owen
Black Pirate . . . . Donald Walcott
Panther . . . . Francis L. Sullivan
Tiger Lily . . . . Nancy Pawley
Liza . . . . Winifred Sutton
Crocodile . . . . Ernest Madden & Reginald
Morgan
Ostrich . . . . Joseph Owen

1925-26

Shaftsbury Theatre

Peter Pan . . . . Dorothy Dickson
Captain Hook . . . . Lyn Harding
Mr. Darling . . . . Bruce Belfrage
Mrs. Darling . . . . Prudence Vanbrugh
Wendy . . . . Angela du Maurier
John . . . . Bruce Baron
Michael . . . . Brian Glennie
Nana . . . . Gordon Carr
Tootles . . . . Audrey Lucas
Nibs . . . . Ivis Goulding
Slightly . . . . Allan Whittaker
Curly . . . . Diana Beaumont
First Twin . . . . Ursula Moreton
Second Twin . . . . J. de la Mare
Smee . . . . George Shelton
Starkey . . . . Charles Trevor
Cookson . . . . Walter Lake
Mullins . . . . F. Rawson Buckley
Cecco . . . . William Luff
Jukes . . . . James English
Noodler . . . . John Kelt
First Pirate . . . . S. Grenville Darling

Second Pirate . . . . Joseph Owen
Black Pirate . . . . Donald Walcott
Panther . . . . Garrett Hollick
Tiger Lily . . . . Nancy Pawley
Liza . . . . Olive Drew
Crocodile . . . . Ernest Madden & Reginald
Morgan
Ostrich . . . . John Thompson

1926-27

Adelphi Theatre

Peter Pan . . . . Dorothy Dickson
Captain Hook . . . . Alfred Drayton
Mr. Darling . . . . Robert Irvine
Mrs. Darling . . . . Dorothy Lynne (replaced
by Jane Baxter in early
January)
Wendy . . . . Annie Kasmir
John . . . . Bruce Baron
Michael . . . . Peter Evans
Nana . . . . Gordon Carr
Tootles . . . . Winnie Sutton
Nibs . . . . Billie Cope
Slightly . . . . Allan Whittaker
Curly . . . . Poppy Redgrove
First Twin . . . . Marina Naiska
Second Twin . . . . Winnie Sheppard
Smee . . . . George Shelton
Starkey . . . . Charles Trevor
Cookson . . . . Thomas Croft
Mullins . . . . F. Rawson Buckley
Cecco . . . . William Luff
Jukes . . . . James English
Noodler . . . . John Kelt
First Pirate . . . . Robert Haslam
Second Pirate . . . . John Hull
Black Pirate . . . . Donald Walcott
Panther . . . . Garrett Hollick
Tiger Lily . . . . Nancy Pawley
Liza . . . . Olive Drew
Crocodile . . . . Stanley Rowan & Reginald
Morgan
Ostrich . . . . Walter Plinge

1927-28

Gaiety Theatre

Peter Pan . . . . Jean Forbes-Robertson
Captain Hook . . . . William Luff
Mr. Darling . . . . Frank Allanby
Mrs. Darling . . . . Marie Lohr
Wendy . . . . Mary Casson
John . . . . Colin Cardew
Michael . . . . Freddie Springett
Nana . . . . Gordon Carr
Tootles . . . . Mary Love
Nibs . . . . Billee Cope
Slightly . . . . Allan Whittaker
Curly . . . . Poppy Redgrove
First Twin . . . . Maudie Bell
Second Twin . . . . Winnie Sheppard
Smee . . . . James C. Wilton

	(replaced by George
	Shelton after a few days)
Starkey	Charles Trevor
Cookson	S. Grenville Darling
Mullins	F. Rawson Buckley
Cecco	James Willoughby
Jukes	James English
Noodler	John Kelt
First Pirate	Percival Owen
Second Pirate	John Hull
Black Pirate	Donald Walcott
Panther	Garrett Hollick
Tiger Lily	Diana Beaumont
Liza	Olive Drew
Crocodile	Claude Bruton &
	Desmond Langdale
Ostrich	John Hull

1928–29

Garrick Theatre

Peter Pan	Jean Forbes-Robertson
Captain Hook	Malcolm Keen
Mr. Darling	Robert Haslam
Mrs. Darling	Marie Lohr
Wendy	Mary Casson
John	Derrick Weale
Michael	Freddie Springett
Nana	Gordon Carr
Tootles	George Howell
Nibs	Leonard Hayes
Slightly	Allan Whittaker
Curly	Harold Reese
First Twin	Peter du Calion
Second Twin	Peter Evans
Smee	George Shelton
Starkey	Charles Trevor
Cookson	Gervis Walter
Mullins	F. Rawson Buckley
Cecco	William Luff
Jukes	James English
Noodler	John Kelt
First Pirate	Richard Allen
Second Pirate	Peter Dixon
Black Pirate	J.W. Alexander
Panther	Garrett Hollick
Tiger Lily	Nancy Pawley
Mermaid	Jane Prinsep
Baby Mermaid	Ruby Cairns
Liza	Olive Drew
Crocodile	Claude Bruton & James
	Skipper
Ostrich	Peter Dixon

1929–30

St. James Theatre

Peter Pan	Jean Forbes-Robertson
Captain Hook	Gerald du Maurier
Mr. Darling	Gerald du Maurier
Mrs. Darling	Marie Lohr
Wendy	Mary Casson
John	Bobbie Jones

Michael	Freddie Springett
Nana	Freddie Page
Tootles	Ralph Hazel
Nibs	Jack Skinner
Slightly	Donald Stuart
Curly	Roger Foster
First Twin	Peter du Calion
Second Twin	Peter Evans
Smee	George Shelton
Starkey	Herbert Ross
Cookson	Tom Woods
Mullins	F. Rawson Buckley
Cecco	William Luff
Jukes	James English
Noodler	John Kelt
First Pirate	W. G. Manning
Second Pirate	Peter Dixon
Black Pirate	Bert Delgarde
Panther	Garrett Hollick
Tiger Lily	Nancy Pawley
Mermaid	Jane Prinsep
Baby Mermaid	Margaret Walker
Liza	Olive Drew
Crocodile	David Koskie & James
	Skipper
Ostrich	Ferdinand Coen

1930–31

Palladium

Peter Pan	Jean Forbes-Robertson
Captain Hook	George Curzon
Mr. Darling	George Curzon
Mrs. Darling	Stella Patrick Campbell
Wendy	Mary Casson
John	Jimmy Hanley
Michael	Freddie Springett
Nana	George Elliston
Tootles	Ralph Hazel
Nibs	Jack Skinner
Slightly	W. G. Manning
Curly	Douglas Beaumont
First Twin	Donald Masters
Second Twin	Michael Jackson
Smee	James C. Wilton
Starkey	Francis Hope
Cookson	Jervis Walter
Mullins	F. Rawson Buckley
Cecco	William Luff
Jukes	James English
Noodler	John Kelt
First Pirate	George A. Boyle
Second Pirate	Percival Owen
Black Pirate	Sam Henry
Panther	Garrett Hollick
Tiger Lily	Constance Cumber
Mermaid	Pauline Saunders
Baby Mermaid	B. Denton
Liza	Verononica Vanderlyn
Crocodile	David Koskie & Alec
	Brown
Ostrich	Billy Speechley

1931–32

Palladium

Peter Pan	Jean Forbes-Robertson
Captain Hook	George Curzon
Mr. Darling	George Curzon
Mrs. Darling	Zena Dare
Wendy	Mary Casson
John	Douglas Beaumont
Michael	Freddie Springett
Nana	George Elliston
Tootles	Ralph Hazel
Nibs	Jack Skinner
Slightly	W.G. Manning
Curly	Graham Payne
First Twin	Charles Hawtrey
Second Twin	F. Hundley
Smee	Cecil Fowler
Starkey	Leedham Stanley
Cookson	Greenville Darling
Mullins	A. E. Johnson
Cecco	William Luff
Jukes	Victor Thornton
Noodler	John Kelt
First Pirate	Harry Frearson
Second Pirate	George Weir
Black Pirate	Ernest Trimmingham
Panther	Charles Apsey
Tiger Lily	Constance Cumber
Mermaid	Pamela Barrett
Baby Mermaid	Marion Lloyd
Liza	Helen Moore
Crocodile	David Koskie & Alec Brown
Ostrich	Harry Glover

1932–33

Palladium

Peter Pan	Jean Forbes-Robertson
Captain Hook	George Curzon
Mr. Darling	George Curzon
Mrs. Darling	Zena Dare
Wendy	Mary Casson
John	Michael Goodwin
Michael	Arthur Payne
Nana	George Elliston
Tootles	Fred Date
Nibs	André Carter
Slightly	W. G. Manning
Curly	Harry Lennard
First Twin	Wilfred Jackson
Second Twin	Frank Hundley
Smee	Cecil Fowler
Starkey	George Howe
Cookson	Arthur Harding
Mullins	A. E. Johnson
Cecco	William Luff
Jukes	John Clements
Noodler	John Kelt
First Pirate	George Hudson
Second Pirate	Richard Turner
Black Pirate	Sam Henry
Panther	Garrett Hollick

Tiger Lily	Constance Cumber
Mermaid	Pat Wood-Samson
Baby Mermaid	Marion Lloyd
Liza	Helen Moore
Crocodile/Ostrich	Harry Glover

1933–34

Palladium

Peter Pan	Jean Forbes-Robertson
Captain Hook	Ralph Richardson
Mr. Darling	Ralph Richardson
Mrs. Darling	Marie Lohr
Wendy	Daphne Courtney
John	Michael Goodwin
Michael	Arthur Payne
Nana	George Elliston
Tootles	J. Cranfield
Nibs	André Carter
Slightly	W. G. Manning
Curly	John Clayton
First Twin	Alphonse Nolin
Second Twin	Arthur Blake
Smee	Cecil Fowler
Starkey	Leedam Stanley
Cookson	Edwin McCarthy
Mullins	Carl F. Wright
Cecco	William Luff
Jukes	Stanley Vine
Noodler	John Kelt
First Pirate	George Hudson
Second Pirate	Richard Turner
Black Pirate	Sam Henry
Panther	Robert Gilbert
Tiger Lily	Constance Cumber
Mermaid	Denise Phillips
Baby Mermaid	Olga Dalglish
Liza	Helen Moore
Crocodile	Albert Kingston & Nina Hill
Ostrich	D. Beaumont (Douglas)

1934–35

Palladium

Peter Pan	Jean Forbes-Robertson
Captain Hook	George Curzon
Mr. Darling	George Curzon
Mrs. Darling	Marie Lohr
Wendy	Pamela Staley
John	Brian Sheridan
Michael	Arthur Payne
Nana	George Elliston
Tootles	Albert Davies
Nibs	Dick Curnock
Slightly	W. G. Manning
Curly	John Clayton
First Twin	Alphonse Nolin
Second Twin	Arthur Blake
Smee	Cecil Fowler
Starkey	Leedam Stanley
Cookson	Edwin McCarthy
Mullins	W. F. George

Cecco .... William Luff
Jukes .... Stanley Vine
Noodler .... John Kelt
First Pirate .... George Hudson
Second Pirate .... H. Garrett
Black Pirate .... Sam Henry
Panther .... Robert Gilbert
Tiger Lily .... Jane Prinsep
Mermaid .... Iris Ashton-Wright
Baby Mermaid .... Margaret Anguish
Liza .... Helen Moore
Crocodile .... Albert Kingston &
                     Derek Blatcher
Ostrich .... D. Beaumont (Douglas)

1935–36

Palladium

Peter Pan .... Nova Pilbeam
Captain Hook .... George Hayes
Mr. Darling .... George Hayes
Mrs. Darling .... Carol Goodner
Wendy .... Violet Loxley
John .... John Clayton
Michael .... Arthur Payne
Nana .... Wallie Scott
Tootles .... S. Axham (Stanley)
Nibs .... Derek Blatcher
Slightly .... W. G. Manning
Curly .... Joseph Hepworth
First Twin .... R. Hyland (Richard)
Second Twin .... Arthur Blake
Smee .... Cecil Fowler
Starkey .... Leedam Stanley
Cookson .... Edwin McCarthy
Mullins .... Victor Thornton
Cecco .... William Luff
Jukes .... Stanley Vine
Noodler .... Granville Darling
First Pirate .... A. Harding
Second Pirate .... R. Turner (Richard)
Black Pirate .... Sam Henry
Panther .... Garrett Hollick
Tiger Lily .... Olive Wright
Mermaid .... M. Milne (Margaret)
Baby Mermaid .... Joyce Alderman
Liza .... Helen Moore
Crocodile .... John Hart & Tony
                     Boothroyd
Ostrich .... S. Bridger

1936–37

Palladium

Peter Pan .... Elsa Lanchester
Captain Hook .... Charles Laughton
Mr. Darling .... Peter Murray Hill
Mrs. Darling .... Cecily Byrne
Wendy .... Pamela Standish
John .... Clive Baxter
Michael .... Paul Dunger
Nana .... Wallie Scott
Tootles .... T. Best (Terence)

Nibs .... D. Blatcher (Derek)
Slightly .... Charles Hawtrey
Curly .... Robert Holland
First Twin .... Stanley Axham
Second Twin .... D. Smith
Smee .... Charles Doe
Starkey .... Harold Scott
Cookson .... Edwin McCarthy
Mullins .... Victor Thornton
Cecco .... William Luff
Jukes .... Hamilton Hunter
Noodler .... Granville Darling
First Pirate .... Claude Talbot
Second Pirate .... Richard Turner
Black Pirate .... Sam Henry
Panther .... Garrett Hollick
Tiger Lily .... Olive Wright
Mermaid .... M. Milne (Margaret)
Baby Mermaid ...... Kathleen Weston
Liza .... Helen Moore
Crocodile .... David Little & Basil
                    MacRae
Ostrich .... T. Bray

1937–38

Palladium

Peter Pan .... Anna Neagle
Captain Hook .... George Curzon
Mr. Darling .... George Curzon
Mrs. Darling .... Cecily Byrne
Wendy .... Pamela Standish
John .... Clive Baxter
Michael .... Christopher McMaster
Nana .... Wallie Scott
Tootles .... P. Scott
Nibs .... Leonard Thorne
Slightly .... Jimmy Hanley
Curly .... P. Sylvester
First Twin .... D. Smith
Second Twin .... Brian Whittle
Smee .... Charles Doe
Starkey .... Max Adrian
Cookson .... Edwin McCarthy
Mullins .... John Lothar
Cecco .... William Luff
Jukes .... Stanley Vine
Noodler .... Granville Darling
First Pirate .... Claude Talbot
Second Pirate .... Richard Turner
Black Pirate .... Sam Henry
Panther .... Garrett Hollick
Tiger Lily .... Olive Wright
Mermaid .... D. Rowley (Destine)
Baby Mermaid ...... Muriel Blatcher
Liza .... Helen Moore
Crocodile .... Ray Smith & Charles
                    Tolman

1938–39

Palladium

Peter Pan .... Jean Forbes-Robertson
Captain Hook .... Seymour Hicks

Mr. Darling .... Anthony Bushell
Mrs. Darling .... Cecily Byrne
Wendy .... Pamela Standish
John .... Geoffrey Atkins
Michael .... David Baxter
Nana .... Wallie Scott
Tootles .... P. Scott
Nibs .... Dane Gordon
Slightly .... Jimmy Hanley
Curly .... Peter Lindsey
First Twin .... Noel Monks
Second Twin .... Michael Monks
Smee .... Charles Doe
Starkey .... Eadie Palfrey
Cookson .... Edwin McCarthy
Mullins .... A. E. Johnson
Cecco .... William Luff
Jukes .... Stanley Vine
Noodler .... Granville Darling
First Pirate .... James Dennison
Second Pirate .... David Glaser
Black Pirate .... Sam Henry
Panther .... Garrett Hollick
Tiger Lily .... Olive Wright
Mermaid .... Roma Rice
Baby Mermaid .... Pat Keefe
Liza .... Helen Moore
Crocodile .... Bruce Miller & Ricky
                      Hyland

1939–40

No London Production Due to War

1940–41

No London Production Due to War

1941–42

Adelphi Theatre

Peter Pan .... Barbara Mullen
Captain Hook .... Alastair Sim
Mr. Darling .... Alastair Sim
Mrs. Darling .... Zena Dare
Wendy .... Joan Greenwood
John .... Ronald Law
Michael .... John Grange
Nana .... Geoffrey Jowitt
Tootles .... Doreen Fischer
Nibs .... Brian Nissen
Slightly .... Eadie Palfrey
Curly .... D. Russell
First Twin .... Pam Warren
Second Twin .... Jeanne Wells
Smee .... Russell Thorndike
Starkey .... Peter Bennett
Cookson .... Frank Worth
Mullins .... Conway Dixon
Cecco .... William Luff
Jukes .... Eric Allbury
Noodler .... Sydney Elliott
First Pirate .... Arthur Taylor
Second Pirate .... Alfred Barnes

Black Pirate .... Harry Crossman
Panther .... Allen Douglas
Tiger Lily .... Jean Kamiya
Mermaid .... Penelope Hughes
Baby Mermaid .... Kinara Kestyn
Liza .... Betty Pollock
Crocodile .... Gordon Hitchins
Ostrich .... Gerald Gordon

1942–43

Winter Garden Theatre

Peter Pan .... Ann Todd
Captain Hook .... Alastair Sim
Mr. Darling .... Alastair Sim
Mrs. Darling .... Iris Hoey
Wendy .... Joyce Redman
John .... Alan Wren
Michael .... John Gilpin
Nana .... Geoffrey Jowitt
Tootles .... Ronnie Perry
Nibs .... Terrence Harvey
Slightly .... Dennis Harkin
Curly .... Michael Payne
First Twin .... Doreen Fischer
Second Twin .... Anne Rogers
Smee .... Mark Daly
Starkey .... Peter Cotes
Cookson .... Laurie Ross
Mullins .... G. Kelly (George)
Cecco .... William Luff
Jukes .... Donald Ross
Noodler .... Gerald Kent
First Pirate .... Stanley Oliver
Second Pirate .... G. Barrett (George)
Black Pirate .... Harry Crossman
Panther .... John Cole
Tiger Lily .... Terri Storri
Liza .... Dacia Battye
Crocodile .... Peter Perry
Ostrich .... Terry Taylor

1943–44

Cambridge Theatre

Peter Pan .... Glynis Johns
Captain Hook .... Baliol Holloway
Mr. Darling .... Baliol Holloway
Mrs. Darling .... Cecily Byrne
Wendy .... Diana Deare
John .... John Deering
Michael .... John Gilpin
Nana .... Stanley Escane
Tootles .... Ann Rogers
Nibs .... Frank Goodwin
Slightly .... Maurice Kelly
Curly .... Katie Bangs
First Twin .... Sylvia Newman
Second Twin .... Audrey Newman
Smee .... Charles Sewell
Starkey .... Peter Bennett
Cookson .... Gerald Lea
Mullins .... Pat Somerset

Cecco . . . . William Luff
Jukes . . . . Alec Collins
Noodler . . . . Gerald Kent
First Pirate . . . . George Barrett
Second Pirate . . . . Charles Mettem
Black Pirate . . . . Harry Crossman
Panther . . . . Dean Hilton
Tiger Lily . . . . Terri Storri
Liza . . . . Doreen Lock
Crocodile . . . . Roy Sergeant
Ostrich . . . . Sheila Smith

1944–45

Stoll Theatre

Peter Pan . . . . Frances Day
Captain Hook . . . . Walter Fitzgerald
Mr. Darling . . . . Walter Fitzgerald
Mrs. Darling . . . . Phyllis Joyce
Wendy . . . . Angela Wyndham Lewis
John . . . . Derek Mayhew
Michael . . . . Brian Parker
Nana . . . . Stanley Escane
Tootles . . . . Denny Spencer
Nibs . . . . Gerald Fox
Slightly . . . . Ian Hardy
Curly . . . . Bernard Hall
First Twin . . . . Billy Darren
Second Twin . . . . James Kenny
Smee . . . . Arthur Sinclair
Starkey . . . . Kenneth Kove
Cookson . . . . Alex Collins
Mullins . . . . Bert Lloyd
Cecco . . . . William Luff
Jukes . . . . John Ellery
Noodler . . . . William O'Connor
First Pirate . . . . Michael Williams
Second Pirate . . . . Peter Adamson
Black Pirate . . . . Harry Crossman
Panther . . . . Ernest Lindsay
Tiger Lily . . . . Mary Windust
Liza . . . . Billie Brook
Crocodile . . . . Laurence Keenan
Ostrich . . . . Laurence Keenan

1945–46

Scala Theatre

Peter Pan . . . . Celia Lipton
Captain Hook . . . . George Curzon
Mr. Darling . . . . George Curzon
Mrs. Darling . . . . Mercia Swinburne
Wendy . . . . June Holden
John . . . . Philip Kay
Michael . . . . Malcolm Sommers
Nana . . . . Eric Hilton
Tootles . . . . Harry Vernon
Nibs . . . . John Walsh
Slightly . . . . Keith Noble
Curly . . . . John Potter
First Twin . . . . Trefor Evans
Second Twin . . . . Jimmy Addison
Smee . . . . Teddy Brogden

Starkey . . . . David Maxwell
Cookson . . . . Alex Collins
Mullins . . . . Bert Lloyd
Cecco . . . . William Luff
Jukes . . . . Oswald Raymond
Noodler . . . . Charles Mettam
First Pirate . . . . John England
Second Pirate . . . . William Newell
Black Pirate . . . . Harry Crossman
Panther . . . . Robert Fuller
Tiger Lily . . . . Mary Windust
Liza . . . . Betty Allaway
Crocodile . . . . Colin Stroud
Ostrich . . . . Colin Stroud

1946–47

Scala Theatre

Peter Pan . . . . Mary Morris
Captain Hook . . . . Alaster Sim
Mr. Darling . . . . John Derrick
Mrs. Darling . . . . Mercia Swinburne
Wendy . . . . Diana Calderwood
John . . . . Colin Simpson
Michael . . . . Brian Parker
Nana . . . . Stanley Escane
Tootles . . . . Michael Brailsford
Nibs . . . . David Simpson
Slightly . . . . Billy Thatcher
Curly . . . . John Potter
First Twin . . . . Freddy Hudson
Second Twin . . . . Alex Ansdell
Smee . . . . Teddy Brogden
Starkey . . . . Donald Pleasance
Cookson . . . . Alex Collins
Mullins . . . . Charles Mettam
Cecco . . . . William Luff
Jukes . . . . Nicholas Brent
Noodler . . . . Max Brimmell
First Pirate . . . . Willam Newell
Second Pirate . . . . R. Wood
Black Pirate . . . . Harry Crossman
Panther . . . . Garrett Hollick
Tiger Lily . . . . Lotte Berk
Mermaid . . . . Eleana Fraser
Baby Mermaid . . . . Joan Sherman
Liza . . . . Marion Harbour
Crocodile . . . . Michael Pocock
Ostrich . . . . Francis Bolleter

1947–48

Scala Theatre

Peter Pan . . . . Phyllis Calvert
Captain Hook . . . . Peter Murray Hill
Mr. Darling . . . . Peter Murray Hill
Mrs. Darling . . . . Jane Welch
Wendy . . . . Christina Forrest
John . . . . Ivan Hyde
Michael . . . . David Cole
Nana . . . . Eric Carr
Tootles . . . . Bryan Crown
Nibs . . . . Michael Lister
Slightly . . . . Michael Medwin

Curly . . . . Timothy Harley
First Twin . . . . David Mercer
Second Twin . . . . Tony Ford
Smee . . . . Teddy Brogden
Starkey . . . . Gordon Murray
Cookson . . . . Alex Collins
Mullins . . . . Charles Mettam
Cecco . . . . William Luff
Jukes . . . . Brian Reilly
Noodler . . . . Gilbert Bailey
First Pirate . . . . Ronald Musgrove
Second Pirate . . . . Eric Burton
Black Pirate . . . . Harry Crossman
Panther . . . . Duncan Robinson
Tiger Lily . . . . Diana Wilson
Liza . . . . Jasmine Burchel
Crocodile . . . . Michael Woolston
Ostrich . . . . Alison Gundle

1948–49
Scala Theatre

Peter Pan . . . . Joan Hopkins
Captain Hook . . . . George Curzon
Mr. Darling . . . . George Curzon
Mrs. Darling . . . . Jane Welch
Wendy . . . . Judith Stott
John . . . . Derek Rock
Michael . . . . Michael Cleveland
Nana . . . . Eric Carr
Tootles . . . . Denis Peck
Nibs . . . . Michael Lister
Slightly . . . . Iain Scott
Curly . . . . Stanley Forman
First Twin . . . . David Mercer
Second Twin . . . . Tony Ford
Smee . . . . Morland Graham
Starkey . . . . Gordon Murray
Cookson . . . . Alex Collins
Mullins . . . . Charles Mettam
Cecco . . . . William Luff
Jukes . . . . Bill Staughton
Noodler . . . . Gilbert Bailey
First Pirate . . . . J. P. Melham
Second Pirate . . . . J. Bladen
Black Pirate . . . . Harry Crossman
Panther . . . . Lionel Gadsden
Tiger Lily . . . . Diana Wilson
Liza . . . . Perlita Neilson
Crocodile . . . . Stanley Connett
Ostrich . . . . Pat Spurlock

1949–50
Scala Theatre

Peter Pan . . . . Margaret Lockwood
Captain Hook . . . . John Justin
Mr. Darling . . . . John Justin
Mrs. Darling . . . . Jane Welch
Wendy . . . . Christina Forest
John . . . . Derek Rock
Michael . . . . Michael Cleveland
Nana . . . . Bernard
Tootles . . . . John Cavanah

Nibs . . . . David Kingston
Slightly . . . . Iain Scott
Curly . . . . Sean Lynch
First Twin . . . . Ross Reed
Second Twin . . . . Bill Croydon
Smee . . . . Philip Ray
Starkey . . . . Desmond Carrington
Cookson . . . . Charles Hersee
Mullins . . . . Giles Cooper
Cecco . . . . William Luff
Jukes . . . . Denis Carew
Noodler . . . . Stanley Platts
First Pirate . . . . Geoffrey Underwood
Second Pirate . . . . Louis C. Wilson
Black Pirate . . . . Harry Crossman
Panther . . . . Johnathan Stewart
Tiger Lily . . . . Mary Windust
Liza . . . . Perlita Neilson
Crocodile . . . . Alan Stebbings
Ostrich . . . . Rosamond Leslie

1950–51
Scala Theatre

Peter Pan . . . . Margaret Lockwood
Captain Hook . . . . Alan Judd
Mr. Darling . . . . Alan Judd
Mrs. Darling . . . . Jane Welch
Wendy . . . . Shirley Lorimer
John . . . . Barrie MacGregor
Michael . . . . Warren Hearden
Nana . . . . Bernard
Tootles . . . . Ross Reed
Nibs . . . . Michael Darlington
Slightly . . . . Iain Scott
Curly . . . . Anthony Selby
First Twin . . . . Donald Hindle
Second Twin . . . . Michael Cleveland
Smee . . . . Russell Thorndike
Starkey . . . . Gordon Murray
Cookson . . . . Michael Peake
Mullins . . . . Arthur Bentley
Cecco . . . . William Luff
Jukes . . . . Peter Mercier
Noodler . . . . Stanley Platts
First Pirate . . . . A. G. Tobin
Second Pirate . . . . R. West-Nelson
Black Pirate . . . . Chick Alexander
Panther . . . . Lionel Gadsden
Tiger Lily . . . . Lisa Veronova
Liza . . . . Enid Kenworthy
Crocodile . . . . Michael Lister
Ostrich . . . . Audrey Pollitt

1951–52
Scala Theatre

Peter Pan . . . . Joan Greenwood
Captain Hook . . . . George Curzon
Mr. Darling . . . . George Curzon
Mrs. Darling . . . . Jane Welch
Wendy . . . . Shirley Lorimer
John . . . . Tony Verner
Michael . . . . Derek Rowe

Nana	. . . .	Bernard
Tootles	. . . .	John French
Nibs	. . . .	Michael Darlington
Slightly	. . . .	Iain Scott
Curly	. . . .	Wilfred Downing
First Twin	. . . .	John Todd
Second Twin	. . . .	Peter Mackie
Smee	. . . .	Russell Thorndike
Starkey	. . . .	Gordon Murray
Cookson	. . . .	Gilbert Bailey
Mullins	. . . .	Jashf Crandall
Cecco	. . . .	William Luff
Jukes	. . . .	Granville Eves
Noodler	. . . .	Stanley Platts
First Pirate	. . . .	John Burton
Second Pirate	. . . .	Edward Roberts
Black Pirate	. . . .	Dan Jackson
Panther	. . . .	Victor Graham
Tiger Lily	. . . .	Babette Renier
Liza	. . . .	Yvonne Prestige
Crocodile	. . . .	Michael Lister

1952–53
Scala Theatre

Peter Pan	. . . .	Brenda Bruce
Captain Hook	. . . .	James Donald
Mr. Darling	. . . .	James Donald
Mrs. Darling	. . . .	Jane Welch
Wendy	. . . .	Hilary Rennie
John	. . . .	Wilfred Downing
Michael	. . . .	Ernest Downing
Nana	. . . .	Eric Carr
Tootles	. . . .	William Simons
Nibs	. . . .	Andrew Haley
Slightly	. . . .	Keneth Williams
Curly	. . . .	Jimmy Verner
First Twin	. . . .	Anthony Adams
Second Twin	. . . .	Peter Mackie
Smee	. . . .	Russell Thorndike
Starkey	. . . .	Gordon Murray
Cookson	. . . .	Gilbert Bailey
Mullins	. . . .	Philip Holles
Cecco	. . . .	William Luff
Jukes	. . . .	Granville Eves
Noodler	. . . .	Brian Panter
First Pirate	. . . .	J. Millen Gallacher
Second Pirate	. . . .	Derek Botell
Black Pirate	. . . .	Astley Harvey
Panther	. . . .	Victor Graham
Tiger Lily	. . . .	Pearl Gaden
Liza	. . . .	Edna Wyn
Crocodile	. . . .	Michael Lister

1953–54
Scala Theatre

Peter Pan	. . . .	Pat Kirkwood
Captain Hook	. . . .	Donald Wolfit
Mr. Darling	. . . .	Richard Vernon
Mrs. Darling	. . . .	Evelyn Laye
Wendy	. . . .	Norah Gorsen
John	. . . .	Sean Barrett
Michael	. . . .	Christopher Beeny

Nana	. . . .	Eric Carr
Tootles	. . . .	Duncan Smith
Nibs	. . . .	Douglas Adams
Slightly	. . . .	Iain Scott
Curly	. . . .	Roy Wingrove
First Twin	. . . .	Melvyn Mordant
Second Twin	. . . .	Christopher Royal-Dawson
Smee	. . . .	Russell Thorndike
Starkey	. . . .	Peter Collingwood
Cookson	. . . .	Gilbert Bailey
Mullins	. . . .	Malcolm Watson
Cecco	. . . .	William Luff
Jukes	. . . .	Peter Cellier
Noodler	. . . .	Noel Carey
First Pirate	. . . .	Peter Brownlee
Second Pirate	. . . .	Jan Lavski
Black Pirate	. . . .	Joseph Layode
Panther	. . . .	Victor Graham
Tiger Lily	. . . .	Annette Chappell
Liza	. . . .	Sheila Fish
Crocodile	. . . .	Colin Freear

1954–55
Scala Theatre

Peter Pan	. . . .	Barbara Kelly
Captain Hook	. . . .	Richard Wordsworth
Mr. Darling	. . . .	Richard Wordsworth
Mrs. Darling	. . . .	Patricia Marmount
Wendy	. . . .	Dorothy Bromiley
John	. . . .	Julian Yardley
Michael	. . . .	Colin Gibson
Nana	. . . .	Eric Carr
Tootles	. . . .	Nicky Edmett
Nibs	. . . .	Peter Murphy
Slightly	. . . .	William Ingram
Curly	. . . .	Robin Willett
First Twin	. . . .	Richard Peters
Second Twin	. . . .	Anthony Lang
Smee	. . . .	Russell Thorndike
Starkey	. . . .	Peter Collingwood
Cookson	. . . .	Gilbert Bailey
Mullins	. . . .	Ronald Vowles
Cecco	. . . .	Joseph Chelton
Jukes	. . . .	George D'Arcy
Noodler	. . . .	Ken James
First Pirate	. . . .	Robert Lowe ("Skylights")
Second Pirate	. . . .	Peter Lindsay ("Cabin Boy")
Black Pirate	. . . .	Ayton Medas
Panther	. . . .	Brian Panter
Tiger Lily	. . . .	Karen Glazer
Mermaid	. . . .	Desne Kniveton
Baby Mermaid	. . . .	Wendy Perschky
Liza	. . . .	Wendy Perschky
Crocodile	. . . .	Bruce Heighley
Badger	. . . .	Richard Ives

1955–56
Scala Theatre

Peter Pan	. . . .	Peggy Cummings
Captain Hook	. . . .	Frank Thring

Mr. Darling .... Frank Thring
Mrs. Darling .... Rosemary Scott
Wendy .... Roberta Woolley
John .... Nicky Edmett
Michael .... John Hall
Nana .... Kenneth Robinson
Tootles .... Cavan Kendall
Nibs .... Adrian Haggard
Slightly .... William Ingram
Curly .... Paul Birrell
First Twin .... Alan Glass
Second Twin .... Peter Stevens
Smee .... Russell Thorndike
Starkey .... Norman Rossington
Cookson .... Gilbert Bailey
Mullins .... James Gill
Cecco .... Joseph Chelton
Jukes .... David Ashman
Noodler .... Lionel Gadsden
First Pirate .... Lionel Wheeler
                        ("Skylights")
Second Pirate .... Kenneth Robinson
                        ("Cabin Boy")
Black Pirate .... Ayton Medas
Panther .... David Ashman
Tiger Lily .... Sally Home
Mermaid .... Lilian Grasson
Baby Mermaid .... Elaine Miller
Liza .... Elaine Miller
Crocodile .... John Ormond
Badger .... John Daw

1956–57
Scala Theatre

Peter Pan .... Janette Scott
Captain Hook .... John McCallum
Mr. Darling .... John McCallum
Mrs. Darling .... Rosemary Scott
Wendy .... Frances Guthrie
John .... Cavan Kendall
Michael .... David Langford
Nana .... Kenneth Robinson
Tootles .... Paul Domanski
Nibs .... Peter Furnell
Slightly .... William Ingram
Curly .... Nigel Green
First Twin .... Robert Petters
Second Twin .... Paul Cole
Smee .... Russell Thorndike
Starkey .... Trevor Ray
Cookson .... Gilbert Bailey
Mullins .... James Gill
Cecco .... Geoffrey Frederick
Jukes .... Brian Cobby
Noodler .... Lionel Gadsden
First Pirate .... Alan John ("Skylights")
Second Pirate .... Brian Tyler ("Cabin Boy")
Black Pirate .... Colin Bean
Panther .... Brian Cobby
Tiger Lily .... Rita Gersohn
Mermaid .... Lilian Grasson
Baby Mermaid .... Rochelle Oberman
Liza .... Rochelle Oberman

Crocodile .... Terry Dyer
Badger .... Derek Freeman

1957–58
Scala Theatre

Peter Pan .... Margaret Lockwood
Captain Hook .... Michael Warre
Mr. Darling .... Michael Warre
Mrs. Darling .... Jane Welsh
Wendy .... Julia Lockwood
John .... Melvyn Baker
Michael .... James Ray
Nana .... Leon Garcia
Tootles .... Paul Domanski
Nibs .... Tony Craze
Slightly .... John Levitt
Curly .... David Rogers
First Twin .... John Freeman
Second Twin .... Sam Jephcott
Smee .... Russell Thorndike
Starkey .... Keith Williams
Cookson .... Gilbert Bailey
Mullins .... James Gill
Cecco .... Robin May
Jukes .... David Drummond
Noodler .... Lionel Gadsden
Skylights .... Raymond Cooke
Cabin Boy .... Leon Garcia
Black Pirate .... Brian Mayhall
Panther .... David Drummond
Tiger Lily .... Elizabeth Hart
Mother Mermaid ..... Sonya Petrie
Baby Mermaid .... Pauline Knight
Liza .... Pauline Knight
Crocodile .... Paul Domanski
Badger .... Derek Freeman

1958–59
Scala Theatre

Peter Pan .... Sarah Churchill
Captain Hook .... John Justin
Mr. Darling .... John Justin
Mrs. Darling .... Jane Welsh
Wendy .... Julia Lockwood
John .... Melvyn Baker
Michael .... James Ray
Nana .... Brian Tipping
Tootles .... Paul Domanski
Nibs .... Peter Craze
Slightly .... John Levitt
Curly .... Tony Craze
First Twin .... Paul Taylor
Second Twin .... Vincent MacLoud
Smee .... Russell Thorndike
Starkey .... Keith Williams
Cookson .... Gilbert Bailey
Mullins .... David Fallon
Cecco .... Leonard Kingston
Jukes .... Geoffrey Rose
Noodler .... Lionel Gadsden
Skylights .... Tenrence Denville

Cabin Boy . . . . Brian Tipping
Black Pirate . . . . Kenneth Baker
Panther . . . . Geoffrey Rose
Tiger Lily . . . . Margaret Riley
Mother Mermaid . . . . . Diane Appleby
Baby Mermaid . . . . Pauline Knight
Liza . . . . Pauline Knight
Crocodile . . . . Paul Domanski
Badger . . . . Michael Hagens

1959–60
Scala Theatre

Peter Pan . . . . Julia Lockwood
Captain Hook . . . . Richard Wordsworth
Mr. Darling . . . . Richard Wordsworth
Mrs. Darling . . . . Pamela Lane
Wendy . . . . Patricia Garwood
John . . . . Jon Skinner
Michael . . . . Peter Craze
Nana . . . . Tony Helm
Tootles . . . . Jeremy Ward
Nibs . . . . Brendan Collins
Slightly . . . . Michael Maguire
Curly . . . . Michael Prater
First Twin . . . . Robert Holford
Second Twin . . . . Charles Petty
Smee . . . . Russell Thorndike
Starkey . . . . Kendrick Owen
Cookson . . . . Gilbert Bailey
Mullins . . . . Terence Denville
Cecco . . . . John Boyd-Brent
Jukes . . . . Anthony Blackshaw
Noodler . . . . Lionel Gadsden
Skylights . . . . Toby McLauchlan
Cabin Boy . . . . Tony Helm
Black Pirate . . . . John Charnley
Panther . . . . Anthony Blackshaw
Tiger Lily . . . . Margaret Latimer
Mother Mermaid . . . . . Margot Hayhoe
Baby Mermaid . . . . Pauline Knight
Liza . . . . Pauline Knight
Crocodile . . . . Jeremy Ward
Badger . . . . James Langley

1960–61
Scala Theatre

Peter Pan . . . . Julia Lockwood
Captain Hook . . . . Donald Sinden
Mr. Darling . . . . Donald Sinden
Mrs. Darling . . . . Pamela Lane
Wendy . . . . Juliet Mills
John . . . . Barry Henderson
Michael . . . . Michael Platt
Nana . . . . Tony Helm
Tootles . . . . Adrian Walker
Nibs . . . . Danny Martin
Slightly . . . . Anthony Wilson
Curly . . . . Dane Howell
First Twin . . . . Christopher Turner
Second Twin . . . . Michael Hammond
Smee . . . . Russell Thorndike

Starkey . . . . Jeffrey Ashby
Cookson . . . . Anthony Ashdown
Mullins . . . . Michael Dawson
Cecco . . . . Gavin Hamilton
Jukes . . . . Robert Russell
Noodler . . . . Lionel Gadsden
Skylights . . . . Toby McLauchlan
Cabin Boy . . . . Tony Helm
Black Pirate . . . . John Charnley
Panther . . . . Robert Russell
Tiger Lily . . . . Jean Robinson
Mother Mermaid . . . . . Anna Carteret
Baby Mermaids . . . . Carol Prince, Linda Green
Liza . . . . Carol Prince
Crocodile . . . . Barry Henderson
Badger . . . . Ray Alderson

1961–62
Scala Theatre

Peter Pan . . . . Anne Heywood
Captain Hook . . . . John Gregson
Mr. Darling . . . . John Gregson
Mrs. Darling . . . . Daphne Jonason
Wendy . . . . Jane Asher
John . . . . Christopher Turner
Michael . . . . Gerald Rowland
Nana . . . . Tony Helm
Tootles . . . . Stephen Marriott
Nibs . . . . Bobby Caetano
Slightly . . . . Barry Henderson
Curly . . . . Michael Reubens
First Twin . . . . Robin Walker
Second Twin . . . . Alan Shortland
Smee . . . . Sydney Bromley
Starkey . . . . Keith Williams
Cookson . . . . Patrick Tull
Mullins . . . . John McGee
Cecco . . . . Peter Torquill
Jukes . . . . Richard Walter
Noodler . . . . Lionel Gadsden
Skylights . . . . Jon Croft
Cabin Boy . . . . Tony Helm
Black Pirate . . . . John Charnley
Panther . . . . Richard Walter
Tiger Lily . . . . Margaret Latimer
Mother Mermaid . . . . . Lezley Fincham
Baby Mermaids . . . . Pauline Knight, Betty Larkin
Liza . . . . Pauline Knight
Crocodile . . . . Barry Henderson
Badger . . . . Oliver Freeman

1962–63
No London Production

1963–64
Scala Theatre

Peter Pan . . . . Julia Lockwood
Captain Hook . . . . Alastair Sim
Mr. Darling . . . . Timothy Parkes

Mrs. Darling .... Pamela Lane
Wendy .... April Wilding
John .... Peter Harvey
Michael .... Paul Martin
Nana .... Tony Helm
Tootles .... David Arden
Nibs .... Alan Jones
Slightly .... Bobbie Bannerman
Curly .... Anthony Mears
First Twin .... Robert Payne
Second Twin .... Paul Large
Smee .... Edward Palmer
Starkey .... John McGee
Cookson .... Patrick Tull
Mullins .... Edmund Dring
Cecco .... Timothy Parkes
Jukes .... Darryl Kavann
Noodler .... John Kobal
Skylights .... Larry Madigan
Cabin Boy .... Tony Helm
Black Pirate .... John Charnley
Panther .... Darryl Kavann
Tiger Lily .... Margaret Latimer
Mother Mermaid ..... Mary Land
Baby Mermaids .... Zena Keller, Linda Harvey
Liza .... Zena Keller
Crocodile .... Bobbie Bannerman
Badger .... Larry Jerome

1964–65

Scala Theatre

Peter Pan .... Dawn Adams
Captain Hook .... Alastair Sim (evenings),
                      Robert Eddison (matinees)
Mr. Darling .... Timothy Parkes
Mrs. Darling .... Jean Harvey
Wendy .... Alison Frazer
John .... David Morris
Michael .... Douglas Mann
Nana .... Tony Helm
Tootles .... Larry Jerome
Nibs .... Trevor Howard
Slightly .... Ian Taylor
Curly .... Michael Cashman
First Twin .... Gregory Paul
Second Twin .... Peter Bonczyk
Smee .... Edward Palmer
Starkey .... Bruce Heighley
Cookson .... Frank McNamara
Mullins .... Roger Swaine
Cecco .... Timothy Parkes
Jukes .... Jonothan Crane
Noodler .... Ralph Carrigan
Skylights .... Peter Kaukas
Cabin Boy .... Tony Helm
Black Pirate .... Rodney Mullinar
Panther .... Jonothan Crane
Tiger Lily .... Jean Shaw
Mother Mermaid ..... Pippa Steel
Baby Mermaids .... Zena Keller, Joy Measures
Liza .... Zena Keller
Crocodile .... Ian Taylor
Badger .... Roland Isaacs

1965–66

Scala Theatre

Peter Pan .... Sylvia Syms
Captain Hook .... Ronald Lewis
Mr. Darling .... Ronald Lewis
Mrs. Darling .... Vanessa Lee
Wendy .... Alison Frazer
John .... Kim Goodman
Michael .... Raymond Ward
Nana .... Tony Helm
Tootles .... Paul Martin
Nibs .... Paul Guess
Slightly .... Ian Taylor
Curly .... Iain Burton
First Twin .... Rufus Frampton
Second Twin .... Edward McMurray
Smee .... James Ottaway
Starkey .... Simon Carter
Cookson .... John Newman
Mullins .... Peter Powell
Cecco .... Peter Forest
Jukes .... Grahame T. Mallard
Noodler .... Scott Tyler
Skylights .... Peter Newby
Cabin Boy .... Richard Mascall
Black Pirate .... John Garretty
Panther .... Grahame T. Mallard
Tiger Lily .... Doran Godwin
Mother Mermaid ..... Mary Land
Baby Mermaids .... Joy Measures, Josephine
                      Garritty
Liza .... Joy Measures
Crocodile .... Ian Taylor
Badger .... Michael Newport
Witch Doctor .... John Garretty

1966–67

Scala Theatre

Peter Pan .... Julia Lockwood
Captain Hook .... Ron Moody
Mr. Darling .... Ron Moody
Mrs. Darling .... Diana Scougall
Wendy .... Mia Martin
John .... Timothy Horton
Michael .... John Watters
Nana .... Tony Helm
Tootles .... Anthony Homes
Nibs .... Peter Kinley
Slightly .... Ian Calvin-Taylor
Curly .... Nicky Peppiatt
First Twin .... Frank Summers
Second Twin .... Barry Newnham
Smee .... Leslie Sarony
Starkey .... David Jason
Cookson .... Roger Fountayne
Mullins .... John Gay
Cecco .... Michael Martin
Jukes .... Guy Saunders
Noodler .... Mark Haskell
Skylights .... Kevin Smith
Cabin Boy .... Hugh Janes

Black Pirate . . . . Hugh Keayes-Byrne
Panther . . . . Guy Saunders
Tiger Lily . . . . Liz Holmes
Mother Mermaid . . . . . Leslie Duff
Baby Mermaids . . . . Julie Weston, Rosemary
                          Booth
Liza . . . . Julie Weston
Crocodile . . . . Ian Calvin-Taylor
Badger . . . . Peter Nobbs
Witch Doctor . . . . Hugh Keayes-Byrne

1967–68
Scala Theatre

Peter Pan . . . . Millicent Martin
Captain Hook . . . . Paul Daneman
Mr. Darling . . . . Paul Daneman
Mrs. Darling . . . . Diana Scougall
Wendy . . . . Mia Martin
John . . . . Philip Croton
Michael . . . . Roland Pickering
Nana . . . . Tony Helm
Tootles . . . . Keith Dewhurst
Nibs . . . . Anthony Peplow
Slightly . . . . Ian Taylor
Curly . . . . Michael Feldman
First Twin . . . . Philip Norton
Second Twin . . . . Paul Alexander
Smee . . . . Dudley Jones
Starkey . . . . Brett Forrest
Cookson . . . . Richard Jones Barry
Mullins . . . . Richard Wardale
Cecco . . . . Darryl Kavann
Jukes . . . . Paul Gregory
Noodler . . . . Harry Ditson
Skylights . . . . Richard Kerley
Cabin Boy . . . . Frank Summers
Black Pirate . . . . Neville Hughes
Panther . . . . Paul Gregory
Tiger Lily . . . . Sheila Irwin
Mother Mermaid . . . . . Sammie Winmill
Baby Mermaids . . . . Gillian Hayes, Angelyne
                          Delmar
Liza . . . . Gillian Hayes
Crocodile . . . . Ian Taylor
Badger . . . . Francis Watters
Witch Doctor . . . . Neville Hughes

1968–69
Scala Theatre

Peter Pan . . . . Wendy Craig
Captain Hook . . . . Alastair Sim (evenings),
                          Richard Wordsworth
                          (matinees)
Mr. Darling . . . . Timothy Parkes
Mrs. Darling . . . . Andrée Evans
Wendy . . . . Caroline Delavigne
John . . . . Philip Croton
Michael . . . . Lee Wilson
Nana . . . . Peter Boyce
Tootles . . . . Ricky Wales
Nibs . . . . Barry Peters

Slightly . . . . Ian Taylor
Curly . . . . John Quinlan
First Twin . . . . Stephen Tye
Second Twin . . . . Martinmus Johnson
Smee . . . . Edward Palmer
Starkey . . . . Brett Forrest
Cookson . . . . Michael Eaton
Mullins . . . . Leonard Gregory
Cecco . . . . Timothy Parkes
Jukes . . . . Adrian Gale
Noodler . . . . John Price
Skylights . . . . Alan Bone
Cabin Boy . . . . Peter Boyce
Black Pirate . . . . Myles Hoyle
Panther . . . . Adrian Gale
Tiger Lily . . . . Sally Goldie
Mother Mermaid . . . . . Laraine Humphrys
Baby Mermaids . . . . Cindy O'Callaghan,
                          Stepanie Colburn
Liza . . . . Cindy O'Callaghan
Crocodile . . . . Ian Taylor
Badger . . . . Andrew Dowling
Witch Doctor . . . . Myles Hoyle

1969–70
New Victoria

Peter Pan . . . . Hayley Mills
Captain Hook . . . . Bill Travers
Mr. Darling . . . . Bill Travers
Mrs. Darling . . . . Gilly McIver
Wendy . . . . Louise Rush
John . . . . Lynton Stock
Michael . . . . Simon Granger
Nana . . . . Richard Mascall
Tootles . . . . Kevan Moran
Nibs . . . . Guy Fraser-Jones
Slightly . . . . John Dryden
Curly . . . . Anton Brooks
First Twin . . . . Eric Hagan
Second Twin . . . . Johannes Hagan
Smee . . . . Edward Palmer
Starkey . . . . Bernard Finch
Cookson . . . . David Hannigan
Mullins . . . . Leonard Gregory
Cecco . . . . Carl Davies
Jukes . . . . Adrian Gale
Noodler . . . . Don Vernon
Skylights . . . . Alan Bone
Cabin Boy . . . . Richard Mascall
Black Pirate . . . . Bill McCabe
Panther . . . . Adrian Gale
Tiger Lily . . . . Lynette Erving
Mother Mermaid . . . . . Peta Mason
Baby Mermaids . . . . Julie Dawn Cole,
                          Wendy Spinks
Liza . . . . Julie Dawn Cole
Crocodile . . . . Richard Mascall
Badger . . . . Geremy Burring
Witch Doctor . . . . Bill McCabe

1970–71
No London Production

1971–72

London Coliseum

Peter Pan	Dorothy Tutin
Captain Hook	Eric Porter
Mr. Darling	Eric Porter
Mrs. Darling	Jane Hilary
Wendy	Belinda Carroll
John	David Arnold
Michael	Christopher Burfield
Nana	Ian Trigger
Tootles	Stephen Leigh
Nibs	Jeremy Woolston
Slightly	Peter Graham
Curly	George Collis
First Twin	Michael Belasco
Second Twin	Richard Belasco
Smee	Ian Trigger
Gentleman Starkey	Brett Forrest
Cookson	Christopher Molloy
Cecco	Ray Edwards
Jukes	Barry Rohde
Noodler	Douglas Anderson (listed as Noodles)
Skylights	Edmund Dring
1st Black Pirate	Ken McGregor
2nd Black Pirate	Joe Iles
Panther	Al Fleming
Tiger Lily	Pippa Reynaud
Mother Mermaid	Julie Neubert
Baby Mermaids	Sheila Dunion, Susan Hannay, Sally Mills, Nikki Thornton, Julia Kerr
Liza	Sheila Dunion
Crocodile	Richarde Mascall
Ostrich	Sally Mills
Raccoon	Lee Goldsmith

1972–73

London Coliseum

Peter Pan	Dorothy Tutin
Captain Hook	Ron Moody
Mr. Darling	Ron Moody
Mrs. Darling	Pauline Jameson
Wendy	Wendy Padbury
John	Benedict Taylor
Michael	Marc Granger
Nana	Peter O'Farrell
Tootles	Jonathan Kiley
Nibs	Keith Lelliott
Slightly	David Arnold
Curly	Jeremy Watts
First Twin	Adam Richens
Second Twin	David Norfolk
Smee	Ian Trigger
Gentleman Starkey	Mischa de la Motte
Cookson	Terry Etteridge
Mullins	David Wells
Cecco	Ray Edwards
Jukes	Barry Rohde
Noodler	Douglas Anderson
Skylights	Jimmy Bell

1st Black Pirate	Namdi (Black Gilmour)
Panther	Bernard Jamieson
Tiger Lily	Jane Lee
Mother Mermaid	Patsy Blower
Baby Mermaids	Wendy Bell, Stephanie Pope, Elizabeth Moorfield, Wendy Ann Baker Beryl Braham, Julia Kerr
Liza	Patsy Blower
Crocodile	Richarde Mascall
Ostrich	Beryl Braham
Raccoon	Paul Barber

1973–74

London Coliseum

Peter Pan	Maggie Smith
Captain Hook	Dave Allen
Mr. Darling	Dave Allen
Mrs. Darling	Jennifer Wilson
Wendy	Gail Harrison
John	Benedict Taylor
Michael	Marc Granger
Nana	Peter O'Farrell
Tootles	Nicholas Dunn
Nibs	David Steele
Slightly	Douglas Rose
Curly	Adam Richens, Paul Barber
First Twin	Julian White
Second Twin	Philip White
Smee	Clifford Mollison
Gentleman Starkey	Brian Peck
Cookson	Ivan Berold
Mullins	Alan Troy
Cecco	Ray Edwards
Jukes	Barry Rohde
Noodler	Jack Eden
Skylights	James Graham
1st Black Pirate	Joe Isles (Black Gilmour)
2nd Black Pirate	Johnnie Kwango (Black Murphy)
Panther	Robin Sheringham
Tiger Lily	Patricia Hammond
Mother Mermaid	Susan Hannay
Baby Mermaids	Beryl Braham, Sue Harwich, Gail Rolfe
Liza	Kim Williams
Crocodile	Richarde Mascall
Ostrich	Beryl Braham
Raccoon	Paul Foster

1974–75

London Coliseum

Peter Pan	Susan Hampshire
Captain Hook	Michael Denison
Mr. Darling	Michael Denison
Mrs. Darling	Marion Grimaldi
Wendy	Stacy Dorning
John	Trevor Hosking
Michael	John Weavers
Tinker Bell	Iris Glow

Nana	Peter O'Farrell
Tootles	Iestyn Mullins
Nibs	Adam Richens
Slightly	Douglas Rose
Curly	Mark Weavers
First Twin	David Parfitt
Second Twin	Colin Cousins
Smee	Tony Sympson
Starkey	Tim Fearon
Canary Rob	Graham Pattenden
Mullins	Alan Troy
Cecco	Barry Wilmore
Jukes	Barry Rohde
Noodler	Kenneth Hale
Skylights	Ken Robson
Black Gilmour	Jules Walter
Panther	Robin Sherringham
Tiger Lily	Jilly Coram
Mother Mermaid	Susan Hannay
Mermaids	Julia Kerr, Joan Maden, Thorey Mountain
Liza	Kim Williams
Crocodile	Peter O'Farrell
Ostrich	Jilly Coram
Raccoon	Matthew Ryan

1975-76

London Palladium

Peter Pan	Lulu
Captain Hook	Ron Moody
Mr. Darling	Ron Moody
Mrs. Darling	Rachel Gurney
Wendy	Tessa Wyatt
John	David Parfitt
Michael	Michael Parfitt
Nana	Malcom Dixon
Tootles	Darren Hatch
Nibs	Bobby Collins, Mark Deamer
Slightly	Graham Kennedy Smith, Adam Richens
Curly	Tracy Plant
First Twin	Darren Ross-Dale
Second Twin	Paul de Freitas
Smee	Tony Sympson
Starkey	Peter Bland
Canary Rob	Bernard Jamison
Mullins	Howard Nelson
Cecco	Kevin Quarmby
Jukes	Barry Rohde
Noodler	Oliver Dunbar
Skylights	Ken Robson
Black Gilmour	Count Prince Miller
Murphy	Jody Hall
Panther	Robin Sherringham
Tiger Lily	Jilly Coram
Mother Mermaid	Susan Hannay
Mermaids	Penny Stevenson, Janet Woodhams, Debbie Hearnden, Suzanne Hywell
Liza	Caroline Ellis
Crocodile	Malcom Dixon
Ostrich	Jilly Coram

1976-77
No London Production

1977-78

London Casino

Peter Pan	Susannah York
Captain Hook	Ron Moody
Mr. Darling	Ron Moody
Mrs. Darling	Sheila Mathews
Wendy	Astrid Clifford
John	Jeremy Ewing
Michael	Michael Parfitt
Nana	Fran Peppard
Tootles	Jon Addison
Nibs	Adam Armstrong
Slightly	Paul Hillman
Curly	Jonathan Willmott
First Twin	Paul Erangey
Second Twin	Kevin Foskitt
Smee	Tony Sympson
Starkey	Paul Mills
Canary Rob	Bernard Jamison
Mullins	Terry Etheridge
Cecco	Kenneth Caswell
Jukes	Rodney James
Noodler	David Calderwell
Skylights	Adrian Le Peltier
Black Gilmour	Trevor Ward
Murphy	Terry Dane
Panther	Robin Sherringham
Tiger Lily	Suzanne Hywel
Mother Mermaid	Susan Hannay
Mermaids	Jackie Bristow, Nikki Heard, Sue Nye, Christine Parkinson
Liza	Jo-Anne Good
Crocodile	Sammy Snapper
Ostrich	Suzanne Hywel
Raccoon	William Smoker

1978-79

Shaftsbury Theatre

Peter Pan	Jane Asher
Captain Hook	Nigel Patrick
Mr. Darling	Nigel Patrick
Mrs. Darling	Sheila Mathews
Wendy	Andrea Kealy
John	Steve Gilroy
Michael	Graham McGrath
Nana	Jonathan Wilmot
Tootles	Jason Mullen
Nibs	Darren Phelan
Slightly	Mark Deamer
Curly	Cleon Spencer
First Twin	James Tapping
Second Twin	Philip Parker
Smee	Tony Sympson
Starkey	Glyn Sweet
Canary Rob	Brian Payne
Mullins	John Harmer

Cecco .... Reynold Silva
Jukes .... Paul Shearstone
Noodler .... Peter Lawrence
Skylights .... John Sherwood
Black Gilmour .... Errol Shaker
Murphy .... Christopher Robinson
Panther .... Robin Sherringham
Tiger Lily .... Jilly Coram
Mother Mermaid ..... Susan Hannay
Mermaids .... Jackie Bristow, Nikkie
                    Heard, Carole Clayton,
                    Rebecca Leigh
Liza .... Jo-Anne Good
Crocodile .... Sammy Snapper
Ostrich .... Jilly Coram
Raccoon .... Amos Hill

1979–80

Shaftsbury Theatre

Peter Pan .... Gayle Hunnicutt
Captain Hook .... James Villiers
Mr. Darling .... James Villiers
Mrs. Darling .... Marion Grimaldi
Wendy .... Briony McRoberts
John .... Craig Stokes
Michael .... Maurice Alister-Hooke
Nana .... Perry Fenwick
Tootles .... Stephen Sweeney
Nibs .... Harvey Hillyer
Slightly .... Steve Fletcher
Curly .... Perry Fenwick
First Twin .... Francis Victory
Second Twin .... Godfrey Williams
Smee .... Ken Randle
Starkey .... Nicholas Frankau
Canary Rob .... John English
Cecco .... Roger Eden
Noodler .... Douglas Anderson
Skylights .... Adrian Gilpin
Black Gilmour .... Basil Patton
Cabin Boy .... Peter Kutzmaida
Panther .... Robin Sherringham
Tiger Lily .... Marisa Campbell
Liza .... Valentine Cavanagh
Crocodile .... Perry Fenwick

1980–82

No London Productions

1982–83

Barbican

Peter Pan .... Miles Anderson
Captain Hook .... Joss Ackland
Mr. Darling .... Joss Ackland
Mrs. Darling .... Sheila Hancock
Wendy .... Jane Carr
John .... Philip Franks
Michael .... Andrew Thomas James
Tinker Bell .... Jan Revere

Nana .... Christopher Hurst
Tootles .... Anthony O'Donnell
Nibs .... Joseph Marcell
Slightly .... James Fleet
Curly .... Dexter Fletcher
First Twin .... Phillip Walsh
Second Twin .... Ken Robertson
Smee .... George Raistrick
Starkey .... Colin Tarrant
Canary Rob .... Anthony Simons
Mullins .... Peter Ellis
Cecco .... Steve Simmonds
Jukes .... Andrew Jarvis
Noodler .... Gary Sharkey
Skylights .... Stewart Mackintosh
Panther .... Mike Murray
Tiger Lily .... Seeta Indrani
The Story Teller ..... Stephen Moore
Mermaids .... Sarah Finch, Noelyn
                    George, Susan Leong, Jan
                    Revere, Susan Jane Tanner
Liza .... Clare Travers-Deacon
Crocodile .... Andrew Jarvis & Steve
                    Simmonds
Ostrich .... Susan Jane Tanner &
                    Anthony Simons
The Never Bird .... Noelyn George
Jane .... Sarah Finch

1983–84

Barbican

Peter Pan .... Mark Rylance
Captain Hook .... Stephen Moore
Mr. Darling .... Stephen Moore
Mrs. Darling .... Frances Tomelty
Wendy .... Katy Behean
John .... David Parfitt
Michael .... John McAndrew
Tinker Bell .... Katherine Levy
Nana .... Alexandra Brook
Tootles .... Mike Grady
Nibs .... Simon Butteriss
Slightly .... Michael Fitzgerald
Curly .... John Tramper
First Twin .... Floyd Bevan
Second Twin .... John Dougall
Smee .... Jimmy Gardner
Starkey .... George Parsons
Canary Rob .... David Phelan
Mullins .... Peter Ellis
Cecco .... Stephen Rashbrook
Jukes .... Andrew Jarvis
Noodler .... Tony Westrope
Skylights .... Ray Llewelyn
Panther .... Mike Murray
Tiger Lily .... Susan Leong
The Story Teller ..... Edward Petherbridge
Mermaids .... Alexandra Brook,
                    Noelyn George, Katharine
                    Levy, Sara Mair-Thomas,
                    Jayne Tottman
Liza .... Sara Mair-Thomas

Crocodile .... Andrew Jarvis & Stephen
                     Rashbrook
Ostrich .... David Phelan
The Never Bird .... Noelyn George
Jane .... Jane Tottman

1984–85
Barbican

Peter Pan .... John McAndrew
Captain Hook .... Stephen Moore
Mr. Darling .... Stephen Moore
Mrs. Darling .... Caroline Harris
Wendy .... Jane Carr
John .... Philip Franks
Michael .... Philip Dupuy
Tinker Bell .... Jenny Dunbar
Nana .... Christopher Hurst
Tootles .... Allan Hendrick
Nibs .... Paul Spence
Slightly .... Christopher Wright
Curly .... Roger Hyams
First Twin .... Raymond Platt
Second Twin .... Piers Ibbotson
Smee .... Timothy Kightley
Starkey .... Clyde Pollitt
Canary Rob .... Jeffrey Robert
Mullins .... Stanley Page
Cecco .... John Nolan
Jukes .... Dean Allen
Noodler .... John Dallimore
Skylights .... Jeremy Wilkin
Panther .... Graham Sinclair
Tiger Lily .... DeNica Fairman
The Story Teller ...... Brian Murphy
Mermaids .... Played by cast members
Liza .... Tina Jones
Crocodile .... Dean Allen & Doyle
                     Richmond
Ostrich .... Jill Connick
Jane .... Sally Jane Jackson

1985–86
Aldwch

Peter Pan .... Bonnie Langford
Captain Hook .... Joss Ackland
Mr. Darling .... Joss Ackland
Mrs. Darling .... Judith Bruce
Wendy .... Annabelle Lanyon
John .... Grant Olding/Ross Dawes/
                     Matthew McNeaney
Michael .... Martin Harver/Julian
                     Wright/Alexander Wright
Nana .... Tim Flannigan
Tootles .... Christopher Chandler
Nibs .... Stephen Speed
Slightly .... Andrew B. Roberts
Curly .... Lee Chappell
First Twin .... Robert Craig-Morgan
Second Twin .... Paul Valentine
Smee .... Edward Phillips
Starkey .... Aidan James
Mullins .... Barry Holland

Cecco .... Philip Tsaras
Jukes .... Christopher Hood
Noodler .... Nick Cursi (listed as
                     Noodles)
Skylights .... James Dundas
Panther .... Richard Chance
Tiger Lily .... Jennie McGustie
Liza .... Lisa Kent
Crocodile .... Tony Parkin
Ostrich .... Tara Syed
Kangaroo .... Michelle Thorneycroft
Wendy Grown Up .... Lynne Winslow
Jane .... Annabelle Lanyon

1986–1987
No London Productions

1987–1988
Cambridge

Peter Pan .... Lulu
Captain Hook .... George Cole
Mr. Darling .... George Cole
Mrs. Darling .... Jan Harvey
Wendy .... Michelle Thorneycroft
John .... Ben Giles, Scott Groves,
                     Matthew McNeaney,
                     Ian Needle
Michael .... Oliver Bardon, Stuart
                     Dawes, James Roberts,
                     Alex Wright
Nana .... Martin Tempest
Tootles .... Russell Nash
Nibs .... Drew Varley
Slightly............. Chris Chandler
Curly .... Lee Chappell
1st Twin .... Steve Jonas
2nd Twin .... Nik Stoter
Smee............... Barrie Gosney
Starkey .... Nicholas Taggart
Mullins............. Christopher Hammond
Cecco .... Jody Hall
Jukes............... Kevin Wainwright
Noodler .... Miles Ambrose (as Noodles)
Skylights .... Nigel Nevinson
Cookson............. Ian Parkin
Panther............. Christopher Hall
                     (Indian Chief)
Tiger Lily........... Celia Belvoir
Liza .... Amanda Dainty
Crocodile........... Martin Tempest
Ostrich .... Maria Clarke
Kangaroo .... Sarah Huntley
Wendy Grown-up ..... Michelle Hockley
Jane .... Sarah Huntley

1988–89
Wimbledon

Peter Pan .... Lulu
Captain Hook .... Christopher Timothy
Mr. Darling .... Christopher Timothy
Mrs. Darling .... Ruth Mayo
Wendy .... Michelle Thorneycroft

John .... Spencer Groves/James
                    Fraser
Michael .... Stuart Dawes, Lee
                    Hoare, Robert Keith
Nana .... Annabel Griggs
Tootles .... Russell Nash
Nibs .... Wayne Howard
Slightly .... Terry Gleed
Curly .... Steve Jonas
First Twin .... Paul Hardy
Second Twin .... Ian Hooper
Smee .... Alan Helm
Starkey .... Patrick Jamieson
Mullins .... Geoffrey Towers
Cecco .... Jody Hall
Jukes .... Kevin Wainwright
Noodler .... Paul Nield (listed as
                    Noodles)
Skylights .... Ian Parkin
Panther .... Desmond Williams
Tiger Lily .... Celia Belvoir
Liza .... Kerry-Jane Beddows
Crocodile .... Andrew Cochrane
Ostrich .... Maria Clarke
Kangaroo .... Benedikte Faulkner
Wendy Grown Up .... Michelle Hockley
Jane .... Benedikte Faulkner

1989–90

Wimbledon

Peter Pan .... Tina Doyle
Captain Hook .... George Sewell
Mr. Darling .... George Sewell
Mrs. Darling .... Sandra Tallent
Wendy .... Debbie Wall
John .... Callum Dixon
Michael .... Susan Mann
Tinker Bell .... Herself
Nana .... John Davitt
Tootles .... Chris Chandler
Nibs .... Zeki Hilmi
Slightly .... Bryce Hamnet
Curly .... Foster George
Rags .... Ethan Stone
Smee .... Stephen Crane
Starkey .... Martin Wimbush
Cecco .... Jonathan Whaley
Jukes .... Martin Rodges
Skylights .... John Davitt
Panther .... Jonathan Whaley
Tiger Lily .... Ava DeSouza
Liza .... Ava DeSouza
Crocodile .... Himself

1993–94

Sadler's Wells presents Black Light Theatre of Prague

Peter Pan .... Martin Rehacek
Captain Hook .... Vladimir Kubicek
Wendy .... Katerina Rejmanova
John .... Monika Mrnkova

Michael .... Jaroslava Stranska
Tinker Bell .... Marcela Skrbkova
Starkey .... Petr Benes
Cecco .... Jan Martinec
Noodler .... Barbara Fiserova (listed as
                    Moodler)
Panther .... Jan Martinec
Mermaids .... Marcela Skrbkova, Barbora
                    Jilkova, Barbara Fiserova

1994–95

Cambridge

Peter Pan .... Nicola Stapleton
Captain Hook .... Ron Moody
Mr. Darling .... Ron Moody
Mrs. Darling .... Rosemary Williams
Wendy .... Debbie Wall
John .... Kieran Snell/William
                    Ullstein
Michael .... Ben Greenberg/Greg Lowe
Tinker Bell .... OPERATOR— Helen
                    Rochelle
Nana .... David Anthony
Tootles .... James Cohen/Gary Croome
Nibs .... James Delaney/Winston
                    Eade
Slightly .... Kevin Bishop/David Wolsey
Curly .... Chris Johns/Scott Robinson
First Twin .... Anselm & Nerada Bearnard
Second Twin .... Jason & Jamie Ravenscroft
Smee .... Harry Dickman
Starkey .... John Foley
Mullins .... David Anthony
Cecco .... Mark Waghorn
Jukes .... Ryk Burnett
Noodler .... Bobby Martino
Skylights .... Sam Newman
Tiger Lily .... Pinky Amador
Liza .... Pinky Amador

1997–98

National Theatre

Peter Pan .... Daniel Evans
Captain Hook .... Ian McKellen
Mr. Darling .... Ian McKellen
Mrs. Darling .... Jenny Agutter
Wendy .... Claudie Blakley
John .... Adrian Ross-Magenty
Michael .... Daniel Hart
Tinker Bell .... VOICE OF— Sally-Ann
                    Burnett
Nana .... Jan Knightley
Tootles .... Wayne Cater
Nibs .... Harold Finley
Slightly .... Daniel Coonan
Curly .... Jonny Hoskins
First Twin .... Mark Channon
Second Twin .... Dominic McHale
Smee .... Clive Rowe
Starkey .... Bryan Robson
Mullins .... Robert Aldous
Cecco .... Anthony Venditti

Jukes . . . . Liam McKenna
Noodler . . . . Jan Knightley
Skylights . . . . Patrick Romer
The Never Bird . . . . Jenny Agutter
Panther . . . . Murray McArthur
Tiger Lily . . . . Natalie Tina
The Story Teller . . . . . . Alec McCowen
Mermaids . . . . Michelle Abrahams,
                              Sally-Ann Burnett,
                              Naomi Capron
Liza . . . . Liza Hayden
Jane . . . . Michelle Abrahams

1998–99
National Theatre

Peter Pan . . . . Justin Salinger
Captain Hook . . . . David Troughton
Mr. Darling . . . . David Troughton
Mrs. Darling . . . . Susannah Fellows
Wendy . . . . Rebecca Johnson
John . . . . Adrian Ross-Magenty
Michael . . . . Jonathan Broadbent
Tinker Bell . . . . Voice of — Inka Magnus-
                              son
Nana . . . . Jan Knightley
Tootles . . . . Kieron Forsyth
Nibs . . . . John Dorney
Slightly . . . . Jonny Hoskins
Curly . . . . Mark Cronfield
First Twin . . . . Peter McCabe
Second Twin . . . . Jason Thorpe
Smee . . . . Christopher Luscombe
Starkey . . . . Hugh Sachs
Wibbles . . . . Ben Mangham
Mullins . . . . Jonathan Kemp
Cecco . . . . Jim Creighton
Jukes . . . . Liam McKenna
Noodler . . . . Jan Knightley
Skylights . . . . Glynn Sweet
Panther . . . . Ben Mangham
Tiger Lily . . . . In-Sook Chappell
The Story Teller . . . . . . Michael Bryant
Mermaids . . . . Kay Curram, Annabelle
                              Dowler, Sarah Lonton,
                              Inka Magnusson
Liza . . . . Annabelle Dowler
Ostrich . . . . Richard Ryder

2001
Royal Festival Hall

Peter Pan . . . . Joe McFadden
Captain Hook . . . . John Thaw
Mr. Darling . . . . John Thaw
Mrs. Darling . . . . Jenna Russell
Wendy . . . . Laura-Michelle Kelly
John . . . . Nathaniel Kelly
Michael . . . . Jorim Kelly
Tootles . . . . Giovanni Spano
Nibs . . . . Gavin Rees
Slightly . . . . Bradley Sowter
Curly . . . . Ricardo Coke-Thomas
First Twin . . . . Nick Woodman

Second Twin . . . . Gregg Lowe
Smee . . . . Tim Healy
Starkey . . . . Simon Green
Mullins . . . . Nolan Frederick
Cecco . . . . Maurice Clarke
Jukes . . . . Graham Bickley
Noodler . . . . David Alder
Skylights . . . . Charles Shirvell
Tiger Lily . . . . Joanna Thaw
The Story Teller . . . . . . Sheila Hancock
Liza . . . . Joanna Thaw
Wendy Grown Up . . . . Sheila Hancock

2003
Savoy

Peter Pan . . . . Jack Blumenau
Captain Hook . . . . Anthony Head
Mr. Darling . . . . David Burt
Mrs. Darling . . . . Kathryn Evans
Wendy . . . . Katie Foster-Barnes
John . . . . Sam Mannox/Joe Prospero
Michael . . . . Jack Dedman/Alexander
                              Rose
Tinker Bell . . . . Voice of — Lorraine
                              Cappell
Nana . . . . Mark Oxtoby
Tootles . . . . Bennett Andrews
Nibs . . . . Tom Ashton
Slightly . . . . Roy Litvin
Curly . . . . Hadley Fraser
First Twin . . . . Leanne Rogers
Second Twin . . . . Amy Rogers
Smee . . . . Jack Chissick
Starkey . . . . David Burt
Mullins . . . . Steve Elias
Cecco . . . . Mykal Rand
Jukes . . . . Mark Oxtoby
Noodler . . . . Scott Cripps
Skylights . . . . Nick Holmes
Cookson . . . . Graham Martin
Tiger Lily . . . . Cezarah Bonner
Mermaids . . . . Kristin Hellberg, Joanna
                              Kirkland, Erlin Wyn Lewis
Liza . . . . Erlin Wyn Lewis

Dec. 18, 2004
Duke of York's Theatre (an afterthought by J.M. Barrie)

Peter Pan . . . . Adam Moore
Nana . . . . Ellen Sheean
The Story Teller . . . . . . Stage Directions —
                              Robin Sneller
Wendy Grown Up . . . . Susan Wooldridge
Jane . . . . Rachel Sternberg

2008–09
West Yorkhire Playhouse (although not in London an important production)

Peter Pan . . . . James Gillan
Captain Hook . . . . David Birrell

Mr. Darling .... David Birrell
Mrs. Darling .... Kirsty Hoiles
Wendy .... Amy Lennox
John .... James Byng
Michael .... Jed Berry
Nana .... Michelle Cornelious
Tootles .... Thomas Aldridge
Nibs .... Simon Schofield
Slightly .... Dominic Ridley
Curly .... Craig Dinnewell
First Twin .... Gregg Lowe
Second Twin .... Tim Edwards
Smee .... Martin Callaghan
Starkey .... Stephen Carlile
Mullins .... Jo Servi
Cecco .... Bradley Jaden
Jukes .... James Bisip
Tiger Lily .... Michelle Cornelious
The Story Teller ...... Alwyne Taylor
Mermaids .... Kirsty Hoiles
Liza .... Clare Halse
Crocodile .... Company member

Spring and Summer, 2009
Kensington Gardens

Peter Pan .... Ciaran Kellgren
Captain Hook .... Jonathan Hyde
Mr. Darling .... Jonathan Hyde
Mrs. Darling .... Karen Ascoe
Wendy .... Abby Ford
John .... Arthur Wilson
Michael .... David Poynor
Tinker Bell .... Itxaso Moreno
Nana .... Moshun Nouri
Tootles .... Ciaran Joyce
Nibs .... Benjamin Chamberlin
Slightly .... Lee Turnbull
Curly .... Ian Street
Smee .... Ian Hughes
Starkey .... Daniel Tuite
Mullins .... Grant Stimpson
Skylights .... Charlie Folorunsho
The Never Bird .... Moshun Nouri
Cookson .... Adam Speers
Tiger Lily .... Amber Rose Revah
Mermaids .... Fiona Lait
Crocodile .... Moshun Nouri
Ostrich .... Moshun Nouri

Private Juvenile Performances

Feb. 20, 1906
Michael's Nursery

Peter Pan .... Winifred Geoghegan
Mr. Darling .... Leslie Oswald
Mrs. Darling .... Phyllis Beadon
Wendy .... Ela Q. May
John .... Harry Duff
Michael .... Geraldine Wilson
Nana .... Master Marini
First Twin .... Pauline Chase
Liza .... Alice Robinson
Cabman .... J. M. Barrie

Feb. 19, 1907
Duke of York's Theatre

Peter Pan .... Winifred Geoghegan
Captain Hook .... George Hersee
Mr. Darling .... George Hersee
Mrs. Darling .... Doris Lytton
Wendy .... Dorothy Le Marchand
John .... Philip Priddis
Michael .... Charlie Chappell
Nana .... Ernest Marini
Nibs .... E. Grata
Curly .... A. Hall
First Twin .... Ben Rose
Smee .... Herbert Hollom
Starkey .... Charlie Chappell
Tiger Lily .... Alice Robinson
Mermaid .... Doris Lytton
Baby Mermaid .... Winnie Delevanti
Liza .... Winnie Delevanti

Cabman .... J. M. Barrie
2nd Cabman .... Marsh Allen

Feb. 9, 1909
Duke of York's Theatre

Peter Pan .... Tessie Parke
Captain Hook .... Herbert Hollom
Mr. Darling .... Ernest Hollom
Mrs. Darling .... Ivy Knight
Wendy .... Beryl St. Leger
John .... Victor Pierpoint
Michael .... Willie Hollom
Nana .... J. Child
Tootles .... Alice Robinson
Slightly .... W. C. Barnes
Curly .... A. Hall
First Twin .... Ernest Hollom
Smee .... W. G. Manning
Starkey .... W. Child
Cookson .... J. Child
Mullins .... Ernest Marini
Cecco .... Gordon Carr
Jukes .... J. Child
Noodler .... Leslie Oswell
Tiger Lily .... Alice Robinson
Liza .... H. Hollom

Feb. 10, 1910
Duke of York's Theatre

Peter Pan .... Herbert Hollom
Captain Hook .... Harry Duff
Mr. Darling .... Ernest Hollom

Mrs. Darling	Maidie Andrews
Wendy	Tessie Parke
John	James Hollom
Michael	Willie Hollom
Nana	Master Marini
Tootles	Ernest Hollom
Nibs	Master Brocknor
Slightly	Master Ben Rose
Curly	Master Searle
First Twin	Maidie Andrews
Smee	Willie Manning
Starkey	Master Marini
Cecco	Gordon Carr
Jukes	Master Grata
Noodler	Master Anderson
Tiger Lily	Alice Robinson
Liza	Little Miss Parke
Crocodile	Masters Searle/Brockner
Ostrich	Master Anderson

Feb. 5, 1911

Duke of York's Theatre

Peter Pan	Mary Glynne
Captain Hook	Herbert Hollom
Mr. Darling	Stephen Thomas
Mrs. Darling	Doris MacIntyre
Wendy	Stephanie Bell
John	James Hollom
Michael	Willie Hollom
Nana	J. Child
Tootles	Ada Glynne
Nibs	A. H. Kent
Slightly	Ernest Marini
Curly	Donald Searle
Smee	Charles Thomas
Starkey	W. Child
Cookson	J. Child
Mullins	W. Anderson

Cecco	Gordan Carr
Jukes	J. Child
Noodler	Walter Scott
Black Pirate	S. Nagle
Tiger Lily	Lois Carruthers
Baby Mermaid	Ada Glynne
Liza	Ada Glynne

Jan. 8, 1925

Adelphi Theatre

Peter Pan	Ivis Goulding
Captain Hook	Brian Glennie
Mr. Darling	Bruce Baron
Mrs. Darling	Joan Buckmaster
Wendy	Dianna Beaumont
John	Ernest Madden
Michael	Wendy Kirby
Nana	Joseph Owen
Tootles	Dillis Greenwood
Nibs	Jane Baxter
Slightly	John Thompson
Curly	Nan Greenwood
First Twin	Jeanne Delamar
Second Twin	Olive Drew
Smee	Leslie Dwyer
Starkey	Ursula Moreton
Cookson	Joseph Owen
Mullins	Rosemary Bamber
Cecco	Betty Talbot
Jukes	George Morris
Noodler	Alan Whittaker
First Pirate	Joseph Owen
Second Pirate	Freddie Hibbs
Black Pirate	Audrey Lucas
Liza	Reggie Morgan
Cabman	Eric Oliphant
Tout	Freddie Hibbs

New York Productions

1905–06

Empire Theatre

Peter Pan	Maude Adams
Captain Hook	Ernest Lawford
Mr. Darling	Ernest Lawford
Mrs. Darling	Grace Henderson
Wendy	Mildred Morris
John	Walter Robinson
Michael	Martha McGraw
Tinker Bell	Jane Wren
Nana	Charles H. Weston
Tootles	Violet Rand
Nibs	Lula Peck
Slightly	Francis Sedgwick
Curly	Mabel Kipp
First Twin	Katherine Keppell
Second Twin	Ella Gilroy
Smee	Thomas McGrath
Starkey	Wallace Jackson

Cookson	William Henderson
Mullins	Thomas Valentine
Cecco	Paul Tharp
Jukes	Harry Gwynette
Noodler	Frederick Raymond
Panther	Lloyd Carleton
Tiger Lily	Margaret Gordon
Liza	Anna Wheaton

The rest of the characters are played by company

1906–07

Empire Theatre

Peter Pan	Maude Adams
Captain Hook	Ernest Lawford
Mr. Darling	Ernest Lawford
Mrs. Darling	Grace Henderson
Wendy	Mildred Morris
John	Walter Robinson
Michael	Martha McGraw

Tinker Bell .... Jane Wren
Nana .... Charles H. Weston
Tootles .... Dorothy Chester
Nibs .... Lula Peck
Slightly .... Francis Sedgwick
Curly .... Mabel Kipp
First Twin .... Katherine Keppell
Second Twin .... Ella Gilroy
Smee .... Thomas McGrath
Starkey .... Wallace Jackson
Cookson .... William Henderson
Mullins .... Thomas Valentine
Cecco .... Paul Tharp
Noodler .... Frederick Raymond
Panther .... Lloyd Carleton
Tiger Lily .... Margaret Gordon
Mermaid .... Minnie Kirby
Baby Mermaid .... Augusta Schendle
Liza .... Dorothy Smith
The rest of the characters are played by company

1912–13

Empire Theatre

Peter Pan .... Maude Adams
Captain Hook .... Robert Peyton Carter
Mr. Darling .... Robert Peyton Carter
Mrs. Darling .... Marion Abbott
Wendy .... Dorothy Dunn
John .... Edwin Wilson
Michael .... Audrey Ridgewell
Nana .... Byron Silvers
Tootles .... Lola Clifton
Nibs .... Dorothy Chesman
Slightly .... William Sheafe, Jr.
Curly .... Margaret Gordon
First Twin .... Dorothy Tureak
Second Twin .... Anna Reader
Smee .... Fred Tyler
Starkey .... Wallace Jackson
Cookson .... August Kraemer
Mullins .... James L. Carhart
Cecco .... Wm. Beckwith
Jukes .... Stephen Wittman
Noodler .... Gustave Strowig
Panther .... Allen Treadwell
Tiger Lily .... Madge Treadwell
Liza .... Helen McDonald
Blackman............ Stafford Windsor
The rest of the characters are played by company

1913–14

Empire Theatre

Peter Pan .... Maude Adams
Captain Hook .... Robert Peyton Carter
Mr. Darling .... Robert Peyton Carter
Mrs. Darling .... Marion Abbott
Wendy .... Dorothy Dunn
John .... Edwin Wilson
Michael .... Audrey Ridgewell
Tinker Bell .... Jane Wren
Nana .... Byron Silvers
Tootles .... Margaret Field

Nibs .... Dorothy Chesmond
Slightly .... William Sheafe, Jr.
Curly .... Elise Clarens
First Twin .... Anna Reader
Second Twin .... Janet Findlay
Smee .... Fred Tyler
Starkey .... Wallace Jackson
Cookson .... Douglas McLane
Mullins .... Byron Silvers
Cecco .... Allen Fawcett
Jukes .... George Hubbard
Noodler .... James L. Carhart
First Pirate .... Willard Barton
Second Pirate .... Gustave Strowig
Black Man .... Stafford Wilson
Panther .... George Hubbard
Tiger Lily .... Marion Abbott
Liza .... Helen MacDonald
The rest of the characters are played by company

1915–16

Empire Theatre

Peter Pan .... Maude Adams
Captain Hook .... Robert Peyton Carter
Mr. Darling .... Robert Peyton Carter
Mrs. Darling .... Adele Prince
Wendy .... Gladys Gillan
John .... Donald McClelland
Michael .... Dorothya Camden
Tinker Bell .... Jane Wren
Nana .... Byron Silvers
Tootles .... Margaret Field
Nibs .... Ruth Gordon
Slightly .... Raymond Hackett
Curly .... Elise Clarens
First Twin .... Katherine Keppell
Second Twin .... Angela Ogden
Smee .... Fred Tyler
Starkey .... Wallace Jackson
Cookson .... Douglas McLane
Mullins .... Byron Silvers
Cecco .... William Barton
Jukes .... George Hubbard
Noodler .... James L. Carhart
Black Man .... Stafford Wilson
Panther .... George Hubbard
Tiger Lily .... Marion Abbott
Liza .... Elizabeth Kennedy
The rest of the characters are played by company

1924–25

Knickerbocker Theatre

Peter Pan .... Marilyn Miller
Captain Hook .... Leslie Banks
Mr. Darling .... Wilfred Seagram
Mrs. Darling .... Violet Kemble Cooper
Wendy .... Dorothy Hope
John .... Charles Eaton
Michael .... John Grattan
Tinker Bell .... Jane Wren
Nana .... Thomas Bell
Tootles .... Virgina Smith

Nibs .... Maureen Dilon
Slightly .... Donald Searle
Curly .... Mary Corday
First Twin .... Sylvia Darling
Second Twin .... Harriet Darling
Smee .... Edward Rigby
Starkey .... Victor Tandy
Cookson .... Horace Pollock
Mullins .... Ashton Tonge
Cecco .... Carl Rosa
Jukes .... Fred Lennox
Noodler .... William Dean
First Pirate .... Eldon Nelson
Second Pirate .... John J. Regan
Black Man .... Phillip McNeil
Panther .... Eugene Weber
Tiger Lily .... Anne Delafield
Liza .... Carol Chase
The rest of the characters are played by company

1928–29

Civic Repertory Theatre

Peter Pan .... Eva Le Gallienne
Captain Hook .... Egon Brecher
Mr. Darling .... Donald Cameron
Mrs. Darling .... Mary Ward
Wendy .... Josephine Hutchinson
John .... Charles McCarthy
Michael .... Vernon Jones
Nana .... J. Edward Bromberg
Tootles .... Glesca Marshall
Nibs .... Lester Salko
Slightly .... Landon Herrick
Curly .... Alfred Corn
First Twin .... David Vivian
Second Twin .... Henry Melvin
Smee .... John Eldredge
Starkey .... Sayre Crawley
Cookson .... Robert Ross
Mullins .... Robert H. Gordon
Cecco .... Harold Moulton
Jukes .... Herbert Shapiro
Noodler .... Walter Beck (as Noodles)
First Pirate .... Lewis Leverett
Black Man .... Ted Fetter
Panther .... J. Blake Scott
Tiger Lily .... Jocelyn Gordon
Liza .... Beatrice De Neegaard
Crocodile .... Gladys Meyer
Ostrich .... Harold Moulton
A Tramp .... Robert H. Gordon
A Cabman .... Robert Ross

1929–30

Civic Repertory Theatre

Peter Pan .... Eva Le Gallienne
Captain Hook .... Walter Beck
Mr. Darling .... Donald Cameron
Mrs. Darling .... Mary Ward
Wendy .... Josephine Hutchinson
John .... Gordon Wallace
Michael .... Vernon Jones

Nana .... J. Edward Bromberg
Tootles .... Florida Friebus
Nibs .... Richard Stokes
Slightly .... Mooney Diamond
Curly .... Patricia Deering
First Twin .... David Vivian
Second Twin .... Amy Chandler
Smee .... Sayre Crawley
Starkey .... Robert H. Gordon
Cookson .... Robert Ross
Mullins .... Joseph Kramm
Cecco .... Harold Moulton
Jukes .... Herbert Shapiro
Noodler .... David Turk (as Noodles)
First Pirate .... Syd Wynne
Black Man .... Leo Hillery
Panther .... J. Blake Scott
Tiger Lily .... Theodosia Dusanne
Liza .... Florence Robinson
Crocodile .... Renne Orsell
Ostrich .... Harold Moulton
A Tramp .... David Kerman
A Cabman .... Robert Lewis

1930–31

Civic Repertory Theatre

Peter Pan .... Eva Le Gallienne
Captain Hook .... Walter Beck
Mr. Darling .... Donald Cameron
Mrs. Darling .... Mary Ward
Wendy .... Josephine Hutchinson
John .... Gordon Wallace
Michael .... Richard Jack
Nana .... Blake Scott
Tootles .... Florida Friebus
Nibs .... Vernon Jones
Slightly .... Lewis Steinhorn
Curly .... Charles Walters
First Twin .... Eugene Soloman
Second Twin .... William Schimmel
Smee .... Sayre Crawley
Starkey .... Robert H. Gordon
Cookson .... Jack Saltzman
Mullins .... Joseph Kramm
Cecco .... Harold Moulton
Jukes .... Herbert Shapiro
Noodler .... Peter Railey (as Noodles)
First Pirate .... David Kerman
Black Man .... DeWitt Kiernan
Panther .... Blake Scott
Tiger Lily .... Jane Kim
Liza .... Beatrice de Neergaard
Crocodile .... Richard Waring
Ostrich .... Howard da Silva
A Tramp .... David Kerman
A Cabman .... Lawrence Levin

1931–32

Civic Repertory Theatre

Peter Pan .... Eva Le Gallienne
Captain Hook .... Walter Beck

Mr. Darling . . . . Donald Cameron
Mrs. Darling . . . . Mary Ward
Wendy . . . . Josephine Hutchinson
John . . . . Gordon Wallace
Michael . . . . Vernon Jones
Nana . . . . J. Edward Bromberg
Tootles . . . . Florida Friebus
Nibs . . . . Richard Stokes
Slightly . . . . Mooney Diamond
Curly . . . . Patricia Deering
First Twin . . . . David Vivian
Second Twin . . . . Amy Chandler
Smee . . . . Sayre Crawley
Starkey . . . . Robert H. Gordon
Cookson . . . . Robert Ross
Mullins . . . . Joseph Kramm
Cecco . . . . Harold Moulton
Jukes . . . . Herbert Shapiro
Noodler . . . . David Turk
                                      (as Noodles)
First Pirate . . . . Syd Wynne
Black Man . . . . Leo Hillery
Panther . . . . J. Blake Scott
Tiger Lily . . . . Theodosia Dusanne
Liza . . . . Paula Miller
Crocodile . . . . Renne Orsell
Ostrich . . . . Harold Moulton
A Tramp . . . . David Kerman
A Cabman . . . . Robert Lewis

1932–33

Civic Repertory Theatre

Peter Pan . . . . Eva Le Gallienne
Captain Hook . . . . Walter Beck
Mr. Darling . . . . Donald Cameron
Mrs. Darling . . . . Beatrice Terry
Wendy . . . . Josephine Hutchinson
John . . . . Burgess Meredith
Michael . . . . Jackie Jordan
Nana . . . . Tonio Selwart
Tootles . . . . Florida Friebus
Nibs . . . . Freddy Rendulie
Slightly . . . . Landon Herrick
Curly . . . . Richard Jack
First Twin . . . . Alexander Lewis
Second Twin . . . . Ben Vivian
Smee . . . . Sayre Crawley
Starkey . . . . Nelson Welch
Cookson . . . . Howard da Silva
Mullins . . . . Robert H. Gordon
Cecco . . . . Harold Moulton
Jukes . . . . John Bauer
Noodler . . . . Joseph Kramm
                                      (as Noodles)
First Pirate . . . . Tomasso Tittoni
Black Man . . . . John Hampshire
Panther . . . . Blake Scott
Tiger Lily . . . . Flora Campbell
Liza . . . . Beatrice de Neergaard
Crocodile . . . . Richard Waring
Ostrich . . . . Howard da Silva
A Tramp . . . . Herbert Marsden
A Cabman . . . . Martin Pollock

1950–1951

Imperial Theatre

Peter Pan . . . . Jean Arthur
Captain Hook . . . . Boris Karloff
Mr. Darling . . . . Boris Karloff
Mrs. Darling . . . . Peg Hillias
Wendy . . . . Marcia Henderson
John . . . . Jack Dimond
Michael . . . . Charles Taylor
Nana . . . . Norman Shelly
Tootles . . . . Lee Barnett
Nibs . . . . Buzzy Martin
Slightly . . . . Richard Knox
Curly . . . . Philip Hepburn
First Twin . . . . Charles Brill
Second Twin . . . . Edward Benjamin
Smee . . . . Joe E. Marks
Starkey . . . . David Kurlan
Cookson . . . . William Marshall
Mullins . . . . Harry Allen
Cecco . . . . Nehemiah Persoff
Jukes . . . . Will Scholz
Noodler . . . . John Dennis
First Pirate . . . . Vincent Beck
                                      (as Wibbles)
Second Pirate . . . . Robert Josias
                                      (as Alf Mason)
Black Man . . . . William Sumner
                                      (as Canary Robb)
Panther . . . . Ronnie Aul
Tiger Lily . . . . Gloria Patrice
Mermaid . . . . Stepanie Augustine
Mermaid . . . . Eleanor Davis
Liza . . . . Gloria Patrice
Crocodile . . . . Norman Shelly

1954

Winter Garden

Peter Pan . . . . Mary Martin
Captain Hook . . . . Cyril Ritchard
Mr. Darling . . . . Cyril Ritchard
Mrs. Darling . . . . Margalo Gillmore
Wendy . . . . Kathy Nolan
John . . . . Robert Harrington
Michael . . . . Joseph Stafford
Nana . . . . Norman Shelly
Tootles . . . . Ian Tucker
Nibs . . . . Paris Theodore
Slightly . . . . David Bean
Curly . . . . Stanley Stenner
First Twin . . . . Alan Sutherland
Second Twin . . . . Darryl Duran
Smee . . . . Joe E. Marks
Starkey . . . . Robert Vanselow
Mullins . . . . James White
Cecco . . . . Robert Tucker
Jukes . . . . William Burke
Noodler . . . . Frank Lindsay
Tiger Lily . . . . Sondra Lee
Wendy Grown Up . . . . Sallie Brophy
Jane . . . . Kathy Nolan

Liza . . . . Heller Halliday
Crocodile . . . . Norman Shelly
Ostrich . . . . Joan Tewkesbury
Kangaroo . . . . Don Lurio
Lion . . . . Richard Wyatt

1979–80

Lunt-Fontanne Theatre

Peter Pan . . . . Sandy Duncan
Captain Hook . . . . George Rose
Mr. Darling . . . . George Rose
Mrs. Darling . . . . Beth Fowler
Wendy . . . . Marsha Kramer
John . . . . Alexander Winter
Michael . . . . Jonathan Ward
Nana . . . . James Cook
Tootles . . . . Carl Tramon
Nibs . . . . Dennis Courtney
Slightly . . . . Chris Farr
Curly . . . . Michael Estes
First Twin . . . . Rusty Jacobs
Second Twin . . . . Joey Abbott
Smee . . . . Arnold Soboloff
Starkey . . . . Jon Vandertholen
Mullins . . . . Steven Yuhasz
Cecco . . . . Trey Wilson
Jukes . . . . Gary Daniel
Noodler . . . . Guy Stroman
Tiger Lily . . . . Maria Pogee
Wendy Grown Up . . . . Neva Rae Powers
Jane . . . . Marsha Kramer
Liza . . . . Maggy Gorrill
Crocodile . . . . Kevin McCready
Ostrich . . . . Maggy Gorrill
Kangaroo . . . . Reed Jones
Lion . . . . Jim Wolfe
Turtle . . . . Cleve Asbury

1990–91

Lunt-Fontanne Theatre

Peter Pan . . . . Cathy Rigby
Captain Hook . . . . Stephan Hanan
Mr. Darling . . . . Stephan Hanan
Mrs. Darling . . . . Lauren Thompson
Wendy . . . . Cindy Robinson
John . . . . Britt West
Michael . . . . Chad Hutchison
Nana . . . . Bill Bateman
Tootles . . . . Julian Brightman
Slightly . . . . Christopher Ayres
Curly . . . . Alon Williams
First Twin . . . . Janet Kay Higgins
Second Twin . . . . Courtney Wyn
Smee . . . . Don Potter
Starkey . . . . Carl Packard
Cecco . . . . Calvin Smith
Jukes . . . . Andy Ferrarra
Noodler . . . . Barry Ramsey
Tiger Lily . . . . Holly Irwin

Wendy Grown Up . . . . Lauren Thompson
Jane . . . . Cindy Robinson
Liza . . . . Anne McVey
Crocodile . . . . Barry Ramsey
Never Bear . . . . Adam Ehrenworth

1991–92

Minskoff Theatre

Peter Pan . . . . Cathy Rigby
Captain Hook . . . . J. K. Simmons
Mr. Darling . . . . J. K. Simmons
Mrs. Darling . . . . Lauren Thompson
Wendy . . . . Cindy Robinson
John . . . . David Burdick
Michael . . . . Joey Cee
Nana . . . . Bill Bateman
Tootles . . . . Julian Brightman
Slightly . . . . Christopher Ayres
Curly . . . . Alon Williams
First Twin . . . . Janet Kay Higgins
Second Twin . . . . Cortney Winn
Smee . . . . Don Porter
Starkey . . . . Carl Packard
Cecco . . . . Calvin Smith
Noodler . . . . Barry Ramsey
Tiger Lily . . . . Michelle Schumacher
Jane . . . . Cindy Robinson
Liza . . . . Anne McVey
Crocodile . . . . Barry Ramsey

1998–99

Marquis Theatre George,
Nov. 23, 1998– Jan. 3, 1999;
Gershwin Theatre,
Apr.7– Aug. 29, 1999

Peter Pan . . . . Cathy Rigby
Captain Hook . . . . Paul Schoeffler
Mr. Darling . . . . Paul Schoeffler
Mrs. Darling . . . . Barbara McCulloh
Wendy . . . . Elisa Sagardia
John . . . . Chase Kniffen
Michael . . . . Drake English
Nana . . . . Buck Mason
Tootles . . . . Aileen Quinn
Slightly . . . . Scott Bridges
Curly . . . . Alon Williams
First Twin . . . . Janet Higgins
Second Twin . . . . Doreen Chila
Smee . . . . Michael Nostrand
Starkey . . . . Sam Zeller
Cecco . . . . Tony Spinosa
Jukes . . . . Buck Mason
Noodler . . . . Randy A. Davis
Tiger Lily . . . . Dana Solimando
Wendy Grown Up . . . . Barbara McCulloh
Jane . . . . Aileen Quinn
Liza . . . . Dana Solimando
Crocodile . . . . Buck Mason

U.S. Touring Companies

1907–08

Peter Pan . . . . Vivian Martin
Captain Hook . . . . Paul A. Tharp
Mr. Darling . . . . Paul A. Tharp
Mrs. Darling . . . . Margery Taylor
Wendy . . . . Violet Hemming
John . . . . Renee Grau
Michael . . . . Carol Pullman
Tinker Bell . . . . Jane Wren
Nana . . . . James Grant
Tootles . . . . May Barton
Nibs . . . . Bertha Mann
Slightly . . . . George Swift
Curly . . . . Florence Stearnes
First Twin . . . . Anna Wheaton
Second Twin . . . . Agusta Gardner
Smee . . . . George K. Rolands
Starkey . . . . Louis Egan
Cookson . . . . George Hebbard (listed
                            as the cook)
Mullins . . . . Hollister Pratt
Cecco . . . . Guy D'Ennery
Noodler . . . . Sidney Northcote
Panther . . . . P. McCoy
Tiger Lily . . . . Margaret Taylor
Liza . . . . Bessie Burt

1909–10

Peter Pan . . . . Eva Lang
Captain Hook . . . . Frank Denithorne
Mr. Darling . . . . Frank Dudley
Mrs. Darling . . . . Marie Hudson
Wendy . . . . Ethel Valentine
John . . . . Walter Voorman
Michael . . . . Veta Bayne
Tinker Bell . . . . Herself
Nana . . . . Clinton Tuston
Tootles . . . . Judith Harle
Nibs . . . . Evelyn Monroe
Slightly . . . . Alice Ballentine
Curly . . . . Mayme Williams
First Twin . . . . Kate Snell
Second Twin . . . . Gene Harold
Smee . . . . Lloyd Ingraham
Starkey . . . . Erville Alderson
Mullins . . . . Wm. T. Hayes
Cecco . . . . Henry Marthy
Noodler . . . . Clarence Ausin
Panther . . . . Mr. Mithers
Tiger Lily . . . . Emma Hepperlin
Liza . . . . Margery Bayne

1911–12

Peter Pan . . . . Beverly West
Captain Hook . . . . Eric Blind
Mr. Darling . . . . Eric Blind
Mrs. Darling . . . . Jane Tyrrell
Wendy . . . . Isoldi Illian
John . . . . Jack Unerti
Michael . . . . Peggy Unerti
Tinker Bell . . . . Herself

Nana . . . . George Leary
Tootles . . . . Isabel Rene
Nibs . . . . Marion Haliday
Slightly . . . . Leona Haliday
Curly . . . . Florence Hunter
First Twin . . . . Mathilda Mohr
Second Twin . . . . Elizabeth Scott
Smee . . . . Walter Dickinson
Starkey . . . . Henry Roberts
Cookson . . . . Larry Ralfe
Mullins . . . . Bryce Oliver
Cecco . . . . Vaughn Morgan
Panther . . . . Theodore James
Tiger Lily . . . . Arline Schmidt
Liza . . . . Marion Haliday
Crocodile . . . . George Leary

1938–39

Peter Pan . . . . Leslie C. Gorall
Captain Hook . . . . John Ireland
Mr. Darling . . . . Howard Whitfield
Mrs. Darling . . . . Elizabeth Dodge
Wendy . . . . Jewel Morse
John . . . . Sheldon Thompson
Michael . . . . Kay Mallory
Nana . . . . Edward Charles
Tootles . . . . Guy Sheldon
Nibs . . . . Bobee York
Slightly . . . . Buddy Harris
Smee . . . . Edwin Hugh
Starkey . . . . Robert Mason Warren
Cecco . . . . Richard Conrad
Panther . . . . Dick Baldwin
Tiger Lily . . . . Bette Morrow
Liza . . . . Inge Adams
Cabman . . . . O. L. Miller
Tramp . . . . Kirk Clive

1951–52

Peter Pan . . . . Joan McCracken
Captain Hook . . . . Boris Karloff
Mr. Darling . . . . Boris Karloff
Mrs. Darling . . . . Jackson Perkins
Wendy . . . . Jennifer Bunker
John . . . . David Frank
Michael . . . . Jackie Scholle
Nana . . . . Frank Neal
Tootles . . . . Lewis Scholle
Nibs . . . . Paul Carter
Slightly . . . . Richard Knox
Curly . . . . Jimmy Grimes
First Twin . . . . Charles Brill
Second Twin . . . . Edward Benjamin
Smee . . . . Joe E. Marks
Starkey . . . . David Kurlan
Cookson . . . . Elwood Smith
Mullins . . . . Lester Brackenbury
Cecco . . . . Keith Taylor
Jukes . . . . John Dorman
Noodler . . . . Alan Lumpkin
Wibbles . . . . Don Elson

Alf Mason . . . . Robert Josias
Canary Rob . . . . William Weaver
Panther . . . . Robert Josias
Tiger Lily . . . . Lucy Hillary
Mermaid . . . . Joyce Homier
Baby Mermaid . . . . Jeanette Goudzward
Liza . . . . Lucy Hillary
Crocodile . . . . Jimmy Taravella

1951

Peter Pan . . . . Veronica Lake
Captain Hook . . . . Lawrence Tibbett
Mr. Darling . . . . Lawrence Tibbett
Mrs. Darling . . . . Ann Blackburn
Wendy . . . . Peggy O'Hara
John . . . . Stanley Martin
Michael . . . . Ray Clarke
Nana . . . . Frank Neal
Tootles . . . . Lee Barnett
Nibs . . . . Peter Freedberger
Slightly . . . . Peter Avramo
Curly . . . . Jimmy Grimes
First Twin . . . . Don Ansell
Second Twin . . . . Ron Ansell
Smee . . . . Bobby Barry
Starkey . . . . Le Roi Operti
Cookson . . . . John Garth III
Mullins . . . . Edward Grace
Cecco . . . . Jerry Stiller
Jukes . . . . Herb Forbes
Noodler . . . . Joe Cusanelli
Wibbles . . . . Del Horstmann
Panther . . . . Ronnie Aul
Tiger Lily . . . . Adeline Hiatt
Mermaid . . . . Leni Barton
Baby Mermaid . . . . Mitzi Wilson
Liza . . . . Adeline Hiatt
Crocodile . . . . Wayne Sheridan/Herb
                             Forbes

1954

Pre-Broadway at the Curran Theatre in San Francisco

Peter Pan . . . . Mary Martin
Captain Hook . . . . Cyril Ritchard
Mr. Darling . . . . Cyril Ritchard
Mrs. Darling . . . . Margalo Gillmore
Wendy . . . . Kathy Nolan
John . . . . Robert Harrington
Michael . . . . Joseph Stafford
Nana . . . . Norman Shelly
Tootles . . . . Arthur Pollick
Nibs . . . . Ronnie Lee
Slightly . . . . David Bean
Curly . . . . Stanley Stenner
First Twin . . . . Alan Sutherland
Second Twin . . . . Darryl Duran
Smee . . . . Joe E. Marks
Starkey . . . . Robert Vanselow
Mullins . . . . James White
Cecco . . . . Meurisse du Ree

Jukes . . . . William Burke (as Juke)
Noodler . . . . Frank Lindsay
Tiger Lily . . . . Sondra Lee
Liza . . . . Heller Halliday
Crocodile . . . . Norman Shelly
Ostrich . . . . Joan Tewkesbury
Lion . . . . Richard Wyatt
Kangaroo . . . . Don Lurio
Woman . . . . Ann Connolly

1959

Peter Pan . . . . Rosemary Harris
Captain Hook . . . . Eric Portman
Mr. Darling . . . . Eric Portman
Mrs. Darling . . . . Sydney Sturgess
Wendy . . . . Chase Crosley
John . . . . George Connolly
Michael . . . . Hayward Morse
Nana . . . . Gus Solomons, Jr.
Tootles . . . . Samuel Waterson
Nibs . . . . James Schuman
Slightly . . . . Charles Lewes
Curly . . . . Bernard Albert
First Twin . . . . David Sullivan
Second Twin . . . . David Fletcher
Smee . . . . Ellis Rabb
Starkey . . . . William Swetland
Cookson . . . . Fletcher Coleman
Mullins . . . . Bowden Anderson
Cecco . . . . Robert Blackburn
Jukes . . . . John Brockington
Noodler . . . . John Peters
Panther . . . . John Peters
Tiger Lily . . . . Angela Wood
Mermaid . . . . Various cast members
Liza . . . . Deborah Ann Gordon

2005

Cathy Rigby has been touring since 1990. See Broadway and TV cast lists for earlier tours. This farewell tour ended in 2009.

Peter Pan . . . . Cathy Rigby
Captain Hook . . . . Howard McGillin
Mr. Darling . . . . Howard McGillin
Mrs. Darling . . . . Tracy Lore
Wendy . . . . Elisa Sagardia
John . . . . Gavin Leatherwood
Michael . . . . Shawn Moriah Sullivan
Nana . . . . Jonathan Warren
Tootles . . . . Lindsay Nickerson
Slightly . . . . Omar D. Brancato
Curly . . . . Jordan Bass
First Twin . . . . Janet Higgins
Second Twin . . . . Theresa McCoy
Smee . . . . Patrick Richwood
Starkey . . . . Michael G. Hawkins
Cecco . . . . Tony Spinosa
Jukes . . . . Jonathan Warren
Noodler . . . . Nathan Balsar
Grown Up Wendy . . . . Tracy Lore

Jane . . . . Theresa McCoy
Tiger Lily . . . . Dana Solimando

Liza . . . . Dana Solimando
Crocodile . . . . Tony Spinosa

Films

December 29, 1924

Peter Pan . . . . Betty Bronson
Captain Hook . . . . Ernest Torrence
Mr. Darling . . . . Cyril Chadwick
Mrs. Darling . . . . Esther Ralston
Wendy . . . . Mary Brian
John . . . . Jack Murphy
Michael . . . . Philippe de Lacy
Tinker Bell . . . . Virginia Brown Faire
Nana . . . . George Ali
Tootles . . . . Maurice Murphy
Nibs . . . . Terrence McMillan
Slightly . . . . Mickey McBan
Curly . . . . George Crane, Jr.
First Twin . . . . Winston Doty
Second Twin . . . . Weston Doty
Smee . . . . Edward Kipling
Starkey . . . . Lewis Morrison
Cookson . . . . Maurice Cannon
Mullins . . . . Ed Jones
Cecco . . . . Ralph Yearsly
Jukes . . . . Charles A. Stevenson
Noodler . . . . Percy Barbat
First Pirate . . . . Robert Milasch (as Kelt)
Giant Blackman . . . . . . Richard Frazier
Tiger Lily . . . . Anna May Wong

1953

Voices for Disney film

Peter Pan . . . . Bobby Driscoll
Captain Hook . . . . Hans Conried
Mr. Darling . . . . Hans Conried
Mrs. Darling . . . . Heather Angel
Wendy . . . . Kathryn Beaumont
John . . . . Paul Collins
Michael . . . . Tommy Luske
Nibs . . . . Jeffrey Silver
Slightly . . . . Stuffy Singer

Curly . . . . Robert Ellis
First Twin . . . . Jonny McGovern
Second Twin . . . . Jonny McGovern
Smee . . . . Bill Thompson
Indian Chief . . . . Candy Candido
Narrator . . . . Tom Conway
Mermaids . . . . June Foray, Connie Hilton,
                            Margaret Kerry, Karen
                            Kester

Dec. 25, 2003

Peter Pan . . . . Jeremy Sumpter
Captain Hook . . . . Jason Isaacs
Mr. Darling . . . . Jason Isaacs
Mrs. Darling . . . . Olivia Williams
Wendy . . . . Rachel Hurd-Wood
John . . . . Harry Newell
Michael . . . . Freddie Popplewell
Tinker Bell . . . . Ludivine Sagnier
Nana . . . . Rebel
Tootles . . . . Rupert Simonian
Nibs . . . . Harry Eden
Slightly . . . . Theodore Chester
Curly . . . . George MacKay
First Twin . . . . Patrick Gooch
Second Twin . . . . Lachlan Gooch
Smee . . . . Richard Briers
Starkey . . . . Frank Whitten
Cookson . . . . Bruce Spence
Mullins . . . . Darren Mitchell
Cecco . . . . Michael Roughan
Jukes . . . . Jacob Tomuri
Noodler . . . . Septimus Caton
First Pirate . . . . Don Batte (as Giant Pirate)
Tiger Lily . . . . Carsen Gray
Mermaid . . . . Various actresses
Skylarks . . . . Alan Cinis
Aunt Millicent . . . . Lynn Redgrave
Narrator . . . . Saffon Burrows

Television Productions

Mar. 7, 1955

*Producer's Showcase — NBC
 (performed live)*

Peter Pan . . . . Mary Martin
Captain Hook . . . . Cyril Ritchard
Mr. Darling . . . . Cyril Ritchard
Mrs. Darling . . . . Margalo Gillmore
Wendy . . . . Kathy Nolan
John . . . . Robert Harrington
Michael . . . . Joseph Stafford
Nana . . . . Norman Shelly
Tootles . . . . Ian Tucker
Nibs . . . . Paris Theodore
Slightly . . . . David Bean
Curly . . . . Stanley Stenner

First Twin . . . . Jackie Scholle
Second Twin . . . . Darryl Duran
Smee . . . . Joe E. Marks
Starkey . . . . Robert Vanselow
Mullins . . . . James White
Cecco . . . . Richard Winter
Jukes . . . . Frank Bouley
Noodler . . . . Frank Lindsay
Tiger Lily . . . . Sondra Lee
Narrator . . . . Patricia Wheel
Wendy Grown Up . . . . Ann Connolly
Jane . . . . Kathy Nolan
Liza . . . . Heller Halliday
Crocodile . . . . Norman Shelly
Ostrich . . . . Joan Tewkesbury
Kangaroo . . . . Carl Erbele
Lion . . . . Richard Wyatt

Jan. 9, 1956

Producer's Showcase — NBC (performed live)

Peter Pan . . . . Mary Martin
Captain Hook . . . . Cyril Ritchard
Mr. Darling . . . . Cyril Ritchard
Mrs. Darling . . . . Margalo Gillmore
Wendy . . . . Kathy Nolan
John . . . . Michael Allen
Michael . . . . Tom Halloran
Nana . . . . Norman Shelly
Tootles . . . . Ian Tucker
Nibs . . . . Paris Theodore
Slightly . . . . David Bean
Curly . . . . Stanley Stenner
First Twin . . . . Harold Day
Second Twin . . . . Alan Sutherland
Smee . . . . Joe E. Marks
Starkey . . . . Robert Vanselow
Mullins . . . . James White
Cecco . . . . Richard Winter
Jukes . . . . Frank Bouley
Noodler . . . . Frank Lindsay
Tiger Lily . . . . Sondra Lee
Wendy Grown Up . . . . Peggy Maurer
Jane . . . . Kathy Nolan
Liza . . . . Heller Halliday
Crocodile . . . . Norman Shelly
Ostrich . . . . Joan Tewkesbury
Kangaroo . . . . Carl Erbele
Narrator . . . . Patricia Wheel
Lion . . . . Richard Wyatt
Black Bill . . . . John Holland

Dec. 8, 1960

NBC

Peter Pan . . . . Mary Martin
Captain Hook . . . . Cyril Ritchard
Mr. Darling . . . . Cyril Ritchard
Mrs. Darling . . . . Margalo Gillmore
Wendy . . . . Maureen Bailey
John . . . . Joey Trent
Michael . . . . Kent Fletcher
Nana . . . . Norman Shelly
Tootles . . . . David Komoroff
Nibs . . . . Carson Woods
Slightly . . . . Edmund Gaynes
Curly . . . . Bill Snowden
First Twin . . . . Brad Herrmann
Second Twin . . . . Luke Halpin
Smee . . . . Joe E. Marks
Starkey . . . . Bob Vanselow
Black Bill . . . . John Holland
Cecco . . . . Richard Winter
Noodler . . . . Frank Lindsay
Tiger Lily . . . . Sondra Lee
Wendy Grown Up . . . . Peggy Maurer

Jane . . . . Maureen Bailey
Liza . . . . Jacqueline Mayro
Crocodile . . . . Norman Shelly
Ostrich . . . . Joan Tewkesbury
Kangaroo . . . . George Zima
Lion . . . . Richard Wyatt
Narrator . . . . Lynn Fontanne

Dec. 12, 1976

Hallmark Hall of Fame — NBC

Peter Pan . . . . Mia Farrow
Captain Hook . . . . Danny Kaye
Mr. Darling . . . . Danny Kaye
Mrs. Darling . . . . Virginia McKenna
Wendy . . . . Briony McRoberts
John . . . . Ian Sharrock
Michael . . . . Adam Stafford
Nana . . . . Peter O'Farrell
Tootles . . . . Nicholas Lyndhurst
Nibs . . . . Adam Richens
Slightly . . . . Jerome Watts
Curly . . . . Michael Deeks
First Twin . . . . Simon Mooney
Second Twin . . . . Andrew Mooney
Smee . . . . Tony Sympson
Starkey . . . . Joe Melia
Tiger Lily . . . . Paula Kelly
Wendy Grown Up . . . . Jill Gascoine
Jane . . . . Linsey Baxter

2000

A & E

Peter Pan . . . . Cathy Rigby
Captain Hook . . . . Paul Schoeffler
Mr. Darling . . . . Paul Schoeffler
Mrs. Darling . . . . Barbara McCulloh
Wendy . . . . Elisa Sagardia
John . . . . Barry Cavanagh
Michael . . . . Drake English
Nana/Jukes . . . . Thomas Buck Mason
Tootles . . . . Hally McGehean
Slightly . . . . Scott Bridges
Curly . . . . Alon Williams
First Twin . . . . Janet Higgins
Second Twin . . . . Joseph Favalora
Smee . . . . Michael Nostrand
Starkey . . . . Sam Zeller
Cecco . . . . Tony Spinosa
Noodler . . . . Randy A. Davis
Tiger Lily . . . . Dana Solimando
Wendy Grown Up . . . . Elisa Sagardia
Jane . . . . Theresa McCoy
Liza . . . . Dana Solimando
Crocodile . . . . Thomas Buck Mason
Mermaids . . . . Barbara McCulloh,
Kaitlin McCoy

Select British Touring Companies

Actors and actresses who played Peter, Wendy, and Captain Hook in touring productions that were basically replicas of the London productions with a different cast. In several cases, such as Jean Forbes-Robertson, leading players would also tour after the London run but these are not included. Asterisk (*) indicates dual role of Captain Hook/Mr. Darling.

Year	Peter Pan	Wendy	Captain Hook
1906 (1st)	Cecilia Loftus	Hilda Trevelyn	*Loring Fernie
1906–07	Zena Dare	Ela Q. May	*Lionel Mackinder
	Pauline Chase	Hilda Trevelyn	*Loring Fernie
1907–08	Pauline Chase	Ela Q. May	Robb Harwood
1908–09	Pauline Chase	Gertrude Lang	Robb Harwood
1909–10	Pauline Chase	Gertrude Lang	Frederick Annerley
1910–11	Pauline Chase	Gertrude Lang	E. Holman Clark
1911–12	Pauline Chase	Gertrude Lang	Loring Fernie
1912–13	Pauline Chase	Gertrude Lang	Loring Fernie
1913–14	Pauline Chase	Mary Glynne	William Luff
	Marjorie Manners	Alice Hattan	Lionel Gadsden
1914–15	Gladys Gaynor	Alice Hattan	Lionel Gadsden
1915–16	Eva Embury	Dot Temple	Scott Leighton
	Stephanie Stephens	Alice Hattan	Lionel Gadsden
1916–17	Eva Embury	Ethel Ward	*Edward Thane
1917–18	Eva Embury	Ethel Ward	*Fred W. Ring
1918–19	Molly Terraine	Ethel Ward	*Edward MacLean
1919–20	Lila Maravan	Ethel Ward	Talbot Homewood
1920–21	Irene Arnold	Marguerite Moreton	*Lionel Gadsden
1921–22	Maisie Darrell	Marguerite Moreton	Lionel Gadsden
1922–23	Doris Littell	Marguerite Moreton	Lionel Gadsden
1923–24	Maisie Darrell	Marguerite Moreton	Lionel Gadsden
1924–25	Maisie Darrell	Marguerite Moreton	Lionel Gadsden
1925–26	Kathleen Vaughan	Miriam Adams	Lionel Gadsden
1926–27	(No touring company)		
1927–28	Doris Littell	Miriam Adams	Lionel Gadsden
1928–29	Sheila Moloney	Judy Hallatt	Lionel Gadsden
1929–30	Sheila Moloney	Judy Hallatt	Lionel Gadsden
1930–31	Kathleen Vaughan	Rosemary Bamber	*Cyril Horrocks
1931–32	Doris Hilditch	Rosemary Bamber	Lionel Gadsden
1932–33	Doris Hilditch	Rosemary Bamber	Lionel Gadsden
1933–34	Moira Lynd	Rosemary Bamber	Lionel Gadsden
1934–35	Betty Marsden	Dinah Sheridan	Lionel Gadsden
1935–36	Ena Moon	Diana Sinclair Hill	Harry Welchman
1936–37	Dinah Sheridan	Diana Sinclair Hill	*George Hayes
1937–38	Anona Winn	Diana Sinclair Hill	Leo Sheffield
1938–39	Joan Shipman	Diana Deare	Leo Sheffield
1939–40	Margaret Cooper	Audrey O'Flynn	*Raf de la Torre
1940–41	(No touring companies due to the war but a recording was made with the following:)		
	Jean Forbes-Robertson	Dinah Sheridan	Gordon Harker
1942–43	Ann Todd	June Holden (last 2 wks)	*Hugh Morton (last 4 wks)
1943–44	Celia Lipton	Barbara White	Baliol Holloway
1944–45	Nova Pilbeam	Rhona Thorndike	*Walter Fitzgerald
	Mary Windust	Rhona Thorndike	*Walter Fitzgerald
1945–46	Celia Lipton	Diana Calderwood	George Curzon
1946–47	Mary Morris	Diana Calderwood	Franklyn Dyall
1950–51	Susan Shaw (replaced Lockwood)	Shirley Lorimer	*Alan Judd
1953–54	Pat Kirkwood	Norah Gorsen	*Stanley Holloway
1956–57	Janette Scott	Frances Guthrie	*Barry Sinclair
1964–65	Dawn Adams	Belinda Carroll	*Richard Wordsworth
1967–68	Millicent Martin	Mia Martin	*Darryl Kavann
1974–75	Anita Harris	Zelah Clarke	*John Gower

Chapter Notes

Introduction

1. Roger Lancelyn Green, *Fifty Years of Peter Pan* (London: Peter Davies, 1954), p. 1.
2. J. M. Barrie, *The Little White Bird or Adventures in Kensington Gardens* (New York: Charles Scribner's Sons, 1902), p. 157.
3. J. M. Barrie, *Peter Pan, or the Boy Who Wouldn't Grow Up* (London: Charles Scribner's Sons, 1928), p. xxix.
4. J. M. Barrie, *Peter and Wendy* (New York: Charles Scribner's Sons, 1911), p. 43.

Chapter 1

1. Viola Meynell, *Letters of James M. Barrie* (New York: Charles Scribner's Sons, 1947), p. 2.
2. Barrie, *Peter and Wendy*, p. 1.
3. Cynthia Asquith, *Portrait of Barrie* (London: Robert Cunningham and Sons, 1954), p. 53.
4. Roger Lancelyn Green, *J. M. Barrie* (New York: Henry Z. Walck, 1960), p. 34.
5. J. M. Barrie, *Margaret Ogilvy* (New York: Charles Scribner's Sons, 1886), p. 12.
6. Janet Dunbar, *J. M. Barrie: The Man Behind the Image* (Boston: Houghton Mifflin, 1970), p. 20.
7. Dunbar, *J. M. Barrie*, p. 44.
8. Barrie, *Margaret Ogilvy*, p. 19.
9. Andrew Birkin, *J. M. Barrie and the Lost Boys*, (London: Constable, 1979), p. 29.
10. J. M. Barrie, *Tommy and Grizel* (New York: Charles Scribner's Sons, 1900), p. 491.
11. *Ibid.*, p. 466.
12. Barrie, *Peter and Wendy*, p. 7.
13. Barrie, *The Little White Bird*, p. 166.

14. *Ibid.*, 257.
15. Lisa Chaney, *Hide and Seek with Angels: A Life of J. M. Barrie* (New York: St. Martin's Press, 2005), p. 213.
16. *Ibid.*, 214.
17. Barrie, *Peter Pan*, p. xxvii.
18. *Ibid.*, vi.
19. *Ibid.*, vii.
20. Birkin, *J. M. Barrie and the Lost Boys*, p. 25.
21. Green, *Fifty Years of Peter Pan*, p. 61.
22. Daniel Frohman and Isaac F. Marcosson, *Charles Frohman: Manager and Man* (New York: Harpers, 1916), p. 255.
23. *Ibid.*, 169.
24. *Ibid.*, 115.
25. *Ibid.*, 169.
26. *Ibid.*, 245.

Chapter 2

1. Nina Boucicault, "When I Was Peter Pan," *Strand Magazine* (January 1923), p. 32.
2. Nicholas Davies, letter, December 15, 1964. V & A Theatre Museum, London.
3. Daphne du Maurier, *Gerald: A Portrait* (New York: Doubleday, 1935), p. 104.
4. Denis Mackail, *Barrie: The Story of J. M. B.* (New York: Charles Scribner's Sons, 1941), p. 347.
5. Hilda Trevelyan to Eric Johns, "The Stories of Famous London Theatres: The Duke of York's," *Theatre World* (January 1940), p. 6.
6. Boucicault, "When I Was Peter Pan," p. 32.
7. Green, *Fifty Years of Peter Pan*, p. 92.
8. George Shelton, *It's Smee* (London: Ernest Benn Ltd., 1928), p. 119.
9. *Ibid.*, p. 111.

10. Boucicault, "When I Was Peter Pan," p. 33.
11. J. M. Barrie, *Peter Pan*, Act 4, p. 108.
12. *Ibid.*, Act 5, p. 27.
13. Nina Boucicault, letter, August 7, 1939.
14. Boucicault, "When I Was Peter Pan," p. 33.
15. Barrie, *Peter Pan*, Act 1, p. 20.
16. Trevelyan, "The Stories of Famous London Theatres: The Duke of York's," p. 6.
17. Boucicault, "When I Was Peter Pan," p. 33.
18. *Ibid.*
19. Unknown 1904 periodical, V & A Theatre Museum, London.
20. *Morning Post*, December 28, 1904.
21. *Daily Telegraph*, December 28, 1904.
22. *Illustrated Sporting and Dramatic News*, January 1905.
23. *Morning Post*, December 28, 1904.
24. *Ibid.*
25. *Ibid.*
26. Green, *Fifty Years of Peter Pan*, p. 89.
27. Unknown 1904 periodical, V & A Theatre Museum, London.
28. Barrie, *Peter Pan*, Act 5, p. 42.
29. *The King*, January 14, 1905.
30. Max Beerbohm, *Saturday Review*, January 7, 1905.
31. Trevelyan, "The Stories of Famous London Theatres: The Duke of York's," p. 21.
32. Mackail, *Barrie: The Story of J. M. B.*, p. 380.
33. Boucicault, letter, August 7, 1939.

Chapter 3

1. Phyllis Robbins, *Maude Adams: An Intimate Portrait* (New

York: G. P. Putnam's Sons, 1956), p. 89.

2. "Peter Pan and Barrie," *Boston Transcript*, October 20, 1906.

3. Ada Patterson, *Maude Adams: A Biography* (New York: Meyer Bros. & Co., 1907), p. 52.

4. *New York Times*, September 28, 1897.

5. *Herald Tribune*, September 28, 1897.

6. Robbins, *Maude Adams: An Intimate Portrait*, p. 43.

7. Perriton Maxwell, *The Stage Story of Maude Adams* (pamphlet, 1908), p. 501.

8. Patterson, *Maude Adams: A Biography*, p. 39.

9. Frohman and Marcosson, *Charles Frohman: Manager and Man*, p. 141.

10. Mackail, *Barrie: The Story of J. M. B.*, p. 264.

11. Robbins, *Maude Adams: An Intimate Portrait*, p. 57.

12. Frohman and Marcosson, *Charles Frohman: Manager and Man*, p. 246.

13. *Ibid.*, p. 170.

14. *New York Times*, November 7, 1905.

15. *Ibid.*

16. *Ibid.*

17. *New York Herald Tribune*, November 7, 1905.

18. *Ibid.*

19. Robbins, *Maude Adams: An Intimate Portrait*, p. 90.

20. *Boston Transcript*, October 23, 1905.

21. Robbins, *Maude Adams: An Intimate Portrait*, p. 93.

22. *New York Times*, November 7, 1905.

23. *Evening Telegram*, November 20, 1905.

24. *Daily Tribune*, November 7, 1905.

25. *Evening Sun*, November 7, 1905.

26. *Ibid.*

27. *World*, November, 1905.

28. *Evening Sun*, November 7, 1905.

29. Mildred Morris, "Behind the Scenes with Peter Pan," *Delineator* (October 1915), p. 10.

30. Barrie, *Peter Pan*, Act 4, p. 10. Original acting version used by Eva Le Gallienne at the Civic Repertory Theatre in New York, 1928–1932. According to Le Gallienne's "On Playing Peter Pan," the Civic Repertory used the same script as Maude Adams. As Adams' script disappeared from the Library of Performing Arts at Lincoln Center sometime in the mid–1980s, this source is being cited.

31. Barrie, *Peter Pan*, Act 4, p. 102–104.

32. "Sally in Our Alley" was written by Henry Carey (1693?–1743), an English composer and playwright. According to *Best Loved Songs of the American People* by Denes Agay (Garden City, NY: Doubleday, 1975), it was published in a collection of Carey's works in 1726. W. Chappell's *The Ballad Literature and Popular Music of the Olden Time* (London: Chappell and Company, 1859) states that Carey's original melody was replaced around 1760 by "a much older ballad-tune," "The Country Lass." This melody, which became popular in America in the eighteenth century, was probably sung by Adams.

33. *Boston Transcript*, October 23, 1906.

34. *Boston Herald*, December 2, 1906.

35. *New York Telegram*, December 25, 1906.

36. Frohman and Marcosson, *Charles Frohman: Manager and Man*, p. 171.

37. *Boston Herald*, November 8, 1906.

38. Stanley Green, *The World of Musical Comedy* (New York: Grosset & Dunlap, 1960), p. 64.

39. *Morning Telegraph*, December 24, 1912.

40. Ruth Gordon, *My Side* (New York: Harper & Row, 1976), p. 169.

41. Robbins, *Maude Adams: An Intimate Portrait*, p. 103.

42. Meynell, *Letters of James M. Barrie*, p. 94.

43. Robbins, *Maude Adams: An Intimate Portrait*, p. 208.

44. *Ibid.*, p. 198.

45. *Ibid.*, p. 199.

46. Meynell, *Letters of James M. Barrie*, p. 97.

47. Robbins, *Maude Adams: An Intimate Portrait*, p. 208.

48. *Ibid.*, p. 209.

49. Letter from Adolph Zukor to Maude Adams, October 18, 1920. Beinecke Library Collection at Yale University.

50. Letter from Daniel Frohman to Adolph Zukor, October 27, 1920. Beinecke Library Collection at Yale University.

51. Letter from Maude Adams to Adolph Zukor, December 3, 1920. Beinecke Library Collection at Yale University.

52. Robbins, *Maude Adams: An Intimate Portrait*, p. 212.

53. Alexander Woollcott, *New Yorker*, December 19, 1931.

Chapter 4

1. Cecilia Loftus, "When I Was Peter Pan," *Strand Magazine* (January 1923), p. 34.

2. *Ibid.*, p. 33.

3. Burns Mantle, July 14, 1943. Cecilia Loftus obituary in unknown periodical.

4. Loftus, "When I Was Peter Pan," p. 34.

5. Barrie, *Peter Pan*, Act 1, p. 33.

6. *Ibid.*, Act 3, p. 7.

7. *Ibid.*

8. "The Lagoon" from *Peter Pan, or The Boy Who Wouldn't Grow Up*. Lyrics by James M. Barrie. Music by John Crook. Copyright 1905 W. Paxton & Co.

9. *Ibid.*, Act 3, p. 15.

10. *Ibid.*, Act 5, p. 1.

11. Green, *Fifty Years of Peter Pan*, p. 123.

Chapter 5

1. Vivian Martin interview, unknown periodical, 1919, New York Public Library of Performing Arts.

2. Vivian Martin interview, unknown periodical, 1907, New York Public Library of Performing Arts.

3. Martin, interview, 1919.

Chapter 6

1. Pauline Chase, "My Reminiscences of Peter Pan," *Strand Magazine* (February 1913), p. 42.

2. Pauline Chase, *Peter Pan's Postbag* (London: William Heinemann, 1909), p. v.

3. Edna Best, "When I Was Peter Pan," *Strand Magazine* (January 1923), p. 40.

4. Chase, "My Reminiscences of Peter Pan," p. 44.

5. Pauline Drummond Chase, letter written to Eric Johns, November 13, 1936.

6. *Morning Telegraph*, December 18, 1906.

7. *Daily Mail*, December 18, 1906.

8. *Daily Chronicle*, December 18, 1906.

9. Mackail, *Barrie: The Story of J. M. B.*, p. 386.

10. *Ibid.*, p. 402.

11. Hilda Trevelyan, letter, December 10, 1957. Beinecke Library Collection at Yale University.

12. Frohman and Marcosson,

Charles Frohman: Manager and Man, p. 246.

13. Chase, *Peter Pan's Postbag,* p. 19.

14. Birkin, *J. M. Barrie and the Lost Boys,* p. 180.

15. *Ibid.*

16. *Ibid.*

17. Cole Lesley, *Remembered Laughter: The Life of Noël Coward* (New York: Knopf, 1976), p. 25.

18. *Ibid.,* p. 26.

Chapter 7

1. Warren G. Harris, *The Other Marilyn* (New York: Arbor House, 1985), p. 13.

2. *Ibid.,* p. 235.

3. *Ibid.,* p. 235.

4. *Ibid.,* p. 41.

5. *Ibid.* p. 45.

6. *Ibid.* p. 45–46.

7. "Look for the Silver Lining" written by Jerome Kern and Bud De Sylva. Copyright 1920.

8. *Ibid.* p. 80.

9. An unknown newspaper article of 1924 inserted in Marilyn Miller's personal scrapbooks at the Lincoln Center Library for the Performing Arts.

10. *Buffalo News,* October 27, 1924.

11. *Buffalo Express,* October 27, 1924.

12. *New York Post,* November 15, 1924.

13. *Ibid.*

14. Heywood Broun, *World,* November 7, 1924.

15. Robert Benchley, *Life,* November 27, 1924.

16. *Ibid.*

17. *Ibid.*

18. Broun, *World,* November 7, 1924.

19. *Ibid.*

20. Charles Eaton, telephone interview, December 7, 1991.

21. Doris Eaton Travis, *The Days We Danced* (Seattle: Marquand Books, 2003), p. 264.

22. Broun, *World.*

23. Alan Dale, *New York American,* November 7, 1924.

24. *Ibid.*

25. *Ibid.*

26. *Ibid.*

27. John McGlinn recorded Kern's contributions to *Peter Pan* for his unreleased complete Jerome Kern collection, which he played for me over the telephone late one evening. He promised to send a CD of "Won't You Have a Little Feather" and "The Sweetest Thing in Life" but passed

away before being able to do so. Hopefully, all of the Kern recordings might someday be released.

28. An unknown newspaper article of 1924 inserted in one of Marilyn Miller's personal scrapbooks housed at the Lincoln Center Library for the Performing Arts.

29. *New York Times,* July 11, 1999.

Chapter 8

1. Myrtle Gebhart, "Peter Pan's Rebellion," unknown film magazine, circa 1925.

2. Mackail, *Barrie: The Story of J. M. B.,* p. 555.

3. J. M. Barrie, "Scenario for a Proposed Film of Peter Pan," in Green, *Fifty Years of Peter Pan,* p. 171.

4. *Ibid.,* p. 182.

5. *Ibid.*

6. Betty Bronson, *The Betty Bronson Papers,* U.C.L.A., p. 2.

7. *Ibid.,* p. 8.

8. *Ibid.*

9. DeWitt Bodeen, "Betty Bronson," *Films in Review,* December 1974, p. 581.

10. *Ibid.*

11. Mary Brian Tomasini, telephone interview, December 7, 1991.

12. Esther Ralston, telephone interview, December 7, 1991.

13. Brian, telephone interview.

14. Ralston, telephone interview.

15. Mordant Hall, *New York Times,* December 28, 1924.

16. *Ibid.*

17. *Ibid.*

18. James R. Quirk, *Photoplay,* December 1924.

19. Mackail, *Barrie: The Story of J. M. B.,* p. 555.

20. Ralston, telephone interview.

21. Brian, telephone interview.

22. *Ibid.*

23. *Ibid.*

24. *Ibid.*

25. *Ibid.*

26. Mordant Hall, *New York Times,* December 26, 1926.

27. Mordant Hall, *New York Times,* January 18, 1926.

28. Joe Franklin, *Classics of the Silent Screen* (New York: Cadillac Publishing Co., 1959) p. 136.

29. Bodeen, "Betty Bronson," p. 585.

Chapter 9

1. James Agate, "This Juliet for Wonder," *Sunday Times,* June 3, 1926.

2. Lesley, *Remembered Laughter,* p. 26.

3. Birkin, *J. M. Barrie and the Lost Boys,* p. 242.

4. Frohman and Marcosson, *Charles Frohman: Manager and Man,* p. 386.

5. Barrie, *Peter Pan,* Act 1, p. 13.

6. Birkin, *J. M. Barrie and the Lost Boys,* p. 296.

7. Green, *Fifty Years of Peter Pan,* p. 125.

8. Stewart Stern, letter to author, September 7, 2009.

9. Angela Du Maurier, *It's Only the Sister* (London: Peter Davies, 1949), p. 78.

10. *Ibid.,* p. 81.

11. St. John Ervine, *Observer,* June 3, 1927.

12. *The Era,* December 28, 1927.

13. *The Times,* December 22, 1927.

14. Barrie, *Peter Pan,* Act 1, p. 29.

15. Charles Morgan, review from unknown periodical, 1928.

16. *The Era,* December 20, 1928.

17. Peter Cotes, *No Star Nonsense* (London: Rockliff, 1949), p. 141.

18. *Ibid.,* p. 142.

19. G. W. B., review from unknown periodical, December 25, 1929.

20. *The Times,* December 27, 1933.

21. Dinah Sheridan, letter to author, January 15, 2005.

22. Elsa Lanchester, *Elsa Lanchester, Herself* (New York: St. Martin's Press, 1983), p. 150.

23. *Ibid.,* p. 151.

24. *Ibid.*

25. *The Times,* December 28, 1936.

26. Stern, letter to author, September 7, 2009.

27. Lanchester, *Elsa Lanchester, Herself,* p. 151.

28. Sheridan, letter to author, January 15, 2005.

29. Anna Neagle, *There's Always Tomorrow* (London: W. H. Allen, 1974), p. 98.

30. *Ibid.,* 99.

31. *The Times,* December 27, 1938.

32. *Ibid.*

33. Sheridan, letter to author, January 15, 2005.

34. Julia Lockwood, email to author, September 9, 2009.

Chapter 10

1. Eva Le Gallienne, "On Playing Peter Pan," p. 1.

2. Eva Le Gallienne, *At 33* (New York: Longmans, Green, 1934).

3. Le Gallienne, "On Playing Peter Pan," p. 17.

4. *Ibid.*, p. 1.

5. Le Gallienne, *At 33*, p. 73.

6. *Ibid.*

7. Josephine Hutchinson, interview with author, April 7, 1990.

8. Le Gallienne, "On Playing Peter Pan," p. 3.

9. *Ibid.*, p. 6.

10. Hutchinson, interview.

11. *Ibid.*

12. Le Gallienne, "On Playing Peter Pan," p. 9.

13. *Ibid.*, p. 10.

14. *Ibid.*, p. 9.

15. Hutchinson, interview.

16. Le Gallienne, "On Playing Peter Pan," p. 2.

17. Stewart Stern, telephone interview, July 2010.

18. Le Gallienne, "On Playing Peter Pan," p. 15.

19. *Morning Telegraph*, November 27, 1928.

20. *Ibid.*

21. *Ibid.*

22. *Herald Tribune*, November 27, 1928.

23. *Ibid.*

24. *New York Times*, November 27, 1928.

25. *The American*, November 27, 1928.

26. *Boston Tribune*, November 27, 1928.

27. Hutchinson, interview.

28. Le Gallienne, "On Playing Peter Pan," p. 12.

29. *World Telegram*, November 7, 1932.

30. Le Gallienne, "On Playing Peter Pan," p. 22.

Chapter 11

1. Tex McCrary and Jinx Falkenburg, "New York Close Up," *New York Herald Tribune*, September 18, 1950.

2. "Portrait of a Press Shy Peter Pan," *New York Times*, May 7, 1950.

3. McCrary and Falkenburg, "New York Close Up."

4. *Ibid.*

5. *Peter Pan* souvenir program, 1950.

6. Lewis Funke, "Rialto Gossip," *New York Times*, December 25, 1949.

7. Norman Shelly, interview with author, July 1989.

8. "Portrait of a Press Shy Peter Pan."

9. *Ibid.*

10. *Peter Pan* souvenir program, 1950.

11. John Chapman, *Daily News*, April 25, 1950.

12. *Ibid.*

13. *Theatre Arts*, July 1950.

14. Howard Barnes, *New York Herald Tribune*, April 25, 1950.

15. *Ibid.*

16. Brooks Atkinson, *New York Times*, April 30, 1950.

17. Daniel Felsenberg, *Leonard Bernstein's Peter Pan*, liner notes, KOCH, 2005.

18. Richard Watts, Jr., *New York Post*, April 25, 1950.

19. Atkinson, *New York Times*.

20. Robert Garland, *Journal American*, April 25, 1950.

21. John Oller, *Jean Arthur: The Actress Nobody Knew* (New York: Limelight, 1997), p. 189.

22. Shirley Temple Black, *Child Star* (New York: McGraw-Hill, 1988), p. 468.

23. Oller, *Jean Arthur*, p. 192.

24. *Baltimore Sun*, 1951.

25. *Variety*, 1951.

26. *Pittsburgh Post-Gazette*, 1951.

27. Green, *Fifty Years of Peter Pan*, p. 166.

28. *Ibid.*, p. 166–67.

29. Paul Taylor, *The Independent*, January 14, 2007.

30. Dominic Cavendish, *Daily Telegraph*, January 4, 2007.

31. Fiona Mountford, *Evening Standard*, December 18, 2006.

32. Taylor, *The Independent*.

33. *Ibid.*

34. Robert Shore, *Time Out London*, December 12, 2006.

35. Peter Flint, *New York Times*, June 20, 1991.

36. Oller, *Jean Arthur*, p. 226.

37. *Ibid.*, p. 218.

38. Mary Martin, *My Heart Belongs* (New York: William Morrow and Company, 1976), p. 202.

Chapter 12

1. Unknown periodical.

2. *New York Times*, August 8, 1949.

3. Leonard Maltin, *The Disney Films* (New York: Crown, 1973) p. 110.

4. Bosley Crowther, *New York Times*, January 23, 1953.

5. Green, *Fifty Year of Peter Pan*, p. 166.

6. Tim Appelo, *Entertainment Weekly*, October 5, 1990.

7. *Ibid.*

Chapter 13

1. Martin, *My Heart Belongs*, p. 202.

2. *Ibid.*, p. 84.

3. Edwin Lester, *Peter Pan* souvenir program, 1954.

4. Mary Martin, letter to author, September 1988.

5. Carolyn Leigh, "On Peter Pan," *The Journal, the Society of Stage Directors and Choreographers* (transcription, June 1982).

6. Sandy Stewart Triffon, interview with author, June 3, 1989.

7. *Ibid.*

8. Leigh, "On Peter Pan."

9. Carolyn Leigh to Christopher Sharp, "Arts and People," *Women's Wear Daily* (August 31, 1929).

10. *Ibid.*

11. Heller Halliday, "Flying is Fun," *Cue* (October 16, 1954).

12. Mary Martin, letter to author.

13. Mary Hunter, "On Peter Pan," *The Journal, the Society of Stage Directors and Choreographers* (transcription, June 1982).

14. Heller Halliday DeMermitt, letter to the author, January 20, 1994.

15. Martin, *My Heart Belongs*, p. 203.

16. Letter from Edwin Lester to Sam Zolotow, May 15, 1954.

17. Kathleen Nolan, interview with author, March 3, 1990.

18. *Ibid.*

19. *Ibid.*

20. Shelly, interview.

21. Sondra Lee, interview with author, August 11, 1989.

22. J. M. Barrie, "A Note on the Acting of a Fairy Play," *Peter Pan*, acting version used by Eva Le Gallienne, 1928.

23. Barrie, *Peter Pan*, Act 1, p. 30.

24. Martin, letter to author.

25. Barrie, *Peter and Wendy*, p. 267.

26. *Ibid.*, p. 267.

27. *Ibid.*, p. 266.

28. *Variety*, August 25, 1954.

29. *Ibid.*

30. *Ibid.*

31. *Ibid.*

32. Nolan, interview with author.

33. Lee, interview with author.

34. Nolan, interview with author.

35. *Ibid.*

36. Lee, interview with author.

37. Nolan, interview with author.

38. Stewart Triffon, interview with author.

39. Hunter, "On Peter Pan."

40. *Ibid.*

41. *Ibid.*

42. Betty Comden and Adolph Green, interview with author, March 1989.

43. *Ibid.*

44. Jule Styne, telephone interview with author, June 1989.

45. *Ibid.*
46. Comden and Green, interview with author.
47. Styne, telephone interview with author.
48. Green, *The World of Musical Comedy*, p. 283.
49. Comden and Green, interview with author.
50. Styne, telephone interview with author.
51. Comden and Green, interview with author.
52. *Ibid.*
53. Moose Charlap, Carolyn Leigh, Jule Styne, Betty Comden, Adolph Green, and J. M. Barrie, *Peter Pan* (New York: Samuel French, 1954).
54. Styne, telephone interview with author.
55. Charlap et al., *Peter Pan.*
56. Comden and Green, interview with author.
57. Leigh, "Arts and People."
58. Nolan, interview with author.
59. Martin, letter to author.
60. Milton Luban, *Los Angeles Times* (1954).
61. Styne, telephone interview with author.
62. Whintey Bolton, *Morning Telegraph,* October 20, 1954.
63. *Ibid.*
64. *Variety*, October 20, 1954.
65. Brooks Atkinson, *New York Times*, October 20, 1954.
66. Walter Kerr, *Herald-Tribune*, October 20, 1954.
67. John Chapman, *Daily News*, October 20, 1954.
68. Richard Watts, *Post*, October 20, 1954.
69. *Variety.*
70. Atkinson, *New York Times.*
71. Thomas Dash, unknown periodical, 1954.
72. Larry Elikann, unknown periodical, Collection of Performing Arts at the Library at Lincoln Center.
73. Nolan, interview with author.
74. Ken Mandelbaum, *Show Music*, 1991.
75. Nolan, interview with author.
76. Martin, letter to author.
77. Transcribed from the tag of the kinescope of *Peter Pan*, March 7, 1955.
78. Joe Mccarthy, "Her Heart Belongs to Forty Million People," *Cosmopolitan* (January 1956).
79. *New York Times*, 1960.
80. *Ibid.*
81. Jack O'Brian, "TView," 1960.
82. Tim Allis, Victoria Balfour, and Doris Bacon, *People Weekly* (March 17, 1989), p. 55.

83. Kenneth R. Clark, *Daily Journal*, March 21, 1989.
84. Letter from Robert W. Sarnoff to Mary Martin, September 23, 1968.
85. Allis, Balfour, and Bacon, *People Weekly.*
86. Lee, interview with author.
87. Allis, Balfour, and Bacon, *People Weekly*, p. 55.
88. Steve Sonsky, *Miami Herald*, March 1989.
89. Hunter, "On Peter Pan."
90. *Ibid.*

Chapter 14

1. Julia Lockwood, email to author, July 31, 2009.
2. Cotes, *No Star Nonsense*, p. 143.
3. Green, *Fifty Years of Peter Pan*, p. 141.
4. *Ibid.*, p. 241.
5. Margaret Lockwood, *Lucky Star* (London: Odams, 1955), p. 110.
6. *Ibid.*, p. 151.
7. *The Times*, December 24, 1949.
8. *Derby Telegraph*, December 24, 1949.
9. Lockwood, *Lucky Star*, p. 152.
10. *Ibid.*, p. 155.
11. *Ibid.*
12. Lockwood, email to author.
13. *The Times*, December 21, 1957.
14. Lockwood, email to author.
15. Julia Lockwood, telephone interview with author, August, 4, 2009.
16. *Ibid.*
17. *Ibid.*
18. *Ibid.*
19. *Ibid.*
20. Lockwood, email to author.
21. Patrick Gibbs, *Daily Telegraph*, December 18, 1959.
22. *Ibid.*
23. Neagle, *There's Always Tomorrow*, p. 99.
24. Lockwood, email to author.
25. Birkin, *J. M. Barrie and the Lost Boys*, p. 1.
26. *Ibid.*
27. Lockwood, email to author, July 31., 2009.
28. Eric Shorter, *Daily Telegraph*, December 19, 1963.
29. *Ibid.*
30. Lockwood, email to author.
31. *The Times*, December 20, 1969.
32. *Daily Telegraph*, December 20, 1969.
33. *Evening Star*, December 22, 1969.

34. Irving Wardle, *The Times*, December 20, 1973.
35. Michael Billington, *Guardian*, December 21, 1973.
36. Anthony Thomas, *Daily Telegraph*, September 20, 1973.
37. *Ibid.*
38. Anita Harris, *Peter Pan* souvenir program, 1974.

Chapter 15

1. Unknown periodical, December 1976, clippings file from NYC Library of Performing Arts at Lincoln Center.
2. *Ibid.*
3. Mia Farrow, *Life*, October 2, 1964.

Chapter 16

1. Sandy Duncan, telephone interview with author, May 1991.
2. *Ibid.*
3. *Ibid.*
4. Sandy Duncan to Helen Newton, "Sandy Duncan of the Hogan Family," *TV Guide*, December 31, 1988.
5. Marilyn Stasio, *New York Post*, September 7, 1979.
6. Sandy Duncan, telephone interview with author.
7. *Ibid.*
8. *Ibid.*
9. Walter Kerr, *New York Times*, September 7, 1979.
10. Douglas Watt, *Daily News*, September 7, 1979.
11. Jack Kroll, *Newsweek*, September 17, 1979.
12. *Ibid.*
13. Kerr, *New York Times.*
14. Howard Kissel, *Women's Wear Daily*, September 7, 1979.
15. *Ibid.*
16. Sandy Duncan, telephone interview with author.
17. *Ibid.*
18. *Ibid.*
19. Fergus McGillicuddy, *Talkin' Broadway*, November 2, 1999.

Chapter 17

1. Cathy Rigby, unknown source, December 1990.
2. Keith Stava, interview with author, June 2010.
3. *Ibid.*

4. Cathy Rigby, interview with author, January 1991.

5. *Ibid.*

6. *Ibid.*

7. Linda Winer, *New York Newsday*, December 14, 1991.

8. Howard Kissel, *Daily News*, December 14, 1990.

9. *Ibid.*

10. Edwin Wilson, *Wall Street Journal*, December 19, 1990.

11. Clive Barnes, *New York Post*, December 14, 1990.

12. *Ibid.*

13. *Ibid.*

14. Mel Gussow, *New York Times*, December 14, 1990.

Chapter 18

1. Bodeen, "Betty Bronson," *Films in Review*, December 1974, p. 585.

2. Meynell, *Letters of James M. Barrie*, p. 61–62. While Henry Ainley was allowed to play Hook and Mr. Darling, actress Edna Best was cast as Peter in 1920. There seems to be no record of the boy whom Ainley spoke so highly of for the part of Peter.

3. Aaron Stein, *New York Post*, February 25, 1936.

4. David Roper, *Daily Express*, December 17, 1982.

5. Michael Billington, *Guardian*, December 17, 1982.

6. *Ibid.*

7. John Barber, *Daily Telegraph*, December 17, 1982.

8. Robert Cushman, *Observer*, December 19, 1982.

9. *Ibid.*

10. John Barber, *Daily Telegraph*, December 23, 1983.

11. Barney Bardsley, *Tribune*, December 23, 1983.

12. Keith Nurse, *Daily Telegraph*, December 20, 1984.

13. Carole Woddis, *City Limits*, January 4, 1985.

14. Giles Gordon, *Punch*, January 16, 1985.

15. Robert Gore–Langton, *Express*, December 18, 1997.

16. Alastair Macaulay, *Financial Times*, December 21, 1998.

17. Kissel, *Women's Wear Daily.*

18. Jack Mathews, *Newsday*, December 11, 1991.

19. David Ansen, *Newsweek*, December 16, 1991.

20. Kathleen Carroll, *Daily News*, December 11, 1981.

21. Ansen, *Newsweek.*

22. Carroll, *Daily News.*

23. Vincent Canby, *New York Times*, December 11, 1991.

24. *Ibid.*

25. Mathews, *Newsday.*

26. A. O. Scott, *New York Times*, December 25, 2003.

27. Roger Ebert, *Chicago Sun-Times*, December 24, 2003.

28. *Ibid.*

29. *Ibid.*

30. Simon Moss, email to author, August 8, 2004.

31. Rodney Milnes, *The Times*, May 1, 2001.

32. *Ibid.*

33. *Yorkshire Evening Post*, December 6, 2008.

34. *Express and Star*, November 22, 2008.

35. Lynne Walker, *Independent*, December 23, 2008.

36. Terry Grimley, *Birmingham Mail*, December 6, 2008.

37. Walker, *Independent.*

38. Fiona Mountford, *Evening Standard*, June 11, 2009.

39. Charles Spencer, *Daily Telegraph*, June 6, 2009.

40. Benedict Nightingale, *The Times*, June 6, 2009.

41. Michael Billington, *Guardian*, June 6, 2009.

42. Karen Fricker, *Variety*, December 9, 2009.

43. *Ibid.*

44. Paul Hodgins, *Orange County Register*, October 5, 2010.

45. Barrie, *Peter and Wendy*, p. 267.

Afterword

1. J. A. Hammerton, *Barrie: The Story of a Genius* (New York: Dodd, Mead & Co., 1929), p. 367.

2. *Ibid.*

3. *Ibid.*

4. *Ibid.*

5. Green, *Fifty Years of Peter Pan*, p. 34.

Bibliography

Barrie's Works

PUBLISHED (CHRONOLOGICAL)

Barrie, James M. *Margaret Ogilvy*. New York: Charles Scribner's Sons, 1886.

_____. *Sentimental Tommy*. New York: Charles Scribner's Sons, 1896.

_____. *The Little Minister*. New York: Grosset and Dunlap, 1897.

_____. *Tommy and Grizel*. New York: Charles Scribner's Sons, 1900.

_____. *The Little White Bird*. New York: Charles Scribner's Sons, 1902.

_____. *Peter Pan in Kensington Gardens*. New York: Charles Scribner's Sons, 1906.

_____. *Peter and Wendy*. New York: Charles Scribner's Sons, 1911.

_____. *Peter and Wendy* (photoplay edition entitled Peter Pan). New York: Grosset and Dunlap, 1924.

_____. *Peter Pan, or the Boy Who Wouldn't Grow Up*. New York: Charles Scribner's Sons, 1928.

_____. *When Wendy Grew Up: An Afterthought*. London: Nelson, 1957 (published posthumously).

UNPUBLISHED

Barrie, James M. "The Boy Castaways of Black Lake Island." The only existing copy is part of the Barrie collection at the Beinecke Library at Yale University.

_____. "A Play." This original draft of *Peter Pan* dated November 23, 1903, is in the collection of the Lillie Library at the University of Indiana.

_____. *Peter Pan, or the Boy Who Wouldn't Grow Up*. A script from the 1910 edition with Pauline Chase is in the collection of the Museum of the City of New York.

_____. *Peter Pan ... Grow Up*. A script of 1927 from the Civic Repertory Theatre is in the collection of the Beinecke Library at Yale University.

_____. *Peter Pan ... Grow Up*. A published script with music cues annotated by Clifford Greenwood for the London Palladium, 1937.

_____. *Peter Pan*. Adapted by Jerome Robbins with Betty Comden and Adolph Green. Lincoln Center Library for the Performing Arts.

Works About Barrie

PUBLISHED

In particular, Andrew Birkin's beautifully written and researched biography, *J. M. Barrie and the Lost Boys*, was of great help and should be of interest to anyone even remotely interested in Barrie. *Fifty Years of Peter Pan* by Roger Lancelyn Green, which documents the early British productions, is also an important and valuable work. Finally, *The Story of J. M. B.*, Denis Mackail's exhaustive biography, remains a work of art itself, seventy years after its first publication.

Asquith, Cynthia. *Portrait of Barrie*. London: Robert Cunningham and Sons, 1954.

Birkin, Andrew. *J. M. Barrie and the Lost Boys*. London: Constable, 1979.

Cable, Lucy Leefingwell. "The Story of Peter Pan." *Ladies Home Journal*. Part I: September 1906; Part II: October 1906; Part III: November 1906.

Chaney, Lisa. *Hide and Seek with Angels: A Life of J. M. Barrie*. New York: St. Martin's Press, 2005.

Dunbar, Janet. *J.M. Barrie: The Man Behind the Image*. Boston: Houghton Mifflin, 1970.

Green, Roger Lancelyn. *Fifty Years of Peter Pan*. London: Peter Davies, 1954.

_____. *J.M. Barrie*. New York: Henry Z. Walck, 1960.

Haill, Catherine, and Nanette Newman. *Dear Peter Pan*. London: Victoria and Albert Museum, 1983.

Hammerton, J. A. *Barrie: The Story of a Genius*. New York: Dodd, Mead, 1929.

Mackail, Denis. *Barrie: The Story of J. M. B.* New York: Charles Scribner's Sons, 1941.

Meynell, Viola. *Letters of James M. Barrie*. New York: Charles Scribner's Sons, 1947.

Walbrook, H. M. *J. M. Barrie and the Theatre*. London: F. V. White, 1922.

Works About the Artists of Peter Pan

PUBLISHED

Best, Edna. "When I Was Peter Pan." *Strand Magazine*, January 1923.

Bodeen, DeWitt. "Betty Bronson." *Films in Review*, December 1974.

Boucicault, Nina. "When I Was Peter Pan." *Strand Magazine*, January 1923.

Charlap, Moose, Carolyn Leigh, Jule Styne, Betty Comden, Adolph Green, and J. M. Barrie. *Peter Pan*. New York: Samuel French, 1954.

Chase, Pauline. "My Reminiscences of Peter Pan." *Strand Magazine*, February 1913.

_____. *Peter Pan's Postbag*. London: Heinemann, 1909.

Cotes, Peter. *No Star Nonsense*. London: Rockliff, 1949.

Davies, Action. *Maude Adams*. New York: Frederick A. Stokes, 1901.

Du Maurier, Angela. *It's Only the Sister*. London: Peter Davies, 1949.

Du Maurier, Daphne. *Gerald: A Portrait*. New York: Doubleday, 1935.

Eaton Travis, Doris. *The Days We Danced: The Story of My Theatrical Family*. Seattle: Marquand Books, 2003.

Farnsworth, Marjorie. *Ziegfeld Follies*. New York: G. P. Putnam's Sons, 1956.

Farrow, Mia. *What Falls Away*. New York: Doubleday, 1997.

Gordon, Ruth. *My Side*. New York: Harper and Row, 1976.

Halliday, Heller. "Flying is Fun." *Cue*, October 16, 1954.

Harris, Warren G. *The Other Marilyn*. New York: Arbor House, 1985.

Kirkwood, James. *Diary of a Mad Playwright*. New York: E. P. Dutton, 1989.

Lanchester, Elsa. *Elsa Lanchester, Herself*. New York: St. Martin's Press, 1983.

Le Gallienne, Eva. *At 33*. New York: Longmans, Green, 1934.

_____. *With a Quiet Heart*. New York: Viking Press, 1953.

Lee, Sondra. *I've Slept with Everybody*. Georgia: Bear-Manor, 2009.

Lesley, Cole. *Remembered Laughter: The Life of Noël Coward*. New York: Knopf, 1976.

Lockwood, Margaret. *Lucky Star*. London: Odams Press, 1955.

Loftus, Cecilia. "When I Was Peter Pan." *Strand Magazine*, January 1923.

Maltin, Leonard. *The Disney Films*. New York: Crown, 1973.

Mank, Gregory. "Josephine Hutchinson." *Films in Review*, November 1980.

Marcosson, Isaac F., and Daniel Frohman. *Charles Frohman: Manager and Man*. New York: Harper and Brothers, 1916.

Martin, Mary. *My Heart Belongs*. New York: William Morrow, 1976.

Maxwell, Perriton. *The Stage Story of Maude Adams*. Pamphlet. No source, 1908.

Mordden, Ethan. *Make Believe: The Broadway Musical in the 1920s*. New York: Oxford University Press, 1997.

_____. *Ziegfeld: The Man Who Invented Show Business*. New York: St. Martin's Press, 2008.

Morris, Mildred. "Behind the Scenes with Peter Pan." *Delineator*, October 1915.

Neagle, Anna. *There's Always Tomorrow*. London: W. H. Allen, 1974.

Newman, Shirlee P. *Mary Martin on Stage*. Philadelphia: Westminister Press, 1969.

Oller, John. *Jean Arthur: The Actress Nobody Knew*. New York: Limelight, 1997.

"On Peter Pan." *The Journal, the Society of Stage Directors and Choreographers*. June 1982. This excellent resource is a transcription of the roundtable panel that consisted of Betty Comden, Adolph Green, Carolyn Leigh, Jerome Robbins, Jule Styne, and Mary Hunter as moderator. An afterword was written by Mary Martin. The S.D.C. Foundation is the only organization in the United States devoted to fostering, promoting, and developing the creativity and craft of professional stage directors and choreographers.

Patterson, Ada. *Maude Adams: A Biography*. New York: Meyer and Bros., 1907.

Ralston, Esther. *Someday We'll Laugh*. Metuchen, NJ: Scarecrow, 1985.

Robbins, Phyllis. *Maude Adams: An Intimate Portrait*. New York: G. P. Putnam's Sons, 1956.

_____. *The Young Maude Adams*. Francestown, NH: Marshall Jones, 1959.

Rose, Jacqueline. "Writing as Auto-Visualization: Notes on a Scenario and Film of Peter Pan c. 1924." *Screen* 16 (Autumn 1975).

Sagolla, Lisa Jo. *The Girl Who Fell Down: A Biography of Joan McCracken*. Boston: Northeastern University Press, 2003.

Schanke, Robert A. *Shattered Applause: The Lives of Eva Le Gallienne*. Carbondale: Southern Illinois University Press.

Sheehy, Helen. *Eva Le Gallienne*. New York: Alfred A. Knopf, 1996.

Shelton, George. *It's Smee!* London: Ernest Benn, 1928.

Steinberg, Mollie B. *The History of the 14th Street Theatre*. New York: The Dial Press, 1931.

Tims, Hilton. *Once a Wicked Lady: A Biography of Margaret Lockwood*. London: W. H. Allen, 1989.

Trevelyan, Hilda (to Eric Johns). "The Stories of Famous London Theatres: The Duke of York's." *Theatre World*, January 1940.

Unpublished

Barrie, James M. *Peter Pan*. Joan McCracken's April 24, 1950, script from the Imperial Theatre is part of the Billy Rose Collection at the New York Public Library of Performing Arts. Also in that collection are several scripts from the 1954 musical, including the stage manager's prompt book and the abridged television script.

Bronson, Betty. The Betty Bronson Papers. A collection of personal scrapbooks, memoirs, and diaries in the Arts Special Collection at U.C.L.A.

Christie, Edith. "Peter Pan Pictures, and Other Pictures of Miss Adams." 1908 scrapbook from the Stephens College in Columbia, Missouri, where Maude Adams taught.

Le Gallienne, Eva. "On Playing Peter Pan." Courtesy of Eloise Armen of the Eva Le Gallienne Estate.

Leigh, Carolyn. All of her unused lyrics are collected with the original drafts of the 1954 musical of *Peter Pan* in the Museum of the City of New York.

Trevelyan, Hilda. A letter describing Barrie's "An Afterthought" dated December 10, 1957, at the Beinecke Library at Yale University.

General References

Agay, Denes. *Best Loved Songs of the American People.* Garden City, NY: Doubleday, 1975.

Barrios, Richard. *A Song in the Dark.* New York: Oxford University Press, 1995.

Black, Shirley Temple. *Child Star.* New York: McGraw-Hill, 1988.

Chappell, W. *The Ballad Literature and Popular Music of the Olden Time.* London: Chappell and Company, 1859.

Darton, F. J. Harvey. *Children's Books in England.* London: Cambridge University Press, 1966.

Epps, William D. "The Empire Theatre." *Marquee: The Journal of the Theatre Historical Society* 10, no. 3 (1978).

Franklin, Joe. *Classics of the Silent Screen.* New York: Cadillac, 1959.

Green, Stanley. *Broadway Musicals.* Milwaukee, WI.: Hal Leonard Books, 1987.

———. *The World of Musical Comedy.* New York: Grosset & Dunlap, 1960.

Howard, Robert. "Duke of York's Theatre." *Then and Now.* London: Battley Brothers, 1972.

Hummel, David. *The Collector's Guide to the American Musical Theatre.* Metuchen, NJ: Scarecrow, 1984.

Jablonski, Edward. *The Encyclopedia of American Music.* New York: Doubleday, 1981.

Knight, Arthur. *The New York Times Directory of the Film.* New York: Arno Press/Random House, 1971.

Leonard, William Torbert. *Theatre: Stage to Screen to Television.* Metuchen, NJ: Scarecrow, 1981.

Mordden, Ethan. *Better Foot Forward: A History of American Musical Theatre.* New York: Grossman, 1976.

Suskin, Steven. *Show Tunes, 1905–1991,* 2nd edition.

Index

Numbers in **bold** italics indicate pages with photographs.